MONROE COLLEGE LIBRARY

3 7340 01020730 3

If I Could

Write This

in Fire

DISCARDED

D0710154

REF
809.89
Smo

30892373

9655
13.00

B&T

If I Could Write This in Fire

An Anthology of Literature

From the Caribbean

Edited by

PAMELA MARIA SMORKALOFF

The New Press   New York

Copyright © 1994 by Pamela Maria Smorkaloff
Permissions Acknowledgments on page 374

All rights reserved. No part of this book may be reproduced in any form without written permission from the publisher and author.

Published in the United States by The New Press, New York.
Distributed by W.W. Norton & Company, Inc., 500 Fifth Avenue, New York, NY 10110

Library of Congress Cataloging-in-Publication Data

If I could write this in fire: an anthology of literature from the Caribbean / edited by Pamela Maria Smorkaloff.
    p.   cm.
  In English: many selections have been translated from the French and Spanish.
  Includes bibliographical references.
  ISBN 1-56584-181-6 :
  1. Caribbean literature. I. Smorkaloff, Pamela Maria, 1956-
PN849.C3I4 1994   94-22578
809 .89729—dc20

Book design by Acme Art, Inc.
Production by Kim Waymer

Printed in the United States of America
    96 97   9 8 7 6 5 4 3 2

Established in 1990 as a major alternative to the large, commercial publishing houses, The New Press is the first full-scale nonprofit American book publisher outside of the university presses. The Press is operated editorially in the public interest, rather than for private gain; it is committed to publishing in innovative ways works of educational, cultural, and community value that, despite their intellectual merits, might not normally be "commercially" viable. The New Press's editorial offices are located at the City University of New York.

CONTENTS

Acknowledgments

I would like to thank Diane Wachtell and André Schiffrin of The New Press, whose support and vision lent encouragement to my own, making this book possible; Max Gordon, Claudia Guerra, and Akiko Takano, also of The New Press, for their unflagging enthusiasm and assistance at every step; and Joseph Murphy, in the same breath, for his continued friendship and for having introduced me to the aforementioned in the first place.

This anthology is influenced by all the friends and colleagues who have listened to my thoughts and strengthened my understanding with their own, and without whom the project could not have been realized.

My thanks to Angela Carreño at New York University, Godfrey Burns, Denise Hibay at the New York Public Library, and to the staff at the Schomburg Center, where I spent many long, pleasant afternoons.

To Rachelle Charlier Doucet my thanks for having brought me back from Haiti years ago a novel by Simone Schwarz-Bart, whose work I didn't know, thus opening up worlds for me.

To Osvaldo Monzón, whose ideas, sharp eye, and knowledge of the plastic arts of the Caribbean were invaluable, and to all the other graduate students over the years whose knowledge, needs, and interests helped give form to this collection.

Special thanks to Christopher Mitchell, Carmen M. Díaz, and Guadalupe Lara Olmos at the Center for Latin American and Caribbean Studies at N.Y.U. for their assistance and patience while I labored on this project.

I also wish to thank all the teachers who allowed me to be Caribbean in my own way—to think, read, and write Caribbean—from Keith Johnson in high school to Moss Roberts in college and Haydée Vitali in graduate school (with more immediate thanks to Haydée for her constant feedback through the many revisions of content and translations).

Lastly, I am eternally grateful to Casa de las Américas, whose marvelous collection of the literature of the Caribbean gave me my first introduction to its rich legacy in the fullest sense.

Introduction

$\mathcal{C}$. L. R. James said of Alexandre Dumas, who had never been to the West Indies, that ". . . in everything that really matters he is a West Indian."[1] The problem with the West Indies, the Indies, the Caribbean—even the name is problematic—is that "what really matters" varies from theorist to theorist and from one epoch to another. "Caribbeanness" is a notion in process, or in flux, as are the very boundaries of the Caribbean as a geographic region. Frank Moya Pons in his 1970 essay "Is There a Caribbean Consciousness?" suggested that the notion of *the* Caribbean "has meaning only as a convenience in geography classes" and that, in practical terms, "it makes more sense to think of several Caribbeans coexisting alongside one another."[2] Gordon K. Lewis, throughout his life's work devoted to the region, attempted "to surmount the linguistic fragmentation that has characterized Caribbean scholarship as well as Caribbean history"[3] by drawing on resources in all the languages of the Caribbean and ultimately broadening the parameters of Caribbean Studies to embrace all of the peoples of the Caribbean, wherever they reside.

1. Ian Munro and Reinhard Sander, eds., *Kas-Kas: Interviews with Three Caribbean Writers in Texas* (Austin: University of Texas at Austin, 1972), p. 23.
2. Frank Moya Pons, "Is There a Caribbean Consciousness?" quoted in Antonio Benítez-Rojo, *The Repeating Island* (Durham: Duke University Press, 1992), p. 37.
3. Gordon K. Lewis, *Main Currents in Caribbean Thought* (Baltimore: The Johns Hopkins University Press, 1987) p. ix.

It is not my intention to add fuel to the long-standing debate on how best to define the parameters of the Caribbean.[4] It is, however, important to note that in 1993 global awareness of the Caribbean has come a long way from Columbus's colossal geographic error, his stubborn belief that he had reached the East Indies, supported by the adventurers of conquering Europe who financed his voyages.

Contemporary approaches to the Caribbean and Caribbeanness tend to be inclusive rather than exclusive, extending up and down the Caribbean coast of continental Latin America, indeed to London and New York, to wherever Caribbeans have made and remade their lives, taking into account the history of fragmentation that has shaped each one of the island nations. Rather than attempt yet another inquiry into how to define the Caribbean in geographical, historical, economic, socio-political, cultural, or literary terms, this anthology aims to offer the reader a panorama of literature(s) of the Caribbean(s) through which to explore what the writers themselves have to say. It brings together for the first time in one volume prose fiction from each of the major linguistic blocks, from Caribbeans writing in French, Spanish, and English.

Suzanne Césaire, referring to her nation's literary expression, boldly declared in 1941, "La poésie martiniquaise sera cannibale ou ne sera pas." [Martinican poetry will either be cannibalistic or it won't be at all.] In the spirit of C. L. R. James's Caribbeanness, "in all that really matters," what has really mattered to the writers collected here is the legacy of resistance to conquest, colonization, and colonialism. As Fernández Retamar makes clear in his essay "Caliban," *cannibal* is a European corruption of *Carib*, those who offered the fiercest resistance to colonization, and thus came to be equated with the fiercest notions of "savagery" in the colonial mind. Guyanese novelist Wilson Harris has observed how the camera, in a contemporary television documentary on Brazil, "polarizes civilization and savagery," and in doing so perpetuates and consolidates the sixteenth-century colonizers' bias.

---

4. A debate which Price-Mars, Mintz, Fernández Retamar, Brathwaite, Carew, and so many others have redirected and shaped with rigor and clarity.

In the conquest of pre-Columbian America, the Spaniards in some degree had to shape a view of the peoples who were overcome and conquered, a view which conscripted those people by and large as cannibals. And this has persisted particularly in regard to Caribs . . . It is something which has pervaded scholarship, institutions, and thus it is there a deeply planted bias, and the curious irony is that the camera in fact may consolidate such a bias. The loathing expressed for the savage is already there and triggered off or consolidated afresh by cinematic stasis in which moving figures occupy one dimension of time and realism.[5]

From Columbus's diaries on, the Caribbean has been the scenario onto which a steady stream of myths and mystifications has been projected. Anthropologist W. Arens in his controversial study, *The Man-Eating Myth*, noted that in the transition from Indian to African slave-labor, "as one group of cannibals disappeared, the European mind conveniently invented another which would have to be saved from itself by the Europeans before it was too late."[6] He sums up his study of European bias by reasoning that although there is legitimate doubt as to who ate whom, "there can be none on the question of who exterminated whom."[7] It is to the legacy of Caliban/cannibal, of those who refused to be colonized, that Suzanne Césaire refers, and which constitutes the common thread encompassing all of the Caribbean writers represented herein. The process of selection has taken a pan-Caribbean approach to the diverse literatures of the region, not in order to reduce or diminish specificity, or to suggest that a pan-Caribbean literature itself exists, but rather to break down the colonialist divisions that isolated the Caribbean societies from one another. Up until recently, the only conceptual bridges allowed were those that linked the French-speaking Caribbean to France, the Spanish-speaking Caribbean to Spain, and the English-speaking to Great Britain. Confining the literatures of the region in linguistic blocks can be yet another form of

5. Wilson Harris in *Kas-Kas: Interviews with Three Caribbean Writers in Texas*, pp. 47–48.
6. W. Arens, *The Man-Eating Myth* (New York: Oxford University Press, 1979) p. 80.
7. Ibid., p. 31.

insularism, not unlike the colonialist monopolies of old that were nevertheless violated by piracy and inter-island channels of communication. It is not accidental that Martinican poet Aimé Césaire's *Cahier d'un retour au pays natal* was first published in a bilingual (French-Spanish) edition in Cuba in 1944. It was not published in its entirety in France until 1947.

There has always been a sustaining undercurrent of inter-Caribbean communication, belying the isolation and fragmentation imposed by the colonial powers. And it is the crucial, though less studied, bridges built from one island society to another, across linguistic divides, to Africa and the Americas, as well as metropolitan Europe, that this anthology hopes to bring to light. All the writers whose work has been collected here share a grounding in a *sense of place*, and that firm anchor in local reality, history, and culture serves as a counterweight to the European and "Europeanizing" tendencies of colonial education. Many of these writers embarked on the process of decolonizing their own language and literary expression while serving out a literary apprenticeship in the capital cities of Europe. Like the indigenist novel of continental Latin America, contemporary Caribbean literature has consciously sought to establish a geography, and to reclaim language in the process of decolonizing it.

Further conceptual links across literary movements are revealing. Indigenist, Andean narrative and contemporary Caribbean narrative—be it that of the English-, Spanish,- or French-speaking nations—share a common philosophical core of historical, social, and cultural reaffirmation; a philosophy that arose in reaction to the fabulous, false, mythical, decorative figures, removed from historical and geographical context, that peopled the exotic *Indianist* literature of the Romantic period and the equally exotic *négriste* literature of the European vanguard. The very terms *Negro, White, Indian, Mulatto*, and *Mestizo* are European inventions; the products of colonial semantics, of a conceptual, classificatory colonialism. In what the United Nations has declared the Year of the Indigenous Peoples of America, it is now well known that the Caribbean "Indian" never existed, that it arose out of Columbus's belief that he had reached the Indies when in reality, he had arrived merely at his own erroneous theory, imposed at all costs. All that could not already be

4

found within European thought, within the conceptual framework of Europe, was "discovered" and, in order intellectually to appropriate all that had been "discovered," given a name. Thus, the inhabitants of the Dominican Republic and Haiti, Cuba, Puerto Rico, all the islands, and later the entire American continent were transformed into "Indians," an ahistorical and antigeographical amalgam. Prior to the adventurism of the African slave trade, the word *Negro,* as applied to human beings, did not exist. During the European Middle Ages, Africans were Moors and Ethiopes and, as Haitian writer René Depestre affirms, human beings "with a mysterious geography because it was unknown,"[8] but nonetheless *possessed of a geography.*

The result, in both cases, is a reduction, a mythological construct emanating from the false consciousness of white, Christian Europe with regard to a "black, pagan" Africa and a "savage, Indian" America. This is the point of departure for the movement toward the indigenist philosophy of Andean narrative and the anticolonialist core of contemporary Caribbean literature. It is against the ahistorical *Negro* and *Indian,* turned into " 'noble savages' to serve as a supplement to the soul" of a Western world in crisis, that the indigenist voice in the Andean region and the Caribbean voice arise, firmly grounded both historically and geographically, and projecting a vision from within.

In the same way that Andean novelists José María Arguedas's and Jorge Icaza's indigenous characters are firmly grasped by geography, within the concrete context of the social and historical life of their countries, it is the African heritage in Caribbean narrative and poetry that traces a profound, historical relationship between man and land, between colonialism, sugar, and slavery; a heritage that is an integral part of the history, geography, economy, and culture of all the inhabitants of the Caribbean in the process of forging society.

In contemporary Caribbean literature, creators interrogate themselves, take the pulse of local reality, and examine their situation within the map and history of the planet, revealing a complex, historical Caribbean. Viewed from a wide angle, as a *corpus,* the literature of

8.   René Depestre, "Aventuras del negrismo en América Latina," in *América Latina en sus ideas,* Leopoldo Zea, ed. (Mexico: Siglo XXI; Paris: UNESCO, 1986), p. 351.

the Caribbean may be read as a dialogue among nations, achieving in literature what has all too often not been possible in the political and diplomatic spheres. Examples of the phenomenon of Caribbean intertextuality abound in contemporary literature, as is the case in Barbadian poet and essayist Kamau Brathwaite's poem "Words Making Man," written in response to Cuban poet Nicolás Guillén's volume, published in English with the title *Man Making Words*, or Guillén's *West Indies, Ltd.*, which explores the common fate of monoculture and the tourist industry throughout the Caribbean, or the historical novel by Cuban novelist Alejo Carpentier, *The Kingdom of This World*, inspired by the Haitian Revolution and written after an extended stay in Haiti, or the pan-Antillean, inter-Caribbean narratives of Puerto Rican writer Ana Lydia Vega, included in this collection. The same intertextual play is evident in contemporary Latin American and Caribbean cinema as well.

On yet another level, as Trinidadian writer and critic C. L. R. James reminds us, it is imperative that we relate dialectically—indeed, as a two-way stream of mutual influences—the literature of the francophone Caribbean with that of France. This holds equally true for the literature of the anglophone Caribbean and that of England. It was in the writings of C. L. R. James that I, along with many others, discovered that two celebrated writers classified in literary dictionaries simply as "French writers," period, are not. They are none other than Alexandre Dumas, *fils*, offspring of Dumas, *père*, and a Haitian woman, and Leconte Delisle, native of La Réunion, an island neighbor to Madagascar; figures who revolutionized French literature. C. L. R. James explains:

> ...I have said enough to show you the integral part West Indian conceptions and West Indian literary activity have played in French literature. Everybody knows that except us. We know everything about Socrates and Dante; but about ourselves, we don't know our own. Nobody has ever taught us so we don't know.[9]

9. C. L. R. James, "A National Purpose for Caribbean Peoples," in *At the Rendezvous of Victory (Selected Writings)*, (London: Allison & Busby, 1984), p. 146.

Ironically, André Breton's first Surrealist Manifesto (1924) served as a powerful stimulus for this odyssey of Caribbean self-exploration and affirmation. Countless Caribbean and Latin American writers had gone off to what was then surrealist Paris to hone their craft. Their encounter with, and rejection of, European surrealism led to a discovery of their native lands and discovery of the "marvelous reality"[10] of the "New World" while living in the "Old World." Sartre himself could not help but admire, albeit with a touch of paternalism, how Caribbean writers transcended the limitations and failings of the movement, particularly Aimé Césaire: "Surrealism, a European movement in poetry, [has been] stolen from the Europeans by a Black man who turns it against them and gives it a well-defined purpose."[11] As Uruguayan critic Angel Rama observed, the Caribbean response to the surrealist tendency in literature ". . . overflowed the bounds, devoured and transmuted it, leading it to unforeseen derivations."[12] Alejo Carpentier transmuted the clichés of European surrealism— "the marvelous, obtained with tricks of prestidigitation, bringing together objects that are never usually associated: the old, deceptive story of the fortuitous encounter between the umbrella and the sewing machine on the anatomy table, which also gives rise to the ermine spoons, the seashells in a rainy taxi, and the head of a lion on the widow's pelvis"[13]—of surrealist expression, into the *real maravilloso* of Latin America and the Caribbean, which had yet to be discovered, to be sufficiently explored, in literature. Aimé Césaire confessed that "Surrealism interested me in so much as it was an instrument of

10. *"Lo real maravilloso"* or "marvelous reality" was a term given resonance by Cuban novelist Carpentier; it is used interchangeably in the U.S. with the term *magical realism*, although both are too often used in relation to the exotic rather than the rich texture of Latin and Caribbean history.
11. Sartre quoted in *Black Writers in French: A Literary History of Negritude*, Lilyan Kesteloot, Ellen Conroy Kennedy, trans. (Washington D.C.: Howard University Press, 1991), p. 45.
12. Angel Rama, *La novela en América Latina: Panoramas 1920–1980* (Bogotá: Instituto Colombiano de Cultura, 1982), p. 196 [translation mine].
13. Alejo Carpentier, *Tientos y diferencias* (Montevideo: ARCA, 1967), p. 115 [translation mine].

liberation, . . . an operation of disalienation."[14] Caribbean writers retained from European surrealism solely the push for liberation and transcendence, and in that sense achieved, as Sartre affirmed, what the surrealist movement had attempted, in vain.[15]

Writers and artists from the Caribbean and Latin America, on the whole, rejected surrealism's forms and formulas while at the same time retaining the spirit of change and the will to individual and collective liberation. This dynamic has a parallel in the principled and uncompromising rejection of colonial education whose form and content served as raw material for the works of many Caribbean authors. The long list of novelists from Zobel and Lamming to the more contemporary writers, such as Vega, Phillips, and Clarke, represented here, reject the premises of a colonial and colonizing education that perpetuates the fragmentation of Caribbeans between "here" and "there," between the island and the metropolitan "center." In working through the theme of education in the coming-of-age novels, acknowledging and exploring the process of fragmentation and the divided self it engenders, they reaffirm the need for grounding in local reality in order to *be*, to fully assume one's identity, to *name*, confront, and artistically transform all the accumulated colonial baggage of Caribbean life.

This is the impetus behind the poetry of Aimé Césaire and Kamau Brathwaite, whose "aesthetic ideal" is to "write a literature of catastrophe, to hold a broken mirror up to broken nature";[16] that is, to combat the colonialist legacy by *recognizing* it, as José Martí did in "Our America" at the close of the last century. Fernández Retamar, his intellectual heir, sets out in his essay "Caliban" to combat the opinion of those in our day who suspect that Caribbeans are "but a distorted echo of what occurs

14. Aimé Césaire, *Poesías*, "Prólogo," (Havana: Casa de las Américas, 1969), p. xxi [translation mine].

15. See Lilyan Kesteloot, "Surrealism and Criticism of the West," *Black Writers in French*, pp. 37–45.

16. Brathwaite quoted in Gordon Rohlehr, "The Problem of the Problem of Form. The Idea of an Aesthetic Continuum and Aesthetic Code-Switching in West Indian Literature," *Anales del Caribe*, No. 6, 1986 (Havana: Casa de las Américas), p. 224.

elsewhere." It is this same rigorous examination of colonial education and its consequences that caused Nobel laureate Derek Walcott to observe: "I am a kind of split writer. I have one tradition inside me going one way and another going another." And Jamaican poet Louis Simpson recalls with irony his own aesthetic formation:

> Even the local landscape was a kind of inferior imitation: the very trees and hills of Jamaica were only a kind of papier-maché. The famous landscapes were in Europe.[17]

This schizophrenic division between Caribbean reality and the dream of Europe is at the heart of the colonial education, examined in the Caribbean novel. The here/there dialectic is a constant in the narrative and poetry of the Caribbean, underlying the themes not only of education and coming of age, but of national and cultural identity, and informing the *ars poetica* and theory of the Caribbean novel. Hence the necessity, returning to our initial theme, of *establishing a geography*, of attaining universality through a deep grounding in, and knowledge of, one's land and historical origins—both the "official" origins celebrated with "official" pride, and the origins denied, the African heritage, revealed and assumed with dignity in the region's literature.

In addition to bringing together contemporary writers from the English-, French-, and Spanish-speaking Caribbean, this collection follows a thematic logic as well. The literary selections presented deal with the foundational themes of the region's literature, common to all across the linguistic divide: the plantation, maroon society, colonial education, rural and urban life, women's changing roles in the modern Caribbean, exile and the diaspora. And the three essays that follow the selections provide a context, a theoretical framework, for the reader. While many contemporary critical theories may shed light on these texts, it is important to listen carefully to what Caribbean theorists themselves have to say, in order to avoid what Henry Louis Gates, Jr., has identified as "the trap, the tragic lure, to which those who believe

---

17. Walcott and Simpson quoted in Michael Gilkes, "Caribbean Identity in the Anglophone Literature of the Region," *Anales del Caribe*, No. 9, 1989 (Havana: Casa de las Américas), p. 281.

that critical theory is color-blind, universal discourse, or a culturally neutral tool like a hammer or a screwdriver, have unwittingly succumbed."[18] Each one of the theorists offers a quintessentially Caribbean perspective on the literature of the region and its sources of meaning, tracing the development of a Caribbean voice and aesthetic.

Now, the creator's task can be none other than that of Adam, naming and defining the things of his or her world, not "from the outside in" as did the envoys of distant empires, but from within, creating a new language, adequate to the creator's task. Whether it is Michelle Cliff's Jamaica, Ana Lydia Vega's Puerto Rico, Austin Clarke's Barbados, or Simone Schwarz-Bart's Guadeloupe, to name only a few, all of the writers represented here are engaged in tracing the history and destiny of their countries; countries placed on a course determined by others' needs, those of monoculture, of sugar and its derivatives. Others "placed" the nations of the Caribbean on the world map, through the logic of international relations, and determined the role they would fulfil in the world economy.

Legend has it that upon receiving the first Spanish grammar, a gift from the Bishop, shortly before she subsidized Columbus's voyage, Queen Isabella asked, "What is it good for?" To which the Bishop of Avila replied, "Majesty, language is the perfect tool of Empire." But as Shakespeare's Caliban, and all the other Calibans have shown us, language is a double-edged sword, equally suited for liberation and the struggle toward autonomy and plenitude, and against isolation and alienation. Caliban's presence is as notable as that of Columbus in the chronicles of the Indies, fragments of which appear as collage and counterpoint in the contemporary literature of the Caribbean, in works that run the philosophical and political gamut, from the poetry of Nicolás Guillén to the novels and essays of V. S. Naipaul. The Caribbean continues to overflow its boundaries, to extend and transcend its borders, resulting in an uprooting, in exile and self-exile as well as in

18. Henry Louis Gates, Jr., "Authority, (White) Power, and the (Black) Critic; It's All Greek to Me," in *The Nature and Context of Minority Discourse*, Abdul R. JanMohamed and David Loyd, eds. (New York: Oxford University Press, 1990), p. 87.

internal odyssey and return. To take in the Caribbean, in its entirety, is difficult, if not impossible; no anthology could hope to embrace it all. Absent in fact, but not in spirit, from this collection of prose fiction, are the Dutch- and Papiamento-speaking Caribbean islands, the Caribbean coast of the continent, Bluefields, Cartagena de Indias, Bahia, and so much more. Along with introducing new readers to a rich and diverse tradition, and providing devotees of the region's literature with a new perspective, the bibliography invites exploration beyond the obvious limits of this initial pan-Caribbean collection.

The Caribbean, in all of its complexity, is, in one sense, as García Márquez claims, "a single country," one that extends to and bears the imprint of the entire world; a region of the planet where, as Angel Rama explains, "the plural manifestations of the whole universe have inserted themselves."[19]

Cuban poet and essayist Nancy Morejón inaugurated a recent colloquium on "The American Caribbean" with a vision of the region that gives eloquent expression both to a deep concern with the complex and changing relations of a borderless Caribbean to the world, and to the will to establish a historical, human geography, which inspires twentieth-century Caribbean writing:

> I always heard people speak of the Caribbean as a whole, as an enormous geographical, political, social, and cultural complex, reduced to the beautiful islands which, of course, belong to it. In my childhood, people spoke of the Antilles (Greater and Lesser), of which Nicolás Guillén wrote as few others have done. And yet, this definition of the contemporary Caribbean . . . includes not only the Antilles, that is, the islands, but reaches the coasts of the Central American and South American nations, and even the United States."[20]

Pamela Maria Smorkaloff

December 1993

19. Angel Rama, *La novela en América Latina* (Bogotá: Instituto Colombiano de Cultura, 1982), p. 194 [translation mine].
20. Nancy Morejón, *Anales del Caribe*, No. 9, 1989 (Havana: Casa de las Américas), p. 8 [translation mine].

Part I

Literary Selections

The Plantation and
Maroon Society

*The story of a grain of sugar is a whole lesson in political
economy, in politics, and also in morality.*
                                        —*Auguste Cochin*

James Carnegie's powerful novella, *Wages Paid*, is, in its own right, a
lesson in the political economy, social structure, and very foundations
of the plantation society whose survival was fueled by slave labor. In
this story, set on a Jamaican sugar plantation, events unfold sometime
between the Haitian Revolution and the demise of the British slave
trade, anticipated by owners like Carnegie's Mr. Johnson who began
"stocking their estates" through "breeding programs" like the one
described in the narrative. The plot develops over the course of one
day, as tensions build to the explosive denouement and its indelible
image of the hierarchy of daily oppression in the plantation structure.

The Autobiography of a Runaway Slave chronicles the development
of maroon society, a revolutionary movement of runaway slaves
poised to undermine the whole structure of the plantation. One of
the earliest contemporary works within the tradition of the testimo-
nial narrative, *The Autobiography of a Runaway Slave* is the life story,
as told in his own words and voice to writer/ethnographer Miguel
Barnet in the 1960s, of Esteban Montejo, at the time more than one
hundred years old. Montejo had been a slave on a sugar plantation,
a *cimarrón*, as the maroons were called, in the mountains of Cuba;
and a soldier in the revolutionary war against Spain. This collabora-
tive effort by Montejo and Barnet provides the first historical account

of social life in the slave barracks, as well as that of the *cimarrones*, relating experiences common to a whole sector of Cuban society, and filling in chapters in the nation's undocumented, unpublished history. I have included Barnet's introduction to the original edition because it offers a more detailed historical framework for the text, and clarifies for the reader the chronology of events, as they unfold in Montejo's life story. Ultimately disillusioned by the kind of post-independence Cuba he had fought for and won from Spain, Montejo returns to the countryside, where the narratives in the next section, Rural Peasantry, take place.

Wages Paid

JAMES CARNEGIE
(JAMAICA)

Part I
Morning

Johnson
I

$\mathcal{T}$he cursing came through the high window at the end of the barracks, the cursing that was monotonous and repetitious, the cursing that was routine.

"Get your arses up. Haul your fucking tails."

It would not be long now before there was an even harsher noise, the noise of the crack of the whips, but there was a difference, a difference between the white voices of the overseer and his book-keepers and the fact that the whips were being wielded by the black slave-drivers. Johnson thought the poor missionaries who had become so abundant in the last few years didn't know what they were facing really when they were talking about brotherhood, because the whip cut just as deep whether wielded by black or white.

It was a day just like any other on an estate just like any other in a year just like any other during a crop season just like any other and the work had to be done.

Although Johnson had something of a special position, he was not one of those slaves fortunate enough to be trusted with their own plots of land or their own huts. Despite his reputation as a stud, he had to share the normal stench of a barracks that was not much different, if his memory served him well, from the barracoon where he had been kept before coming to Jamaica 15 years before as a boy of 15.

II

They moved out the barracks in the usual way, with some brave or stupid ones remaining behind as usual pretending to be sick. Some of them were sick for true, Johnson thought, but whether they really were or not, Johnson had no doubt that by the time Mr. Johnson—the fucker—in the Great House finished with them they would be a good deal sicker. Johnson respected Mr. Johnson although trouble was growing between them. His name showed that Mr. Johnson had once regarded him highly, since the name was only passed down normally through sons, but Mr. Johnson—and Johnson in his own mind could not really leave off the title "Mister"—now was apparently regarding him, Johnson, as a rival, although he still belonged to him, and not as a troublemaker like those far across the water in St. Domingue.

III

They went into the field and began to eat. Johnson looked at the women and wondered whether the poor bitches really had an easier time than them, the male-animals who they were feeding. Both men and women had their bodies used, but with the men it was only their outsides that suffered since, if you survived, the external muscle-aches were soon long gone, but the women-bitches had to take the men inside them and then bear the results for months, then years afterwards, in a long tiring cycle which only ended with the end of their usefulness, and they had to do other work meanwhile. Johnson laughed because—as usual—he had got a piece of meat *and* a piece of fish with his yam and vegetables. Few of the others had got either because *none* of them were entitled to it before mid-day when their bodies and spirits were both dry and when the food was just fuel and had no enjoyment.

At the same time Johnson thought it was fucking funny and he laughed at the right word when he thought how he paid for this special treatment at night. He bit off the laugh quickly though and not just for the immediate fear of the lash but by the repetition of the thought about his namer Mr. Johnson.

IV

They had finished eating and Johnson thought about the fuel that would be burnt out now and in the same cane fields after dark, but even while chopping and piling he was thinking about Mr. Johnson and their rivalry. This rivalry was over the women, not any particular woman but the women in general. Mr. Johnson of course had first pick first fuck, second pick second fuck, third pick third fuck, last pick last fuck, any pick any fuck, and he, Johnson, who had grown into a stud because of his size, his looks, and his endurance, had to take what he could get as well as what he was not particular for and which was sometimes even forced on him, but Mr. Johnson was supposed to be angry because a few of his house women had supposedly been show-ing reluctance to enter his own bed after they had been serviced by *him*—Johnson. Worse yet, Mr. Johnson was angry because the laugh-ing story had been going round that Mr. Johnson had been given a dose by one or more of the women, and the untrue story had been spread by one or more of these same women in their frightened defense that they had caught the said clap from Johnson.

V

"Clap"—the word and the lash of the whip with the same sound and feeling hit Johnson at the same time. The whip had been handled by fat black Cho-Cho, the driver of his gang. Johnson knew that he must have been idling in his daydream with the painful results he had just felt. The bitch Cho-Cho knew that he could not afford to harm Johnson too much, but at the same time he knew just how far he could go to hurt him. If he ever got the chance Johnson would kill Cho-Cho's rass. Johnson also thought that the whip was as painful as the clap that he had been thinking about and he felt that it was just like the fucking white to blame the Indians who had been here long before both of them for giving them clap or whatever they wanted to call it. He had first heard the word used by some naval officer guests of Mr. Johnson.

VI

Johnson did not want to kill Cho-Cho's rass for any special reason but pride. Johnson knew within himself that he would be just like Cho-Cho if he was a driver, but he figured that in his special position that Cho-Cho should not trouble him at all, because he was expensive, because he was a prize, because he was a stud. At the same time that he was thinking this, Johnson knew that he was really not being reasonable, because if Cho-Cho did do that the other slaves would not have stood for it. They might wink their eyes at the extra food because they probably felt that he deserved the food for his extra "work," but they would not take kindly to it if he did not get his own ass cut now and again like the rest of them.

VII

There were somewhere between two hundred and fifty and three hundred slaves on Mr. Johnson's estate and only four or five of them had the kind of importance or special treatment that Johnson and Cho-Cho had. Johnson did not really know exactly how many slaves there were on Bonavist estate—and what a fucking name he also thought—for several reasons, and one of them was because it was none of *his* business since he was just one of them at the start anyway. Another reason was that some died, some got sick, more got sold, some were bought and even one or two escaped from month to month. But the figure was between two fifty and three hundred on a stable basis, and of these perhaps one hundred and fifty of them were stable. Johnson hadn't died and he didn't intend to die just yet, although his middle passage had been a bad one even as those went. Johnson didn't get sick very often either because he was well fed and well exercised, and he perhaps did not really have any time to get sick between his day and night duties, although he *had* heard of slaves like him who had been killed by their *night* duties. Johnson didn't intend to get sold either because he had also heard, and he stopped to think that he had *heard*, a lot of things that when you were sold to another estate or another master that things seldom got better but only worse. As for being bought, well he was here, and he thought that Mr. Johnson sure as hell wouldn't buy him again. As for escape, some had tried that but not *he*, Johnson. There were two reasons why *he* wouldn't do that— The first was that he would *probably* get caught, and the second was that he would almost *certainly* get caught. If he got caught, Mr. Johnson wouldn't kill him, although he was certainly entitled to do so. He would probably just cut off his balls, which was his life, in a move that would leave him strong enough to do the donkey work. He even knew the words associated with this act—"castration," "gelding," and "eunuch." Even as a boy on his home coast he had heard rumors of strange practices in the north by some of the Muslims. What might be even worse however was that he would succeed in escaping and be forced to go to the Maroons in the mountains, or worse yet be set upon by them. The Maroons of Jamaica had realized for many years now, and especially since the last war, that the white men would only allow them to exist if they did not grow much further or faster in numbers and if they did not spread out of their own areas and affect the estates. Because of this they had become hunters, and as hunters they were as good as the whites who had hunted *them* before were bad. They knew everywhere, they thought like slaves themselves, and they did not tire—so people like Johnson suffered.

VIII

The whip cracked again and Johnson was stung out of his thoughts— he was not prepared to take much more of Cho-Cho, but on the other hand he was not ready to move, so he figured that he had better get cracking properly again. He wasn't ready yet but he would be ready soon, he thought as he bent to the restoration of his rhythm.

Mary

I

The women were working not far from the cane fields. They were also working near some of the food that they were preparing, in the shade of some breadfruit trees.

To the older slaves the breadfruit was still a strange taste. A few of them liked it, but most of the older ones did not eat it as if they liked it. They had heard that it had come to the islands through a mad white captain about whom even some of the slave owners— some of whom were mad themselves—still talked. The women were in the shade unlike the men and some of their own sex who Mr. Johnson made work in the fields. Mr. Johnson tried to keep his women for particular purposes and he tried to keep his men and women apart most of the time, but he also made sure that they were together when he wanted to, and when Mr. Johnson said together he *meant* together. The women were in the shade, but they were still hot.

II

They were hot because they were cooking for the men, because it was hard work, because the wood and charcoal fires were hot, and because they had to stay close to them. They had to fan them, they had to keep them going—they had in fact to cool one fire to get it hot—and they also had to get the food ready in time and when called for. During crop nothing really stopped and everything was supposed to be ready when due. When something was not ready, there was even more cursing and beating and noise and anger than was the normal pattern of life on the estate. Mary was one of the women cooking, she was one of the chief regular cooking women cooking in the shade. Mary was no longer very young or else she would still have been somewhere nearer Mr. Johnson in his Great House, in his great bedroom, perhaps even wiping him down when he got off his great commode in his great bedroom beside his great bed, in his Great House. It was one of Mr. Johnson's nice peculiarities that he liked his women to do. Mary had

22

passed that stage however and, partly because she had deliberately wanted to pass that stage, she had in fact got fatter.

III

Mary had got fatter in the body but not in the head. Too many of the girls who performed house and bed duties were good for nothing else and so got sold or passed down for common stud use to their fellow niggers when Mr. Johnson and his white overseers got tired of them. Mary had made sure however that she could cook well enough and be strong enough to earn her place. Mary was also a troublemaker of sorts. It was she who had put up the girls to telling Mr. Johnson that Johnson had spread the dose among them.

IV

Mary was a troublemaker for a good reason as she saw it. During her best years as a filly she had enjoyed certain privileges and outward powers on the estate because of her special position. She had lost these sooner than she need have, and in order to save herself from a worse situation, she saw to it that she was the unofficial mother-figure and advisor of the girls as well as the head cook of the cooking women, in fact if not in name. She had not found it difficult to attain these positions in fact because on the female side of the estate there was very little of the structure of authority that there was on the male side. The old women did have certain positions, it was true also, but they did not have the energy to follow up on this, which suited Mary just fine.

V

Mary's story about Johnson to Mr. Johnson was not done just out of *idle* calculated mischief but out of *planned* calculated mischief. As a woman of substance, as she saw herself justifiably, she had been fucked by Johnson and fucked up by Johnson. To tell the truth, she had not minded being fucked by Johnson—as a stud he was good at his job and she had not minded that part of her duty, when she had been passed down by Mr. Johnson, and to tell the truth she had not minded that part of Mr. Johnson either, but whereas she recognized that Mr. Johnson had the right to turn her out of his bed and everything else, she had not expected a similar type of disregard or callousness from Johnson. She had hoped that Johnson would have seen what she was trying to do for herself on the estate and would have respected her for it, but he had thrown her aside in due time too, as if to show Mr. Johnson that he respected and feared his judgment on everything, that he was no different from any other man—black or white.

VI

The slow idea of revenge was thus built up in Mary's head and she did not let anyone else see what was happening. Thus, she did not do anything as obvious as poisoning or fouling Johnson's food because this would have been too clear. Everything might have been over too swiftly and, worst of all, she too would have been inevitably punished. Her desire for revenge was certainly strong but it did not run as far as self-sacrifice, self-sacrifice of position, or, worse yet, of life. If anybody's life was going to be lost, it was going to be Johnson's—not hers, no sir, not hers. Her plan involved women since women, being one herself, were what *she* knew about and since women were the weaknesses of Johnson and Mr. Johnson, and since both Johnson and Mr. Johnson thought that women were in fact one of their strengths. She knew better however, she certainly knew better and her plans involved the obeah-man, Wiseman, who was also looking out for himself. Not that she felt that she could trust *him* or *any* man, after her experience with the Johnsons.

Wiseman
I

Wiseman had been given his name by Mr. Johnson, some said because he was afraid, some said because he was joking. At any rate Mr. Johnson, who liked all of his slaves to have English names, had called his obeah-man Wiseman and the name stuck because it was so suitable. Every estate had at least one obeah-man like Wiseman on it, although they served different purposes on different estates. On some the masters thought they were frauds and charlatans but kept them just the same in order that they could control the other slaves. On some, the masters were not sure about their powers or their values, but they kept them just in case they had either.

Other masters feared them just as much as the slaves did and treated them specially almost as if they were not slaves in fact, but people on the same level as the whites. It was not clear exactly which category of master Mr. Johnson was in as far as this was concerned, because he did treat Wiseman very well, although the slaves were equally sure that Mr. Johnson feared neither God nor man—nor woman nor child, nor animal, nor slave for that matter.

II

Wiseman worked neither as a house or field slave nor did he seem to do very much work for the estate. Most of the time he was allowed to cultivate his own plot of land all the time unlike the few others who could only do so after hours and on weekends when it was not crop time. Even this Wiseman did not seem to do, since he usually managed somehow during even the heaviest of crop times to have some young slaves to do the work for him and allow him to walk around appearing from place to place and from time to time as if he were one of the overseers.

III

As he was doing now. Wiseman himself had no doubt of where he stood. He had power because of it, he had power because he *really* had *power*. He was a big black man with deep-set brooding eyes and he did not talk much. Which all meant that he was very rarely challenged as a man quite apart from not being challenged as an *obeah*-man. As long as he could remember the power had been in his family with his father and grandfather and doubtless those before them too. When he cursed somebody he stayed cursed and on occasion he had even seen to it that a man was killed if he seemed at all reluctant to die once he was supposed to. Wiseman did not normally do business as an obeahman on the estate since he was already comfortable enough so that he could comfortably terrorize everybody and anybody impartially.

IV

Wiseman was probing now with something particular in view because he had sensed what was building up on the estate over Johnson, Mr. Johnson, and the girls, and he didn't like it since he couldn't control it and he didn't like things that were not under his control. He had also noted, because it was his business to do so, that Mary was building up to something, that she was planning to approach him judging by the way in which she had been glancing at him recently, glances which he knew were not those of sexual attraction but something much more significant. Because of his strong position in the place Wiseman did not bother with questions of sexual attraction. He was no stud either but when he wanted a woman he took her or, as was more likely, it happened during the course of one of his Dahomey rituals. His business was observation, however, and he wanted to know what was brewing in Mary's mind. He had watched the way in which she had carried herself over the years on the estate and he had watched carefully in order to make sure that she was not doing anything that would affect his own position. He had nothing against Mary, in fact he rather liked her, but if he had to he would crush her. He was the most powerful black man on the estate—even more powerful than Cho-Cho the head driver—and he intended to stay that way or else . . . there would be no estate worth speaking of left.

Cho-Cho
I

The subject of Wiseman's last meditation, Cho-Cho, was not given to much meditation himself, or he had not been so since taking on the job of head slave-driver for Mr. Johnson, some four years before.

The head slave-driver was always the most hated and feared person, because he wielded the white man's whip, because he was black, because he shouldn't have been flogging other blacks, because he himself was a fucker, because only a fucker ever became a slave-driver, because slave-drivers were always fuckers. Cho-cho had been sour from the start, perhaps even before the start. One of the reasons why he had survived *his* particular Atlantic crossing had been because he was a miserable rass. He had fought in the hold, he had killed and he had caused to die. At the auction he had been in better shape than most of his fellows, but it must have been what the others called his "crossness" which had caught Mr. Johnson's eye.

II

He had sure to rass given Mr. Johnson trouble. He was a fighter, a malingerer, and a potential rebel. He tended to know just where to stop so that he could live, so that he could survive, thus he was never in real danger of being beaten within an inch of his life, nor in danger of being put to death. Nowadays, Cho-Cho thought, anyway only a madman would kill valuable property like a slave, although they did not worry a shit about turning the old and sick ones out to die. It had not taken Mr. Johnson long to see through Cho-Cho really, though by figuring that the same things in his character which made him a hell of a hell-raiser would make him a very devil of a hell-queller.

III

None of the other slaves had ever liked Cho-Cho, it was true, but there were those who secretly admired him for his spirit of rebellion. This admiration quickly went, however, when it was expressed through the whip on their backs. Cho-Cho had not wasted much thought on taking the job if he really had a choice. To shy away from such a job would have served as a kind of statement to his owner-master that he intended to be a perpetual troublemaker and that he would have to be disposed of one way or the other eventually before *he* reached the point of *thinking* of disposing of his master by rebellion or personal action. Being the driver meant, of course, that Cho-Cho always had to be on the watch-out for a literal stab-in-the-back and that he had to have a hut by himself, but this suited Cho-Cho just fine—his own company was *all* he wanted most of the time anyway and his own company was what he generally got.

IV

Cho-Cho was watching Johnson as well as flicking him with the whip. He believed in his heart, or his soul or his mind—he was not really sure which—that Johnson was somebody like him—a man who had to have his own way and had additional facts to back him up as Johnson did with his stud prowess. Cho-Cho knew that he was playing with fire and almost needlessly when he was provoking Johnson, because he did not feel that Johnson had anything in mind in particular as far as he, Cho-Cho, was concerned, yet he could not resist the temptation to annoy him or hit at him. He also wanted to make it clear to the others in the gang that he, Cho-Cho, was not afraid of Johnson or any other fucker—even Wiseman. Cho-Cho was aware however that this could *really* make Johnson his enemy and that he, Cho-Cho, could then *really* have some trouble on his hands since he would *have* to face up to what would come after—*whatever* that was.

Part II
Mid-Morning

Mr. Johnson
I

Mr. Johnson himself appeared long after breakfast and long after the work had started. He did this because it was his policy and not because he was lazy, although he did like to lie late in bed in the mornings as a consequence of being up late at nights or being down at nights, as the case was, with vigorous activity. Mr. Johnson liked to believe that his estate was well run, and he liked to feel that the routine would go

28

on even if he or his few European employees were temporarily absent from the estate. For that reason he always made sure that things got going before he himself came on the scene, although inevitably things were always tighter when he appeared. Several slaves became syco-phantic or, as they were termed by the others behind his back, the "balls-suckers" got into operation and began to shine up.

II

Mr. Johnson was an unusual master in more ways than one and was clearly different from most of his neighbors and even "colleagues" throughout the entire island—even an island as big as Jamaica which was the biggest of the British Indies without any doubt at all. The chief thing that made Mr. Johnson different was that he was an educated man, he read books—a fact which he generally tried to keep quiet or to cover up when he was in the company of other whites, but which still had in fact been spread around by certain of the Baptist missionaries who not only disapproved of Mr. Johnson as a slave owner, but also of his moral character and of the fact that as an educated and cultured person they felt inwardly somehow that he should *know* better or at least *act* better.

III

Mr. Johnson had come out to the islands in a very strange manner, a manner which explained why he was so unusual a member of the plantocracy. He had been the second son of a wealthy family and as such had been educated to go into the Church, but before actually taking orders his father, older brother, and younger sister had been burnt to death in a fire which also razed the family estates suspi-ciously near in time to the Gordon riots of 1780. In order to reshape the family fortunes, Mr. Johnson had come out to the islands himself in order to take over the management from the attorney who had let the place run down in line with the general disinterest that the Johnson family had itself shown at a time when sugar prices were already declining and when the Revolutionary War was treating the island colonies even more roughly than it was treating England herself.

Mr. Johnson had thus had a trying time from the very start as he saw it and he was not helped by the fact that his arrival virtually coincided with that of the first group of effective missionaries who had begun to stir up trouble in the islands by contrasting the gospel of Brotherly Love with the institution of slavery. Mr. Johnson thought wryly to himself how he had been tempted by the Wesleyans in England, yet how he could not face up to the necessities of their actions in Jamaica.

IV

As he rode around his plantation, Mr. Johnson continued to muse and to worry because he was in fact a secret pessimist—secret because he did not dare let either his fellow owners or his slaves know how he really felt, the former because they would have felt that he was mad and was letting down the side, and the latter because they would probably have felt encouraged towards rebellion or other direct action. Yes, Mr. Johnson thought, he *was* a pessimist, or perhaps it would have been more accurate to say that he was a *realist*. He did not see himself how the slave and sugar systems could last very much longer and, feeling the way that he did, he did not know, or rather did not want to think, what his own physical and financial positions would be once the system collapsed with him and others like him somewhere underneath in the ruins. He had thought these heretical thoughts for some time before the Revolution in St. Domingue, which was now several years old, and he still felt that way although the Maroons had been crushed here in Jamaica the year before and although the troubles in St. Domingue showed no immediate signs of spreading across to Jamaica. He just could not believe, however, that a new century could and would come without the dangerous ideas bred in Europe and to the north having some effect in this part of the Indies. The cursed missionaries had come quickly enough after the activities of the brothers Wesley in England, but at the same time his brother planters had shown an astonishing resistance to some of the mechanical developments that had been taking place at home over the last generation, and he and one or two others who felt like him did not dare go ahead on their own.

V

At the same time Mr. Johnson *had* to admit to himself—and he smiled at the thought of the idea of compulsion since he was not really trying to hide anything from himself—that he was very guilty of obtuseness and traditionalism in the running of his very own estate, and he was guilty for a combination of reasons none of which were very good or very commendable, such as his mental laziness and the pleasures of the flesh, although he now and then rationalized to himself that if the estate, the system, and he himself were all going to the devil then he might as well do so in style and comfort.

VI

It was certainly inaccurate to speak of comfort now, since he was literally paying with pains for the pleasurable use of his penis every time he had to piss these days, and one of the peculiar things about his particular variation on the venereal disease was that he had to keep making his water over and over again, and every time he looked at and felt the offending organ he thought with painful irony that his and other diseases of their type should have been blamed on the goddess Venus especially as portrayed by Botticelli whose original he had seen on his Grand Tour which now seemed such a long time away.

VII

Mr. Johnson was worried about his "dose" because he had known of men dying from this complaint or if not even dying being obviously disfigured and raddled and unfit for human companionship. He had been bled and purged, and he had even stepped up his alcoholic consumption as had been recommended by the local quacks, but he was in fact no better off—if anything he was worse—and he was in fact being really sorely tempted by necessity—despite his strong scepticism—to contact Wiseman soon and find out what were the African remedies for such an unfortunate situation. He would have to do something about the bedroom attendants—and he smiled at the euphemism—who had passed the dose on to him. He would also have to consider what should be done about his once-favorite stud Johnson.

VIII

Mr. Johnson did not for one moment believe the story that Johnson had passed on the disease to him through the attractive intermediaries, but there were sound reasons for giving the impression that he did. He felt in fact that such a situation was indeed possible but not probable, since his stud Johnson had so much personal pride that he would have taken great pains to avoid being caught in such a situation. Johnson also knew that he could be checked at any time on the state of his health since his position was important in the stocking of the estate and definitely likely to become more so since he, Mr. Johnson, felt that once the war with the French let up the slave trade would have to go, since even First Minister Pitt himself was reported to have given his support to Wilberforce and the other hypocrites on the last occasion that the matter had come up in the Commons—in other words it was just a matter of time, and not necessarily a *long* time either. He was one of the first planters in Jamaica to definitely make this a policy practice, and he had been doing it for some time, although not systematically, until he had heard of the work of the well-known Codringtons of Barbados on one of the smaller islands.

IX

There was also a problem with European numbers, although Mr. Johnson did not let that concern him too much *whatever* the so-called Deficiency Laws said. Quite apart from their almost total lack of cultivation, he had tended to be prejudiced against Europeans and Creoles in the islands because of the careless and dishonest way in which his family's estates had been managed and the consequent amount of work that he had had to do and the lack of cooperation with which he had been faced even at that point and even with what he considered were his own rational and liberal ideals. Mr. Johnson also did not want too many others like him who shared his own weakness as far as the women were concerned, because they might not be able to discipline themselves as well as he could in that he could control himself when he wanted—he liked to feel. He liked for instance to give them up for Lent just to show that he could do so, although he had long since lost any orthodox or other religious convictions. Thus he had only one European overseer and one European book-keeper and no others.

X

Mr. Johnson rode up at last to the spot where the main gangs of slaves were working and as he neared he could sense the tempo rising as far as the work, the whips, and the voices of the drivers were concerned, the tempo of life rising although during crop time it often seemed as if the tempo could rise no higher, although he knew from his own experience that this did not mean that everybody was thinking about the work even if they appeared to be very busy. Nor did Mr. Johnson make the mistake of thinking like most of his associates on his own estates and his fellow planters on the others that the slaves did not have minds to think. If the St. Domingue rising had shown nothing else it had shown this, but there were still those who refused to see and these were many, and these many were the main reasons why Mr. Johnson did not feel optimistic.

Johnson
I

Johnson's and Mr. Johnson's eyes met. As he rode past, Mr. Johnson said, "Listen nuh Johnson, I want to see you at the House tonight." Johnson did not answer, he had no need to, it was not expected, he had nothing to say, he did not want to say anything, he could not say anything, he did not *feel* like saying anything, he said nothing. He even tried not to think anything, although he knew very well what Mr. Johnson wanted with him. He tried to think of other things and other people in his small world, although he knew that even this would bring him right back eventually to Mr. Johnson.

II

Johnson thought of his children unknown and known on the estate—unknown because before Mr. Johnson had introduced his breeding program he could not be sure what the tally was, although he had a very good idea in some instances who was who because of physical resemblances on both the male and female sides. In other cases he could not be sure, and in some cases he could never be sure, because some were sold and some died. Mr. Johnson did not have any particular policy as far as keeping or breaking up families and relationships were concerned and he seemed to sell or not to sell as the whim, fancy, or the money took him, most notably the latter. In any event, Johnson figured that not even Mr. Johnson, who was smarter than most among the Europeans, really understood the wide family system of the Guinea Coast, and the responsibilities over a large area—if they ever did come to understand it, they would realize how futile many of their efforts at breaking-up were and how, in some instances anyway, their property, their cattle, their stock, their playthings were actually laughing at them instead of crying on account of them, as they often pretended to do on these occasions.

III

Since the breeding program, however, Johnson knew of a couple of dozen on the estate who definitely belonged to him. Because of the numbers and because of his nature, however, he only followed up very few of them and he was only really interested in fewer, but he had to pretend more interest than he really had because it was expected of him as a man, it was expected of him as a tribesman in particular, and as a seeker of position especially. It was true of course that Johnson, because of his occupation, did not have to have or recognize or claim children to prove his virility since he was a stud, and a stud was of necessity virile or he wasn't a stud, and if he *was* a stud and then was no *longer* a stud, then he was nothing, and if he was nothing after such a background, then he was *really* nothing.

IV

Johnson had a particular pride in certain of his daughters. He had this pride for two reasons—not that he was ashamed of his sons he let it be known speedily. The first and most important was that he was *not* expected, as a man and a stud, to be particularly interested in girl children—since usually they only wanted the boys to show concrete proof of the virility continuously through life and to carry on the tradition so they were not fussy normally about girls who they thought were more or less clutterers up and useful only eventually for cooking and for other men's pleasures when they grew up or even perhaps *before* they did. Johnson, however, liked girls as children because no one else in his line normally did, he liked them when they grew up to be pretty and to attract other men, and he liked them when they reminded him of their mothers—since their mothers had usually been well chosen women—and they in their turn would be the fillies for future generations of his successors as studs—if the life continued as it was, which it probably would, but which he hoped for their sake would not.

He hoped that they would not mate them with any of his own sons by other women—he did not know very much about the body apart from its various pleasant and not-so-pleasant functions, but he knew that this was not good and that the products never lived for long and, even if they did, they were always sickly. He had seen this both in Guinea and in Jamaica and he felt also that it was the kind of mistake that Mr. Johnson—whatever he thought of him—was not likely to make.

V

He wondered on continuing to think of Mr. Johnson and on being hit for a third time—a third time too much—by Cho-Cho this morning

35

whether he, Mr. Johnson, would live long enough or whether he would remain vigorous long enough to enjoy any of his daughters—which in a few years could very well have been some of his own, since the complexion was not always diluted and sometimes it was very much thinned out. When he looked up again he saw Mary talking to Mr. Johnson while the rest of the women were getting ready to serve the lunch.

Mary
I

Mary was indeed talking to Mr. Johnson and not only was she talking to him, but she was setting her plans into motion by baiting Mr. Johnson:

"Mr. Johnson, I hear you not so well sah," with a sly, half-smile. "In fact sah I hear that you feeling poor sah, perhaps you need me to take care of you like old days sah." She smiled, openly this time, but bit it off swiftly when Mr. Johnson casually stung her across her face with his riding crop as he stormed off with an even more sour look than normal on his face.

II

Even with the blood running down her chin and the public hurt to her claims on dignity, Mary was well satisfied. She wanted to get Mr. Johnson vexed and she had succeeded in doing so, even at some risk to herself, but hurt dignity and a cut mouth were small prices to pay if her larger plans were going to work out and these plans definitely depended on getting Mr. Johnson vexed and moving him out of his normal frame of mind—in other words to get him acting rashly without his normal thinking and care. She had done this. She now had to set into motion the other parts of her plan, which concerned other people, unfortunately. Wiseman had to be brought in and she had to figure out a way in which Wiseman could be used without his getting too much out of it and without too much risk to *her* own plans.

III

She was now able to go and see Wiseman and she had to work up her courage and work out her thoughts before she could do so, since Wiseman was no joker and had to be convinced that things would work out well for him too before he could take any *particular* course of action. She also could not afford to go and see him in full sight of everybody—at least not in the *day*. People would then begin to wonder, whereas if she went at night they would not think anything of it, or rather they would only think of the obvious reasons for her going there—this kind of thought might have worried her at one time even quite recently, but it did not *now*. On second thought, however, Mary decided to brave it and go and see him immediately. She did not think that there was very much time to waste, nor was she sure for how long Mr. Johnson could be kept on the boil, so she calculated that she had better act very quickly.

IV

She waited for a while, while watching over the cooking process. Wiseman had been around before on his "supervisory" rounds and she was sure that he would be round again since he, like everybody else, had to eat or wanted to eat and more often than not he would eat his mid-day meal with the rest of the slaves—it was in fact one of the few ways in which he showed that he was like them in any real respect apart from their doubtful humanity, although again, as far as *he* was concerned, he did not really show any animal status as far as work and usages were concerned.

She looked around, trying to concentrate on the figures looming in the distance. What she was looking for was a black figure walking free and not hurrying—that would be Wiseman, because even the drivers hurried. She wondered meanwhile whether she should really wait for him to come *round* or whether it would be better to go *to* him—which plan would look worse, which one would be the *least* worst, which one would be the most effective and at the same time the most misleading or the most confusing.

V

She went up to him, but with a plate of food at the same time, walking
with a little more deliberation and slowness, and consciously moving
her bottom with a little more play than she normally employed or at
any rate was conscious of employing. She went up to him, handed him
the banana leaf with the food and walked off again, a little more slowly
though than on her original approach in order to make sure that the
point was not lost on anybody. She had also made sure that the others
could see that Wiseman had got portions of food like Johnson—this
would not have surprised the other slaves of course who appreciated
the influence of Wiseman's position constantly, but they would have
noted Mary's approach to him as being something new and she hoped
that they would draw what seemed to be the very obvious conclusion
when Wiseman followed her as he was now in fact *doing*.

VI

Mary walked along knowing that Wiseman was right behind her, but
she did not look around until she had reached the tree and her shade.
She sat down and heard Wiseman say directly, "What you want?" He
grunted again directly, "You not like them other women—no mind,
wha you goin on wid?" He paused, "What you want?," again. Mary
looked at him for a long time. Wiseman looked at her for a long time
and noticed the blood stains on one side of her nose and her mouth.
He looked at her for a long time again and hit her deliberately and
very forcefully on the other side to bring a matching but fresher stain
of blood. "You wastin me fuckin time," he said and turned to go away.
"Stop," said Mary. "Ah wan talk to you." "Den why the rass you wont
talk?" said Wiseman. "Ah fraid," said Mary. "You not fraid a rass," said
Wiseman. "Look how you get two rass lick since morning and you jus
tek them. What you want?" said Wiseman again. "Ah wan some help,"
replied Mary. "Ah wan fuck up Johnson. Ah wouldn't mind fuckin up
Mr. Johnson too. You been hearing the story dem." Her voice now
changed to a querulous questioning note. "Yes," said Wiseman. "You
can do anything wid it? You can do anything bout it?" "Praps," replied

38

Wiseman. "Praps." And he left. He left, leaving Mary more than a
little worried since he had not in fact asked for any reasons or any
explanation or any profit and this was unlike him and she was in fact
very worried.

Part III
Lunch

Cho-Cho
I

Cho-Cho stepped up the tempo of the whip a bit more—he always
did this near meal times because he liked to give the impression that
on his gang at any rate there would be no slackening up for meals,
while at the same time it really indicated that he wanted his lunch.
On this particular day he also wanted time to think out what was
happening, because he sensed that something *was* happening that *he*
was being left out of and this he did *not* like.

He had seen the clash between Mr. Johnson and Mary and he had
seen what appeared to be another clash between Wiseman and Mary
and of course there had been his own use of the whip on Johnson more
often than he had had to do normally and these all added up to an
unpleasant situation, much more unpleasant than the normal unpleasantness of the estate. He was especially concerned about what seemed
to be Mary's odd behavior which was not like her at all at all.

II

Cho-Cho decided that he would go to Mary herself for his food instead
of taking it from the first of the women who came along as was his normal
custom. He noted right away that Mary saw this and made an effort to
control herself and to act as if she did not notice anything in particular.
Cho-Cho did not say anything while he was actually *taking* the food and
he even turned as if he was *not* going to say anything at all and then he
suddenly snapped his head round and said, "Ah know what you goin on

wid." Pause, "Ah doan like it. You better doan fuck wid me at all." He was pleased to see that she changed color despite her blackness and that her eyes seemed to reflect what was happening in her head and her belly and what was happening there was not nice as far as she was concerned. Yes, he was *very* pleased to see that, on second thought and on third and forever thought, although he didn't really feel that what Miss Mary was doing concerned him directly, but one of the reasons that he had survived for so long and had in fact got to where he was, was because he did not let situations like this slip.

III

Cho-Cho also saw another funny thing when he sat down to eat his food which he normally enjoyed but which he was not really noticing today, but only shoveling down like the slaves who stoked the boilers in the factory at the height of the crop who seemed to be oiled by their own sweat which was produced by their own work, which was fueled by food which had taken energy to eat, which enabled them to burn more energy which put out more sweat which oiled them. The food Cho-Cho was now eating was oiling him and oiling his mind. The funny thing that was now exercising his mind additionally was the sight of Wiseman sitting down and doing nothing after he had eaten— not that Wiseman's doing nothing was an odd sight, but Wiseman usually did nothing upright or walking or on his own ground or lying down and did not often do nothing sitting down.

IV

Cho-Cho continued to eat his food and to find food for thought at the same time. What Wiseman was doing could not even be considered as part of the short rest that the slaves were sometimes given when it was very hot since he would then be stretched out under a tree or sleeping with a woman beside him, but there could be no mistake that *Mister* Wiseman was actually thinking and what was actually worse, he could guess or actually be sure that Wiseman was thinking about what Mary had said to him despite the fact that he had hit her. In other words,

Wiseman may very well have been angry but he still listened to her and not only listened to her but was evidently thinking of taking some course of action on what she had said to him. Considering this he now began to wonder whether he had been wise in his approach to Mary and he figured that he could just about handle Mary by herself although to tell the truth he was not so really sure about that, but like everybody else on the estate he was afraid of Wiseman or steered clear of him, although he was more afraid of Wiseman as a *man* than as an *obeah-man*, but a combination of Mary and Wiseman was something else again entirely with which he did not want to meddle and with which he was now very much afraid that he had already meddled too much.

V

Cho-Cho now had to figure out what to do to protect himself from getting burnt by the sparks that would almost certainly fly from whatever might happen, yet it was not in him to go back to Mary and try to recover his ground. His position would not really be worth anything if he was to do that with a woman. This meant that he had to go to Wiseman or better yet talk to Wiseman the next time he came around past his gang, all he would do would be to offer his services in any capacity. This might of course make him a puppet of Wiseman as far as future actions were concerned but this was much better than being thought an enemy.

VI

As he got up trailing his whip, Cho-Cho saw a sight which distracted him temporarily—a gang of small and not so small boys and girls under the supervision of one of the older women, and he wondered how some of those boys and some of his own children would accept the life when they grew up. He had heard of other slaves on other estates who were being brought up in the Christian religion, but he did not think that that was very important because most of the owners did not seem to take it very seriously as far as they themselves were concerned, although some of them seemed to be worried by the missionaries' effect on the slaves.

What he was thinking of though, was that these boys were actually born on the island and had no memory of anything else, so that he actually wanted to know whether they would be easier to handle than the older slaves who could always explode at any time—in fact even after several years of being a driver Cho-Cho rarely turned his back on his own gang unless he was being covered. Cho-Cho also thought of the possibility/probability that some of the said future possible troublemakers could be his own children and those of other drivers and he laughed, but the laugh did not sound nice.

Wiseman

I

Wiseman *knew* that his unusual posture was attracting attention and he sensed that even Cho-Cho was watching him, but he was not really worried although he was concerned, concerned not worried. He was not worried because he was still in control of the situation and that control was not yet threatened nor had any crisis really developed, but he was concerned because Mary looked as if she might do something desperate if she were not helped or aided in her problems or imagined problems or desire for revenge. He was also concerned about what would happen after whatever he chose to do or not to do. In thinking it over he came to two plain conclusions—that he didn't mind cutting down Johnson or even doing away with him, but Mr. Johnson was an entirely different business—definitely. It might be useful and even pleasant to cause him pain but not permanent harm since, unknowingly, he shared Johnson's view that it was better to stick with the known evils and if he *did* arrange for anything to be done to Mr. Johnson he had to make sure that there would be no reaction on *his* head—although he did not really care very much about Mary's.

II

He thought about what he could do and how many people he could or should involve in his plans and in what way he could involve them. He thought about whether he should use his position as a man and his strength instead of or as well his obeah status, and if he should just use his obeah status whether he should have a public ritual or a private one? Should it be done in the night or in the day? Whether in fact he could afford to postpone any action beyond today and whether in fact he had time for *anything* at all that would take elaborate preparations in view of the time at his disposal. He could *always* set up something of course, even in the limited time, but this might involve *so* many people as to create a major upheaval on the estate and Wiseman was comfortable enough as not to want to do this whatever anybody else on the estate might think—but *he* definitely *had* to think.

III

Sitting down did not seem to help, however, so Wiseman got up and resumed his rounds noting with satisfaction that Mr. Johnson seemed to have gone in—they never normally met, in fact they tried to avoid each other on most occasions but Wiseman did not in particular want to meet him today and would not like it to appear as if he were avoiding him especially since he felt that Mr. Johnson would sense—on this day—that there was something in the air, and although he was a skilled trickster and dissembler he did not feel up to tricking Mr. Johnson at *this* point in time on this day at this hour. Almost as unwelcome a sight, however, was that of Cho-Cho sidling towards him and trying to pretend with not very much success that he was not doing so.

IV

Although Wiseman was annoyed at Cho-Cho, in view of his sense of order he did not dare slap him down in front of the slaves in the gang since that might cause trouble before he was ready. He even went as far as to speak first to make things seem not too strange since he sometimes did this not just with Cho-Cho but the other gang-drivers too. "Wha you want?" he said. "Ah want to talk to you." "Ah know, me cyan see dat." "Listen no old man," this from Cho-Cho. "Ah never mean anyting wid Mary. Ah never really mean fe trouble har. Ah did lose my temper." Wiseman replied, "Boy you have fe careful who you lose yu temper wid." He said it with a half-laugh though and not with too much apparent annoyance. This reassured Cho-Cho and he changed too. Any of the slaves might have thought that they were talking about women as they were, yet as they were not, for the conversation was not really about Mary, although it involved her, and even then, Mary was far from being a typical woman—certainly not on this estate.

V

Wiseman had not really gained anything direct from the conversation but this was not entirely true, he thought. Cho-Cho had not told him anything positive, apart from the fact that he had confessed to losing his temper—which was normal in a slave-driver anyhow, although he had not bothered to point this out to Cho-Cho. Cho-Cho should have realized this weakness but it stressed what he had to do—he had to make the people concerned, Johnson and Mr. Johnson, lose their tempers. He had to prevent them from thinking straight, he had to make them not think at all if possible, although that was not very likely when he considered who were the people involved, so it boiled down again to women and to *bringing in* women.

Johnson
I

Johnson meanwhile was feeling the pressures of the morning and he had also begun to sense something that he did not like at all. He had begun to feel without any real evidence—since he was not really thinking about *all* that he had seen—that events were being aimed at him as if he were being pressed and within four walls with no escape. Eating his lunch was no help either and he was very conscious of this because he normally enjoyed his food like all the pleasures of the flesh and he was especially conscious because he had deliberately gone to Mary, who had been the center of so much activity, and she had given him even more than his usual extra-special share—which he did not like at all since he could not understand *what* was going on and she had *no reason* to give it to him.

II

He *had* to find something to take his mind off his worries. He not only had to *find* something, he had to *do* something and he thought about his children again. He wanted to look for some of them although this meant that he would have to ask Cho-Cho's permission to do so. Not that he felt that Cho-Cho would refuse, but he did not want to face him so soon after their clashes of the morning. The slaves were supposed to have what the Spaniards had called a siesta for an hour or two, although this usually went by the way during crop-time. The pressure was on now, of course, but Johnson hoped that the fact that he had hurried through his lunch would not give Cho-Cho any excuse at all to stop him. When he asked Cho-Cho, he saw an expression on Cho-Cho's face as if to swallow him, but then it was as if Cho-Cho swallowed it himself—although he had made the request with a bitter sullenness—yet Cho-Cho almost seemed to be in haste to grant him the request after everything. Later, when it was too late, it crossed his mind to wonder—although at *this* point he did not bother.

III

To get to the children was a good walk in the hot sun, but Johnson did not really notice it, or at any rate he was not conscious of physical heat tearing through his mentally burning worries as he walked along. The walk was far because the children worked their way through the fields already reaped and after they had weeded and/or cleared, the planting and ratooning process would continue in a cycle that never stopped although some who kept the cycle going would die year to year, month to month, week to week, or in the bad times of the mosquito diseases or the flux, even hour to hour. He saw the figures of the many children and the few old women in the distance and he wondered for the second time what would happen to them. The contrast with the old women stressed it here—they had survived, but they too had been young once and had been desired by people like him or other Mr. Johnsons, and he wondered whether it was worse being dead or faded.

IV

Johnson skirted several gangs before finding the one he wanted, not that he could not have found his children in any others, but he was looking for some special children in a special gang which contained specially bred children, the results of Mr. Johnson's specially controled experiment, a gang which contained young beauty and strength, a gang in short that contained Johnson himself. He was looking for a special child, a special girl—Alice.

V

This gang also had a boy who Johnson thought might be one of his—a boy whose name he believed was Abel, though he was not sure of the name or the son, whereas Johnson could be sure of Alice because she looked like him and because he remembered what her mother had looked and felt like. Her mother had actually been sent to another estate because Johnson believed that Mr. Johnson—who had taken her over—did not want to pass her on. Johnson saw Alice and called her and he noticed while she was coming that his son was watching them strangely and intently, probably, Johnson felt and he could only feel thus, because he was supposed to be the supposed father. The clumsiness and the force of the thought struck him at the same time, but it was the way in which they hit him and it was the way he was—although if the thoughts had really struck him as they should, perhaps he might have thought that the boy/son Abel looked strange and intent because the nature of the society was such that children were not particular about their parents—perhaps their mothers early, but certainly not their fathers—which fitted the boys to become similar fathers—though Mr. Johnson's breeding system and similar ones on other estates had kept down the scattering and dispersal.

VI

Alice came. Johnson looked at her, and after this long look said only, "Alice, you look like you modder but fresher." Alice looked back and replied "Yes." Johnson grasped her hands and said, "Chile you look like you modder fe true," and waited for a reply though tempted to go right away. Alice replied, "Ah believe you but ah didn't know her." She blurted this out and smiled—again like her mother who had not so much to smile about, but had done so. Just at this point the boy/son Abel came up and pulled at her arm glancing crossly at Johnson.

"Cho, come mek we go back," he muttered. "Mek we go back." The girl smiled and Johnson said, "Gwan bout you business, ah just come to see you. Is all right." Johnson turned away noting again out of the corner of his eye that the boy Abel was staring again, more at him than the girl, with what seemed to be anger, and he wondered why. He hadn't done the boy anything, except perhaps to create him, and the boy looking at him as if he had commited some *personal* offense.

Part IV
Early Afternoon

Mary
I

Johnson's departure had been noticed by Mary and she had sent one of her assistants to watch him under the pretext that she was sending for more firewood—this was not unusual since things kept going almost perpetually during crop and firewood was not only necessary for cooking, lighting the fields and factory areas at night, and most important, as fuel by the slaves fueling the factory boilers too. She waited impatiently on the girl although this was not obvious, because her face was, as normally, placid, but her curiosity was boiling. Since she herself had already been a target for the day, however, she did not want any more outbursts even if a new one came from her and was not *directed* at her. She was nervous whether Johnson had noticed anything and was making counter-plans. She did not really believe this, but wanted to keep abreast of what was happening, and whatever was happening was whatever Johnson or the others were doing. Their business was *her* business.

II

The girl reported that she had seen Johnson talking to a girl though not for very long. She did not know who the girl was from a distance, and she did not think it important because she was not near enough to see the way in which the boy had been staring at Johnson and the girl or to know that this would have meant anything to the sharp Miss Mary. She just passed that part of the information out of her mind like water. Mary guessed who the girl was although not precisely, though she calculated it was one of his daughters. She had already had the glimmerings of an idea and these became stronger when she thought again about the weaknesses of Johnson and Mr. Johnson. She now needed help, careful calculation, and time. But of this latter commodity she did not think she had very much at all.

III

Mary had to work out her plans since she had already spent time on thought and there was not much left. She now had an idea of what she was going to do too if she could manage it, although she would have to handle herself carefully if she was not to be carried away in the disaster that she hoped would ensue. She had to get close to Mr. Johnson in a way that would not make him unduly suspicious. Perhaps the only way she could do this would be to make it seem that she was not only trying to get back into his good graces but his bed. Knowing Mr. Johnson's temperament, she could easily get back into his bed and be humiliated in such a way that she would lose her position on the estate with the other slaves and particularly with the women who *she* knew only too well, as a powerful woman herself, were the key individuals and, though suffering, were the powers behind the powers behind the powers, although *under* the powers.

IV

Mary decided to work up a pretext to see Mr. Johnson and get the words she wanted to his ear and let them stay there, sink into his system, penetrating down to his painful cock and burning balls which was the point and the content of her whole effort, and Mary thought that this was quite funny, although the joke could very well come back and land on her with great pain and sad consequences. She however preferred not to think about it not only because the thought was frightening but because it would interfere with what she had to do constructively if her destructive plans were to work and because she had to ensure that Mr. Johnson would not think very much.

V

Mr. Johnson would almost certainly be at his siesta so he would have to be disturbed and so he would be even more annoyed and choleric than had been his norm which was saying something since his norm was like a devil when aroused, although he still did not say very much at the best of times, if slightly more so at the worst of times. How then to disturb him in a way that would not reveal her hand, and in a way that would not be or be thought *too* inconsistent in her own pattern of behavior? How to start a disturbance that would be *sure* to pass the portals of the Great House and reach Mr. Johnson wherever he might be?

VI

Said Mary, "Dis food taste funny." They were beginning the preparation of the evening meal—although during crop time was comparatively unimportant, except that it was continuous and feverish, so that it did not matter *what* meal, but that it was one. "Dis food taste damn funny," repeated Mary. "Who fuck wid it? Must be one a dem gal inna de Big House." "Yes, Miss Mary," chorused the others who had *not* noticed, but were not prepared to cross her since they had to deal with her daily and to suffer if anything, and also in case something went wrong with the food and they were suspected.

49

VII

"Ah gwine fe see wha ah gwan," said Mary. She now had an excuse for leaving the field, although she was not sure it would stand up when she reached the Great House. She also had to worry what Cho-Cho might swallow as an excuse if he chose to ask her *why*. She suddenly decided to anticipate him and cut his suspicion so she went up noticing that as soon as he saw her coming he began to swing his "supplejack" whip a little wider and wilder. She did not pause, however, noticing with a sense of small triumphant satisfaction that as she got nearer, he began to take more care. "Ah goin go see massa," she growled. "Wha for?" Cho-Cho growled back. "Somebody ah fuck wid de food," she responded. "Gwan den," said Cho-Cho adding a dig. "Ah jus' hope ah no you because you is a *real* fucker."

VIII

Mary did not like Cho-Cho's remark one bit, but she went to the Great House generally satisfied just the same—she knew there was no guarantee Cho-Cho would believe her, but felt there was a better chance since she had told him herself, and *had* taken the trouble, a lot of *rass* trouble, to lug one of the smaller but still heavy pots right along with her. It was quite a walk to the Great House, mercifully most on open level ground. It was like this on *most* estates that she had heard of or seen—the planters always wanted to *see* what was happening even if they were not able to control it. Being on a hill was naturally safer too if slaves were attacking the House, but if the ground was level it made for a safer ride by carriage or on horse if the whites felt it was safer to escape than to fight.

IX

Mary realized that Mr. Johnson could see her coming if he was on his front verandah or in one of his front rooms. Even if hot, however, there were sure to be House slaves hanging about since *someone always* had

to be at the planter's beck and call, *all* part of the image and appearance of being a planter. Sure enough, one of the younger and facety
sweet-mouth gals soon came out.

Mr. Johnson
I

Mr. Johnson was not on his front verandah, but at the east, the Great
House having been built on a rough north to south pattern—unlike most
of the others on the island, but Mr. Johnson's father, like himself, had
liked to be different in his surroundings as in everything and had not
thought overmuch about the sun or rain or anything else. Mr. Johnson
was not asleep, or it was more accurate to say he was *no longer* asleep,
since he had been asleep, having dozed off with his pipe in his mouth
and ashes on his belly while the damned lazy gal who had been fanning
him had faded off to sleep or to fuck, he was not sure, but anyway was
nowhere around. As he thought of that woman, he was suddenly aware
that women's voices were disturbing him and that there was a fight on.

II

Mr. Johnson bawled out, "What is all that noise?," and, "Who the hell
is that?," adding to himself, "Somebody is going to pay for this," and
again, "Manasseh," his head personal male slave, "find out what is
going on." "Ya sar," came a faint reply as he heard the heavy slap-slap
of powerful bare feet on the wooden floor indicating his commands
were being obeyed although the noise of the fight was still going on
and on. Mr. Johnson vexationally and annoyingly decided that he
might as well get up himself, since there was no more rest for him *now*.

III

He tried to flex himself out of the lace hammock which he considered
one of the few real assets of his position, life, wealth, status, or
whatever had you. He tried to flex and failed. He failed with fire in
his groin and his loins, but not the usual kind that could be spent

pleasurably, but fire that was contained and pent up and that would kill him if he could not rid himself of it—although he thought with ironic self-shame/knowledge that it was the pleasant fire that had led to the painful one.

IV

Mr. Johnson finally got up and went outside to deal with the problem. Out there he saw Mary and one of his younger house-girls being held apart with disheveled difficulty by Manasseh and two of the other boys. Mr. Johnson thought wryly of the description of women as the weaker sex and the pressure that the supposedly stronger men were having, and he also thought of how women could pressure men and tear them apart in ways that were not necessarily physical, but which were even more painful and destroying than the violence that the handy boot or instrument of man could devise, although he felt that *he* was now being destroyed by physical contact with a woman or women.

V

Mr. Johnson glowered though he was only too aware that the slaves could see through his bluff, and he was even more aware that his glowering bluff was *not* going to work with this particular slave even if it might have temporary success with others. He was also glowering because he did not know what to say, and he was glowering because he knew that *he* should say nothing, that he should leave the first talking to Mary, but that he should not make this obvious. He was, truth to tell, glowering at himself.

VI

"Mis*ter* Johnson," the stress on *er* not *ah* and with a sneer. "Dis facety rass gal messin with me and your business. *Your business.*" A heavily stressed repetition with a meaning he would later discover, if she so desired. He suddenly decided to take the offensive to see whether it would do him any good for information or in the contest of "face." "My business?" he said. "What business?," in what he liked to hope was a cool flat yet staccato-effective tone of voice. He was countered right away, however, by an equally flat, equable cool, "Ah your business, yes," longish-just-barely-insolent, "sir." Repeated, "All right, so it is my business. But does that mean you have to wake me and the whole blasted place up for that matter? I have a good mind to break you as you have broken my sleep. Manasseh."

VII

"No bodder wid dat *sir*, any way you know me can tek lik anyway is only you on de estate was asleep, although," a little pause which seemed to show she knew she had gone too far in the "face" contest also for her own purposes. "Is your Estate, an you own we, an you have de right to sleep or do anything, but anyway sah," *sah* this time ingratiatingly, "ah really your business."

VIII

"All right, *what* kind of business?" Mr. Johnson was satisfied he had won the contest of face and that violence would no longer be necessary, so he could withdraw the threat without acknowledging that he had in fact made it. "Somebaddy mess wid de food." Mr. Johnson's stomach sank and his head spun. "Somebody what! I do not believe you. I *refuse* to believe you!," and more weakly to himself, "It's just not possible."

IX

Mr. Johnson was frightened. He was so frightened that he almost had to hold back for fear that he would soil himself, and he was frightened with very good reason. Planters were afraid of poisonings because they were so insidious—even if poisoners on estates could be traced, it would only normally be after very heavy damage in terms of loss of life.

X

Mr. Johnson spoke again, and again he thought about his words and about how *this* particular one did not apply to his new worries, but he had begun and forced himself to ask Mary for details. "Tell me everything," he barked, and not so loudly, "Everything!" Mary paused—apparently to catch both her breath and her mind. "Ah doan say it pizen but somebaddy mess wid de food." Pause. "Dem really do it." Pause. "It kina taste bad to me, aldo you would haffe know good fe pick it up, ah no everybody would notice it." Triumphant pause. Then, "Ah spec, smaddy fuck wid it and ah wan feel ah know is who." Pause again and Mr. Johnson knew that the time had now come for *him* to start blustering, looking, or fishing.

Mary
X

Mary was well satisfied so far. She had upset Mr. Johnson, turned the tables on him without his really knowing, while he was feeling that *he* was in control whereas *she* was on top. He was now ready to be set up for the next stage, and she waited for Mr. Johnson to make the next move so that *she* could counter him, for which *she* was ready.

XI

Mr. Johnson duly moved. "*Who* do you think did it?" Pause, "Who did it? Why?" Mary replied, "Ah who you think do it?" Pause again. "Who you feel woulda wan fe do it, eh sah?" She finished her speech smiling slightly after the insolent gap in her speech. She knew that he would not get the message immediately, but that when he got it it would hit him as hard or even harder than she had hoped or expected with results.

XII

Mr. Johnson, "Wait, wait, wait, wait," in a strong but tapering tone of voice, building and waning with anger. "That blasted boy wouldn't dare, he wouldn't damn dare." Mary, slyly, "Which bwoy sah? Which bwoy you ah talk bout? Is a whole heapa bwoy dem have on de estate, a hole heap." Mr. Johnson, "*You know*, don't play with me. I am not in the mood for it."

XIII

Mary smiled inwardly, because she *had* been playing with him all along and his statement, true-in-anger, made her realize her plans were working and that the game was going in her direction with little trouble. She broke her thoughts to answer still slyly, "You mean Johnson sah? Johnson? You really feel dat bwoy would do dat?" "Who do *you* feel?" said Mr. Johnson. "*Me* did feel so, sah, but me never know dat *you* would, aldo de bwoy damn brave and fool fe true."

XIV

Mary sneaked that in, nicely, slyly, under Mr. Johnson's anger. She had successfully got it taken for granted that it was Johnson who was guilty and she had gone even further, because Mr. Johnson was now so angry that he had not even bothered to finish investigation of the original story, so mad was he now at the thought of Johnson, but then she noticed that Mr. Johnson was turning to go inside, which did not suit her at all, although she ought to have known that Mr. Johnson was the type who would want to go inside to think. She now had to act and did.

XV

"But s'pose de rass bwoy *fuck* wid de food again sah. You haf fe decide what you gwine do." Stop. "You cyan leave it ya sah, next time he may ketch smaddy." These quick-succession comments halted Mr. Johnson while almost in mid-flight. "Not only dat eider, sah. You really a go mek dis bwoy fuck up you *business all-de-while?*" Querulously, Mary had shot in a low blow and she saw Mr. Johnson recoil, as if kicked in the groin or gripped in his belly, which *was* very probably true whether physical or mental.

Mr. Johnson
XI

Mr. Johnson did have a mental and physical pain in his belly, because Mary had jolted him badly and caused him personal physical fear that his precarious world was falling and also the pain in his crotch which had been buried by all the disturbance had now returned with more strength and fire because his concentration was now intensified down there with no possibility of relief.

XII

Mr. Johnson knew he should try to control himself and try to settle the situation privately, but it had been brought into the open and he could not retreat. Before he knew it, he had blurted out, "I wonder what to do," and worse, "What am I going to do about that boy?" as if appealing as he was in fact doing, but did not do. Mary, "Licks too good for him sah—too easy—him too strong, you got fe really hurt him, make him really feel. You should know whey him weaknesses dey." Significant pause, "*You* should know, sah."

XIII

Mr. Johnson paused, tried to cool himself so he could think over what Mary had said, but he could not, because there was something in what she had said which seemed to hint at *his* own weaknesses, and he had had enough of facing up to his own weaknesses for the day. "Weakness, what weakness? What are you talking about. How should I know about Johnson? What do I care about him?" Mary, "No woman, sah, no woman, nearly *all* man love woman, but you and Johnson *really* love woman." Smile-smirk. Mr. Johnson remained stony-faced, although he was realizing more and more how this was.

XIV

"We were talking about poisoning and then Johnson. I don't know how women and I, I or women came into this." He realized that he was now talking to Mary like an equal which should have worried him, but which he did not have the time to worry about now. He did not really mean what he had just said, however, but was only trying to pull Mary's tongue since he was under no illusion that *he* knew his slaves better than the other slaves themselves did.

XV

He looked at Mary and Mary looked at him. It seemed to be what the chess players called stalemate, in which no one really was able to get anywhere and there was nothing to do but stare. So he decided to use the heavy-handed approach and more and if necessary not bluff this time, because he had to get on top of the situation. "Come on woman, speak up or I will have to assume that you are responsible. I will have you flogged and worry about Johnson later, but *you* might not be in a position to worry about that, if *you* are skinned alive."

Mary

XVI

Mary thought of answering Mr. Johnson right away, but on thinking of the game she was playing and what she was aiming at decided to risk punishment so that her plans would not be suspected or recognized at any time, or at any rate not before it was too late to do anything positive about it. So she just stared back.

XVII

Mr. Johnson went inside and brought out *his* rarely used supplejack, the common implement for immediate punishment. Mary continued to stare and received the first slash across the face with his comment, "So you won't talk, eh," and on the backhanded return, "we'll see." After the third and fourth passes Mary had more than welts and some bleeding was starting. On the seventh stroke she turned to run and was caught on the back of her neck, which was held by Manasseh, the girl she had fought, and some slaves who had gathered around as interested listeners. At this point, Mr. Johnson called for a whip which was promptly supplied, and just as promptly used by the boiling master himself, red with fury and lathered with sweat. After the fourth cutting lash and uncontrollable kicks, Mary shouted, "Awlright, me will tell you!" A forced concession, but not yet an out-of-character begging.

XVIII

"What are you going to tell me now?" Mr. Johnson shouted while his chest heaved down and up, up and down, then down, down, down. "Ah gwine tell you what a believe sah!," said Mary. "What ah feel will help you and mek yu fuck Johnson up!" Pause, "Ah did tell you dat Johnson love woman." "Yes you did," said Mr. Johnson, "I know that, that's nothing new." "Yes sah, but is not just big woman him love, him love him daughter dem."

XIX

"*What* have his daughters got to do with this? I never heard of a slave interested in daughters!" The last was made with definite scorn. Mary realized that Mr. Johnson was baffled and also that she was definitely on the right path. "Him daughter dem might help you to soak him. Dem can serve two purposes." "What two purposes?" "Him love him daughter dem sah, specially one, and you can use her two way."

XX

"What two ways, I don't know what you are talking about." "You ever hear bout virgin and your troubles sah, how fresh gal good for dat." "What foolishness are you talking about? I have never heard anything about virgins before on this estate."

XXI

Mary responded, "When man cock get sick de only way it can cure is by virgin ting, it have fe get fresh taste." Mr. Johnson responded, "I have never heard such nonsense, what rubbish is this?" Mary hit back, "How much slave you ever see wid dat sickness, how much?" Mr. Johnson did not reply and he was definitely given pause, even if the doubt remained on his face. "And anyway," Mary added, "you *cyan* tink of a betta way fe frig up de bwoy Johnson and bring him to heel. Him won' like it and him won' give you more trouble, *me can promise you dat*."

Part V
Late Afternoon

Johnson

I

A message had come down to Johnson that he was wanted at the Great House. This was after he had, with his shift, been allowed back to his barracks after the day's work and Johnson was wondering why it was that he was wanted, what was it that he had done, or what was it that he had *not* done, or what combination or variation of both, or something in between. By nature he was not a worrier, but he wondered what was the reason, and he tried to cast his mind's eye back over the events of the day to see if he could find out the reason for the invitation and to figure out what was happening.

II

He remembered Mary's leaving the field mysteriously and suspiciously, so much so that he and others had enquired and had heard something that was equally mysterious about the food. He had seen her coming back and had seen her consult with Wiseman, and he had seen them both talking to Cho-Cho. All this *was* unusual, but not so unusual, or at least not so unusual with immediate consequences as to disturb him or to worry him unduly, and he saw no reason before receiving his summons to figure that *he* was in any way connected with these events.

III

Since receiving the summons, however, he had begun to wonder again and to calculate that in some way he would be involved—perhaps because Cho-Cho had to make an unusual report about his behavior, but even then, that in itself would not normally have merited a visit to the Great House or more rather a summons. He felt concerned, he knew he ought to be worried, but he did not know what *precisely* he had to fret about. In *any* event, going up to the House could not be delayed, so he just had to make the best of it and proceed.

Wiseman
I

Wiseman had returned to *his* own private area and then gone back to make his afternoon patrol round the fields in what appeared to be his usual style, but he wanted to find out what Mary had done when she had gone up to the Great House so that he would know in detail what she had had in mind, what she had done, and what she now wanted him to do, whether she had gone too far, or whether she had gone far enough or whether she had gone just the right and safe distance, which would again be for *him* to decide.

II

He found her as he had expected, back at her pots with a worried expression on her face although Wiseman could see that *this* was not really genuine at all, although he told himself that *he* could only say that because *he* knew her inside story and that she was not being genuine only because he knew her inside story, which he thought, however, was *not* necessarily genuine *either*.

III

Wiseman reached and, "Wha' happen? Wha did gwan up dey?" Mary half-smiled. "Ah set him up rass," she replied.

Wiseman, "A fe who rass you set up, Johnson or Mr. Johnson?" "Bot a dem, a set up bot' a dem rass!" She sighed with another half-smile, "Ah gwine fuck bot' a dem. Betta still, if tings work out dem gwine fuck each other." She actually laughed and then added, "But yo mus help me." Wiseman, "All right, woman, but tell me how it go."

IV

"Ah mess up him rass head dat's how it go, ah mess up him head but you mus follow tru' fe mek sure him no come back and straighten himself out." Wiseman asked, "Wha you tell him, mek him head mess up, and wha you wan me fe do fe keep it so." Mary, "Ah tun him min pon gal." Wiseman, "You tun him mind pon gal. Ah wha de rass you a tell me, him min no always pon gal. Dat a nuttin new at all. You mus be really a joke effen a dat a you big news. You must be a fuck wid me." "No, man," Mary responded. "No man," even a little frightened, "no man a not so it go at all, a special gal me a tun him on to, a no jus gal gal, a Johnson, daughter." "Johnson daughter?" Wiseman almost screamed and shouted, "Wha you mean Johnson daughter. Johnson no ha no daughter big nuff fe really interes man who cyan get any amount a big woman him want." Here Wiseman's voice relaxed into its usual confident authority.

V

"Ah jus dat," Mary replied. "Ah jus dat. Ah tell him bout de virgin business." Wiseman, "De virgin business? Virgin business?" Mary, "You know man Wiseman..." Wiseman interrupted. "Oh, Oh!!! Den you tink him believe you, dat man head hard, an him no fool you know." "Ah feel him believe me," responded Mary. "But you mus' follow up." "You wan' me to talk to him? After you and him well know say me no talk plenty, him gwine tink dat someting really funny and it funny fe true, an 'im will realize it." "No man, me no wan you fe talk, but if you sen him de gal, him will know say you no joke. Him respect you, praps him even fraid fe you little bit." Wiseman, "Ah no, ah no tink him fraid me but him know me, praps a will do dat." "Ah no praps," said Mary boldly. "De iron hot, you haffe lick it." "No push me woman," said Wiseman. "No woman mustn't push me, an fe me bisness set up you know. Me no really need what you a frig roun wid, me no need it at all, me can manage jus' as how it ah gwan, me just a use yu cause it convenient to me, wedder yu like it or not."

VI

"All right, *Mr.* Wiseman," stressed Mary. "Me appreciate dis, but tings wi wuk out even better if you follow tru." Wiseman softened noticeably. "Whey you find de gal, sen fi har, mek har come see me." "She down a one a de sout' fiel dem. Mi wi get har and bring har." Wiseman, "No bring har yuself or go find har yuself woman. Dat wi track tention." "Me know, me no fool so, me sen one o de cooking gal dem." And with a three-quarter smile, "Me do enuff walkin' and talkin' fe de day or de month or any time fe dat matter. Me really get a wuk-out today, but me no min if business wuk out O.K." and she smiled at her own joke, which she thought was to be no joke for some other people she knew—thinking also that *they* were going to get a different kind of work out *altogether*.

Cho-Cho

I

Cho-Cho had observed the last meeting between Mary and Wiseman and had begun to feel that he should try somehow to get himself into the action even if at a safe distance. He had decided this even before the last encounter. When he had intercepted the messenger sent to Johnson after he had been to Johnson with the message that Johnson was to go up to the Great House. Cho-Cho figured correctly that he could always find some excuse to follow Johnson up there on the excuse that he had to find particular reasons to follow a particular troublemaker up to the Great House for the protection of the master.

II

Since they were coming to the end of the normal working day, Cho-Cho felt that he would have a good excuse even if he were challenged when he went up to the Great House, but he calculated that if Mr. Johnson were going to be occupied with Johnson he would not want to bother noticing him, Cho-Cho. He also figured that somehow Mary and Wiseman would be in on the act and would clutter up whatever scene there was to be even more. He realized too that he would have to be cautious with Mary and Wiseman in view of his previous encounters with them for the day—which he had no real desire, to say the least, to have repeated and certainly not in front of other people too since to lose face individually before either of them *was* bad enough and had been bad enough.

III

On that train of thought, Cho-Cho soon glimpsed Johnson on the path going up to the Great House, but having seen him he did not move yet since he had a good view of anyone going up in that direction and he calculated also that Mary and/or Wiseman would both be going up shortly as well and he did not want to reach up there before they did since that would not do at all. It would not do from several points of view—the fact that his doing so might prevent events from taking place, the fact that he might be forced to play the type of part in the events that he had not really anticipated, and thus could not cope with, and the fact that really he was just curious and wanting to see what would happen and making sure that it did not involve him in any adverse way.

Mary

I

Mary called the same girl who had spied on Johnson earlier. "You 'member de gal you did see Johnson was a talk to?" "Yes mam." "Go find har and bring har." "Wha me wi tell de ol lady mam?" Mary shouted, growled, "Tell har say *mi* want har for Mr. Johnson business, dat wi satisfy har," and to herself, "It betta." "S'pose Mr. Cho-Cho stop me pon de way back wid de chile mam," persisted the doubting girl. "Tell him de same damn ting, him won't frig wid my business afta dis morning." Mary then remembered her status, Cho-Cho's status, and the girl's status. "Jus talk to Mr. Cho-Cho nice and tell im is Mr. Wiseman, Mr. Johnson and fi me concern." She noticed, however, by her expression, that the girl had got down the order of importance and degree of status of the names she had called. This was just as well, because Mary, though bent on causing an upheaval herself, had no intention of risking or losing her own position from below, although she was very much aware of the fact that she was doing both from above.

II

The girl went, with trepidation, more with anxious and unreassured fear, but Mary was very pleased to see, though she had expected it, that the girl was more terrified of her and the consequences of her than she was even of Cho-Cho. The lash of her tongue and the back of her hand were more feared than the cutting literal edge of Cho-Cho's lash. Although she had herself suffered both the lash and the back of a hand on this particular day and from more than one of the estate's top men and in public view too, the girl went and Mary was willing her on.

III

Mary was not really worried about either Mr. Johnson or Johnson watching her various transactions. Not Mr. Johnson, because he was unlikely to reappear again for the day no matter how nervous he felt because that would have indicated panic. And the same point applied to Johnson because he was under control and not now in the area. She felt safe and secure, as safe and secure as one could feel on the estate, that estate, any estate, in those times.

IV

The girl returned with the other girl, a feminine burden. They both looked frightened and Mary asked her messenger, "Mr. Cho-Cho ask you anyting?" "Yes mam," came the timid reply. "Me did tell him what yu say." Mary turned away from her and made an effort to cool herself down because it was very important that Johnson's daughter not be frightened until it was too late to make a difference to anyone who mattered. So softer, "What you name chile?" The girl muttered something under her breath and Mary almost, but not quite, got annoyed enough to shout at her, "Speak up me dear, ah cyan hear you." "Alice mam," was the soft reply, "me name Alice, mam."

V

"You know who me is Alice?" "Yes mam, you is Miss Mary." "No a mean you know who me is." "Yes mam, you in charge of de cook dem, you is de chief woman on de estate, you in charge a all we gal dem." "Dat's right gal, you know me den." "Yes mam." "Ah wan you do sometin for me gal, lickle later from dis." "Yes mam, anyting yu say, anyting at all." "Me wi tell you what me wan you fe do but you musn't tell anybody, in fact yu mus' tan right yah, tan ya wid me.'

VI

Mary turned to the other girl. "Go look fah Mr. Wiseman now." The tone of astonishment was even deeper this time, since Mary knew that the girl or anyone else on the estate for that matter could not comprehend *anyone* on the estate *summoning* Wiseman, not even Mr. Johnson, who whenever he had anything to do with him always met him in the course of both their rounds. "Yes chile, me dey tired of how yu a gwan, ask him to come dis way, him wi know why, ah cyan come wid de gal." The messenger nodded mutely. She had had a most interesting day, but she was also aware that it was in her own interests not only that she should not appear too astonished but also that she should not try to find out why the day *had* been so astonishing lest she should receive a nasty shock for herself, instead of what she sensed was being built up for some other people.

Wiseman
VII

Wiseman had practically reached the Great House himself on his way to see Mr. Johnson proceeding in his usual leisurely way, or rather even more leisurely than usual, since it was very important not to reveal what was going on by his manner when he was passed by the athletic and vigorous Johnson. Wiseman thought, spoke and acted quickly. "Bwoy wait dey fe me, whey you a go?" It was a low-key order-question aimed just at its target with not much offense meant or given.

VIII

"Mr. Johnson sen fi me." Respectful, yet not a fearing answer, the two men both knew their measure. "Hol' down dey, praps me know what it about," said Wiseman. "Me wi talk to Mr. Johnson," he added. "Yu know wha Mr. Johnson want me fo?" "Me tink so," replied Wiseman, "anyway, you mek me go up dey fus go talk to him." Johnson spoke again however, "Me nah mess wid dat man tho, him sen' fi me, so me a go up dey, me nah gi him no excuse at all fi fuck wid me. Me get fuck wid too much time fe de day already." "Alright bwoy," and the "bwoy" was not said in the usual fashion that the word was used on the estate. "Mi wi talk to him fus. You jus res' lickle way down whey you can see him an him can know say dat you no ignore him."

IX

They approached the Great House, Wiseman with contained anticipation and, he could see, Johnson with contained fear although he was fighting it. Wiseman did not know the details but he would not have been surprised to know at all that his approach would be rather different from the one that Mary had seen fit to adopt. Wiseman just went straight up to the first slave he saw on the verandah, who happened to be the same Manasseh, and said, "Ah come to see Mr. Johnson." A statement, not a request, and the slave-houseboy realized it.

X

Manasseh went inside, he too being somewhat fearful of this turn in the turn of events. He was not accustomed to seeing so many slaves coming up to the Great House during the normal course of events, particularly slaves like Mary and Wiseman, and Wiseman thought to himself, as he assessed Manasseh's reaction, that he did not in fact make it a habit to go up to the Great House and only did so on very important occasions, which led him to think to himself that he hoped that Johnson did not stop to figure out to think why should he, Wiseman, be taking up his, Johnson's, case.

XI

Wiseman congratulated himself on having had the foresight to make Johnson remain some distance away even while he heard Mr. Johnson storming out and toning down his steps even while coming down the passage once he saw who it was waiting for him. Wiseman reflected to himself that Manasseh, messenger-boy Manasseh, had very probably told Mr. Johnson who it was waiting for him on the verandah but that it had not sunken in, with Mr. Johnson being in a confused and an irritated state which suited what he and Mary had in mind more and more to cope with Mr. Johnson who was no fool even in an irritated state.

XII

"What do *you* want now, Wiseman? You know that I think I have had enough of a hard time for the day already." Wiseman noticed that he spoke of a "hard time" and thought that Mr. Johnson would not have spoken like that wherever over the water that he had originally come from. "Me no come to give you no hard time, Mr. Johnson," Wiseman responded gently but scoldingly at the same time. "Me come mebbe fe help you, cos if me no help you, fe mi business may mash up too." As he said this, Wiseman thought to himself that this note of confessed selfishness was rather clever.

XIII

He followed up swiftly with another self-thought-to-be-selfish-and-smart-confession, "Miss Mary come to me and say she tell you someting dat you might not believe, so dat I mus come and tell you say it true," he blurted and spouted out in one rapid mouthful for him. "What is all that?" asked Mr. Johnson. "You are going much too quickly for me." "Is bout wha Miss Mary tell you bout de gal, sah." "The girl?" Mr. Johnson queried repeating the phrase more than once although Wiseman could see that he was just pretending, that he knew well what was happening. Wiseman played up to him all the same. "Johnson daughter sah," and he dropped his voice and unconsciously, unwillingly, turned around to look at Johnson although he was aware that Johnson was standing a sufficient distance away and could not in fact hear him and he only hoped that if Johnson noticed what was happening that he would think they were talking about him which in a sense they were, in fact. On thinking it over, he hoped that Johnson would observe what they were doing.

XIV

"De gal name Alice sah, ah tink Miss Mary ave har ready, but anyway sah, de pint is sah, me know of dat ting fe wuk, out yah an back on de Guinea Coast." Wiseman saw a glint in Mr. Johnson's eye and saw that he was going to be taken up for his mention of the Guinea Coast. He was not disappointed and so he had time to prepare himself. "What do you know of the Guinea Coast?" a question followed by an equally forceful statement. "You were not old enough to remember anything there, even if you were born there, were you?" another question in the tail. "No sah, but me hear it from me fader, who did hear it from him fader before him and no forget sah, all a we did in a de same line from long time—it enna me family and *me* see it wuk down yah." Wiseman knew that he had Mr. Johnson on unsure ground here, because he himself was sometimes unsure whether he had the power, and although he was lying when he was saying that he himself knew of cases, he had certainly *heard* of some!

XV

"Anyway it wi teach de damn bwoy a lesson," and then Wiseman poised for his most effective and most powerful thrust so far. "We feel fe de good a de estate sah, dat him need fe learn a lesson." As he had figured, this woke up Mr. Johnson completely and brought him fully to life. "What is that about the estate?" Again Mr. Johnson was going on as if he had not heard clearly, whereas it was really intended to give him more time to think. "Ah feel dat dis bwoy should punish sah, and ah doan mean lick, slave dem on de estate *ah laugh at you* tru tis bwoy." "How?" replied Mr. Johnson. "In what way?" "You know de story dem a spread sah say a him mek you get de clap indirect, or even tru purpose. Sah, you cyan afford fe have dem a say dat sah, no sah you cyan afford dat at all—even if ah true—ya cyan afford fe have all slave dem a laugh after you. Next ting dem wi wan do wuss da laugh and effen dem a laugh after you dem gwine do bout and wid me?" He ended his question plaintively intending to give Mr. Johnson the incorrect impression that he was still very concerned with his own position.

XVI

Mr. Johnson spoke as if to himself, "Yes, I had not really considered that, no, not at all." Wiseman butted into his thoughts, "Den doan bodder talk to de bwoy at all sah, or not till de business done, me wi jus mek him res dey and say dat you wi call him later and him wi think is nuten while we sen fi de gal. Eh sah, what you say to dat, you no tink dat say is a good idea?" The question was put almost like a suggestion, in fact it was even more like a polite command than a suggestion, and Wiseman did not really expect any resistance, nor did Mr. Johnson offer any.

XVII

Wiseman suddenly got the impression that Mr. Johnson was a very tired man and was willing to go on along with almost anything that was suggested to him so that he could get some peace of mind, body, soul, spirit, what have you, which was just the state of mind that Wiseman and Mary before him had wanted to get him into.

XVIII

Wiseman did not dally further, he summoned one of the Great House girls, "Go dung a field and tell Miss Mary mus sen' de gal come." The girl looked hesitantly sideways at Mr. Johnson to see if he approved, but she must have noticed the same deadness in him because she swiftly looked back at Wiseman, "Which gal sah?" Wiseman looked piercingly, frighteningly at her, then decided not to let his anger show overmuch for fear of awakening Mr. Johnson from his state of deadness, then replied, "Miss Mary wi know which gal. Gal, gwan bout de business quick and no talk to de bwoy Johnson when yu a go dung *or a lick out you clart.*" He added the last few words with a great deal of force and intensity and made the girl start again just as he had intended to, and she pelted off keeping at a safe distance from Johnson and running at what appeared to be an unsafe speed.

Part VI
Dusk

Mr. Johnson, Johnson, Wiseman, Mary, and Cho-Cho
I

They were all now assembled in front of the Great House at the end of the day, all the main characters of the day's events and some additional ones besides, and they were all thinking similarly but differently.

MR. JOHNSON: was wondering to himself how he had got into this situation and whether he should make an exhibition of himself, but realized indeed that whatever he did he was going to make an exhibition of himself or that he had *already* made an exhibition of himself so that he might as well do something that could just possibly cure his pain and should definitely give him pleasure.

JOHNSON: was still not sure what was happening. He got the impression that the gathering was because of him, yet he was not the central or most important figure in it, or at least not yet; he knew that he was in some kind of trouble, maybe even very bad trouble as indicated by the additional presence of his daughter, but even then he could not be sure, because she might just be there by accident since he did not feel that any of the others could really be sure that she was his daughter, so how could he and she be involved; at the same time he did not like it.

WISEMAN: was satisfied he knew what was happening, what was going to happen and he felt confident that it would happen as he and Mary—in his satisfaction he nearly forgot Mary although she was right beside him—wanted it to happen.

MARY: was not satisfied, she felt uneasy at what appeared to be her moment of triumph, she looked around and sensed that only Wiseman was cool and the girl, for whom she was almost sorry for a moment, looked just bewildered, since she did not know what was happening. Mary was not at all sure that Mr. Johnson would not back off and do something sudden.

CHO-CHO: had arrived after Johnson and Wiseman but before Mary and the girl and he was just looking around rapidly since he was not at all sure that he should have come, but what made him even more uncomfortable was the fact that he was being ignored—an experience that he had *never* had before on the estate and he was hurt, yet somehow easier in his mind. As it was, he was the only one who saw a young boy approaching stealthily yet hurriedly—normally he would have taken the necessary disciplinary precautions, but this was not a normal situation and Cho-Cho was not sure what part the boy might be playing, so he did nothing. The others were so preoccupied with setting up a tableau that they were paying little attention to anyone but themselves, which would prove to their cost.

Mr. Johnson, Johnson, Wiseman, Mary, and Cho-Cho
II

There was some life now and some stir in the group and at the same time a hesitancy. *Mary* spoke first, "See di gal yah sah, see har yah." *Wiseman* spoke next, "Yas sah, tek har and teach de rass bwoy a lesson, learn him proper." *Johnson* moved forward as if to answer or to hit someone and immediately, almost out of nowhere, four slaves materialized to hold him at each arm and leg as if they intended to quarter him. "Wha de rass ah gwan," he shouted. "Wha de fuck a you do wid me and me daughter." *Mr. Johnson* laughed to himself then and spoke out softly, so that he could barely be heard, "Perhaps you have said the right thing there Johnson, perhaps you have said it all," and while the excitement was going on and the ten people in the little group were milling around and talking with one another, only Cho-Cho noticed another slim shape coming up behind them in the dusk.

Mr. Johnson, Johnson, Wiseman, Mary, and Cho-Cho
III

While the four slaves tried to hold down *Johnson*, who was now shouting, screaming, struggling, and scraping, in a vain effort to get at his daughter, *Mary* and *Wiseman* held down the terrified girl and tore off her clothes, and *Mr. Johnson*, as if in a trance, began to mount her. As he did so despite her struggles, he suddenly spoke out surprisingly, "She's no virgin, this girl is no virgin. You have tricked me." He said nothing more because at the same time the boy Abel rushed through with a stone in hand to Johnson's great surprise but pleasure which quickly turned to horror, and crashed it down on Mr. Johnson's head, screaming, "Leave me sister alone, leave mi gal alone, leave har a say." The four slaves who had been holding Johnson pounced on him and in the same horrible moment in which the boy went down under their weight, on top of Mr. Johnson, who must now be dead, on top of the girl, who might just as well be dead, both underneath the boy himself, who was going to be dead, Johnson stood now quietly in shock, remembering Mr. Johnson's last words, "No virgin." As for Mary, Wiseman, and Cho-Cho, they just stood.

From: The Autobiography of a Runaway Slave

ESTEBAN MONTEJO
(CUBA)
EDITED BY
MIGUEL BARNET (CUBA)

Introduction

I first met Esteban Montejo in the summer of 1963. He struck me as a lonely, aloof, almost severe character. He received me coldly and with considerable reserve. I wanted to meet this man of a hundred and five years because he had lived through experiences which seem extraordinary to people today. The most attractive of these, perhaps, was his time as a runaway slave in the forests of central Cuba.

With time and the requisite patience, I managed to get him to talk naturally and frankly, and these conversations became the material for a book about his life. I filled shoe-boxes with notes and filing-cards, and taped a lot of our talks—somewhat haphazardly, I must admit. This took about two years. I wanted his story to sound spontaneous and as if it came from the heart, and so I inserted words and expressions characteristic of Esteban wherever they seemed appropriate. My particular concerns were the social problems of life under slavery, the promiscuity in the barracoons, Esteban's celibate life as a runaway and his part in the War of Independence, which he describes from a lively, personal angle—the anti-romantic, anti-ideological standpoint of a man who joined the fight purely from a hunger for freedom, without petty motives or the hope of easy privileges.

Esteban soon became the real author of this book. He was constantly looking at my notebook, and he almost forced me to write down everything he said. His vision of the creation of the universe particularly appealed to me because of its poetic, surrealist slant.

The need to check facts and dates which cropped up in these sessions of ours led me to conversations with other old men more or less his contemporaries. I pored over reference books and city records, and revised the whole period under review so that my questions should be as precise as possible. Not that this book is primarily a work of history—history merely enters it as the medium in which the man's life is lived.

I have necessarily had to paraphrase a good deal of what he told me. If I had transcribed his story word for word it would have been confusing and repetitive. I have kept the story within fixed time limits, not being concerned to recreate the period in minute detail of time and place. I have concentrated on things like agricultural methods, ceremonies, fiestas, food, and drink, although in many cases my informant was unable to remember when precisely he had been involved with them. I have checked the facts where they seemed important—as in the account of slavery and of the two wars, the Ten Years' War of Carlos Manuel de Cespedes and the War of Independence. Esteban's life in the forest is a remote and confused period in his memory.

The book helps to fill certain gaps in Cuba's history. None of the orthodox, schematically-minded historians would ever have bothered with the experiences of a man like Esteban. But Esteban appeared on the scene as if to show that one voice from the heart of the action is worth a vociferous chorus from the sidelines.

The war against Spain, our "motherland," lasted almost a century. After the Haitian Revolution and the Negroes' seizure of power there, led by Toussaint L'Ouverture, the Spanish Government was forced to adopt measures to prevent a similar conflagration in Cuba. Nationalist feeling grew, and there were several important rebellions. Esteban refers to two of these. The first, which sprung from the *Grito de Yara** in 1868, was headed by a patriot from Bayamo, in Oriente Province, Carlos Manuel de Céspedes. This war, in which much of the Negro population was involved, was a strange, remote and disconcerting experience for Esteban. During that time, the decade from '68 to '78, he was a runaway in hiding in the mountains and he only occasionally heard a shot or caught sight of a platoon traveling across the plains. It was bewildering to see horses charging and men cutting each others' heads off with machetes and not knowing what it was all about. Esteban told me once that the experience was like standing drunk in front of the sea.

Then, in 1880, two years after what Cubans call the Ten Years' War, the abolition of slavery was declared. Esteban left the forest and his celibate existence there, to take up a new life. The Ten Years' War was a failure for the Cubans, but at least slavery had been abolished.

Political turmoil continued. Cuba swarmed with different parties and factions. Men like Esteban wanted nothing less than total freedom: Cuba's independence of Spain and solid economic advantages. Consequently, whenever he mentions annexationism, the movement in favor of Cuba's annexation to the United States, or autonomism, which proposed that Spain should concede certain trading advantages on the island but keep political control, he does so in vague, pejorative terms. Independence, though, the one dignified solution, was the cause which united the whole revolutionary population of Cuba, including this one unknown man. On February 24, 1895, the *Grito de Baire* was heard in a poor village in Oriente Province and gave birth to the War of Independence which freed Cuba from Spanish rule. Esteban talks, in his very subjective and individual way, of such great and distinguished figures as Máximo Gómez and Antonio Maceo, both generals in this war. Maceo was a Negro, and consequently Esteban's attitude to the two men differs widely, a fact which throws

* Literally "the Shout of Yara." This refers to the patriotic outcry raised in the village of Yara which sparked off the Ten Years' War of Carlos Manuel de Céspedes.

light on certain aspects of the war as well as on the racial attitudes he shared with other Negroes. He admired Maceo as much as he distrusted Gómez, whom he believed to be a puppet of the Americans.

During the war Esteban went through testing experiences. He first fought under bandit leaders who turned out traitors to the revolution, then under a more honest officer, but always in difficult and distracting circumstances. When the war ended the ex-slave, ex-runaway and ex-revolutionary was humiliated to see an unexpected and unpleasant development. The Americans intervened after the Cubans had fought and won the war and seized power for themselves. As a pretext for intervention they used the blowing up of their warship, the *Maine,* then at anchor in our waters. We believe that they blew up the ship themselves, and then accused Spain of having done so.

Esteban was further disillusioned to find himself the object of racial discrimination, and jobless, after having fought bravely and honorably. So he went back to the countryside, to his old life of cutting cane, clearing the ground, and hunting pigs. But this did not break his spirit. He carried on the hard struggle for existence and overcame poverty and pain. Now, after forty years of retirement, he tells his life story, sitting in a leather chair, and stoutly maintains that he does not want to die so that he can take part in any battles to come. "And I'm not going into the trenches," he explains, "or using any of those modern weapons. A machete will do for me."   **Miguel Barnet**

Life in the Barracoons

There are some things about life that I don't understand. Everything about Nature is obscure to me, and about the gods more so still. The gods are capricious and willful, and they are the cause of many strange things which happen here and which I have seen for myself. I can remember as a slave I spent half my time gazing up at the sky because it looked so painted. Once it suddenly turned the color of a hot coal, and there was a terrible drought. Another time there was an eclipse of the sun which started at four in the afternoon and could be seen all over the island. The moon looked as if it was fighting with the sun. I noticed that everything seemed to be going backwards—it got darker and darker, and then lighter and lighter. Hens flew up to roost. People were too frightened to speak. Some died of heart failure and others were struck dumb.

I saw the same thing happen again in different places, but I never dreamed of trying to find out why. You see, I know it all depends on Nature, everything comes from Nature, which can't even be seen. We men cannot do such things because we are the subjects of a God; of Jesus Christ, who is the one most talked about. Jesus Christ wasn't born in Africa, he came from Nature herself, as the Virgin Mary was a señorita.

The strongest gods are African. I tell you it's certain they could fly and they did what they liked with their witchcraft. I don't know how they permitted slavery. The truth is, I start thinking, and I can't make head or tail of it. To my mind it all started with the scarlet handkerchiefs, the day they crossed the wall. There was an old wall in Africa, right round the coast, made of palm bark and magic insects which stung like the devil. For years they frightened away all the whites who tried to set foot in Africa. It was the scarlet which did for the Africans; both the kings and the rest surrendered without a struggle. When the kings saw that the whites—I think that the Portuguese were the first—they were taking out these scarlet handkerchiefs as if they were waving, they told the blacks, "Go on then, go and get a scarlet handkerchief," and the blacks were so excited by the scarlet that they ran down to the ships like sheep and there they were captured. The Negro has always liked scarlet. It was the fault of this color that they put them in chains and sent them to Cuba. After that they couldn't go back to their own country. That is the reason for slavery in Cuba. When the English found out about this business, they wouldn't let them bring any more Negroes over, and slavery ended and the other part began: the free part. It was some time in the 1880s.

I haven't forgotten any of this. I lived through it all. I even remember my godparents telling me the date of my birth. It was the 26th of December 1860, St. Stephen's Day, the one on the calendars. That is why I am called Stephen. One of my surnames is Montejo, after my mother who was a slave of French origin. The other is Mera. But hardly anyone knows this. Well, why should I tell people, since it is false anyway? It should really be Mesa, but what happened is that they changed it in the archives and I left it that way because I wanted two names like everyone else, so they wouldn't call me "jungle boy." I stuck to this one and, well, there you are! Mesa was the name of a certain Pancho Mesa who lived in Rodrigo. It seems this gentleman cared for me after I was born. He was my mother's master. I never saw him, of course, but I believe this story because my godparents told it to me, and I remember every word they told me.

My godfather was called Gin Congo and my godmother Susanna. I got to know them in the Nineties before war began. An old Negro from their sugar plantation who knew me gave me the introduction, and took me to see them himself. I got into the way of visiting them in Chinchila, the district where they lived near Sagua la Grande. As I had never known my parents, the first thing I did was ask about them, and that was when I found out their names and other details. They even told me the name of the plantation where I was born. My father was called Nazario and he was a Lucumí* from Oyó. My mother was Emilia Montejo. They told me too that they had both died at Sagua. I would very much like to have known them, but if I had left the forest to find them I would have been seized at once.

Because of being a runaway I never saw my parents. I never even saw them. But this is not sad, because it is true.

Like all children born into slavery, *criollitos*+ as they called them, I was born in an infirmary where they took the pregnant Negresses to give birth. I think it was the Santa Teresa plantation, but I am not sure. I do remember my godparents talking a lot about this plantation and its owners, people called La Ronda. My godparents were called by this name for a long time, till slavery left Cuba.

Negroes were sold like pigs, and they sold me at once, which is why I remember nothing about the place. I know it was somewhere in the region where I was born, in the upper part of Las Villas, Zulueta, Remedios, Caibarién, all the villages before you come to the sea. Then the picture of another plantation comes to mind: the Flor de Sagua. I

---

* Cuban name for a Negro slave who came from Nigeria or the Gulf of Guinea.
+ Little Creole. Creole was a first-generation Cuban, black or white.

don't know if that was the place where I worked for the first time, but I do remember running away from there once; I decided I'd had enough of that bloody place, and I was off! But they caught me without a struggle, clapped a pair of shackles on me (I can still feel them when I think back), screwed them up tight and sent me back to work wearing them. You talk about this sort of thing today and people don't believe you, but it happened to me and I have to say so.

The owner of that plantation had a funny name, one of those long ones with lots of parts. He was everything bad: stupid, evil-tempered, swollen-headed. . . . He used to ride past in the fly with his wife and smart friends through the cane fields, waving a handkerchief, but that was as near as he ever got to us. The owners never went to the fields. One odd thing about this man: I remember he had a smart Negro, a first-rate driver, with gold rings in his ears and everything. All those drivers were scabs and tale-bearers. You might say they were the dandies of the colored people.

At the Flor de Sagua I started to work on the *bagasse** wagons. I sat on the box and drove the mule. If the wagon was very full I stopped the mule, got down and led it by the rein. The mules were hard-mouthed and you had to bear down on the reins like the devil. Your back began to grow hunched. A lot of people are walking around almost hunchbacked now because of those mules. The wagons went out piled to the top. They were always unloaded in the sugar-mill town, and the *bagasse* had to be spread out to dry. It was scattered with a hook and then it was taken, dried, to the furnaces. This was done to make steam. I suppose that was the first work I did. At least, that's what my memory tells me.

All the indoor parts of the plantation were primitive; not like today with their lights and fast machinery. They were called *cachimbos*, because that is the word for a small sugar mill. In them the sugar was evaporated and drained. There were some which did not make sugar, but syrup and pan sugar. Almost all of them belonged to a single owner; these were called the *trapiches*. There were three sugar-boilers in the *cachimbos*—big copper ones with wide mouths. The first cooked the

---

* The fibers left after the juice has been extracted from the sugar cane.

79

cane juice, in the next the froth was taken off, and in the third the treacle was boiled till ready. *Cachaza* was what we called the froth that was left over from the cane juice. It came off in a hard crust and was very good for pigs. When the treacle was ready, you took a ladle with a long wooden handle and poured it into a trough and from there into a sugar-locker, which stood a short distance from the boilers. That was where they drained the *muscovado*, or unrefined sugar, which had most of the syrup left in it. In those days the centrifuge, as they call it, did not exist.

Once the sugar in the locker had cooled, you had to go in barefoot with spade and shovel and a hand-barrow. One Negro always went in front and another behind. The barrow was to take the hogsheads to the *tinglado*, a long shed with two beams where the hogsheads were stacked to drain the sugar. The syrup which drained off the hogsheads was given to the mill-town people and was given to the pigs and sheep. They got very fat on it.

To make the refined sugar there were some big funnels into which the raw sugar was poured to be refined. That sugar looked like the sort we have today, white sugar. The funnels were known as "moulds."

I know that part of sugar-making better than most people who only know the cane as it is outside, in the fields. And to tell the truth I preferred the inside part, it was easier. At Flor de Sagua I worked in the sugar-locker, but this was after I had got experience working with *bagasse*. That was spade-and-shovel work. To my mind even cane-cutting was preferable. I was ten years old then, and that was why they had not sent me to work in the fields. But ten then was like thirty now, because boys worked like oxen.

If a boy was pretty and lively he was sent inside, to the master's house. And there they started softening him up and . . . well, I don't know! They used to give the boy a long palm leaf and make him stand at one end of the table while they ate. And they said, "Now see that no flies get in the food!" If a fly did, they scolded him severely and whipped him. I never did this work because I never wanted to be on closer terms with the masters. I was a runaway from birth.

All the slaves lived in barracoons. These dwelling places no longer exist, so one cannot see them. But I saw them and I never thought well of them. The masters, of course, said they were as clean as new pins. The slaves disliked living under those conditions: being locked up stifled them. The barracoons were large, though some plantations had smaller ones; it depended on the number of slaves in the settlement. Around two hundred slaves of all colors lived in the Flor de Sagua barracoon. This was laid out in rows: two rows facing each other with a door in the middle and a massive padlock to shut the slaves in at night. There were barracoons of wood and barracoons of masonry with tiled roofs. Both types had mud floors and were dirty as hell. And there was no modern ventilation there! Just a hole in the wall or a small barred window. The result was that the place swarmed with fleas and ticks, which made the inmates ill with infections and evil spells, for those ticks were witches. The only way to get rid of them was with hot wax, and sometimes even that did not work. The masters wanted the barracoons to look clean outside, so they were white-washed. The job was given to the Negroes themselves. The master would say, "Get some whitewash and spread it evenly." They pre-pared the whitewash in large pots inside the barracoons, in the central courtyard.

Horses and goats did not go inside the barracoons, but there was always some mongrel sniffing about the place for food. People stayed inside the rooms, which were small and hot. One says rooms, but they were really ovens. They had doors with latchkeys to prevent stealing. You had to be particularly wary of the *criollitos*, who were born thieving little rascals. They learned to steal like monkeys.

In the central patio the women washed their own, their husbands', and their childrens' clothes in tubs. Those tubs were not like the ones people use now, they were much cruder. And they had to be taken first to the river to swell the wood, because they were made out of fish-crates, the big ones.

There were no trees either outside or inside the barracoons, just empty solitary spaces. The Negroes could never get used to this. The Negro likes trees, forests. But the Chinese! Africa was full of trees, god-trees, banyans, cedars. But not China—there they have weeds, purslaine, morning glory, the sort of thing that creeps along. As the rooms were so small the slaves relieved themselves in a so-called toilet standing in one corner of the barracoon. Everyone used it. And to wipe your arse afterwards you had to pick leaves and maize husks.

The bell was at the entrance to the mill. The deputy overseer used to ring it. At four-thirty in the morning they rang the Ave Maria—I think there were nine strokes of the bell—and one had to get up immediately. At six they rang another bell called the line-up bell, and everyone had to form up in a place just outside the barracoon, men on one side, women the other. Then off to the cane fields till eleven, when we ate jerked beef, vegetables, and bread. Then, at sunset, came the prayer bell. At half-past eight they rang the last bell for everyone to go to sleep, the silence bell.

The deputy overseer slept in the barracoon and kept watch. In the mill town there was a white watchman, a Spaniard, to keep an eye on things. Everything was based on watchfulness and the whip. When time passed and the *esquifación*, the slaves' issue of clothing, began to wear out, they would be given a new one. The men's clothes were made of Russian cloth, a coarse linen, sturdy and good for work in the fields—trousers which had large pockets and stood up stiff, a shirt, and a wool cap for the cold. The shoes were generally of rawhide, low-cut with little straps to keep them on. The old men wore sandals, flat-soled with a thong around the big toe. This has always been an African fashion, though white women wear them now and call them mules or slippers. The women were given blouses, skirts, and petticoats, and if they owned plots of land they bought their own petticoats, white ones, which were prettier and smarter. They also wore gold rings and earrings. They bought these trophies from the Turks and Moors who sometimes came to the barracoons, carrying boxes slung from their shoulders by a wide leather strap. Lottery-ticket sellers also came round, who cheated the Negroes and sold them their most expensive tickets. If any of the tickets came up on the lottery you wouldn't see them for dust. The *guajiros*, or white countrymen, also came to barter milk for jerked beef, or sell it at four cents a bottle. The Negroes used to buy it because the owners did not provide milk, and it is necessary because it cures infections and cleans the system.

These plots of land were the salvation of many slaves, where they got their real nourishment from. Almost all of them had their little strips of land to be sown close to the barracoons, almost behind them. Everything grew there: sweet potatoes, gourds, okra, kidney beans, yucca, and peanuts. They also raised pigs. And they sold all these products to the whites who came out from the villages. The Negroes were honest, it was natural for them to be honest, not knowing much about things. They sold their goods very cheap. Whole pigs fetched a doubloon, or a doubloon and a half, in gold coin, as the money was then, but the blacks didn't like selling their vegetables. I learned to eat vegetables from the elders, because they said they were very healthy food, but during slavery pigs were the mainstay. Pigs gave more lard then than now, and I think it's because they led a more natural life. A pig was left to wallow about in the piggeries. The lard cost ten pennies a pound, and the white countrymen came all week long to get their portion. They always paid in silver half-dollars. Later it became quarter-dollars.

Cents were still unknown because they had not crowned Alfonso XIII king yet, and cents came after his coronation. King Alfonso wanted everything changed, right down to the coinage. Copper money came to Cuba then, worth two cents, if I remember right, and other novelties in the way of money, all due to the king.

Strange as it may seem, the Negroes were able to keep themselves amused in the barracoons. They had their games and pastimes. They played games in the taverns too, but these were different. The favorite game in the barracoons was *tejo*. A split corn cob was placed on the ground with a coin balanced on top, a line was drawn not far off, and you had to throw a stone from there to hit the cob. If the stone hit the cob so that the coin fell on top of it, the player won the coin, but if it fell nearby, he didn't. This game gave rise to great disputes, and then you had to take a straw to measure whether the coin was nearer the player or the cob.

Tejo was played in the courtyard like skittles, though skittles was not played often, only two or three times altogether that I can remember. Negro coopers used to make the bottle-shaped skittles and wooden balls to play with. This game was open to all comers, and everyone had a go, except the Chinese, who didn't join in much. The balls were rolled along the ground so as to knock down the four or five skittles. It was played just like the modern game they have in the city except that they used to fight over the betting money in those days. The masters didn't like that at all. They forbade certain games, and you had to play those when the overseer wasn't looking. The overseer was the one who passed on the news and gossip.

The game of *mayombe** was connected with religion. The overseers themselves used to get involved, hoping to benefit. They believed in the witches too, so no one today need be surprised that whites believe in such things. Drumming was part of the *mayombe*. A *nganga*, or large pot, was placed in the center of the patio. The powers were inside the pot: the saints. People started drumming and singing. They took offerings to the pot and asked for health for themselves and their brothers and peace among themselves. They also made *enkangues*, which were charms of earth from the cemetery; the earth was made into little heaps in four corners, representing the points of the universe. Inside the pot they put a plant called star shake, together with corn straw to protect the men. When a master punished a slave, the others would collect a little earth and put it in the pot. With the help of this earth they could make the master fall sick or bring some harm upon his family, for so long as the earth was inside the pot the master was imprisoned there and the Devil himself couldn't get him out. This was how the Congolese revenged themselves upon their master.

The taverns were near the plantations. There were more taverns than ticks in the forest. They were a sort of store where one could buy everything. The slaves themselves used to trade in the taverns, selling the jerked beef which they accumulated in the barracoons. They were usually allowed to visit the taverns during the daylight hours and sometimes even in the evenings, but this was not the rule in all the plantations. There was always some master who forbade the slaves to go. The Negroes went to the taverns for brandy. They drank a lot of it to keep their strength up. A glass of good brandy costs half a peso. The owners drank a lot of brandy too, and the quarrels which brewed

---

*African word meaning evil spirit; hence name given to the branch of the Stick Cult which concentrates on black magic.

were no joke. Some of the tavern-keepers were old Spaniards, retired from the army on very little money, five or six pesos' pension.

The taverns were made of wood and palm bark; no masonry like the modern stores. You had to sit on piled jute sacks or stand. They sold rice, jerked beef, lard, and every variety of bean. I knew cases of unscrupulous owners cheating slaves by quoting the wrong prices, and I saw brawls in which a Negro came off worse and was forbidden to return. They noted down anything you bought in a book; when you spent half a peso they made one stroke in the book, and two for a peso. This was the system for buying everything else: round sweet biscuits, salt biscuits, sweets the size of a pea made of different-colored flours, water-bread and lard. Water-bread cost five cents a stick. It was quite different from the sort you get now. I preferred it. I also remember that they sold sweet cakes, called "caprices," made of peanut flour and sesame seed. The sesame seed was a Chinese thing; there were Chinese pedlars who went around the plantations selling it, old indentured laborers whose arms were too weak to cut cane and who had taken up peddling.

The taverns were stinking places. A strong smell came from all the goods hanging from the ceiling, sausages, smoked hams, red mortadellas. In spite of this, people used to hold their games there. They spent half their lives at this foolishness. The Negroes were eager to shine at these games. I remember one game they called "the biscuit," which was played by putting four or five hard salt biscuits on a wooden counter and striking them hard with your prick to see who could break them. Money and drinks were wagered on this game. Whites and blacks played it alike.

Another competition was the jug game. You took a large earthenware jug with a hole in the top and stuck your prick in it. The bottom of the jug was covered with a fine layer of ash, so you could see whether a man had reached the bottom or not when he took it out again.

Then there were other things they played, like cards. It was preferable to play with oil-painted cards, which are the correct ones to play with. There were many types of card games. Some people liked playing with the cards face up, others with them face down, which was a game where you could win a lot of money, but I preferred *monte*, which began in private houses and then spread to the countryside. *Monte* was played during slavery, in the tavern and in the masters' homes, but I took it up after Abolition. It is very complicated. You have to put two cards on the table and guess which of the two is the highest of the three you still have in your hand. It was always played for money, which is what made it attractive. The banker dealt the card and the players put on the money. You could win a lot of money, and I won every day. The fact is, *monte* is my weakness, *monte* and women. And with some reason, for you would have had to look hard to find a better player than me. Each card had its name, like now, except that cards today are not so colorful. In my day they had queens, kings, aces, and knaves, and then came all the numbers from two to seven. The cards had pictures on them of men on horseback wearing crowns, obviously Spaniards, because they never had fellows like that in Cuba, with those lace collars and long hair. They had Indians here in the old days.

Sunday was the liveliest day in the plantations. I don't know where the slaves found the energy for it. Their biggest fiestas were held on that day. On some plantations the drumming started at midday or one o'clock. At Flor de Sagua it began very early. The excitement, the games, and children rushing about started at sunrise. The barracoon came to life in a flash; it was like the end of the world. And in spite of work and everything the people woke up cheerful. The overseer and deputy overseer came into the barracoon and started chatting up the black women. I noticed that the Chinese kept apart; those buggers had no ears for drums and they stayed in their little corners. But they thought a lot; to my mind they spent more time thinking than the blacks. No one took any notice of them, and people went on with their dances.

The one I remember best is the *yuka*. Three drums were played for the *yuka*: the *caja*, the *mula*, and the *cachimbo*, which was the smallest one. In the background they drummed with two sticks on hollowed-out cedar trunks. The slaves made those themselves, and I think they were called *catá*. The *yuka* was danced in couples, with wild movements. Sometimes they swooped about like birds, and it almost looked as if they were going to fly, they moved so fast. They gave little hops with their hands on their waists. Everyone sang to excite the dancers.

There was another more complicated dance. I don't know whether it was really a dance or a game, because they punched each other really hard. This dance they called the *maní* or peanut dance. The dancers formed a circle of forty or fifty men, and they started hitting each other. Whoever got hit went in to dance. They wore ordinary work clothes, with colored print scarves round their heads and at their waists. (These scarves were used to bundle up the slaves' clothing and take it to the wash: they were called *vayajá* scarves). The men used to weight their fists with magic charms to make the *maní* blows more effective. The women didn't dance but stood round in a chorus, clapping, and they used to scream with fright, for often a Negro fell and failed to get up again. *Maní* was a cruel game. The dancers did not make bets on the outcome. On some plantations the masters themselves made bets, but I don't remember this happening at Flor de Sagua. What they did was to forbid slaves to hit each other so hard, because sometimes they were too bruised to work. The boys could not take part, but they watched and took it all in. I haven't forgotten a thing myself.

As soon as the drums started on Sunday the Negroes went down to the stream to bathe—there was always a little stream near every plantation. It sometimes happened that a woman lingered behind and met a man just as he was about to go into the water. Then they would go off together and get down to business. If not, they would go to the reservoirs, which were the pools they dug to store water. They also used to play hide-and-seek there, chasing the women and trying to catch them.

The women who were not involved in this little game stayed in the barracoons and washed themselves in a tub. These tubs were very big and there were one or two for the whole settlement.

Shaving and cutting hair was done by the slaves themselves. They took a long knife, and, like someone grooming a horse, they sliced off the woolly hair. There was always someone who liked to clip, and he became the expert. They cut hair the way they do now. And it never hurt, because hair is the most peculiar stuff; although you can see it growing and everything, it's dead. The women arranged their hair with curls and little partings. Their heads used to look like melon skins. They liked the excitement of fixing their hair one way one day and another way the next. One day it would have little partings, the next ringlets, another day it would be combed flat. They cleaned their teeth with strips of soap-tree bark, and this made them very white. All this excitement was reserved for Sundays.

Everyone had a special outfit that day. The Negroes bought themselves rawhide boots, in a style I haven't seen since, from nearby shops where they went with the master's permission. They wore red and green *vayajá* scarves around their necks, and round their heads and waists too, like in the *maní* dance. And they decked themselves with rings in their ears and rings in all their fingers, real gold. Some of them wore not gold but fine silver bracelets which came as high as their elbows, and patent leather shoes.

The slaves of French descent danced in pairs, not touching, circling slowly around. If one of them danced outstandingly well they tied silk scarves of all colors to his knees as a prize. They sang in patois and played two big drums with their hands. This was called the French dance.

I remember one instrument called a *marímbula*, which was very small. It was made of wickerwork and sounded as loud as a drum and had a little hole for the voice to come out of. They used this to accompany the Congo drums, and possibly the French too, but I can't be sure. The *marímbulas* made a very strange noise, and lots of people, particularly the *guajiros,*[*] didn't like them because they said they sounded like voices from another world.

As I recall, their own music at that time was made with the guitar only. Later, in the Nineties, they played *danzones*[+] on pianolas, with accordions and gourds. But the white man has always had a very different music from the black man. White man's music is without the drumming and is more insipid.

More or less the same goes for religion. The African gods are different, though they resemble the others, the priests' gods. They are more powerful and less adorned. Right now if you were to go to a

[*] Peasants, originally white settlers, but by this time black and Mulatto also.
[+] *Danzón:* a slow, stately Cuban dance popular in the last century.

Catholic church you would not see apples, stones, or cock's feathers. But this is the first thing you see in an African house. The African is cruder.

I knew of two African religions in the barracoons: the Lucumí and the Congolese. The Congolese was the more important. It was well known at the Flor de Sagua because their magic-men used to put spells on people and get possession of them, and their practice of sooth-saying won them the confidence of all the slaves. I got to know the elders of both religions after Abolition.

I remember the *Chicherekú** at Flor de Sagua. The *Chicherekú* was a Congolese by birth who did not speak Spanish. He was a little man with a big head who used to run about the barracoons and jump upon you from behind. I often saw him and heard him squealing like a rat. This is true. In Porfuerza there was a man who ran about in the same way. People used to run away from him because they said he was the Devil himself and he was bound up with *mayombe* and death. You dared not play with the *Chicherekú* because it could be dangerous. Personally I don't much like talking of him, because I have never laid eyes on him again, and if by some chance. . . .Well, these things are the Devil's own!

The Congolese used the dead and snakes for their religious rites. They called the dead *nkise* and the snakes *emboba*. They prepared big pots called *ngangas* which would walk about and all, and that was where the secret of their spells lay. All the Congolese had these pots for *mayombe*. The *ngangas* had to work with the sun, because the sun has always been the strength and wisdom of men, as the moon is of women. But the sun is more important because it is he who gives life to the moon. The Congolese worked magic with the sun almost every day. When they had trouble with a particular person they would follow him along a path, collect up some of the dust he walked on and put it in the *nganga* or in some little secret place. As the sun went down that person's life began to ebb away, and at sunset he would be dying. I mention this because it is something I often saw under slavery.

* African word for bogey-man.

If you think about it, the Congolese were murderers, although they only killed people who were harming them. No one ever tried to put a spell on me because I have always kept apart and not meddled in other people's affairs.

The Congolese were more involved with witchcraft than the Lucumí, who had more to do with the saints and with God. The Lucumí liked rising early with the strength of the morning and looking up into the sky and saying prayers and sprinkling water on the ground. The Lucumí were at it when you least expected it. I have seen old Negroes kneel on the ground for more than three hours at a time, speaking in their own tongue and prophesying. The difference between the Congolese and the Lucumí was that the former solved problems while the latter told the future. This they did with *dilog-gunes*, which are round, white shells from Africa with mystery inside. The god Eleggua's* eyes are made from this shell.

The old Lucumís would shut themselves up in a room in the barracoon and they could rid you even of the wickedness you were doing. If a Negro lusted after a woman, the Lucumís would calm him. I think they did this with coconut shells, *obi*, which were sacred. They were the same as the coconuts today, which are still sacred and may not be touched. If a man defiled a coconut, a great punishment befell him. I knew when things went well, because the coconut said so. He would command *Alafia*,[+] to be said so that the people would know that all was well. The saints spoke through the coconuts and the chief of these was Obatalá, who was an old man, they said, and only wore white. They also said it was Obatalá who made you and I don't know what else, but it is from Nature one comes, and this is true of Obatalá too.

The old Lucumís liked to have their wooden figures of the gods with them in the barracoons. All these figures had big heads and were called *oché*. Eleggua was made of cement, but Changó and Yemayá were made of wood, made by the carpenters themselves.

* Eleggua, Obatalá, Changó, Yemayá: gods of the Yoruba, a Nigerian tribe, worshipped in Cuba by followers of *santería*.

[+] Lucumí expression meaning "all goes well," used particularly in the system of divination with sacred coconuts.

They made the saints' marks on the walls of their rooms with charcoal and white chalk, long lines and circles, each one standing for a saint, but they said that they were secrets. These blacks made a secret of everything. They have changed a lot now, but in those days the hardest thing you could do was to try to win the confidence of one of them.

The other religion was the Catholic one. This was introduced by the priests, but nothing in the world would induce them to enter the slaves' quarters. They were fastidious people, with a solemn air which did not fit the barracoons—so solemn that there were Negroes who took everything they said literally. This had a bad effect on them. They read the catechism and read it to the others with all the words and prayers. Those Negroes who were household slaves came as messengers of the priests and got together with the others, the field slaves, in the sugar-mill towns. The fact is I never learned the doctrine because I did not understand a thing about it. I don't think the household slaves did either, although, being so refined and well-treated, they all made out they were Christian. The household slaves were given rewards by the masters and I never saw one of them badly punished. When they were ordered to go to the fields to cut cane or tend the pigs, they would pretend to be ill so they needn't work. For this reason the field slaves could not stand the sight of them. The household slaves sometimes came to the barracoons to visit relations and used to take back fruit and vegetables for the master's house; I don't know whether the slaves made them presents from their plots or whether they just took them. They caused a lot of trouble in the barracoons. The men came and tried to take liberties with the women. That was the source of the worst tensions. I was about twelve then, and I saw the whole rumpus.

There were other tensions. For instance, there was no love lost between the Congolese magic-men and the Congolese Christians, each of whom thought they were good and the others wicked. This still goes on in Cuba. The Lucumí and Congolese did not get on either; it went back to the difference between saints and witchcraft. The only ones who had no problems were the old men born in Africa. They were special people and had to be treated differently because they knew all religious matters.

Many brawls were avoided because the masters changed the slaves around. They kept them divided among themselves to prevent a rash of escapes. That was why the slaves of different plantations never got together with each other.

The Lucumís didn't like cutting cane, and many of them ran away. They were the most rebellious and courageous slaves. Not so the Congolese; they were cowardly as a rule, but strong workers who worked hard without complaining. There is a common rat called Congolese, and very cowardly it is too.

In the plantations there were Negroes from different countries, all different physically. The Congolese were black-skinned, though there were many of mixed blood with yellowish skin and light hair. They were usually small. The Mandingas were reddish-skinned, tall and very strong. I swear by my mother they were a bunch of crooks, too! They kept apart from the rest. The Gangas were nice people, rather short and freckled. Many of them became runaways. The Carabalís were like the Musundi Congolese, uncivilized brutes. They only killed pigs on Sundays and at Easter and, being good business-men, they killed them to sell, not to eat themselves. From this comes a saying, "Clever Carabalí, kills pig on Sunday." I got to know all these people better after slavery was abolished.

All the plantations had an infirmary near the barracoons, a big wooden hut where they took the pregnant women. You were born there and stayed there will you were six or seven, when you went to live in the barracoons and began work, like the rest. There were Negro wet nurses and cooks there to look after the *criollitos* and feed them. If anyone was injured in the fields or fell ill, these women would doctor him with herbs and brews. They could cure anything. Sometimes a *criollito* never saw his parents again because the boss moved them to another plantation, and so the wet-nurses would be in charge of the child. But who wants to bother with another person's child? They used to bathe the children and cut their hair in the infirmaries too. A child of good stock cost five hundred pesos, that is, the child of strong, tall parents. Tall Negroes were privileged. The masters picked them out to mate with tall, healthy women and shut them up in the barracoon and forced them to sleep together. The women had to produce healthy babies every year. I tell you, it was like breeding animals. Well, if the Negress didn't produce as expected, the couple were separated and she was sent to work in the fields again. Women who were barren were unlucky because they had to go back to being beasts of burden again, but they were allowed to choose their own husbands. It often happened that a woman would be chasing one man with twenty more after her. The magic-men would settle these problems with their potions.

If you went to a magic-man to ask his help in getting a woman, he would tell you to get hold of a shred of her tobacco, if she smoked. This was ground together with a Cantharis fly, one of the green harmful ones, into a powder which you gave to the woman in water. That was the way to seduce them. Another spell consisted of grinding up a humming-bird's heart to powder and giving this to a woman in her tobacco. If you merely wanted to make fun of a woman, you only had to send for some snuff from the apothecary's. This was enough to make any woman die of shame. You put it in a place where they used to sit down, and if only a little touched their bums they started farting. It was something to see those women with cosmetics all over their faces farting about the place!

The old Negroes were entertained by these carryings-on. When they were over sixty they stopped working in the fields. Not that any of them ever knew their age exactly. What happened was that when a man grew weak and stayed huddled in a corner, the overseers would make him a doorkeeper or watchman stationed at the gate of the barracoon or outside the pigsties, or he would be sent to help the women in the kitchen. Some of the old men had their little plots of ground and passed their time working in them. Doing this sort of job gave them time for witchcraft. They were not punished or taken much notice of, but they had to be quiet and obedient. That much was expected.

I saw many horrors in the way of punishment under slavery. That was why I didn't like the life. The stocks, which were in the boiler house, were the cruelest. Some were for standing and others for lying down. They were made of thick planks with holes for the head, hands, and feet. They would keep slaves fastened up like this for two or three months for some trivial offense. They whipped the pregnant women too, but lying down with a hollow in the ground for their bellies. They whipped them hard, but they took good care not to damage the babies because they wanted as many of those as possible. The most common punishment was flogging; this was given by the overseer with a rawhide lash which made weals on the skin. They also had whips made of the fibers of some jungle plant which stung like the devil and flayed off the skin in strips. I saw many handsome big Negroes with raw backs. Afterwards the cuts were covered with compresses of tobacco leaves, urine, and salt.

Life was hard and bodies wore out. Anyone who did not take to the hills as a runaway when he was young had to become a slave. It was preferable to be on your own on the loose than locked up in all that dirt and rottenness. In any event, life tended to be solitary because there were none too many women around. To have one of your own you had either to be over twenty-five or catch one yourself in the fields. The old men did not want the youths to have women. They said a man should wait until he was twenty-five to have experiences. Some men did not suffer much, being used to this life. Others had sex between themselves and did not want to know anything of women. This was their life—sodomy. The effeminate men washed the clothes and did the cooking too, if they had a "husband." They were good workers and occupied themselves with their plots of land, giving the produce to their "husbands" to sell to the white farmers. It was after Abolition that the term "effeminate" came into use, for the practice persisted. I don't think it can have come from Africa, because the old men hated it. They would have nothing to do with queers. To tell the truth, it never bothered me. I am of the opinion that a man can stick his arse where he wants.

Everyone wearied of the life, and the ones who got used to it were broken in spirit. Life in the forest was healthier. You caught lots of illnesses in the barracoons, in fact men got sicker there than anywhere else. It was not unusual to find a Negro with as many as three sicknesses at once. If it wasn't colic it was whooping cough. Colic gave you a pain in the gut which lasted a few hours and left you shagged. Whooping cough and measles were catching. But the worst sicknesses, which made a skeleton of everyone, were smallpox and the black sickness. Smallpox left men all swollen, and the black sickness took you by surprise; it struck suddenly and between one bout of vomiting and the next you ended up a corpse. There was one type of sickness the whites picked up, a sickness of the veins and male organs. It could only be got rid of with black women; if the man who had it slept with a Negress he was cured immediately.

There were no powerful medicines in those days and no doctors to be found anywhere. It was the nurses who were half witches who cured people with their home-made remedies. They often cured illnesses the doctors couldn't understand. The solution doesn't lie in feeling you and pinching your tongue; the secret is to trust the plants and herbs, which are the mother of medicine. Africans from the other side, across the sea, are never sick because they have the necessary plants at hand.

If a slave caught an infectious disease they would take him from his room and move him to the infirmary and try to cure him. If he died they put him in a big box and carried him off to the cemetery. The overseer usually came and gave instructions to the settlement to bury him. He would say, "We are going to bury this Negro who has done his time." And the slaves hurried along there, for when someone died everyone mourned.

The cemetery was in the plantation itself, about a hundred yards from the barracoon. To bury slaves, they dug a hole in the ground, filled it in, and stuck a cross on top to keep away enemies and the Devil. Now they call it a crucifix. If anyone wears a cross around his neck it is because someone has tried to harm him.

Once they buried a Congolese and he raised his head. He was still alive. I was told this story in Santo Domingo, after Abolition. The whole district of Jacotea knows of it. It happened on a small plantation called El Diamante which belonged to Marinello's father, the one who talks a lot about Martí.* Everyone took fright and ran away. A few days later the

* Martí, often known as the "Apostle" or "the Father of Cuba," was the leader of Cuba's national War of Independence and also a poet and essayist of great influence in the Spanish-speaking world. Juan Marinello, one of Cuba's leading Communists, is an important critic of Martí's literary work.

Congolese appeared in the barracoon; they say he entered very slowly so as not to scare everyone, but when people saw him they took fright again. When the overseer asked what had happened, he said, "They put me in a hole because of my cholera and when I was cured I came out." After that, whenever anyone caught cholera or another disease, they left him for days and days in the coffin until he grew cold as ice.

These stories are true, but one I am convinced is a fabrication because I never saw such a thing, and that is that some Negroes committed suicide. Before, when the Indians were in Cuba, suicide did happen. They did not want to become Christians, and they hanged themselves from trees. But the Negroes did not do that, they escaped by flying. They flew through the sky and returned to their own lands. The Musundi Congolese were the ones that flew the most; they disappeared by means of witchcraft. They did the same as the Canary Island witches but without making a sound. There are those who say the Negroes threw themselves into rivers. This is untrue. The truth is they fastened a chain to their waists which was full of magic. That was where their power came from. I know all this intimately, and it is true beyond doubt.

The Chinese did not fly, nor did they want to go back to their own country, but they did commit suicide. They did it silently. After several days they would turn up hanging from a tree or dead on the ground. They used to kill the very overseers themselves with sticks or knives. The Chinese respected no one. They were born rebels. Often the master would appoint an overseer of their own race so that he might win their trust. Then they did not kill him. When slavery ended I met other Chinese in Sagua la Grande, but they were different and very civilized.

Life in the Forest

I have never forgotten the first time I tried to escape. That time I failed, and I stayed a slave for several years longer from fear of having the shackles put on me again. But I had the spirit of a runaway watching over me, which never left me. And I kept my plans to myself, so that no one could give me away. I thought of nothing else; the idea went round and round in my head and would not leave me in peace; nothing could get rid of it, at times it almost tormented me. The old Negroes did not care for escaping, the women still less. There were few runaways. People were afraid of the forest. They said anyone who ran away was bound to be recaptured. But I gave more thought to this idea than the others did. I always had the feeling that I would like the forest and I knew that it was hell working in the fields, for you couldn't do anything for yourself. Everything went by what the master said.

One day I began to keep my eye on the overseer. I had already been sizing him up for some time. That son-of-a-bitch obsessed me, and nothing could make me forget him. I think he was Spanish. I remember that he was tall and never took his hat off. All the blacks respected him because he would take the skin off your back with a single stroke of his whip. The fact is I was hot-headed that day. I don't know what came over me, but I was filled with a rage which burned me up just to look at the man.

I whistled at him from a distance, and he looked round and then turned his back; that was when I picked up a stone and threw it at his head. I know it must have hit him because he shouted at the others to seize me. But that was the last he saw of me, because I took to the forest there and then.

I spent several days walking about in no particular direction. I had never left the plantation before. I walked uphill, downhill, in every direction. I know I got to a farm near the Siguanea, where I was forced to rest. My feet were blistered and my hands were swollen and festering. I camped under a tree. I made myself a shelter of banana leaves in a few hours and I stayed there four or five days. I only had to hear the sound of a human voice to be off like a bullet. It was a terrible thing to be captured again after you had run away.

Then I had the idea of hiding in a cave. I lived there for something like a year and a half. The reason I chose it was that I thought it might save me wandering about so much and also that all the pigs in the district, from the farms and smallholdings and allotments, used to come to a sort of marsh near the mouth of the cave to bathe and wallow in the water. I caught them very easily because they came up one behind the other. I used to cook myself up a pig every week. This cave of mine was very big and black as a wolf's mouth. Its name was Guajabán, near the village of Remedios. It was very dangerous because there was no other way out; you had to enter and leave by the mouth. I was very curious to find another exit, but I preferred to stay in the mouth of the cave with the *majases* which were very dangerous snakes.* They knock a person down with their breath, a snake breath you cannot feel, and then they put you to sleep to suck your blood. That was why I was always on guard and lit a fire to frighten them off. Anyone who dozes off in a cave is in a bad way. I did not want to see a snake even from a distance. The Congolese, and this is a fact, told me that the *majases* lived for over a thousand years, and when they got to a thousand they turned into marine creatures and went off to live in the sea like any other fish.

The cave was like a house inside, only a little darker, as you would expect. Ah, and the stink! Yes, it stank of bat droppings! I used to walk about on them because they were as soft as a featherbed. The bats lead a free life in caves. They were and are the masters of caves. It is the same everywhere in the world. As no one kills them they live for scores of years, though not as long as the *majases*. Their droppings turn to dust and are thrown on the ground to make pasture for animals and fertilize crops.

Once I almost set fire to the place. I struck a spark and flames leapt through the cave. It was because of the bat droppings. After Abolition I told a Congolese the story of how I lived with the bats, and the liar—the Congolese were even worse than you could imagine—said, "A Creole like you doesn't know a thing. In my country what you call a bat is as big as a pigeon." I knew this was untrue. They fooled half the world with their tales. But I just listened and was inwardly amused.

The cave was silent. The only sound was the bats going "Chui, chui, chui." They didn't know how to sing, but they spoke to each other. They understood each other. I noticed that one of them would go "Chui, chui, chui" and the whole band would follow him wherever

* In fact they are harmless.

98

he went. They were very united in everything. Bats don't have wings. They are nothing but a scrap of black rag with a little black head, very dark and ugly, and if you look closely at them they are like mice. In that cave I was, as it were, just summering. What I really liked was the forest, and after a year and a half I left that dark place and took to the forest tracks. I went into the Siguanea forests again and spent a long time there. I cared for myself as if I were a pampered child. I didn't want to be taken into slavery again. It was repugnant to me, it was shameful. I have always felt like that about slavery. It was like a plague—it still seems like that today.

I was careful about making sounds or showing lights. If I left a trail they would follow me and catch me. I walked up and down so many hills that my arms and legs became as hard as wood. I came to know the forest gradually, and I began to like it. Sometimes I forgot I was a runaway and I started whistling. I used to whistle to dispel the fear of the first days. They say whistling drives away evil spirits. But in the forest a runaway had to be on his guard, and I stopped in case the *ranchadores* came after me. To track down runaway slaves, the masters used to send for a posse of *ranchadores*, brutal white countrymen with hunting dogs which would drag you out of the forest with their teeth. I never ran into any of them or even saw one close up. They were trained to catch Negroes; if one of them saw a Negro he would give chase. If I happened to hear barking nearby I would take off my clothes immediately, because once you are naked the dogs can't smell anything. Now I see a dog and it doesn't mean a thing, but if I had seen one then you wouldn't have seen my heels for miles around. I have never felt drawn to dogs. To my mind they have wicked instincts.

When a *ranchador* caught a slave, the master would give him money, a gold onza or more. In those days an onza was worth seventeen pesos. There's no knowing how many white countrymen were involved in that business!

To tell the truth, I lived very well as a runaway, hidden but comfortable. I did not let the other runaways catch sight of me: "Runaway meets runaway, sells runaway." There were many things I didn't do. For a long time I didn't speak to a soul. I liked this solitude. The other runaways always stayed in groups of twos and threes, but this was dangerous because when it rained their footprints showed up in the mud, and lots of idiots were caught that way.

There were some freed slaves around. I saw them going into the forest to look for herbs and *jutías*, edible rats. I never spoke to them or went near them, in fact I took good care to hide from them. Some of them worked on the land, and as soon as they left the coast clear, I took advantage of their absence to steal their vegetables and pigs. Most of them raised pigs on their plots of land. But I preferred to steal from the smallholdings because there was more of everything and it was easier. The smallholdings were bigger than the plots, far bigger, almost like big farms. The Negroes didn't have such luxuries. Those *guajiros* really lived well in their palm-bark houses. I used to watch them at their music-making from a safe distance. Sometimes I could even hear them. They played small accordions, kettledrums, and gourds, maracas, and calabashes. Those were their favorite instruments. I didn't learn their names till after I left the forest because, as a runaway, I was ignorant of everything.

They enjoyed dancing. But they didn't dance to the black man's music. They liked the *zapateo* and the *caringa*.* They all used to get together to dance the *zapateo* in the evenings, around five o'clock. The men wore colored scarves around their necks and the women wore them around their heads. If one man excelled in the dance, his woman would come up and put a hat on top of the one he was wearing. This was the prize. I watched it all from a safe distance, taking it all in. I even saw them playing their pianolas. They played every sort of instrument there. They made a lot of noise, but it was as pretty as could be. From time to time one of the men would grab a gourd to accompany the pianola. The pianolas played the music that was popular at the time, the *danzón*.

On Sundays the *guajiros* wore white and their women put flowers on their heads and wore their hair loose, then they joined the rest of the festive company and got together in the taverns to celebrate. The

* Folk dances popular in the nineteenth century, especially among white country people. The *caringa* was of African origin and usually took the form of a scurrilous song accompanied by a dance.

men liked linen and drill. They made themselves long shirts like jackets, with big pockets. The *guajiros* in those days lived better than people realize. They got tips from the masters almost every day. Naturally the two got along very well and did their dirty work together. But in my view the runaway lived better than the *guajiro;* he had greater freedom.

I had to forage for food for a long time, but there was always enough. "The careful tortoise carries his house on his back." I liked vegetables and beans and pork best. I think it is because of the pork that I have lived so long. I used to eat it every day, and it never disagreed with me. I would creep up to the smallholdings at night to catch piglets, taking care that no one heard me. I grabbed the first one I saw by the neck, clapped a halter round it, slung it over my shoulder and started to run, keeping my hand over its snout to stop it squealing. When I reached my camp I set it down and looked it over. If it was well fed and weighed twenty pounds or so, I had meals for a fortnight.

I led a half-wild existence as a runaway. I hunted animals like *jutías*. The *jutía* runs like the devil, and you need wings on your feet to catch it. I was very fond of smoked *jutía*. I don't know what people think of it today, but they never eat it. I used to catch one and smoke it without salt, and it lasted me months. The *jutía* is the healthiest food there is, though vegetables are better for the bones. The man who eats vegetables daily, particularly malanga roots, has no trouble from his bones. There are plenty of these wild vegetables in the forest. The malanga has a big leaf which shines at night. You can recognize it at once.

All the forest leaves have their uses. The leaves of tobacco plants and mulberry trees cure stings. If I saw some insect bite was festering, I picked a tobacco leaf and chewed it thoroughly, then I laid it on the sting and the swelling went. Often, when it was cold, my bones would ache, a dry pain which would not go away. Then I made myself an infusion of rosemary leaves to soothe it, and it was cured at once. The cold also gave me bad coughs. When I got catarrh and a cough, I would pick the big leaf and lay it on my chest. I never knew its name, but it gave out a whitish liquid which was very warming; that soothed my cough. When I caught a cold, my eyes used to itch maddeningly, and the same used to happen as a result of the sun; in that case I laid a few leaves of the *ítamo* plant out to catch the dew overnight, and the next day I washed my eyes carefully with them. *Ítamo* is the best thing for this. The stuff they sell in pharmacies today is *ítamo*, but what happens is that they put it into little bottles and it looks like something else. As one grows older this eye trouble disappears. I have not had any itching bouts for years now.

The macaw-tree leaf provided me with smokes. I made tight-rolled neat little cigarettes with it. Tobacco was one of my relaxations. After I left the forest I stopped smoking tobacco, but while I was a runaway I smoked it all the time.

And I drank coffee which I made with roast *guanina* leaves. I had to grind the leaves with the bottom of a bottle. When the mixture was ground right down, I filtered it and there was my coffee. I could always add a little wild honey to give it flavor. Coffee with honey strengthens the organism. You were always fit and strong in the forest.

Townsfolk are feeble because they are mad about lard. I have never liked lard because it weakens the body. The person who eats a lot of it grows fat and sluggish. Lard is bad for the circulation and it strangles people. Bees' honey is one of the best things there is for health. It was easy to get in the forest. I use to find it in the hollows of hardwood trees. I used to make *chanchánchara*, a delicious drink made of stream water and honey, and best drunk cold. It was better for you than any modern medicine; it was natural. When there was no stream nearby I hunted around till I found a spring. In the forest there are springs of sweet water—the coldest and clearest I have seen in my life—which run downhill.

The truth is I lacked for nothing in the forest. The only thing I could not manage was sex. Since there were no women around I had to keep the appetite in check. It wasn't even possible to fuck a mare because they whinnied like demons, and if the white countrymen had heard the din they would have come rushing out immediately. I was not going to have anyone clap me in irons for a mare.

I was never short of fire. During my first few days in the forest I had matches. Then they ran out, and I had to use my *yesca*, a black ash that I kept in one of the tinderboxes the Spaniards sold in taverns. It was easy to get a fire going. All you had to do was rub a stone on the tinderbox until it sparked. I learned this from the Canary Islanders when I was a slave. I never liked them as they were domineering and petty. The Galicians were nicer and got on better with the Negroes.

As I have always liked being my own man, I kept well away from everyone. I even kept away from the insects. To frighten off snakes I fired a big log and left it burning all night. They did not come near because they thought the log was a devil or an enemy of theirs. That's why I say I enjoyed my life as a runaway. I looked after myself, and I protected myself too. I used knives and half-sized machetes made by the firm of Collins, which were the ones used by the rural police, to clear the undergrowth and hunt animals, and I kept them ready in case a *ranchador* tried to take me by surprise—though that would have been difficult, as I kept on the move. I walked so much in the sun that at times my head began to burn and become, I imagined, quite red. Then I would be seized with a strong fever which I got rid of by wrapping myself up a bit or putting fresh leaves on my forehead, plantain as a rule. The problem was that I had no hat. I used to imagine the heat must be getting into my head and softening my brain.

When the fever passed, and it sometimes lasted several days, I dipped myself in the first river I came across and came out like new. The river water did me no harm. I think river water is the best thing for health, because it's so cold. This is good, because it hardens you. The bones feel firm. The rain used to give me a touch of catarrh which I cured with a brew of *cuajaní* berries and bees' honey. So as not to get wet I sheltered myself with palm leaves, piling them on top of a frame made of four forked sticks to make a hut. These huts were often seen after slavery and during the war. They looked like Indian shacks.

I spent most of the time walking or sleeping. At mid-day and at five in the afternoon I could hear the *fotuto*,* which the women blew to call their husbands home. It sounded like this: "Fuuuu, fu, fu, fu, fu." At night I slept at my ease. That was why I got so fat. I never thought about anything. My life was all eating, sleeping, and keeping watch. I liked going to the hills at night, they were quieter and safer. *Ranchadores* and

* A large conch used as a trumpet in the country districts.

wild animals found difficulty in getting there. I went as far as Trinidad. From the top of those hills you could see the town and the sea.

The nearer I got to the coast the bigger the sea got. I always imagined the sea like an immense river. Sometimes I stared hard at it and it went the strangest white color and was swallowed up in my eyes. The sea is another great mystery of Nature, and it is very important, because it can take men and close over them and never give them up. Those are what they call shipwrecked men.

One thing I can remember really clearly is the forest birds. They are something I cannot forget. I remember them all. Some were pretty and some were hellishly ugly. They frightened me a lot at first, but then I got used to hearing them. I even got so I felt they were taking care of me. The *cotunto* was a real bastard. It was a black, *black* bird, which said, "You, you, you, you, you, you, you ate the cheese up." And it kept on saying this until I answered, "Get away!" and it went. I heard it crystal clear. There was another bird which used to answer it as well; it went, "Cu, cu, cu, cu, cu, cu," and sounded like a ghost.

The *sijú* was one of the birds which tormented me most. It always came at night. That creature was the ugliest thing in the forest! It had white feet and yellow eyes. It shrieked out something like this: "Cus, cus, cuuuus."

The barn owl had a sad song, but then it was a witch. It looked for dead mice. It cried, "Chua, chua, chua, kui, kui," and flew off like a ray of light. When I saw a barn owl in my path, especially when it was flying to and fro, I used to take a different way because I knew it was warning me of an enemy nearby, or death itself. The barn owl is wise and strange. I recollect that the witches had a great respect for her and worked magic with her, the *susundamba*, as she is called in Africa. The barn owl may well have left Cuba. I have never seen one again. Those birds go from country to country.

The sparrow came here from Spain and has founded an immense tribe here. Also the *tocororo*, which is half a greenish color. It wears a scarlet sash across its breast, just like the one the king of Spain has. The overseers used to say it was a messenger from the king. I know it was forbidden even to look at a *tocororo*. The Negro who killed one was killing the king. I saw lots of men get the lash for killing sparrows and *tocororo*. I liked the *tocororo* because it sang as if it was hopping about, like this: "Có, co, có, co, có, co."

A bird which was a real son-of-a-bitch was the *ciguapa*. It whistled just like a man and it froze the soul to hear it. I don't like to think how often those creatures upset me.

I got used to living with trees in the forest. They have their noises too, because the leaves hiss in the air. There is one tree with a big white leaf which looks like a bird at night. I could swear that tree spoke. It went "Uch, uch, uch, ui, ui, ui, uch, uch." Trees also cast shadows which do no harm, although one should not walk on them at night. I think trees' shadows must be like men's spirits. The spirit is the reflection of the soul, this is clear.

One thing it is not given to us men to see is the soul. We cannot say whether it is such or such a color. The soul is one of the greatest things in the world. Dreams are there to put us in touch with it. The Congolese elders used to say that the soul was like a witchcraft inside you and that there were good spirits and bad spirits, or rather, good souls and bad souls, and that everybody had them. As far as I can see, some people have only the magic sort of souls, while others have ordinary ones. But the ordinary ones are better, I think, because the others are in league with the Devil. It can happen that the soul leaves the body—when a person dies or sleeps—and joins the other souls wandering in space. It does this to rest itself, because so much strife at all times would be unbearable. There are people who don't like being called while they are asleep, because they are easily frightened and could die suddenly. This is because the soul travels far away during sleep and leaves the body empty. I sometimes get the shivers at night, and the same used to happen in the forest. Then I cover myself well because this is God's warning to one to take care of oneself. People who get the shivers need to pray a lot.

The heart is very different. It never leaves its post. If you put your hand on your left side you can make sure that it is beating. But the day it stops no one can help but go stiff. That is why you should not trust it.

Now the most important thing of all is the guardian angel. It is he who makes you go forwards or back. To my mind, the angel ranks higher than the soul or the heart. He is always at your feet, watching over you and seeing everything. Nothing will ever make him go. I have thought a lot about these things, and I still find them a bit obscure. These are the thoughts which come when one is alone. Man is thinking at all times. Even when he dreams, it is as though he were thinking. It is not good to speak of these thoughts. There is danger of decadence setting in. You cannot put much trust in people. How many people ask you questions so as to be able to use the information against you afterwards! Besides, this business of the spirits is infinite, like debts which keep piling up. No one knows the end. The truth is I don't even trust the Holy Ghost. That was why I stayed on my own as a runaway. I did nothing except listen to the birds and trees, and eat, but I never spoke to a soul. I remember I was so hairy that my whiskers hung in ringlets. It was a sight to inspire fear. When I came out of the forest and into the villages an old man called Ta Migue cropped me with a pair of big scissors. He gave me such a close crop I looked like a thoroughbred. I felt strange with all that wool gone, tremendously cold. The hair started growing again in a few days. Negroes have this tendency—I have never seen a bald Negro, not one. It was the Galicians who brought baldness to Cuba.

All my life I have liked the forest, but when slavery ended I stopped being a runaway. I realized from the way the people were cheering and shouting that slavery had ended, and so I came out of the forest. They were shouting, "We're free now." But I didn't join in, I thought it might be a lie. I don't know…anyway, I went up to a plantation and let my head appear little by little till I was out in the open. That was while Martínez Campos was Governor, the slaves said that it was he who had freed them. All the same, years passed and there were still slaves in Cuba.

When I left the forest and began walking, I met an old woman carrying two children in her arms. I called to her, and when she came up I asked her, "Tell me, is it true we are no longer slaves?" She replied, "No, son, we are free now." I went on walking the way I was going and began to look for work. Lots of Negroes wanted to be friends with me, and they used to ask me what I had done as a runaway. I told them, "Nothing." I have always been one for my independence. Idle gossip never helped anyone. I went for years and years without talking to anyone at all.

Rural Peasantry

The Caribbean countryside is the setting in which Simone Schwarz-Bart places her characters in *Between Two Worlds*. Like Montejo and Barnet, she fills her novels with the social life and history of those not often found in official records. Her novel of the rural peasantry of her native Guadeloupe sets out to bridge the gaps left by the experts who "have once and for all dismissed [the nation's] history as insignificant," but which the narrator affirms is "quite worthy of educated people's attention." Schwarz-Bart blends legend and African and Créole belief systems, and chronicles local history in a work that takes on epic proportions. Book One, reprinted here, opens: "The island on which our story takes place is not well known. It floats, forsaken, in the Gulf of Mexico, and only a few especially meticulous atlases show it." With this novel, Schwarz-Bart places Guadeloupe firmly on the map and secures her own place in literary history.

Silvester, the protagonist of Pedro Mir's novel of the Dominican Republic, *When They Loved the Communal Lands*, through a series of "discoveries," places his nation in context. The novel spans fifty years, from 1916 to 1965, chronicling the aftermath of the U.S. invasion of 1916 and its effect on national consciousness. The occupation led to a change in the Constitution of 1920 concerning land tenure, and it is the resulting break-up of the communal lands of the rural peasantry around which the novel revolves. Through a gallery of characters and perspectives, Mir captures "the major and minor tragedies that have befallen major and minor characters throughout the course of this century," their "physical and mental geography," and thus recreates "a complete picture of national life . . . " For Mir, the national reality is one that extends from the Dominican Republic to Riverside Drive and the Dominicans on the island of Manhattan who also harbor "a treasure of native experiences."

From: Between Two Worlds

SIMONE SCHWARZ-BART
(GUADELOUPE)

BOOK 1

Which tells the history of the world
up to the birth of Ti Jean L'horizon,
and of our hero's early life

1

The island on which our story takes place is not well known. It floats, forsaken, in the Gulf of Mexico, and only a few especially meticulous atlases show it. If you were to study a globe you could wear your eyes out peering, but you'd be hard put to it to find the island without a magnifying glass. It arose out of the sea quite recently, a mere couple of million years ago. And rumor has it that it may go as it came, suddenly sink without warning, taking with it its mountains and little sulphur volcano, its green hills where ramshackle huts perch as if hung in the void, and its thousand rivers, so sunny and capricious that the original inhabitants called it the Isle of Lovely Streams.

Meanwhile it still floats on a sea that brings forth cyclones, on waters always changing from calmest blue to green or mauve. And it supports all kinds of strange creatures, men and beasts, devils, zombies, and the rest, all seeking something which has not yet come but which they dimly hope for without knowing its name or shape. It also serves as a stopover for birds that come down to lay their eggs in the sun.

To tell the truth, it is a completely unimportant scrap of earth, and the experts have once and for all dismissed it as insignificant. And yet it has had its bad times, its past great upsurges, fine copious bloodlettings quite worthy of educated people's attention. But all that was forgotten long ago. The very trees have no memory of it, and as for the people, they believe nothing happens on the island, never has and never will until the day it goes to join its elder sisters at the bottom of the sea.

They have adopted the habit of hiding the sky with the palms of their hands. They say that real life is somewhere else, and even that this speck of an island can reduce anything to nothing; so much so that if God were to descend there in person, he would end up like all the rest, up to his neck in rum and women.

In this back of beyond there is a place yet further remote, and that is the hamlet of Fond-Zombi. If Guadeloupe itself is hardly more than a dot on the map, it may seem even more hopeless and futile to try to summon up an atom like Fond-Zombi. And yet the place does exist. Moreover, it has a long history, full of wonders, bloodshed, and frustrations, and of desires no less vast than those that filled the skies of Nineveh, Babylon, or Jerusalem.

The first inhabitants of Fond-Zombi were men with red skins who lived on the banks of the Leafy River, beyond where Ma Vitaline's hut now stands, just after the Bridge of Beyond; you can still see great rocks there carved with suns and moons. They had their own special way of looking at the landscape; hence the sparkling name they gave to their little world—Karukera, or, as I have said, the Isle of Lovely Streams. The name Guadeloupe came later, with the arrival of pale, long-eared men, harassed and uneasy, who seem not to have noticed the beauty of the rivers, though they made a great fuss about the heat of the tropical sun. Having driven out the men with red skins, these philosophers turned to the coasts of Africa for men with black skins to sweat for them. And so, just because of the sun, slavery came to the ancient island of Karukera, and there were cries and supplications, and the sound of the whip drowned the sound of the mountain streams.

But all that was a thing of the past when my story begins, and the blacks of Fond-Zombi thought there was not a single event about the island worth remembering. Sometimes, deep down, some of them wondered whether after all there might not be some glory in their past, some radiance which might reflect on them a little; but fearing ridicule, they were careful to keep their thoughts to themselves. Others went so far as to doubt their ancestors had come from Africa, despite the little voice whispering in their ear that they had not always lived there, that they were not native to the country in the same way as the trees and stones and beasts that had sprung from its pleasant red soil. And so, when they thought of themselves and their fate, arisen out of nowhere in order to be nothing, hardly more than shades roaming Fond-Zombi on a tuft of wild grass, these forgetful ones would be seized by a kind of bitter, feverish longing, which would make them miserable for a moment or two. But then they would drearily shake their poor, battered heads, and reassured by a familiar face or shrub or a broken-down hut still standing among the rocks, would send a great shout of laughter skyward. All was well: they knew where they were again.

For, you see, they were men of sand and wind, born of words and dying with them. They knew life as an ox knows ticks, and they did their best day after day to make it anew, even amid the sharp sugar cane and the itch of the red ants among the bananas. Their feet were not quite firmly on the ground. And when two village women parted after one of those little chats when time is forgotten, instead of bidding each other "au revoir" they would shorten it to "au rêve"— meaning "till the dream."

In those old long-gone times, the days before light and tarred roads, before the electricity posts that give no shade, Fond-Zombi was quite different from what it is today. The only ones who remember it as it was are the few white-haired mongooses who every year convey the latest news underground.

Listen, youngsters: The Fond-Zombi of those days was not the forest, but beyond the forest, not the back of beyond but the back of the back of beyond. The traveler would leave the township of La Ramée with its town hall, its school, its graveyard with the flame trees, its dilapidated wharf humming with mosquitoes. Then he would go along a little wandering path that led off the main road and seemed to take off like a bird toward the mountains, as if it could not wait to disappear into the clouds. There were bananas on the left, cane fields on the right—all the property of the white man, one single estate from the sea to the foothills of the volcano. On either side of the track there sprang up little wooden shacks supported on four stones. They looked as if they were joined together in big clumps, but these groups got sparser as you left the coastal plain behind and went farther into the interior. Then the clumps became only thin tufts, two or three thatched huts shimmering in little mud yards, smooth and shiny as marble.

After an hour's journey the forest sprang up on all sides, fighting a rearguard action against the sugar plantations that inched farther up every year, up one hill after another. And there were shadows lying easy and dense across the track—mahogany and galpas, geni-paps and locust trees, the now-extinct bois rada, and balatas en-twined in lianas, screening you in, shutting you away in a separate world. Then came the little Bridge of Beyond, hanging over a dried-up gully, a dead river haunted by a troop of evil spirits writhing and beckoning in the hope that some human being would miss his footing, slip, and come and join them below. And then you would reach Fond-Zombi itself, in a fantastic clearing of light, built on a string of hillocks, its little cabins dotted about crazily and seeming to hang from invisible ropes: a mere handful of human habitations, the dwellings of zombies abandoned in the great forest and clinging to Mount Balata, itself apparently about to collapse into the void.

The actual village was no more than a row of shanties beside a dusty track which petered out there below the solitudes of the volcano. Strung out like that, they looked like the coaches of a little train setting out to climb the mountain. But this train didn't go anywhere. It had come to a halt long ago, half buried under the vegetation, and had never started off again. The huts faced the sea and looked out at the world; but the world didn't see them. For wherever you stood you could see a distant strip of water below, about five miles away, a longish cycle ride for those who made their living by fishing. Most people worked on the white men's estates, flatlands spiky with sugar cane or rich slopes planted with bananas. But there were also a few fishermen, craftsmen, shopkeepers who sold oil and rum and salt cod; two or three women who hawked fish; and, holding themselves somewhat aristocratically aloof, some sawyers who cut planks in the forest, on scaffolding up near the mist-shrouded peaks. All these people seemed to have ground to a halt, like the track. Everyday life was hardly different from what the oldest of them had known in the days of slavery. The shape and arrangement of the houses went back to the same period, as did their poor and wretched appearance: mere boxes perched on four stones, as if to signify how precariously the black man was rooted in the soil of Guadeloupe.

And yet it was a land of verdant hills and clear waters, beneath a sun every day more radiant. When there was no wind, clouds would form and slightly veil its splendor; but usually it shone as bright as could be, the breezes and trade winds keeping heaven clear and solacing man.

These people of wind and sand were not the entire population of Fond-Zombi. Beyond the village, across the Bridge of Beyond, a narrow path rose up hills piled one on the other like a giant ladder climbing the hazy steeps of the volcano. There, on an almost inaccessible plateau, lived a small group of real solitaries, people who had cut themselves off from the world once and for all, and who were called the folk Up Above.

The hermits of the plateau were the poorest of all the inhabitants of Fond-Zombi, of Guadeloupe and the neighbouring islands, and perhaps among the poorest people in the whole world. But they regarded themselves as superior to all, for they were the direct descendants of the slaves who in the past had risen in revolt, and had lived and often died bearing arms on the very spot where their huts now stood. Unlike the villagers, these people did not fret or wonder about the color of their guts; they knew, they knew that a noble blood ran in their veins; the blood of the braves who had built these same round whitewashed huts. Nor did they ask themselves whether Guadeloupe was of any importance in the world; they knew, they knew that rare happenings and unparalleled glories had been seen in the wretched forest they now haunted, and that these deeds had been the exploits of their ancestors.

Every evening the wild folk would sit by the edge of the plateau facing the twinkling lights in the valley, and tell their children stories of African animals, stories about hares and tortoises and spiders that thought and behaved like human beings, and sometimes better. And then, in the middle of one of these stories, some old veteran would point at the grass which the evening breeze pressed down under their naked feet and say earnestly: "Look, children, that's the hair of heroes that fell here." The people would speak of the dead blacks, and of their fate in this world, on this very spot, the desperate battles in the dark, the hunt and the final fall. And suddenly, at an always unpredictable moment, a strange silence would fall from the sky, during which the heroes rose up out of the earth and were visible to all.

These people were very tall, much taller than the people of the valley, with impassive countenances, broad yellow cheekbones, and slanting, elusive eyes. They did not go in much for cultivation. They did not work in the cane fields, and they neither bought nor sold. Their only currency was crayfish and game, which they exchanged in the villages for rum, salt, paraffin and matches for the days when it was too damp to use flints. After the abolition of slavery they had tried to talk to those in the valley, the folk Down Below as they called them, to tell them of the heroes' flight in the dark and the final defeat and fall. But the others had laughed, a strange, shrill little laugh, and said that these things were never of great importance—they couldn't be, for where were the books they were written down in? Some of the villagers even cast doubt on the truth of the stories. They said that as far as they knew, never, since the devil was a little boy, had any fool of a black ever done anything so illustrious. Though free, they uttered these words with a kind of triumphant bitterness, as if they prided themselves on admitting their own insignificance, and found secret pleasure and special virtue in being beyond all doubt the lowest of the low. But the wild folk thought otherwise, and as a result there was considerable animosity between them and the people in the valley. They did not marry or intermingle their blood with one another. They did not drink together. If they happened by chance to encounter one another in the forest they would ostentatiously avert their eyes. In short, their paths no longer crossed.

The folk Up Above called the people of the valley chameleons, snakes continually casting their skin, experts at apery—not to put too fine point on it, consummate imitators of the white man, delighting in doing just what they were not born to do. For their part, the respectable villagers sneered at the barbarians up on the plateau, steeped in ignorance, madmen of the dark who still wiped their arses with stones. But they were careful to stop there and lower their voices, for the "people of the dark" had the power of changing themselves into dogs and crabs, birds and ants, which could come and spy on and plague you even in bed. They could also strike from a distance and make you fall into nonexistent pits. And no sorcerer in the lowlands could counter their spells or undo what they had tied up or fastened up there in the dark. For their lore came straight from Africa, and against the blows they struck there was no defense.

Their chief had been present at the struggles of the heroes of old; his powder had added to the smoke of the battles fought ages ago in the wild woods. His comrades' bones had whitened, turned to dust and been washed deep into the earth, while he still told the children of their exploits, every evening, facing the setting sun. The man's name was Wademba, the same name he had brought with him from Africa in the hold of a slave ship. But after it became known that he was immortal, the people of the plateau just called him the Green One, or the Green Eel, because he had coiled himself up on the heights like his namesake in a hole in the rock, and nothing would ever get him out again.

Things dawdled along like this for a hundred and fifty years, with now the sun and now some flashes of lightning, until the day when the tarred road and its electricity posts shot Fond-Zombi right into the twentieth century.

2

That fateful day found the man still perched up on his plateau with his old comrades from the deluge, who were still holding out, though they didn't quite remember against what. When the tarred road went through Fond-Zombi and got as far as the Bridge of Beyond, the former rebels realized the battle was lost; and two or three of the gloomier ones, shattered by the spirit of defeat, crept down the path, followed by others and yet more in a positive cascade, leaving behind only the wildest ones, in other words all the green eels. Most of the women had drifted down, drawn by the magic of the plain, the tarred road, and the electricity posts. So the majority of those who remained were men, and the traditional balance was upset. But after a period of indecision a new system was established among them, a strange and unexpected harmony whereby several men's houses were grouped around one woman who serviced them all alike.

For a long time Wademba enjoyed the privilege of having a wife to himself, a woman called Aboomeki, also known as the Silent One. She was a very simple creature, completely lacking in coquetry, whose only definite liking was for the long grass skirts she would make twirl and eddy about her hips when she thought no one was looking. But after a few years she began to hanker after the exciting life of the folk Down Below, and she asked her husband's permission to leave, down the path now referred to as the cascade.

The man agreed, but on condition that she left him the little girl they'd had together, to keep him company: the child was called Awa.

Awa, Aboomeki's daughter, was scarcely ten years old when her mother went down the cascade. She was rounder and curlier than a breadfruit, with eyes far apart like hanging droplets— drops of water after the rain, trembling, quite willing to fall.

With her two sous of hips behind and her little Chinese dates in front, she nevertheless gave off the radiance of a woman, and the old Negresses would smile as she went by. "See how flesh springs from flesh all of a sudden," they would say, enchanted by the sumptuous, promising curve of her hips, which might soon bring new strength to the plateau. Fortunately these crude old ladies never dreamed of the fancies filling the child's brain. Her eyes already looked for what they could not see, and perhaps that was what made them so fine so young. That was why, when she indulged in love play, instead of flailing around softly in the grass as convention required, she would suddenly take off into the air and float mentally, at a height of at least fifteen feet above the ground, towards a youth from another place, whom she had never seen but whose countenance attracted her more than anything else in the world.

Perhaps that was the only pleasure she got out of rolling in the hay—that all-powerful attraction that drew her away elsewhere.

She dreamed also of the plain, of her mother's skirts now seen no more; and she wouldn't have been ashamed to go down the cascade herself in due course. She had never had the feeling that noble blood ran in her veins. From the middle of that round head she secretly looked at the folk Up Above and the folk Down Below with the same affectionate eye, full of both melancholy and desire, as that with which she saw the creatures of the air and the water and the forest, who all belong to the great family of the living, and who all die. But she never said anything of all this, but concentrated on anticipating the wishes of Wademba, who tended to treat her as a servant, or some domestic pet to fondle or kick out of the way as the fancy took you.

The Immortal One might let whole weeks go by without saying a word to her. Despite the fact that she lived in his shadow and in his smell, lit his fire, did his cooking and his washing, and wove his cotton belly bands, he just did not see her. Every now and again he would seem to remember her, and then he'd take her into the forest and teach her about the plants and their secret virtues, their subtle connections with various parts of the human body. Often, in the middle of the lesson, he would fly into a rage and heap on her all the insults he could lay his tongue to: she had no talent for this sort of thing, her head was full of water, and as for her brains . . . just beads without a thread, all jumbled up together. But if she'd been a good pupil he'd tickle the top of her head and ask her to tell him what she'd like as a reward—anything, so long as it wasn't to do with the degenerate existence of the blacks Down Below. Awa knew what she wanted, but lowered her eyes and kept her own counsel. One day, however, when he actually smiled at her with a sort of affection, she plucked up her courage and confessed her long-felt desire to know what fish from the sea tasted like. Wademba, surprised, gave a mocking laugh. "Is that all?" he said. Then he picked up a basket, drew the outline of a boat on the side of the hut, stepped coolly into it and vanished as if swallowed up by the soot-blackened wall. Soon afterward Awa saw him return by the same magic means, his naked body streaming with water leaving little white trails, and the basket full of small fishes of various colors.

Another time, when she'd been to fetch water and was coming back with a calabash balanced on her round frizzy head, the Immortal One's slanting eyes suddenly gleamed with a strange light. Pointing as if to show her to beings present but invisible, he proclaimed that she was like the little black vanilla bean, able to perfume the whole world. Then he broke a twig off the pawpaw tree that grew by the house, dipped it in carapa oil, led the child inside, and made her lie down on the bed. Then very gently he slid the pawpaw twig into the most secret hollow of her being. He seemed pleased to find she'd already been opened by young scamps her own age. He continued this procedure for several weeks, gradually widening and shaping and easing the opening, until the child could receive him as a guest at the narrow table of her body. In his big hands she felt light, absorbed in her role as a properly opened vanilla bean giving off its perfume. But a sadness came over her because of the unknown youth whose face had suddenly ceased to appear to her on the crest of the wave. And more than ever her eyes would turn towards the little lights that shone up from the valley in the evening, as tales were told of heroes of the past.

She grew bolder now, and would sometimes slip away to a little hill near Fond-Zombi from which you could see the villagers without being seen yourself. She would have liked to walk along the tarred road—her feet tingled at the thought of it—and go into one of those funny wooden houses, get to know the people, find out at last what those folk thought about life. From a distance everything about them charmed and excited her, including the exuberance that made them bubble like boiling water, and their ways of sending up roars of laughter into the sky, as if to mock the judgments always raining down on them from the wretched thickets up on the plateau.

To her their young men looked smoother and shinier in the sun than those of the plateau. It was whispered that they made love more delicately. And this thought disturbed and bewildered her as she stood there on her little hill, for she didn't really know what it meant.

Growing from Chinese plums to guavas, apples of Venus, her breasts swelled gently in the sun. The year they reached the size of mangoes, two young sawyers set up a scaffolding in the mountains, a stone's throw or so from the plateau. They streamed with sweat, shining all over, even to their short oiled hair. Each wore a leather thong round his wrist and a large-linked silver chain round his neck. The poor girl, lurking behind a clump of trees, compared them bitterly to the shabby youths of Up There, all hairy and unadorned, their fingernails blue and hooked like claws.

She liked best to be there about noon, for the pleasure of watching this brilliant couple eat: they used a metal fork to select morsels from a bowl held between their knees, and then popped the food into their mouths without ever letting a spot of grease fall on their chins. One day they quarreled in the middle of this ceremony, and one of them flung off, cursing his friend, while the other just shrugged his shoulders and went on with his meal regardless. He ate like a great artist, sitting up straight and putting the food away in small mouthfuls, chewing slowly and judiciously, the veins in his temples scarcely moving. Awa, bewitched, emerged from her refuge and went over to the stranger, who stood up in the sunshine in the still air of the clearing, his skin shining like lacquer in the sunshine, the sort of skin that looks cooked to a turn and transparent as a grilled corn cob. At first he stepped back, rather startled at the sight of this wild, barefooted creature. Then she laid her hands on his shoulders and pressed down, smiling, cool, a straight red canna, and he, dazzled, forgot all fear and dropped unresisting onto the grass. She had already pulled up her shift, and with her legs bare to the sky was politely opening with her fingers the pearly edges of her shell. But to her surprise the young man quickly pulled the fold of cotton down again, saying with a worried expression:

"You are pretty, more charming than a coconut flower, but I don't hold with such goings-on. I belong to the L'horizon family, and that's not how we set about it."

"How do you do it, then?" she asked with a sigh of delight, enraptured at the thought of a world where people made love delicately.

"We start off by saying sweet words. . ."

"Words?" she stammered.

Tears ran down Awa's cheeks as he declared his eternal passion for her. Then they had something to eat, went down and drank from a spring, then returned to the clearing and did the same things to the same music. Awa now knew, and followed, the proper order to be observed in making love. And when at last she took off from the ground, she was not at all surprised to find that the face on the crest of the forty-foot wave was that of the sawyer.

He still gazed at her, dazzled, fascinated, unable to credit this manna fallen from heaven practically naked, wearing just an old shift with a vine instead of a belt. Awa, fulfilled, bright-eyed as a tench, now examined him at leisure, and saw that he was tall on his legs and well set up, perfectly proportioned from head to foot. But somehow she felt there was something frail about him. Then she suddenly realized that he belonged to the nebulous race of the blacks Down Below, creatures of sand and wind who according to Wademba were upset at every tremor of the earth. But wasn't that also true of herself, who had always found it so hard to maintain the shape of her body in space?

When darkness fell she went down with him into the valley, where he had just built a little hut of new, sweet-smelling planks.

The coming of Awa sent a wind of panic through the anxious souls of Fond-Zombi. Her sweetheart's many friends advised him to send her back home right away; otherwise her father's spells would reach him, Jean L'horizon, even in the shelter of his own house and no matter how many charms and countercharms he weighed himself down with. When the evil day came, the loftiest and most subtle protections would avail him nothing, for no one could set himself up against the Immortal One.

Run away? Cross the sea? But distance did not exist for that old mesmerizer of darkness. He might be that fly there on the table, apparently preening itself in all innocence. Or that ant on your arm, listening to what you say and its jaws really grinning all the time at the useless ploys you were inventing. The young man listened to all this in a dream, not taking his eyes off Awa's face, determined to follow his misfortune through to the end—his complete and final undoing, people called it, but he called it his fine one. So people gave way before that fateful smile, and one smooth peaceful morning overflowing with serenity the whole population accompanied the new child of God to the church at La Ramée, where the priest made her promise to renounce the devil and all his works. Then, without warning, the white man flicked a few drops of water into the wild girl's eyes; and that was how she became Eloise.

In the twinkling of an eye she had learned to wash and mend, how to make a nice Christian stew and lay the table, and how to eat with a fork as daintily as if she'd never done anything else all her life. Then she squared her shoulders and went into the blaze of the sugar canes; and that was her second victory in the eyes of the people of Fond-Zombi. But her real hour of triumph was yet to come. For one night before Lent, an especially warm and sweet-scented night, the neighbors were woken by extraordinary cries, full and splendid, enough to carry even the most unwilling away.

Musicians of the dark were not rare among the village women, and sometimes their cries would answer one another from house to house.

"Ah, what a journey!"

"Yes indeed. But let's keep on, my lass, further, further!"

And the cries would go on with renewed vigor, for what was the use of having a man if it wasn't to journey with him, sail, float, fly?

Musicians of the dark were not rare among the village women, but from the latest one, from the throat of Eloise, there came such a wealth and variety of sounds it was like a whole orchestra, with drums and violins, flutes, guitars, and rattles, all mounting up toward the sky. Other voices were immediately caught up in it, rising up in the dark and all rolling from roof to roof as far as the outskirts of the village, like a living wave forcing all, willy-nilly, into the concert. People talked long afterward of the night when human beings started to fly together like angels hand in hand. Even the shyest and most modest of the women, whose cries usually sank to the soles of their feet, let themselves go. And more than one of them came and thanked poor Eloise, and congratulated her on the heavenly beauty of her song, which had almost plucked Fond-Zombi up off the ground and sent it whirling among the stars.

In their enthusiasm everyone had forgotten she was a sorcerer's daughter: that was ancient history, a useless trifle, to be put away on the shelf with the broken china. But Jean L'horizon remembered night and day, and sometimes he feared he would be stricken with some horrible disease, a vile snake-like thing that would for a long while writhe unknown in his heart and then suddenly burst out in the sight of all. What he was most afraid of was the "tying of the knot," this of course being particularly apt as he had led into wrong courses the precious blood of the Immortal One. This fear always came upon him unexpectedly. He would seem quite content with life and glad that his mother had borne him, and then suddenly two fingers would stray between his legs and he would say sadly:

"Here I am, eating and drinking like a fool, but who knows? Perhaps my glory will never rise again."

Then Eloise would stretch out a helping hand, and there would be laughter and eternal vows, soft bread and sweet words, as it was under the scaffolding in the clearing, the first time.

But Eloise could see he was soaking in a brine of sadness, and every day that God wove, as the people in the valley used to say, she was tempted to go up the path and ask her father's consent, as Aboomeki the Silent One had done in her day. But she was afraid he might keep her, having grown used perhaps to her young live body and her scent of ripe vanilla. And she loved her sawyer, who dazed her with the soft words he lavished on her day and night, for, he said, a kiss without words is like a pretty black girl's neck without a necklace. And as she could not bear to lose him, every day that God wove she put things off till the next day.

Their bloods went so well together that she became pregnant the same year as she was baptized. But there was no weight in her womb, which felt full of air, like a gold-beater's skin; and in the sixth month all her hopes turned to water and blood. Ten years went by like this. Jean L'horizon became like a man gone mad over the spell, in which everyone recognized the brand and the touch, the unique claw mark of the Immortal One. And when his wife was with child again he looked thoughtful, and people saw he was giving up and getting ready to haul down the flag. One day when Eloise was asleep, worn out with carrying another dead child, he quietly packed a case and went to the main road to wait for the bus. It was driven by one Max, Max Armageddon, well known as having the easiest and the luckiest hand at the job in the whole service. Max could drive drunk as an owl, or leaning back with his feet on the steering wheel to amuse the passengers; but all his charges always arrived safely. On this occasion, however, just outside La Ramée and the bend where the ice factory stood, a rock suddenly appeared in the middle of the road, forcing the driver to swerve right into a tree. One of the doors flew open and one of the passengers, as if propelled by an invisible hand, was thrown onto the horns of an ox grazing peacefully a few feet from the road. The man flying without wings was Jean L'horizon himself. The driver looked back along the road. The rock had vanished.

At that very moment Eloise was sitting in her hut, swollen with pain, her hand on the enigma in her womb, thinking of the years that had gone by and been lost with the man who, according to what a neighbor had just told her, was now on his way to Point-à-Pitre. Suddenly something forced her legs open and she felt herself being assailed and penetrated by an invisible body; and as she recognized the fabulous drive and attack of the Immortal One, she was carried away on a wave of foam, and dimly knew that this child would live, would not, not this one, come unstuck from her womb.

Once the departed was buried, Eloise began to contemplate her womb, which already thumped and leaped about like a second heart. Then her sorrow abated, and she even tried to smile from time to time, for it is well known that a mother's sorrow is not good for her child. And when the time came, moved by some obscure piety, she gave birth in the manner traditional among the people Up There, kneeling at the foot of the bed, her hands joined at the nape of her neck, her elbows finding support and courage in the wooden crossbar. When she was shown the *ti-mâle*, the little boy, she at once recognized the thick, obstinate, frontal bone which projected like the peak of a cap from the ancient skull of Wademba. But the attendant matrons paid no attention to this sign, for they were overcome by the enormous length of the infant and the darkness of his gleaming skin. One of them clasped her hands together and said:

"If he had been a bit longer the scoundrel would never have got out."

"Yes," said another, "and he's already eager for the fray."

And she pointed to how the *ti-mâle* was clenching his fists, thumbs tucked well inside, as if to strengthen the blows he would one day rain on her, that madwoman who runs through the streets seeking whom she may devour, that madwoman called life.

After a tortuous and passionate debate in which some of the old women exhibited the wildest imagination, it was decided that the young warrior should simply bear the name of his father, the late lamented Jean L'horizon. But this seemed useless to Eloise, a farce which left the child without protection in life, like a nestling without beak or feathers. An African name was what she wanted, a real and effective shield which would give her son weight and prevent him from becoming upset at every tremor of the earth, like people of the valley. And so on the eighth day, after taking the baby to be baptized, she left him with a neighbor and secretly went along the path that led to Up Above.

It was a long time since it had rained and the earth was dry, shiny and coppery. Eloise went through limp vegetation trying to struggle against the sun for no other reason than that it had gone to the trouble of putting down roots. She stopped at the edge of the plateau, taken aback at the picture of abandonment that confronted her: dilapidated huts open to the sky, on ground broken here and there by mounds of termites. A single hut stood upright among the desolation, and the old man sitting in the shade of the sooty walls on a carved wooden stool seemed to her eternal. She immediately felt certain that the ancient mesmerizer of darkness was waiting for her behind those old tortoise-shell eyelids.

"You know why I've come," she whispered.

"I know why you've come. I also know you've come for nothing."

"But the child is yours, sprung from the foam of your loins?"

"So you say, Awa," he answered with a sarcastic smile.

"It is your child—the evening breeze itself knows it. It is your child, and have you no name for him, nothing to put over his little shoulders? Do you want him to be at the mercy of the forces of evil, to go through life unprotected, the prey of anyone who wants to take his soul and throw it to the dogs? Do you want him to be exposed to the weather like an animal—is that it?"

"Awa, Awa," he said, "don't waste your breath spitting at me. There is no name I can give to your child, for as you yourself said, he will go through life like an animal, a wild animal that finds its own path. And if I gave him an African name it would wind itself round his throat like a collar and strangle him. You don't want anything like that for him, do you?" He ended with a sneer.

"I went down among the people Below, but you wanted me to, or else you could have stopped me with a lift of the finger. And now you take your revenge on the child you yourself made, on your own flesh and blood, Wademba. Why did you let me go if you wanted me to stay? And why did you make the child only to abandon him to the Powers of Evil?"

"The way these young females carry on!" he said. "Now listen, little water flea. Dry your tears and try to understand what I say. There is no name for this child because his name is waiting for him, his name is somewhere in front of him, and when the time comes it will come and alight on his head. Do you see?"

But Eloise was far away and no longer listening. She had clasped her hands over her head, covering her face, and was rocking mechanically to and fro like a mourner. After a while she heard a strange sound, and coming back to earth saw her father's mouth opening in frail laughter. Sitting up scaly and naked on his stool, with his knees drawn up to his shoulders, shining like an old tree polished by the wind, Wademba was gazing at her with his eternal eyes and laughing.

Then for the first time in her life the young creature was swept by a wave of anger. She had fallen back a step, trembling all over, and suddenly she had an inspiration and said, her voice still tearful:

"I see now. It was you who sent me among the people Down Below, and now you're laughing at me, eh?"

She was like one distracted. She saw the old man's stick leaning against the door of the hut, seized it, and gave him a violent thump on the head.

"You sent me down there, and now you laugh?"

Then she hit him again, and yelled in stupefaction:

"You dried my babies up in my womb, and you laugh?"

She said a lot more that day, going back over her despoiled childhood, her darkened youth, and finally the strange flight to death of the late Jean L'horizon, whose only sin was to have made her happy. And she punctuated each grievance with a great ringing blow which disheveled the white tufts on the unfathomable skull of the Immortal One.

"The way this young female carries on!" he said suddenly, as if absentmindedly.

Then there was a great dark gush, and he toppled off his stool on the ground, like a tree. Eloise looked vaguely at the huge body lying at her feet. But the old man raised himself on one elbow, wiped the blood away from his eyes, and started to laugh again, louder and louder, with a sort of terrifying gaiety that made Eloise draw back, drop the stick, and draw back further still. Then she turned and took to her heels, across the ruined plateau and down through the thickets and sharp-grassed undergrowth, which only stopped right down below, with the evening and the first gleams of light in Fond-Zombi.

3

He had been baptized with his father's name, but the people of the valley avoided calling him Jean, Jean L'horizon, lest the departed take the opportunity of answering in his stead. Eloise didn't like mixing up the living and the dead like that either, and to avoid the confusion her son for a long while answered only to the names of Hey, Hi, and Psst. Then someone had the idea of calling him Little or Ti Jean, and it was under this modest appellation that our hero made his entry into the world—he who was one day to overturn the sun and planets.

As a child, scarcely fallen from the breast, he had the somewhat ponderous grace of a young pachyderm, with legs like small bronze columns and round feet which had difficulty getting a purchase on the ground and made him stumble. He was a fierce animal, his fist always clenched tight as in his mother's womb. Eloise, seeing him look so surly and discontented, wondered how it was she had not given birth to the joy of living personified. In fact, as she discovered, the lad's whole being was concentered then on his muscles and bones, which still had need of him, of his constant attention, in order to reach their full perfection. He had so many things going on deep down in his body that it made his mouth forget to smile or speak, and he didn't utter a single word until he was four years old. But once he did make up his mind to it he spoke whole sentences straight away, in a high, clear, precise voice strangely reminiscent of the tones of the Immortal One.

This gave Eloise an opportunity to see that the valley people were cultivators of forgetfulness. The child moved among them with the face of Wademba, his voice, and the same excess of spirit emanating from slanting, impregnable eyes; and no one seemed to notice it. The only thing they did remark was how his little tail stood up when he got into fights, and returned to its usual position when hostilities ceased. Ti Jean was still going about quite naked when this phenomenon first occurred. The people, amazed, took pleasure in making him angry just to see his organ stick up stiff as a spike. But this glory didn't strike anyone in Fond-Zombi as suspicious, and after the show the men would just say to one another with a touch of wistfulness:

"The world is full of all sorts of rods, some that are sumptuous and others that are less so, and even some that are supposed to be forked, apparently. In short, God always provides more than the mind of man can imagine, that and more." And they concluded that Eloise's child had inherited a veritable rod of gold!

Although the boy grew quickly, he made little more use of his tongue than Ma Eloise made of hers, and their hut was the quietest in Fond-Zombi, if not in the whole of Guadeloupe. Sometimes he would prick up his ears for no apparent reason, as if he had just heard a call, but although Eloise looked all round the hut she would see only an ordinary fly on the table, or an ant running over the slats of the floor, or some bustling insect. Then she would ponder, strangely uneasy, wondering whether Wademba had ever let the child out of his sight since the hour he was born. And whenever a big black dog came wandering nearby, she would panic and throw stones at it.

Yes, the child was about as talkative as an oyster. But as soon as he could stand up on his round feet he was always to be seen out of doors, trotting about and nipping under the verandas, on the alert for anything that was said in the village. Sometimes his mind would draw strange conclusions from what he heard. One day he was there when a neighboring housewife said, "Ah, if the earth could speak it would tell us some things we don't know!" It was just one of those throwaway remarks one makes without thinking. But later the same day Eloise found her son lying in the garden, his ear to the ground, listening for mysterious voices rising from the depths. Another time someone said that only the trees know what man is, and unfortunately they are dumb. Eloise turned at once to her son, and saw him making off, with his slightly clumsy, hesitant step, and a little while afterwards couldn't help laughing when she found him clinging lovingly to the guava tree in the yard, his face all lit up with expectancy as he listened for the voices lurking in the knots of the wood. She laughed again during the days that followed, every time she saw him clasping the trunk of the guava tree. Then suddenly the laughter died on her lips: the boy had taken to rushing round the village, with eyes that looked as if they had become sightless and didn't recognize anything, and open-mouthed as if asking, "Is it really true—what I see, what I hear?"

The rushing about stopped the day he first went to school in La Ramée down on the coast. He came back wearing an air of deep serenity. And then the second surprise for the people of the village: despite his lack of speech, Eloise's boy had a brain as vast as the belly of a whale, a brain just like a white man's, with columns for arranging everything in his mind. In the evening, by the light of the oil lamp, she watched with amazement as he sat immersed in his books, touching them with the same look of radiant expectation as that with which he used to caress tree trunks in order to hear the voice of the world.

Things went on in this way for one or two seasons, and then the joy in books vanished and Eloise found herself once more with a child who came home from school silent, who would work a bit in the garden, fetch a drum of water for his mother, and then sit in a shady corner with his little hands clenched on his knees, suddenly still and stiff as death.

It was plain that the books had fallen silent and that the boy had given up the voices of the world; he no longer went out, even to bathe in the river. Sitting there in the dark, his eyes quiet and dull, he seemed to be constantly pondering and cultivating some insult or outrage committed against him. And seeing him like this, Eloise wondered how it had happened that she had not brought forth the joy of living personified, when during her pregnancy she had tried so hard, so hard, to smile.

So it went on until Ma Justina's fall, which for a long while provided a topic of conversation in Fond-Zombi and round about. Ma Justina was not a real witch but a sort of reservist, one of those people weary of human form who sign a contract with the devil so as to be able to change themselves at night into a donkey or a crab or a bird as the fancy takes them. One fine day she was found drowned in her own blood on the way into the village. Returning from a nocturnal flight, she had been surprised by the first rays of dawn and immediately flattened on the ground, struck down by the holiness of the light. As she lay in the middle of the road her bird's body slowly resumed its human form: hands sprouted at the tips of her wings and long dazzling white tresses mixed with the lusterless feathers on the head of an owl. The people stood a little way off taking note of all the details one by one, for it was a sight extremely rare, to be recounted carefully to those who happened to be away, to distant relations, even to strangers who might be met with later along the road of life. It was a Thursday, and the children slipped between the grown-ups' legs, but they didn't seem unduly surprised at the spectacle. They'd seen much more in dreams, they seemed to be saying, since they drank in such stories with their mothers' milk. Only the oldest among them made any comment, the "doctors" studying for their school-leaving certificate, each with his or her pen sticking proudly out of a mop of hair. According to them, people turned into dogs or crabs as naturally as water turned to ice, or as electricity was changed into light or lamps or into words and music on the radio. In their view Ma Justina was just a little slice of life which wasn't mentioned in books because the white men had decided to draw a veil over it.

The police from La Ramée, alerted by the secretary at the town hall, arrived after the battle, on the stroke of noon. Ma Justina had just finished with the birds, and all the policemen found was an old Negress lying shattered in the middle of the road. Despite all the witnesses present, the police refused outright to listen to the explanations offered by the people of Fond-Zombi, determined not to understand and getting angry and rough with them as if they were concealing something unmentionable, perhaps some crime in which the whole population was involved. And it was only after weeks combing the entire district, joking and mocking and straining the charity of not a few, that they resigned themselves to the mystery of the tall naked Negress lying in the middle of the road as if fallen from the sky. This persecution was painful to all the blacks, but those who felt it most bitterly were the schoolchildren, especially the "doctors," who could not understand why the testimony of the people of Fond-Zombi had been rejected. Did not they themselves, at their desks, accept the white men's stories about the earth, the sun, and the stars, which weren't all that easy to swallow?

Yes, the whole population was present at the metamorphosis, but it was our hero whose eyes were opened the widest. Ti Jean seemed to be contemplating at last the secret sought in vain under the earth and in the trunks of trees and in books brought back for one or two seasons from school. By the following day the little fellow was reconciled with the world, and returned to the river and games appropriate to his age. From his whole person there flowed a sort of happy magic, and when they saw him people said: "Well, well, Ma Eloise's boy is coming out of his cocoon. Is he making up his mind to take his place in the sun?"

From: When They Loved the Communal Lands

PEDRO MIR
(DOMINICAN REPUBLIC)

Part I
"Romanita Hears Panic"

1

*R*omanita was there facing the dumping ground, her back to the street, completely immobile, ecstatically inert, without the smallest movement of her hands or eyelashes infringing the standards of rigidity imposed on her entire figure, as if it had suddenly crystalized upon reaching the last wall of cosmic time and had been incapable of adopting a more purely cadaver-like pose or a more eloquent gesture of eternity, having been surprised, as well, in a position not quite lucidly balanced, and not only completely irrational but also inopportune if the brief period of adaptation to reality required by the natural instinct for survival had elapsed, since at that very moment she was about to hurl into the void of the dumping ground a large package she was holding in her right hand, grasping it by the cord wound around it from one end to the other and whose weight forced her to keep her right arm rigid and

131

extend the left arm straight out, level with her shoulders, so that it formed
a kind of horizon on which her inert head rested like a setting sun when
her eyes cast a rapid glance which descended like a lightning bolt toward
a fixed point down the road around which and for exactly forty seconds
her corporal structure was outlined and her bodily functions were suspended as she concentrated on that distant point of fear, which had
become the nucleus of life and death, all possible attention and her concentration was such that it hindered her from making the slightest
movement until she gave the impression of having been petrified and of
having lost in one fell swoop the ability to breathe, her pulse, and perhaps
even causing the decomposition of her perspiration and saliva and
bringing about the involuntary descent of a trickle of urine down the
interior wall of her thighs, which under other circumstances might have
made that bashful and delicate zone cringe in a stupor and that was how
she came to be suddenly immobilized in a pose of absolute inertia in
which, to be more precise, one could observe the two distinct intentions
simultaneously paralyzed on the same threshold of reality, one of which,
A, was oriented toward the dumping ground and the frustrated intent to
hurl the bundle, while the other, B, continued in the horizontal path of
her left arm above whose trajectory her glance radiated in the direction
of a point in the street, conspicuous to her alone, upon which her whole
vital system was condensed because during those forty seconds neither
of those intentions caused her to realize a plan of action or the supposed
resolution it contained, or resume the natural breathing on which she
depended or anything else except the resounding nothing in whose
center Romanita remained, fixed, exotic, exorbitant, and ecstatic in the
infinite void, the unfathomable abyss, the somber well, the gap between
yes and no, which the most renowned philosophers say mediates between the potential and the act or, to put it yet another way, between
brain and muscle or, to put it another way, between the swing of the
pendulum that confronts us in the middle of the street when it occurs to
us to investigate whether the automobile coming up fast is going to kill
us or whether it is more advisable to start running immediately and leave
the investigation for a more academic occasion and this was more or less
the situation Romanita found herself in in the fabulous lapse of those
forty seconds with the difference that this indescribable tension had a

lot to do with the fact that they called her none other than Romanita since before her name was known, or it was presumed to be known that she came from La Romana, that place launched by the tourist agencies as the best-kept secret in the world although at that time it wasn't and that detail of having come from La Romana was enough to decide on the name they would give her in the heart of a family that kept her busy with domestic tasks without any interest at all in the labyrinths of significance contained within a name and assigning her among other daily tasks that of showing up every afternoon at the dump, called that because people used to dump all kinds of objects and no-longer-wanted substances there even though it wasn't a garbage dump authorized by the sanitary agencies and that is where Romanita was throwing out a large bundle supposedly filled with refuse from the house although no one had stopped to stealthily inspect it after she hurled it in order to verify the contents and it was of course enough to observe that it remained intact when those who were in charge of picking up the garbage threw it onto the truck without worrying about the possibility that it contained a fetus or a time bomb or important quantities of counterfeit bills or marijuana leaves destined for some conventional location taken over by a band of delinquents in cahoots with one of the men from the above-mentioned garbage truck since sometimes the most apparently unimportant events can have the most extraordinary consequences and this is what an image as rich as that of Maupassant is based on, Maupassant who submerged one of his characters in the most terrible of tragedies simply for having leaned over to pick up a banal piece of rope he found on the ground during one of his walks, thinking of its eventual usefulness, because the unfortunate guy had never done that before and it aroused in him a curiosity that, mixed with calumny and suspicion, led to his downfall, being an innocent, but in Romanita's case the opposite happened because the frequency of the action of hurling the package robbed it of any significance since habit wears away interest and attention and no one is interested in investigating a mystery that repeats itself even if it is murder and that's why Romanita took that same route back every day without feeling at all perturbed after carrying out her afternoon operation, completely free of her load and her intentions, whatever they might have been, with that same walk of a direct and persuasive Créole, with her chest held high and an air of contempt, until the day that produced the situation abruptly suspended at the very instant she went to hurl the package and it was really as if a finger had pressed a button and stopped the passage of time and her glance had remained electrically cast in the direction of her left arm all the way down the street from her frozen pupils to one of the street corners where the virile splendor of Bonifacio Lindero had burst onto the scene or at least someone who looked very much like him since that was the same way he walked and he had the same density to his body and the same height covered with clothes like the ones he wore although from that distance Romanita couldn't have been sure, even with a gaze as committed and as intense and as suspended as hers, that it was Bonifacio whom she had taken as her legally wedded and certifiably documented husband and naturally it could be him since Romanita had escaped from the home they had established together in La Romana and come to the Capital leaving behind not only her identity as a married woman but even her maiden name and had also left Bonifacio Lindero completely in the dark as to her whereabouts, which were just vaguely suggested by the information received from the lips of the driver who let her off at the gasoline station, which is the habitual stopping off point for travelers who either have no place to stay in the Capital or wish to keep their address hidden and all of this meant, as Romanita knew very well, that if Bonifacio found her all of the gods of the Créole Mount Olympus couldn't keep him from taking her back to La Romana, dragging her by the hair if he had to, and without any need to appeal to the Law because he was Bonifacio Lindero and it would seem that that was an inevitable fate for Romanita and for Bonifacio as well it seemed to be an irreparable fate because Romanita had the fiercest determination to shape reality to her will and in those very terms she had spent several weeks, dispelling her initial fears, giving herself a daily dose of self-confidence and filling her existence with new stimuli and rounding out a new set of illusions centered on the alternative of a home of her own, that is to say independent of Bonifacio, without implying dependent on another man, although no one has ever been able to say they'll *never* drink the water, which is a healthy attitude and so the immediate thing was to make the time pass quickly so that her life could begin again within an atmosphere of change, instinctive in the young because it's based on the real elasticity of their tissues and the natural resistance to adversity even though it might only be because a young man believes himself capable of waiting long years if necessary to right a wrong but everything was going to fall apart for Romanita if the individual poised on one of the street corners about four or five blocks from the dump where she came every afternoon to hurl her bundle turned out to be Bonifacio Lindero since in those very seconds the denouement of her drama had exploded and that's why the package had to remain suspended in her right hand waiting for her left hand to resume its uninterrupted movement in order to give it the final push which would send it flying through the air according to a program which normally ran its course but then time doesn't belong only to Romanita but also to the package, and time continued on its imperturbable course, going around the sphere of the faces of all the watches with the disagreeable consequences of its passage both for the destiny of people and of packages and so they both remained trapped within the limits of those forty seconds during which Romanita remained completely petrified while her gaze moved swiftly and intensely toward the individual who had turned one of the distant corners and had come into view and the truth is that that look was completely improper since its conduct was so undesirable that if instead of a gaze it had been something else, something other than a gaze like a shot of light according to the poets, or like a vibration of the ether according to classical physics, if it had been say a person, a Christian, of flesh and blood, it would have been considered insolent and crude because in order to be sure that the individual on the corner was Bonifacio Lindero and none other she began to ignore the sacred inviolability of faces, like that of houses and letters, scrutinizing the most minute figuration of his wrinkles and the most intimate characteristics of his nose and mouth visible to the eye without finding any of the physical traits which would allow her to establish beyond a shadow of a doubt that it was not Bonifacio Lindero but rather some person who could be mistaken for him in a situation like this one, determined, of course, by the dramatic circumstances Romanita was in and this meant a resounding failure for that turbulent gaze hastily convinced of having made a precipitate voyage, engaged in censurable conduct, with the severity that all failure inspires, which is terribly discouraging even for the most simple of gazes and the worst thing of all was that having arrived at the precipitous determination that the individual was Bonifacio Lindero her gaze was obliged to transform itself and exchange for humiliation what had only seconds earlier been haughtiness and that was how her face had come to deposit on the face of the guy she had taken to be Bonifacio all its electric vibrations like the daggers that flew through the air in the old-fashioned cloak-and-dagger adventures and were dealt a blow by the moon before decapitating a phantom and suddenly lost their sparkle upon re-entering the sheath after discovering that their adversary was not a phantom at all but merely an innocent abandoned suit of armor, and with the frustration of the bashful had to return as speedily as it had departed and deposit in Romanita's eyes a humble balance of naiveté at the precise moment when the forty seconds of the voyage were up, during which time Romanita had remained completely still like a photographic image, as if all vital undulation had left her, spent in the adventure of that gaze and as if the passage of time had been suspended, paralyzing all the watches including the sundial on Damas Street that had been functioning for more than two centuries without interruption, not even at night or when it rained, and therefore it was not difficult to observe how the flow of life returned to Romanita's eyelids and the color, which at a certain age reveals the hidden but certain manifestation of the will to live or to allow oneself to die by the same impulse, returned to her cheeks and that was how Romanita's sojourn to the realm of eternity came to an end as her left arm broke the horizon that extended itself between passion and uncertainty, with gestures and pulsations, descending finally with a great sensuality to rest, like a dove, on the package in order to assist the right arm in loosening its rigidity and carrying out the ritual of the early evening hurling of the package, which was finally thrown into the dump without harboring any contents other than the usual garbage and Romanita's gaze, propelled by the internal imperative that forces us to constantly demonstrate that we are important

136

and good for something in this world, moved in the direction of the package and followed its course taking the same turns the package did in the afternoon light and falling with a dull thud somewhere on the dumping ground where its new fate would commence as it was hauled away by the municipal truck to an unknown end and at that point Romanita's arms returned to the spot they normally occupied when she was walking and her svelte anatomy revolved around her own vertical axis like the carriage of a watch that has begun to tick again and she began the trip back without her destiny having been modified in order to return tomorrow and the day after tomorrow with a new package equally devoid of significance or mystery, which her gaze would follow in its flight toward the void, a gaze much more serene now that it had been put to the test of humility and failure in the thunderous school of human passions

Hay dos modos de conciencia:
Una es luz y otra paciencia.
Una estriba en alumbrar
Un poquito el hondo mar;
Otra, en hacer penitencia
Con caña o red, y esperar

— *Proverbios y Cantares**

2
Bonifacio and the Automobile

an automobile
an automobile is approaching
an automobile is rapidly approaching
an automobile is rapidly approaching and someone is waiting in the shadow while his solitary heart beats rhythmically in time with

---

* This and all of the other epilogues appearing at the end of chapters or sections are from Antonio Machado.—ED.

the acceleration of the automobile in the silence of the night in a remote city on the eastern end of the Republic where these small sounds resonate in a place originally meant for the mating cries of cicadas and crickets until they become frightful harsh sounds capable of causing delirium in those whose brains aren't tough enough to resist when it comes to the motor of an automobile and the experience only lasts forty seconds or the approximate time required by this infernal machine to make its explosions heard from a distance and reach the desperate person who is listening for it if you take into account that its speed is measured in kilometers per hour and not in meters per second because if in one hour an automobile can travel 120 kilometers then the total meters per second are almost exactly equal, point for point, to the explosion of emotional processes and the uncontainable outburst of desperation and this is precisely the situation in which Bonifacio Lindero found himself submerged night after night after his wife abandoned him in such an incredible and therefore terrifying manner, and added to that was the additional aggravating factor of his having moved within an atmosphere of grandeur and power recognized by all around since his earliest childhood, and which he believed he deserved because of the hard work and industry of his father, more shrewd than intelligent, which is an important distinction because it lies at the core of this narration and reaches back to a period in the history of our scenario that is only distant for the new generations of the last few decades of the century but is known to many people who still have full use of their faculties and it centers on a peculiar practice since, in contrast to what occurs in the majority of nations, here the peasants showed little interest, if any, in putting fences around the lands that provided the goods necessary for their existence, in fact they considered this as absurd as attempting to put a fence around the ocean's waters or the meadows in the sky where the clouds circulate or the emotions that would eventually be dispelled from their hearts, but as it turned out in 1920 a modern system of registering land holdings was established to provide the means to ensure and guarantee the demarcation of private property and this system consisted of a procedure so crudely articulated that it permitted any quick-witted adventurer to set about marking boundaries here and boundaries there as the peasants looked on in passive contemplation, peasants who had grown accustomed over the centuries to consider the demarcation of boundaries an ingenuous occupation if not a foolish one and that's why people began calling Bonifacio's father Lindero,* which stuck and eventually became a respectable last name since as a consequence of his activities he became the illustrious owner of a good portion of the nation's territory and in this he was superbly protected by the Constitution and Laws of the Republic and this allowed Bonifacio, his son, solemn entry into these lands in a golden cradle, as they say, guaranteed the respect and consideration of his compatriots and because of all the consideration he received it is not difficult to understand Bonifacio's agitation when people became aware of the fact that despite his notorious grandeur he was incapable of keeping his wife at his side or once he lost her of dragging her back by the hair, all of which meant that poor Bonifacio was becoming the object of public scorn and to a certain degree making a fool of himself or losing a social position that had been established for him when he made his solemn entry into a world that belonged to him but he still believed in his own attributes and awaited from one moment to the next the voluntary and submissive return of the fugitive so that the first

five seconds

that allowed him to identify the sound of the engine of an automobile coming down the road toward his house put all of his organic parts in a state of alarm because the human organism's unity is astounding, forming a subtle interweaving of the most apparently unrelated functions and effecting a formidable coherence of the entire system so that in moments of conflict like this one between the idea Bonifacio has of himself and the ideas that others have of him he begins to register on the most external surface layer of skin, apparently indifferent to gossip, the processes that are occurring in the deepest internal zones, those supposedly not disconnected from what is taking place on the outside, and this explains why in those first five seconds Bonifacio felt as if a light cold breeze was blowing across his skin and lifting up each one of his body hairs, including the hairs in his beard, which are naturally tough and even more so for being shaved and generally indifferent to the action of the breeze or any other similar

* *Lindero* means "boundary" in Spanish.—ED.

external agent but this sensation, which was in itself alarming, was soon to be felt as a whole fugue of sensations moving though the interior layers of his organism and so naturally after the

first ten seconds

in the approach of the automobile had elapsed in a catastrophe of cicadas and crickets, forced to suspend the propagation of the species and abruptly stop their sacrosanct mating cries, Bonifacio felt the first organic shudder in the part of the system considered the most noble probably because it is the one that responds most immediately to any stimulus from the surrounding world and particularly to the conflicts of love suffered mostly by the young or to episodes of broken pride, which are suffered mostly by the old particularly if they are rich and wield power, without it being necessary to consider the heart the most noble and sensitive part of our organism and this explains the high incidence of heart disease among millionaires and among people of breeding and position and that is how it happened that Bonifacio felt his heart beat hard first in his jugular, which automatically caused his throat to close as if to prevent any foreign body from entering under those circumstances through the pipes that normally carry food and this produced in Bonifacio a feeling of strangulation, which caused saliva to flow into his mouth, which he then couldn't swallow and it began to have a strange bitter taste caused not by the saliva itself but by the conjunction of other processes of a saline or acid nature because when the automobile had now been approaching for

fifteen seconds

the sensation that had originally been confined to his skin and had subsequently passed to his throat then descended to his chest squeezing it as if a leather belt had been tightened around it altering the rhythm of his breathing and blocking the entry of oxygen into his lungs, which caused three organic changes to enter into conflict beginning with the outermost fibers of the nerve tissue on the surface of the skin, followed by circulatory tensions, and joined at that stage by the respiratory processes, all of which was sufficient to bring on a torturous syndrome since one of the most painful symptoms is that of having difficulty breathing, which conjures up images of death by asphyxia and that is why the execution of those condemned to death in the gas chambers earned the

Nazis their reputation as cruel and inhuman, which in great measure led
to their defeat because it provoked the hatred of the entire human species,
which identified with the Nazis' victims, but by that time it had been

twenty seconds

during the course of which the sound of the approaching automobile's
engine grew louder and Bonifacio should have taken the few steps
necessary to accommodate the entrance of the recent arrival by first
opening the door and placing himself to one side with a soothing smile
but the imminent arrival of the fugitive produced the opposite effect and
the pressure in his chest sent a quick message to his pylorus, which is a
very intelligent and sentimental little door located at the mouth of the
stomach and in cases of conflict it abruptly closes off the passage of
nourishment to the rest of the system through a series of spasms that are
usually extremely painful and as he became aware of this new symptom,
which rocked his organism, since up until then he had not felt any pain,
it happened that the moving automobile passed the twenty second mark
and approached

twenty-five seconds

in its advance with a considerable increase in the volume of the roar of
its engine, which was accompanied by the perturbation of the mecha-
nisms of Bonifacio's pancreas and since these glands are known for their
capacity to excrete into the blood certain liquids which they produce
when disturbances occur at the external level in the emotional life of the
individual, not unlike the disturbances the Benedictines created when
the social and political atmosphere outside the convent was altered, and
the effect was similar to that which occurs when an individual takes a
drink of an energizing substance like brandy or potash, which shakes up
the whole anatomical structure even in people like Bonifacio whose
anatomy is resilient and prepared to withstand confrontation with material obstacles and in whom the effects are felt in central points like the
knee joints which renders them incapable of moving from one place to
another or even of shifting position in order to walk if standing or stand
up if sitting down, all of which must have produced in him a profound
state of alarm in that his conduct did not correspond to the image people
had of him and even less to the image he had of himself, forged in the
heady feeling of his own power and his control of others as well as himself,

141

and this could easily be resolved by masking reality but the material facts were implacable given the rush of the oncoming vehicle which had passed the twenty-five second mark and

thirty seconds

had in fact now passed, spreading the disturbances throughout his organism and threatening to make him lose consciousness and fall to the ground if the unfolding of events did not take a different turn and produce an explosion in his brain, which would leave him abruptly and irrevocably insane, and that's what was going on while the automobile was approaching and you could hear from far away the rather slow shifting of the gears, which gave the impression that it was not moving at all but once the sound barrier had been broken the shifting gears that could be heard increased their pace rapidly and now it was not only the sound of the engine but that of the carriage as it bumped against the irregularities in the road and this created the impression that it had picked up speed and that it was approaching faster and faster as it went from thirty to

thirty-five seconds

an agonizing few moments for Bonifacio who by making a supreme effort had managed to slip out of the strange ligaments that had him bound and make a mad dash for the front door of his house, not so much to greet his consort as to flee from that inferno almost hoping that she wouldn't arrive and find him in such a deplorable state and he finally managed to grab hold of the rings and latches and with one formidable push opened the door at the precise instant that the formidable

forty seconds

of his agony had elapsed and the automobile passed through his visual and emotional field with the speed of a missile enveloped in a gust of wind and dust and this positively confirmed the objective fact that his wife would not be returning on this trip and that perhaps she would never return, establishing as public knowledge that he was a nobody and powerless, but by then the process was beginning again in reverse, not from silence to noise but from noise to silence, using up exactly the same forty seconds but this time back from forty to

zero

during which Bonifacio himself had to find the necessary means to transform his organism from the catastrophic state it was in to one of serenity and peace and to achieve this he first had to go back into the house and carefully close the door while looking for a chair to sit in without heading for the bed because there was always the danger that a brusque cessation of the successive processes unleashed in his organism might trigger a whole new process which could lead to a cerebral hemorrhage or an explosive crisis of nerves without guarantee of recovery, that is if certain thoughts didn't come into play, which can be more frightening than the material dangers themselves and can precipitate an even worse outcome, but in fact none of these dangers materialized because Bonifacio began on a new course of meditation, comforting himself with the idea that his wife's return could have been prevented for any number of acceptable reasons and there was no reason why what didn't happen today couldn't happen tomorrow and with that his organism began to orient itself in the opposite direction, adapting all of its functions to the presence of that optimistic image which foretold the advent of happiness and joy, and with the same natural wisdom that had earlier set off all his functions in the reverse, his endocrine glands changed the composition of the liquids they sent into the bloodstream and his saliva was able to pass the message on when it filled with a sugary sensation and the tightness of his throat eased as did the pressure in his chest, which brought on a general sense of relaxation like the euphoria of convalescents when they first see the sky again, and to this process contributed forcefully the movement of an automobile as it drives away quickly, and takes hope with it

an automobile that drives away quickly
an automobile that drives away
an automobile

Dije a la noche: Amada misteriosa,
Tú sabes mi secreto;
Tú has visto la honda gruta
Donde fabrica su cristal mi sueño.
Y sabes que mis lágrimas son mías,
Y sabes mi dolor, mi dolor viejo,
—¡Oh! Yo no sé, dijo la noche, amado,
Yo no sé tu secreto. . .　　　　　　　　*—Del camino*

Memorabilia

Moving with a haughty ease and slow, measured pace down the surface of the avenue which hugs the coast while the strong breeze is still blowing away, back toward the sea, the salty residue caused by the crashing waves, leaving in peace the eyes of the passersby as well as the glass that protects them, one invariably finds a gentleman of venerable age out in the early morning hours every day, whose fatigued organism demands this morning exercise in order not to become definitively paralyzed sooner rather than later, and even though this is unavoidable no matter how much he manages to push back the hands of the clock, his fate will be an immensely deplorable one although one recognizes its inevitability and even the possibility that it might be desired or welcomed because it responds as we know to a natural law that is universally acknowledged as the rule of humanity and to which we are all reconciled and the fact that we are already beginning to lament, even now, this eventuality, viewing it as a catastrophe, is due to the fact that this gentleman is a walking treasure like those that the native pirates of the nineteenth century left inconspicuously buried in unknown places along our shores, and in whose innermost recesses most probably lay hidden jewels still youthful and worthy of the homage of a woman's neck or precious stones and flaming doubloons and other coins spectacularly snatched from English convoys returning to Britain after having pillaged the Spanish galleons and just as these treasures hold a destiny of eternal promise, this gentleman should be by all rights eternal and conserve for future generations the riches of memory, but you must understand that we are not talking about a character from any novel or work of fictional literature and that in this respect the gentleman is not only not the product of fantasy as can be evidenced by a simple early morning walk and a cursory inspection of the passersby scattered across the same avenue who are for the most part either athletes or persons subjected to slimming regimes and can be identified by the severity and mental concentration they exhibit as compared with the majestic movement, the leisurely pace of his grave and advanced years, and so it is plain that quite to the contrary, this gentleman is in fact the most ardent protection and defense against the temptation to succumb to fantasy, one to which many writers of all styles and tendencies are exposed, precisely because he had been a vibrant and active witness to the historical life of this country and because he constituted a part of the patrimony of the people and had as a consequence accumulated within his memory an enormous wealth of experiences, tales, countenances, memorable and lapidary expressions on the faces of the infinite beings who ran by his side and at times through his veins, as well as the places, regions, customs, and paths that flowed under him or the public events, government officials, and hurricanes that had flowed over him together with major and minor tragedies that befell major and minor figures throughout the course of the century, and the physical and mental geography, which taken together make up a complete picture of national life and much more importantly an explanation, theory, treaty, and *vade mecum* or shared consciousness of its inhabitants, solidly valid for all epochs and stages, and since we are dealing with a simple man his vision of the world and the responses he has given to all that faced him belong to a completely logical order, distinct, although no less intelligible, and perhaps endowed with the force of conviction and an air of authenticity that studies conducted by better cultivated minds and more illustrious personalities, with one or two exceptions, never reach, theories meant to explain the vital, historical essence of those who have populated this territory, hence the importance and appeal of this gentleman whose tired organism parades its weighty anonymity up and down the avenue that parallels the coast while the salt air hovers over the waves unable yet to advance toward the morning pedestrians or the hungry carriages of automobiles and so it deposits itself on this thankful memorial where the small ornaments and minute gold links that have come loose from his most intimate baggage have been recognized and restored, and with which the present record or memorabilia has been composed, and superimposed, in effect on his collaboration if not voluntary or conscious, at least effective and complete, and in which have been incorporated diverse steps or levels of recollection and reflection, duly backed up by testimony, events, experiences, and instances in his personal life, easily manifest in the infinite interconnections of practical life and day to day existence, but by an incredible accident of fate, some days before if not on this very day, walking with the same ease and slow pace but naturally for very different reasons, and this time on Riverside Drive, the famous avenue that runs along the Hudson River in New York City, was a woman from the same country, also worthy of being considered a treasure of native experiences and who in intimate, private circumstances was called *la bonaerense* although she had never lived in Buenos Aires nor had she ever acquired that gratifying nationality, but rather for comic reasons since people believed her to be a native of a much more modest population, situated at the halfway point between two more important cities of this Antillean nation among whose semi-bucolic, semi-cosmopolitan inhabitants could be heard the mixture of the rural sounds of birds and brooks and the city noise of horns and motors, which proudly bore the original name of *Bonao*, and it turns out that she, like our itinerant gentleman, had her own image of this common reality contemplated from a perspective that was feminine but equally straightforward or, if you prefer, modest and clear, and as a consequence, uncommon and rare, that is, memorable and severe, and whose transparent tangibility was most apparent in the atmosphere of New York because of the contrast created by the sovereign metropolis' stamp on the native image, just imagine the Créole expressions, gestures, vehemence, and shock, expressed in counterpoint to the supercivilized and psychopathological cosmopolitanism that emanates from the corner of 42nd Street and Broadway and spills over onto the rest and even Riverside Drive itself when autumn whirls it around in golden gusts of wind that rise to meet the Brooklyn Bridge or it gets submerged in the downtown or uptown flow of the metropolitan subway where the spirit of our people, Indian, Black, or white Spaniard, or a mixture of all of them, instead of vaporizing is purified by nostalgia and condenses into a beloved evocation, rendering a vision quite different from that of the old gentleman although similar in intensity and objectivity, so that given the strange coincidence that two people passionately constitute, in themselves, the same treasury

of documentary history, although separated by time, space, style, and
age, as well as by the gender and region within which they developed
their spirituality, fate or chance or fortune wanted them to come
together in such a striking manner in these pages that it made it
possible for them to materialize in a direct and textual account and
it is they who validate this document and give it its authenticity or,
to put it another way, its adherence to the reality we all live in
although of course there are other memories and some reflections
mixed in that don't belong to them, as well as a certain intellectual
and stylistic inflection, which though it never deviates for a moment
from the desire to get inside their spirit or essence comes from other
sources, notably from one in particular, which happens to be one of
those obscure characters, the hidden characters with bit parts, the
fellow travelers who, as often happens in anyone's life, only appear
when certain lines in the palm of the hand intersect, and who only
come to light when summoned through the magical methods and
transcendental faculties of the gypsy women who appear when they
are least expected in the most guileless regions of the Republic or at
least used to appear years ago with golden hoops in their ears and
their long, silky black hair wrapped in a colorful head scarf underneath which was visible the profile of an extremely seductive swarthy
face, if it held the glow of youth, or quite convincing, if it was clouded
over by age, and generally surrounded by a halo of mystery and an air
of wisdom that seemed to slip inside of you when they spoke and you
heard the accent of remote and legendary countries with an ancient
culture since they most commonly came from Spain and spoke the
language that founded the nations of Hispanic tradition, which hold
a kind of fascination and evoke a kind of respect behind the old
fascination with their dominion and it is precisely through the strange
spell cast by one of these gypsies that the triangle would become
complete, the triangle that is the source that generates the testimony
that follows, made complete by the addition of the third figure of the
cabala who will now be introduced and who joins the tired old
gentleman making his way slowly along the avenue of the capital that
borders the sea and the Créole woman who is, like him, making her
way along an avenue that hugs the coast of New York City, so that

they could come to life in these pages, fulfilling the prophecy of the gypsy woman, and all of this has been stated in order to reaffirm the absolute objectivity of this narrative and its total independence from any convention, precept, requirement, aspiration, or persevering trait applicable to literary narrative or to the atmosphere of rhetoric in vogue at present when what should take priority here as the most essential characteristic is the close and intimate kinship with the notarial genre, which is supposedly constrained to note strictly and without the slightest spark of fantasy the course of events submitted for record even though we know full well how much the record can benefit from the myths, legends, fables, and tales held in common by the people or the support it might gain from the absurd, the incoherent, or the rapture peculiar to old, now tired, literatures and above all the imponderable resources that the spirit of adventure and exploration on the psychic plane or the stylistic and aesthetic experimentations of contemporary literature have placed at writers' disposal enabling them to make their approximation of reality more powerful and complete but unfortunately these have not yet reached the notary's realm or the ledgers of the civil registry, which pride themselves on the prestige of their objectivity and independence although sadly wedded to a formula that is incapable of gathering and giving testimony to the drama of a wedding or a birth or the inevitable tragedy contained within the documentary evidence that upholds a deed of ownership to some barren lands or simply the marking of a boundary around an indivisible piece of property or an undefined stretch of land, all of which would permit us to include the present document among those usually orchestrated by one of those notaries or civil court judges who enjoy the privilege of *public trust*, which this testimony feels itself worthy of, and having made the previous declaration may it remain there like a net designed to catch the most sought-after reader on which to feed, one who should be appetizing, and if possible juicy, and perhaps even fleshy and above all free of spines or thorns, but having the same grace as the delicious creatures that emerge trembling and resplendent from the depths of the ocean or of love, when the hook is clean and the bait convincing, and when, incidentally, the line is strong and the dawn is clear

Silvester Discovers His Homeland

Sporting a pair of pants that were brand new or at least appeared to be and had come to their new owner through the generosity of some woodland spirit whose inclination was to protect the good peasants, Silvester was walking down the main road to the school presided over by *Maestro* Francisco Villamán when he heard the steady footsteps behind him of someone who could be one of his classmates because when he turned around to see who it was there was no one there, which could only have been possible if that someone was hiding in order to play the kind of trick on him that schoolboys are fond of, and so, with a scornful look on his face, he began walking again but hadn't even taken seven or eight steps when he again heard the steady, rhythmic sound of the same measured footsteps behind him and would have caught the trickster *flagrante delicto* if he had turned around suddenly to catch him as Silvester, half playful, half curious, finally did with all the agility of his young muscles but this time, just as before, he was surprised not to find anyone to his right or his left or up or down the road behind him and there was no hiding place around there capable of harboring a stranger and besides Silvester had learned to read that dusty road and the slightest alteration in the terrain would have tipped him off to the presence and even the nature of the being that had left its marks in the dust and this time he stopped to think because for Silvester this mystery was not cause for fear but for reflection and according to his still immature but well-reasoned criteria there had to be an explanation for the mysterious footsteps, which would in the first place indicate that it wasn't someone who wanted to do him any harm since he could by now already have done so and it was also true that he was not completely alone since the other boys who took the same route to school and had gotten a head start on him couldn't be so far away that they wouldn't hear his cries for help unless the mysterious enemy's plan was to distance him even further from the other boys and take advantage while he was alone and unprotected but what could be the motive behind all this strategy and unable to arrive at a convincing answer Silvester decided that the best thing to do would be to walk even faster in order to catch up with his classmates and make any unforeseen occurrence more difficult but no sooner had he begun to move again, reestablishing his pace, when he heard the sound of someone behind him again walking at exactly the same speed as if what he wanted was to always maintain exactly the same distance between them and in truth the situation couldn't have been stranger since legends generally state that apparitions don't occur to people during the day but under cover of night when absolute solitude reigns and then on the other hand Silvester repeated this walk daily since he lived quite a ways from the school and had never heard of anything like this occurring and besides the trip took up the better part of his day since in addition to simply going to school he had to find something to eat by going deep into the woods to look for mangos or wild legumes or cashews and avocados or guavas and star apples or rose apples and snails, depending on the season and his luck, or perhaps even a pair of good eggs or a couple of quails or doves if he was shrewd and had good aim all of which proves that dreamers sometimes steal and thieves sometimes dream, as one of our famous writers said, and this is only fair since Silvester lived with his grandfather in a hut they built together and their small plot only yielded enough food for the evening meal but it also means that there had been ample opportunities for this situation to occur in conditions much more favorable to the supposed enemy if he could get close enough because it was obvious that Silvester wasn't old enough for love or vices so that excluded a rival for someone's affection or a disgruntled gambling partner, which would be the first thing to consider, and as to the boy's personal qualities we need hardly make any additional comments if you take into consideration the effort invested in walking miles and miles every day to listen to a teacher whose wisdom was normally established by the severity of the blows he dealt with his rod, and above all when you don't have shoes or books or an atmosphere for learning or any direct and demanding guidance in your lessons so we cannot attribute to Silvester any internal contradictions that might explain the mystery that surrounded him and we don't know what he would have done if this situation had prolonged itself indefinitely because an event of a very

different kind made him forget the mysterious sound that had been
following him around when he heard a wild gallop behind him and
felt compelled to turn around and see what it was and this time he
was much more fortunate in that he could actually see a man on
horseback approaching furiously, raising an impressive cloud of dust,
and you don't have to be a genius to figure out that when a galloping
horseman like that disturbs the peace of the countryside and the
marvellous order of nature there must be an overwhelmingly powerful motive because no one is going to mistreat their beast that way,
probably their only and highly prized inheritance, unless the mayor
has been assassinated or there's been a flood that could kill the cattle
or a woman's giving birth to a breech baby, or something else of that
magnitude, so this time Silvester stopped to take a good look and
make sure that it was at least the beast that belonged to old man
Villamán, his teacher's father, and he could make out that it was in
fact exactly the person he thought it might be, which only added to
his curiosity because old man Villamán was held in high esteem for
his peace of mind and good sense and only in circumstances of
extreme importance would he have been riding at such a fierce
gallop, endangering himself, given his age, and putting his horse at
risk, but this mystery didn't last as long as the other one because as
soon as the old man got to where Silvester was standing he began to
yell, loud enough for his classmates to hear
boys, turn back, our homeland is in danger
and so naturally Silvester realized that it was not a woman in labor or
even the region that was in danger but the nation itself and that was
a catastrophe greater than any other he could imagine since up until
then for him the homeland had been something they talked about in
school and was mentioned in the readings they assigned but he had
never seen in his travels through the woods or in the countryside any
concrete manifestation of the homeland and had become convinced
that the homeland must be one of those civilized products found in
the Capital or some other far off place, maybe even in Cuba since he
had heard his teacher repeat so often that Máximo Gómez had gone
off to fight for his homeland in Cuba and it seemed clear to Silvester
that if the homeland were here Máximo Gómez wouldn't have had

151

to make such a long trip and when he arrived at this point in his
reasoning he decided to continue on to school and not return home
to the hut and the garden where he was absolutely sure the homeland
wasn't to be found because if it was he would have felt it with his
own hands whereas in school he would no doubt find an explanation
for the old man's ominous prediction and it was a very wise decision
because when he finally got to the schoolhouse he would have
sufficiently overtaken the horseman to discover for himself and in
detail the reason for Villamán's profound alarm but in the meantime
something occurred to Silvester that in the midst of the circumstances at hand seemed totally devoid of significance and unworthy
of attention except for the fact that it made him uneasy for a few
disagreeable moments and it was that the presence of old man
Villamán, preceded by the majestic cloud of dust, had distracted him
from the noise that had mysteriously followed him around and this
gave his mind much greater elasticity and common sense which
allowed him to realize that the sound of mysterious footsteps he
heard at his back was made by the fabric on the hem of his new pants,
which were much wider than he was used to wearing and the hems
of the pant legs rubbed against each other when his feet crossed as
he walked and since the sound was as new to him as the pants he
couldn't at first tell where it was coming from and his own mind
played tricks on him projecting the sound backwards so that it
perfectly simulated the sound of another person's footsteps and the
whole episode might have turned into a story for cheerful conversation if it weren't for the much greater mystery that hovered over the
homeland in terms that were for him profoundly impressive and had
been until then unfamiliar because the events recorded here occurred exactly as they are told according to the testimony of eyewit-
nesses who lived through them in all their intensity from 1916 on,
for example, old man Villamán is still remembered by many in Puerto
Plata, age permitting, and they even recall the words with which he
gave out the first news of the U.S. military intervention that took
place that year and shook the national and patriotic consciousness
hard all over the country even in its most bucolic and isolated corners
and by then Silvester was a strapping boy approaching puberty since

as we know primary education starts late in the countryside, and we are also aware that this is the age, at least for males, when they begin to express an interest in and babble about public affairs in the same way that females become conscious of the maternal instinct and all of this made it possible for Silvester to comprehend a lapidary phrase like that one, pronounced in the midst of such a spectacular scene from which a fiery steed emerged enveloped in a cloud of dust, and it must have produced a veritable explosion of emotions in the young lad's soul already conditioned by the personal excitement and predisposition toward mystery he had for a few brief moments experienced on his way to school but the most important thing was that the whole affair would not simply end when he met up with the other boys, just as worried as he was, who were closing up the school with *Maestro* Villamán and his father, but would prolong itself indefinitely as was clear from the comments as well as the speculations and predictions coming from the mouths of old man Villamán and his son, and this was merely a prelude to an infinite number of comments and concrete references that from then on spread to every corner of the precarious Republic because a military intervention is not simply a political event produced at the highest levels of the government, it also profoundly affects the nature of the most intimate relations in the life of the people and the citizenry and extends in all directions, paralyzing the very core of national life in such a way that what had initially been an almost theatrical surprise for young Silvester was later substantiated in his own life because it took that life at the very point of its awakening and accompanied it over the course of its development since the invading forces didn't leave the country until 1924 when Silvester had completed his physical development, passed through all the cycles of anatomical and biological transformation, making him a grown man, and there is another circumstance that should be taken into account, which is that Puerto Plata was the port of entry chosen by the waves of political refugees from Cuba during the course of that country's War of Independence against Spain and the fighters and activists brought with them a fervor for patriotic action that led to the creation of numerous public organizations passionately supported by their native hosts and in which they continually held cultural and political functions in solidarity with those who struggled for Cuba's independence, and in these organizations none other than Máximo Gómez figured prominently, instilling in every fiber of the citizenry an identification with the Cuban people, and even though some years had passed and almost all of the immigrants had returned to Cuba, quite a few remained in the country because of the ties that had grown up while they were in exile and which they later could not break and in any case that experience continued to float over the public consciousness in the region creating a foundation that subsequent events would give greater meaning to and it was in that scenario that Silvester's life began and old man Villamán's phrase was engraved upon his still-limpid consciousness like a kind of destiny that would never fade from his memory and to the circumstance of history would be added another, which would be reflected in the aristocratic sectors of the country around which the most influential of the intelligentsia revolved, since in 1915 Haiti had been occupied militarily and these sectors had made themselves believe that what had happened there could never happen here so when they found themselves face to face with the inexorable reality of occupation they suffered a kind of humiliation, followed by immeasurable indignation, and all around the most cultured and prestigious voices of the nation were mobilized, including some that resonated throughout the Latin American continent, and still others whose flight reached the other continent and rang out over the skies of Europe like that of the poet Fabio Fiallo whose exquisitely delicate poetry was matched by the gallant and elegant figure he cut very much in keeping with and in the style of what had survived of romanticism during that period, reflected in the mirror of Rabindranath Tagore, and although Silvester found himself at the opposite end of the universe from such a distinguished milieu, and along with Silvester vast sectors of society's dispossessed, the truth is that the entire nation experienced a common feeling of humiliation expressed in the concept of a tarnished, wounded homeland, and creating a national consciousness and conscience in whose breast Silvester's budding virility found its first nourishment

Dime tú: ¿Cuál es mejor?
¿Conciencia de visionario
que mira en el hondo acuario
peces vivos,
fugitivos,
que no se pueden pescar,
o esa maldita faena
de ir arrojando a la arena,
muertos, los peces del mar?

—Proverbios y Cantares

Decolonization and the
Colonial Education

$\mathcal{A}$ustin Clarke's coming-of-age novel opens with a numbing enumeration of the identifying markers of the Combermere School, Lower Second Form, designed to confer an identity on the narrator—that of belonging to the Barbadian middle class. Education was a vehicle that would, in the narrator's words, "turn me into a civil servant, if I did well," and if not, a "book-keeper on one of the many sugar plantations." Clarke's wry, young first-person narrator takes the identity of the Barbadian middle class apart, piece by piece, in order to construct another, quite distinct one. As the self-conscious narrator, the Calibanesque protagonist, observes at the outset: "I was at the beginning of having a choice in life." His school days are framed by the Second World War and anticipate the shift from British to U.S. dominance in the economies of the West Indian nations, as well as the cultural influence that comes with it: "We all wanted to be either Americans, or else to live in America. So, we lived through the defeats and victories of the British Empire and her allies."

The young Barbadians who people Austin Clarke's novel of colonial education know that those who went to war went, "not to die for the Empire," as the schoolmaster reminded them, but "as we knew, because we were to be the beneficiaries, to make a living." And so, *against* and *because of* their colonial preparation, they forged another identity, one that combatted the false identification as "black Britons" of "Little England." Throughout, the scattered bits of decontextualized knowledge that passed for education are contrasted with *home*, in its own terms. The narrator turns the precepts of colonial education on their head, being taught by rote about the "'men of resolution and independence' who walked beside a sea and picked up seashells," while thinking, "We picked welts and 'sea beefs' ourselves. The fools in our Village and the doatish old women had been doing this all their lives, and nobody in Barbados wrote a poem about it." The instinctively anticolonialist narrator of *Growing Up Stupid Under the Union Jack* knows the answer, he knows *why* they weren't given poems about the Barbados seashore written by Barbadians at school, and that knowledge provides the radical tension underlying the novel.

"Journey Back to the Source," one of Cuban novelist Alejo Carpentier's early works, is a coming-of-age tale in reverse. In it, we retrace the steps of aristocratic Marcial's life, from death, through old age, youth, adolescence, and back into the womb. A normal life, taken out of its normal order or sequence, offers infinite possibilities for reflection, for choosing another path, as does the young narrator of Austin Clarke's novel. The Marquis, sadly, does not choose, either over the course of a lifetime or during the temporal regression back to the source. All of Carpentier's novels are journeys through history, on the double axis of time and geography, in search of origins, of roots. His characters move back and forth through time, through layers of culture, ideology, and philosophy, in order to clarify perspective, to examine critically prevailing attitudes and explain apparently recurring phenomena in Latin American and Caribbean reality. In "Journey Back to the Source," the novelist peels off layers—legal, social, cultural—in the formation of the nineteenth-century Créole aristocracy of Havana, later to become the dependent bourgeoisie of our own century. Marcial's has been a passive, unreflective life, and as he moves backwards in time and layers of "constraint" drop off, the attainment of freedom is equally unconscious and unwilled. The theme of liberty, of liberation and false liberation, is one Carpentier will return to again and again. Here he suggests that the mere freedom from constraint, with no social ethic, leads quite literally to nothingness.

From: Growing Up Stupid Under the Union Jack

AUSTIN CLARKE

(BARBADOS)

I was admitted to Combermere School, a secondary school in Barbados, on Roebuck Street, in Town, on September 1944, and placed in the "L2D," the Lower Second Form, with thirty other boys. For all these years, I have been wondering whether the "D" in L2D stood for "duncc." And nobody so far has told me.

But that was a day of personal rejoicing for my mother. She had at last achieved something beyond the expectations of the Village. The Village of St. Matthias rejoiced with her on that day. The poor and ambitious mothers gave me their blessing, and in their stern and frightening voices, they said, "Go 'long, boy, and *learn!* Learning going make you into a man." And Delcina, the tallest, blackest, and most beautiful woman I had ever seen, smiled and broke into a hymn. She lifted her operatic voice, trained in the hot broiling sun as she bent over tubs of many sheets and shirts, with her black hands on the heavy soap suds, for the rich *out the front road,* and she sang on that morning. The washing would be carried later in the week, to the Marine Hotel, white as snow and ironed like glass. Delcina sang a beautiful hymn that morning as I walked down the gap from my house, on my way to a new, but uncertain world. Delcina sang, "O God, Our Help in Ages Past." My book bag was filled with books of interminable pages, with puzzles of new knowledge undreamed of by my mother and by anybody else in the Village, for that matter. There was the shining gold-painted set that contained the compasses; the Rankin biscuit tin, scrubbed clean and looking now like a small silver coffin, with a flying-fish sandwich in it; and my Ferrol bottle of "clear" lemonade, without the label on it. One of the "uncles" in that vicious circle of men with a pair of scissors and a broken "glass bottle" for a razor, had on the previous Sunday, sat me down on the throne of a chair, under the clammy-cherry tree, and when I got up, my head was *clean*. "Don't mind them few scratches and bumps I had to leave round the back of your head, boy. You is a Combermere boy now!" The finished product had the impact and the look of a bowl put on your head, and all the visible hair beneath it and around it, wiped clean away, with soap and water, by the blade of the sharp piece of "glass-bottle." The smell of Limacol was strong even as I entered the large iron gate of Combermere School, on that shaking, quivering morning, grabbed by the hand by my equally scared mother.

Combermere School was the school for middle- and lower-middle-class boys. It was a second grade school. It would turn me into a civil servant, if I did well. If I didn't do well, it would turn me into a sanitary inspector. If I did even worse than that, into a "book-keeper," on one of the many sugar plantations, to ride about in the sun, under a khaki helmet, dressed in a khaki suit, on a horse, to drive some of my less fortunate friends and neighbors to work in the fields. The prospect of the sanitary inspector appealed more to me in those days. I had seen them, flitting about the Village like black mosquitoes, a ladle in their hands, dipping into people's drinking water buckets, and into pigs' urinals, and pronouncing ruin and plague and pestilence, at the sight of "larvees"; and having more drinks than doing work. That kind of drama and tragedy has always impressed me. I was at the beginning of having a choice in life.

But to be a civil servant, that was beyond my wildest dreams! Could I be like one of those powerful young men, walking up and down the corridor of the Old Public Buildings, on the second and third floors, with huge important files of all colors, blue, red, white, faded and musty, dressed in white shirts and ties like the white Colonial officers who ruled and ran the country at that time, and who had the knack of looking important?

"Not on your blasted bottom dollar!" my mother said, imaging greater things. "I want you to be a *doctor*, hear?" To be a doctor in those days, you had to know Latin backwards and forwards. You had to be a "Latin fool": *amas, amat*, and *amamus* would be the only things to save me from the hot sun of the book-keeper; the *larvees* of the sanitary inspector, dressed like a soldier of health; and from the low salary of the civil servant. The other possibility was to be an elementary school teacher. But you had to have brains, and slightly more patience than brains in those days if you wanted to be a school teacher; and you had to love children, and even lower wages, even more. I was tempted by my own dreams, to settle for the "*amo-amas-amat*."

On that terrifying morning, ignorant about the meaning of higher education, and of Combermere School for Boys, and big books, and foreign languages of Latin and French, I waited in the Hall with the other one hundred new boys, all of us stiff in our new khaki uniforms, clean heads, new ties of blue and gold which were the school colors, and which choked us; with our book bags made out of blue denim, some of leather boasting about the goodwill of a "relative" who lived Away, meaning most likely America. Our book bags were filled with every conceivable heavy book, priced at more than most of our parents worked for, in wages, in a month. To those of us who did not win scholarships to get here, or who did not receive government bursaries, the tuition fees were the devastating amount of eight dollars a term. A term lasted three months. But we were to be the new leaders of the country, and members of the Barbados middle class. Combermere meant that in those days.

The headmaster was a Santa Claus of a man. A man of the cloth. He was bull-frogged and deep-voiced, but loveable as a cherub; a man who liked cricket, and who would take your ability to play it into consideration when you were sent to him for a flogging. The Reverend A. E. Armstrong, B.A. (Durham), M.A. (Someplace). In our unexplained tradition of giving almost every living person a nickname, he was known as "The Buff." We called him "The Buff" behind his back, naturally; and we tipped our caps in his white-suited presence, and called him "Sir!"

During my first term, I never came within his Church-of-England presence; never sat at his feet, for he taught Scripture in the first form, and Latin in the higher forms; and I was in L2D. But at the end of that first year, before he left for retirement and England, I was "sent" to him, for a flogging. I had to stand on the long wooden bench in front of his office. And while I waited for him, I wilted with uncertainty from the rumors about his strength and cruelty and dexterity with a tamarind rod. All the time, boys, smaller boys, big boys, the school prefects, and the master who had *sent* me, paused and jeered and "skinned" their teeth at me, imitating in mock drama and with antics, the rod of Buff's justice "in your arse!" I was old enough, after one academic year, and wise in the ways of the school, to know that I should shriek with pain even before the first smooth tamarind rod's blow landed on my starched khaki trousers. For the offense I was reported for: making a whistling sound with a mechanical pencil my friend Kenny had got from his mother in America, I could get three lashes. But this was nothing like the flogging orgies I witnessed, and sometimes suffered through, at St. Matthias Boys' School, my previous school.

There, the headmaster used the belt from a sewing machine. Rumor among the boys said that the headmaster soaked it every night, in pee. And during the long hot afternoons, he walked through the empire of benches, and blackboards and *desses*, with the whip around his neck, hanging like a black dead snake, or like a dew worm coiled and held between the thumb and index fingers.

But the Reverend Armstrong, a man of great theological tolerance and knowledge, close to the altar and the communion cup, was a saint in comparison.

"Clarke!"

His voice was like large stones in a deep bucket. It was an authoritarian English voice. The water had already settled in my eyes. My body was waiting for the explosion of the rod. All I had to do now, was screel so loud, that the Reverend's understanding of Christian love and charity and pity would freeze his hand, or lighten the blow; and he would say, "Dismiss, Clarke!"

"Bend over!" he said instead. The voice was still hoarse.

Wap!

"Go!" and I left, laughing to myself the moment I was out of sight; eager again to dare the form master, and inform the boys, "Man, 'The Buff' can't lick, in truth! I didn't feel nithing. . . ." And then to be welcomed back into the class as a hero, a "bad boy."

But one morning at St. Matthias, the sun was already hot. The perspiration was mixing with the coconut oil, or the Brilliantine, or the Vaseline which we wore on our hair. When I reached the school gate and bolted to the entrance to the school, crossing the yard which had no grass, which never had any grass, and up the single step, the headmaster was already there. Something had happened. Something was going to happen. The entire school of two hundred boys were singing. "Rock of Ages." They had reached the last verse.

But the headmaster loved singing, and loved that song. He delighted in leading the bass section among his teachers: tenors, altos, and less profundo basses; and so, the hymn had to be sung from the beginning again. He could sing a hymn, or a song, ten times.

I stood at the door. Five other boys who were late stood silently beside me. We were three minutes late. We had no excuse. The headmaster accepted no excuses for coming late. Once a boy told him, "Please sir, I had to go 'cross the road five times to bring water for my mother and for the sheeps, 'cause my mother sick with badfeels." The headmaster listened carefully, and patiently. In our hearts, we cheered for the little boy. There could no better excuse. But when the confession was over, the pee-soaked black snake was wrapped six times across the boy's back, like the Cross of St. Andrew. And when it was over, we had to carry the boy out, like a casualty, four of us, to the pipe across the school yard, and wash the feces from his legs and pants. We all swore then, as we stood under the pipe, in the frightened secrecy of our hearts, to become men soon, strong men, and come back for the headmaster, with a bull pistle whip.

This morning, I stood at the door, facing the Union Jack. I was pinned against the wall below the grandfather clock, which the headmaster wound every morning with a key which he kept in his pocket. Once, he asked me to wind the clock, and I knew that something had happened to me, and certainly to him. The boys were now singing "O God, Our Help in Ages Come." The voices were beautiful voices. Some of these voices belonged in the choir of the church which was separated from our school by a thick wall. It was made out of stone and marl and lime and dust, and it covered our hands each time we jumped over it, to steal the almonds which grew in the churchyard. Now, the school had become a church.

The hymn had come to an end. The school became very quiet. I could imagine the vicar walking up the aisle with the choir. It was still, like the hour before the school inspector was due to arrive, and inspect our progress and send his results and our results back to England.

The headmaster wore white. He always wore white. He wore white as if it meant something to him which we boys could never aspire to; and he wore a tie that had no tropical color in it. Around the knot, he wore a pure, real, "true-true gold" as the boys said, gold ring. He walked like a tall black king, from the bottom of the one-roomed school right up to the platform. He held the bell, a dinner bell in size to the larger brown one which summoned the beginning of classes, and he touched its tongue with a finger. But the school was already at attention. Nobody, including his teachers, who feared him as we trembled in his presence, was breathing. He took a black object, something that looked like a huge hairpin from his side pocket. It was his tuning fork. He struck it against the desk, and it spoke the correct note and pitch he wanted. He hummed, "Do, re, me, faaaaaa!" He had won competitions in his youth for his voice. He struck the tuning fork again, and listened to its hum, and again he hummed, "Do, re, me, *faaaa.*"

" 'Ride on!' " he said, announcing the hymn. When he announced hymns, and sang the first few lines, he was calm and loving like a choir master. He loved singing hymns, and he transferred some of that love on to us.

164

But this morning he rushed from the platform and reached the door where we were standing, in three strides. He became like a giant. So, we galloped into the hymn "Ride on, Ride on, in Majesty," careful to let him know that we loved singing, and that we knew the words.

He was towering above us now. The long desk at the back was cleared of exercise books, nib pens, pencil boxes, and boys. It looked clean, cleared-away like a tribunal or scaffold.

The entire school and the teachers were singing at the top of their voices.

Ride on! Ride on in majesty!
In lowly pomp ride on to die. . . .

"Fingers!" he said to the five of us at the door. The boy at the head of the line held his hand out. The headmaster inspected his fingers and his fingernails. They were dirty. They were always dirty. No one of us in that school had ever held a nail file in his hands. Nail files were not common in our Village. When the time came, we cleaned our fingers with a stick. And we pitched marbles morning, noon, and night, and our nails bore the guilt of that evidence. He knew they were dirty; he knew they would always be dirty; he knew that not one of the five of us in the "late line" would remember to use the piece of stick. One went with the other.

He held the boy's ear, and looked inside it, and then the other. Then he pushed him gently, like an approved piece of merchandise, aside. And he inspected the rest of us, and pushed us aside. We were now thinking of the brimstone and ashes of his fierce temperament. And in all this time, the school was singing, like a choir of a cathedral, at the top of their voices.

Ride on! Ride on in majesty!
The last and fiercest strife is nigh. . . .

He threw the black snake across the neck of the boy nearest him. Then he was flogging all five of us, at the same time, across our backs, our heads, our feet as we jumped in stupid attempts to avoid the snake, criss-crossing, horizontal, diagonal like the various English crosses in the flag, and in other flags of countries he had taught us about, in his class of Social History of the British Empire. We smelled his perfume of chalk. We smelled his breath. And we could hear from that close, chilling distance, the deep profundo of his voice, for he was flogging and singing along with the teachers and the rest of the school; singing and flogging with the presoaked, pee-soaked fan belt from his wife's sewing machine.

Look down with sad and wondering eyes
To see the approaching Sacrifice.

And when it was over, when we had come galloping and exhausted and *whemmend* to the end of the hymn; and he was perspiring, and his black skin was jewelled with beads of his morning, corporal exercise, he touched the tong of the dinner bell. Silence reigned.

Beyond us, in the meantime, the Second World War was raging on seas and battle fields in strange countries. In the magazines which trickled through the blockades of ships and reached us, in the pages of *Life* and *English Country Life*, *Punch* and *Reader's Digest*, we would see the war in pictures. We would see American GI's, stronger than Charles Atlas, drinking cans of grapefruit juice, and overturning German tanks with their bronzed bare hands. We all wanted to be either Americans, or else to live in America. So, we lived through the defeats and the victories of the British Empire and her allies. We praised Churchill, for a time; and thought of praising Stalin, too. We hated Hitler and Mussolini, as if we were on the Field of Flanders. The church wall meanwhile, was painted with the swastikas of our graffiti.

The headmaster cleared his throat. He was about to make an important announcement. It could be, too, a speech of sorrow and of patriotism. It was a speech of sorrow. The Germans had sunk another merchant ship. The headmaster called the ship by name, and he read off the names of the dead at sea. Some were men who had walked about our streets, unemployed and barefooted a few months before; men whom we had passed, whistling along the streets that had no paving, no macadam, streets which kicked up the dust of their cocky former independence. Men we knew. Men from our Village, and from neighboring villages had gone to sea, not to fight the Germans whom they didn't know, not to die for the Empire, as the headmaster told us in his stern, sad voice, but had ventured forth, as we knew, because we were to be the beneficiaries, to make a living. Unemployment, "work" we called it in our Village, was so prevalent, as in the dust in the public road.

We stood for the three silent minutes of respect for the dead of our Village, "lost at sea." Our eyes filled with tears for the unfairness and the frightening imagined photographs of men falling out of ships, in seas higher than the crown of the clock in the tower of the Garrison Savannah, higher than any building in our island-country, higher than any wave we had seen off the Gravesend Beach; and blacker, too.

He told us it was in the Atlantic Ocean that it happened. He told us about the Atlantic again, and called it "one of the biggest bodies o' salt water, boys." The men, whom he had told us, on other occasions of enlightenment, had discovered us, would themselves have crossed this very Atlantic, hundreds of years and miles before. And now the Germans were ruling these same waves and waters, and killing fathers, brothers, and uncles from our Village. And as black Britons, we wanted to do something about it.

That morning, the headmaster said a very long prayer. We prayed for the King and the Royal Family, and the Prime Minister of England, and for all our Allies, and we asked God, with closed eyes and bended heads, to give our English leaders good counsel, wisdom, and strength to kill more Germans and Italians than the Axis Powers could do to us, "in these days of peril." He read from the Book of Common Prayer, something about us *calling out of the depth of misery, and out of the jaws of death, which is now ready to swallow us up. . .* and I got very scared and was glad that it was not night. Then he said something about our sins *now crying out against us for vengeance; but hear us thy poor servants begging mercy, and imploring thy help, and that thou wouldest be a defense unto us against the face of the enemy.* We knew he meant the Germans and the "Axes."

The headmaster brought the sad proceedings to a close, by leading us into the singing of "Rule Britannia, Britannia Rules the Waves." And in all the singing, nobody remembered to pray for the families of the Barbadian seamen, lost or dead, at sea.

Combermere School could never match the drama of learning and instruction, that was staged daily, at St. Matthias Boys' School. At Combermere, a new school at this time, with two stories and a corridor on both floors, which we used to practice the hundred yards dash, at this school we sat at individual *desses* and marked our initials "on the *desses* of time" as one bright boy said; and gouged secret coded protestations of love for girls. Inside our desses we kept our almost unaffordable books; along with our lunch. And when the last bell rang at three in the afternoon, we secured these possessions with a padlock, and kept the key tied to a long piece of string, and showed it proudly on a school bus, or in the street in our Village, arrogant in this display of the fact that we were "Cawmere boys."

At Combermere, I learned about the two sides of an isosceles triangle; was told that x was equal to 2, and y to 3, if certain things happened; and was left in fear, alone, to figure out the value of z. we were taught the capitals of almost every known country in the British Empire; *amo, amas, amat; je suis, tu suis, il suit;* about the birth and life of Christ, in the Gospels; and I learned how to pronounce *pseudonym*.

But the way the master taught Scripture at Combermere was nothing like the way Miss Smith taught it in Sunday School. Miss Smith was a young, round-faced woman in her twenties, when I was eight or nine or ten. All of us Sunday School boys fell in love with Miss Smith. We married her many times before she knew; and some brave boys who had heard of "woman things" beyond the reach of my tender carnal knowledge, or had read about it in magazines, or in the underlined passages of the Bible about David and Bathsheba, they talked about taking Miss Smith to bed. They would then tell me in details bigger than their imaginations, what it was all about. But Miss Smith made the Scriptures live. On Sunday evenings, we went to bed with our minds made up to be "good little boys;" or else filled with the damnation and the everlasting darkness that was the lot of Lot, or of Goliath. Our houses had no electricity in those days, and the hell of her voice and of her threats, were blacker even than the pictures she painted of sinners. One boy, impressed by the moral of David's advantage before Goliath, challenged the village bully to a fight. As a result, he did not attend Sunday School for the next three weeks, while the swelling to the left side of his face where the blow landed, went down gradually, to disclose again an eye, whose safety he had lost sight of.

The master at Combermere enters the classroom. He sits at his elevated *dess*, which is at the front, in the middle of the room, below the large blackboard, nailed into the wall. And he opens his book for the lesson.

"What's the lesson for today?" he asks. He had himself set the lesson.

The monitor stands and says, "*Axe*, chapter one, sir?"

He had told us to study chapter one, in the Acts of the Apostles, the previous time; but this is the way they do things at the "big schools." He would then ask each one of us, sitting in the order of the alphabet, or in academic order, to recite a line, or if he was in a bad mood, two, three, four sentences. Even the way he is dressed and the clothes he wears, is strange to me. At the elementary school, the teachers (they were not called "masters") wore long-sleeved shirts and ties, and large baggy long trousers. Their shirts were sometimes discolored and "high" from sweating. And when they put their jackets on, at the end of the day, and jumped on their bicycles, the perspiration on their jackets could be seen, too; for it had eaten through the underarms of the jackets themselves. All their jackets looked old and slept in. But these men were brave, poor honest men who studied hard at night, and put themselves on a higher plane of academic degrees. They were beautiful black men.

At Combermere, the masters (they were not "teachers") wore shorts of khaki, and clean white sweet-smelling shirts. Some of them wore suits.

In this class now we are seated in alphabetical order.

The master points a finger, as if he is too tired; points with a glaring eye, and nods at the first boy, in the first row of scared boys.

"Armstrong," he says, and smiles. We become tense.

Armstrong stands up, between his chair, made of wood by the school carpenter, and his *dess*, made of wood by the school carpenter. The room is quiet. Like those mornings at St. Matthias, when a flogging was in the air.

"Begin!" the master says.

Armstrong tries to look wise. And when that fails, he relaxes and looks stupidly at the ceiling. Bright students at our school always look up at the ceiling before answering a question. They would close their eyes once or twice, to make the question more difficult. No one wanted to be well-known for answering easy questions. *"The former treatise have I made . . . ,"* Armstrong says.

"Next boy, go on!"

Armstrong, E. E., who came after Armstrong A. E., stands up.

"Spell *treatise*, EE!"

EE spells *treatise*. EE is bright.

"Next boy!"

And Babb stands up, and says, *". . . O, Theophilus, of all that Jesus began to teach and do."*

The master loses his temper, and bellows, *"Next idiot!"*

Something is wrong. He says, *"Next! Next idiot!"* as each boy jumps up, and tries to figure out what is wrong with Babb's answer. Then all of a sudden, a genius among us, who has remembered the lesson by heart, sees the point. He raises his hand in the air. He cannot speak, before he is given permission to do so. In a weak, uncertain voice, he says, "Both to do and teach." He answers as if he is asking a question.

"Yess!" the master hisses. He smiles. Somebody in his class has an eye for detail, even if it is useless detail. He is gratified. "Come up above the *asses!*" The smiling little genius, hated now by all of us, exchanges his seat and takes that of the first boys who had missed the point in the question. There is shuffling and snickering and threats under the breath, for this little genius. The room becomes quiet again, and the master offers to "enlighten our darkness."

"The important word," he says, "in the first sentence of the *Axe* is *both*. *Both* show you that there is two things involved here. The doing *and* the teaching. Jesus wanted his disciples to walk about the place teaching, not like the reverends we have running 'bout this place, but like real social workers." He was doing an External Degree by correspondence from Wolsey Hall College, in Sociology. By the end of our first term, we learned that this master who taught us Scripture was an atheist, and a Communist.

"That is what studying all them big books on Sociology does to a man's brain," the little genius enlightened our darkness.

Apart from Scripture, we learned the declension of Latin nouns, and the first conjugation of Latin verbs. But we had more fun inventing our own Latin verbs.

We soon covered *amabo, amabis, amabit, amabitis, amabamus, amabunt.*

And the little genius who was fast becoming an atheist himself, and who borrowed *Das Kapital* from the Public Library, introduced us to the new Latin verb, *mary-hairy-co, mary-hairy-cit, mary-hairy-citis, mary-hairy-camus, mary-hairy-cunt!*

"What is the longest word in the whirl?"

"Mississippi."

"Spell it!"

"Who is the oldest man in the Bible?"

"Nicodemus?"

"No, he is the fellow who walk by night!"

"Who is the King of Englunt?"

"George the Six, man! Everybody know that!"

"Betcha can't tell me the King wee-wees, when he's on parade shaking hands and inspecting the Guards!"

"I have a' uncle who uses to live in Amurca, and from there he went to live in Englund, and he tell me that the King have this thing, like a long piece o' rubber, yuh know?

"Tie-on to the King's waist, just below the King shoe, and when the King want to wee-wee, or fire a shit, all the King got to do is . . . that is the meaning of a King, to be a King."

And we laughed, and learned and pitched marbles in the soft ground, and ran races in the large playing field, larger than any one of us had ever played on, before; and we played cricket and football, and went home drowned in perspiration, but proud "Cawmere boys," wearing the school tie, slightly loosened because that was the style.

I remember that first Christmas. It came soon after the end of the first term. I had passed the Michaelmas Examinations. I was now a *high school boy*, for I had passed my first exams. I was a choirboy, too. I was moving up in the world, my mother concluded.

"Take off my clothes, please!" she commanded, the moment I reached home from Combermere. I was now within the sphere of her domain. "Take off my clothes, and put on your home-clothes." My "home-clothes" were any clothes not good enough to be worn at church, or to school, or to Town, or to visit the countless uncles and aunts I had, who lived in the country, in St. James; or to be worn at the Empire Theatre on Saturday afternoons, where we met to see American movies, and eat parched peanuts, "a penny for a big bag, look muh here! You want me, young fellow?"

"You got your work to do. Don't play no sport with me, this evening, boy! You not at Cawmere now!"

Latin and French and the ability to spell the longest word *in the whirl*, did not change my status in her eyes, in her book. The Village had its rituals and its customs; and these rituals and customs swallowed me up again, the moment I entered its precincts. It was as if I was a laneway, or a path, or a "cane-brek" which was suffocated, swallowed up and hidden in a short time after the rains, by the strangulating vines and weeds and wild flowers that grew everywhere.

Christmas meant work. I never knew it to be a religious festival, only. All our old furniture had to be scraped and painted, or varnished. The house had to be cleaned from top to bottom. And since we did not sleep on factory-made mattresses, I had to cut fresh Guinea-grass and Cush-Cush grass for our "mattresses." Sometimes, I stole it, or begged for it. I would bring it home in the hot sun, and my neck would burn, and scratch for days. I laid it out in the backyard in the sun, which turned it from green into makeshift down.

Christmas meant also lots of food and torture. Shoes were bought deliberately too small. And my mother made me spend the two weeks before Christmas, walking in the golden light of the weak kerosene lamp with the red seeds in its bottom, on old newspapers, to "stretch" the shoes to my size. For Christmas, she kept me sitting up with her, beyond the nodding time, my neck heavy and stricken by a palsy of exhaustion, while she made, and taught me how to make, cushions from pieces of cloth she got from the dressmaker of the Village, and leftovers from the silk dress lengths she bought from the Indian man. Or we would make "artificial flowers," roses, out of crepe paper, of pink and red and yellow and green and mauve. The roses in the school garden at St. Matthias were only red. I could smell these real roses, all along the dark close road to my house.

Always on these nights just before Christmas, when the house was filled with women (there were few men around), the women would tell stories of the War, of previous wars, of the Village, of the volcanic dust that came from St. Vincent and covered the land and made the fowls jump on their *rooses* before it was mid-day; and stories of village boys who were "good" and who were "bad" and who were "too mannish"; of girls who got "in trouble" and of boys who got girls "in trouble." The best stories they liked to tell were about boys who supported their parents. No one ever talked about the fathers. Only after they were dead. And the night would sometimes be filled with ghosts from stories, and the long imagination of women who worked "obeah" on men to get them to marry them, or to turn them doatish after that first "dose of obeah didn' work, child"; stories of superstition and monsters and men with three heads. Once they told a story about a train which ran in Barbados. But I fell asleep before I could hear the end.

I would be sitting, frozen with the sleep in my body and from the story, and with the scissors in my hand, and my mother would catch me idle and nodding, and say, as if her love had been itself napping, say so kindly, in her soft voice, "Boy, why you don't turn-in, and get some sleep?"

And my sleep would be torment. I would writhe in greater terrors than those which chilled me from the Bible stories of sinners which Miss Smith told, like Judy Garland. I would run on the unmoving bed of Cush-Cush grass, and shout and call out, for voiceless help, from the clutches of a nightmare of white horses that were trampling me; and in the middle of that kind of arthritis of limbs and of voice, hear my mother calling out to the fisher-woman, to buy flying-fish, "all-a-penny," over the front window, at this graveyard hour. At this late hour, no later than ten o'clock, but to my small mind, an hour of cobwebs and ghosts, the fish tasted better than during the day. My mother would buy as many as she could clean. She boned them, and washed them in lime juice, and seasoned them and floured them, and fried them over a fire made of dried sugar-cane roots. In good times, the fire was stimulated and made more ferocious by the seeds of the mahogany tree. The War had made coal scarce. But our way of living had, at this time, never accommodated coals.

"Come boy, get up and run 'cross the road for a fresh bucket o' water for me. You sleeping?" She was terrified of the dark.

The dark road, which never had street lamps, but which would always have people, bright with talk, perhaps a man and a woman hiding beneath a window to steal a kiss, would, without wishing it, keep me company along the somnambulating fifty yards to the public stand pipe, with the galvanized bucket in my hand. I would return to the nightmares and the riding horses in my turning dreams, and then, in the middle of peace and good "wet dreams," be awakened from the soaked bed mistaken for the school yard where we played, to be given six crispy fried flying fish, golden brown and hot with pepper.

"Nobody in this whirl should ever go to sleep hungry, boy," my mother always told me.

In the morning, it would be time enough to surrender my Cush-Cush mattress to the sun to dry. If my mother woke up "on the wrong side," I would surrender my body for a flogging, for wetting-up the bed. "You too old to be always pissing-up your bed!" The biology of the reason was never known to me; and my mother didn't care.

But the smells of Christmas! The new paint and varnish and the golden apples and the sugar-apples and mammy-apples; the ham which had come wrapped in tar paper, and which had to be soaked in water for days, before it was boiled; the great cake, soaked since Easter in rum; and the currants and raisins themselves soaked in rum along with the boiled peelings of grapefruit and orange; the coconut bread, the sponges and the puddings made with more eggs than I had seen our hens laying, and mixed by hand in one long night, and done in one day of baking: mixing the butter from Australia, rancid as the sheep of the Pampas that I would learn about in my Geography classes at Combermere; and the fresh artificial flowers and the Christmas dinner of roast pork with a crackling of dark brown flavored skin which you chewed in a boastful "chaw" for hours after the meal, and walked through the lanes of the Village as you chewed it, as if it was chewing gum; and rice and peas, and doved peas, and a thick porridge-like dish called "jug," something my mother told me had come "with her, from Africa;" and sweet potatoes and tomatoes and rivers of sorrel, one lip-wetting taste of rum, because "I don't want you to be growing-up liking rum, you hear me?" Rum was our national product. And then, after the meal, which we ate in silent, jaw-moving seriousness, because the rule in our house said you "don't talk whilst you have food in your mouth," my belly would be full and extended on this day of food, Foodmas; and at the end, I would literally have to be rolled on the floor, and my mother would rub down my belly with coconut oil. That was the way we ate on Christmas Day. It was as if it was our last meal on earth.

Briggs and Mickey and George-Ben and Johnny, my four friends, lived nearby. We would compare foods and presents, and plan to meet early on Boxing Day to run races.

"Wha' you get for Christmas?"

"Man, I ain't get nothing this time. My uncle in Amurca didn't send the letter."

"My mother give me a' apple. It come from Canada. It was wrap in a piece of paper that come from Canada, too. She pay a shilling for it in Town. I keeping it till Old Year's Day before I eat it."

"You not going eat it till then?"

"You is a fool? Nobody don't eat a Canadian apple the same day. My mother say yuh have to watch it for a few days."

"Tomorrow is races."

"I'm going to be a jockey."

"I is a horse!"

"Man, you can't be a horse, because you not fast enough. Man, you have to be a jockey!"

I do not remember getting presents wrapped in pretty paper at Christmas. The War was on. But after the War, there were other "wars" of money, "wars" of drought, "wars" of unemployment. Presents were never put under a tree. We never had Christmas trees in

175

my days. And of course, snow never fell, even at Christmas, so there were no white Christmases. But we all loved Bing Crosby, and tried to sing like him. We dreamed and sang, sang and dreamed, but never saw a white Christmas. The holly and the ivy were just words to us. We had all heard of a man named Father Christmas who brought presents for boys and girls. And Miss Smith always said that he brought presents for boys and girls who were good. I was therefore not in that choir of angels. But we had balloons and red bells made of crepe paper, which opened in frills, and which were pinned in the rafters where there were cobwebs my mother could not reach with her broom. It was my job to get the "snow" to put around the house, on Christmas Day. The "snow" came from the rock quarry in the Village. I would scrape up the whitest, prettiest marl, and put it in the back yard, and keep it under great security, until four o'clock Christmas morning. Then I would spread it around the house, from the front, leading up the single step made of limestone. The front step stood like a white sentry. All around the back, covering up the haphazard paths beaten back and forth by neighbors' feet to our house. And some was thrown under the chickens' coops to make them know it was Christmas.

The bells of the church began to ring half an hour before five o'clock. Five o'clock on Christmas morning when there were stars in Bethlehem and Barbados, was the time to test one's Christianity, one's charity, one's finery, one's successes in getting the new clothes in time, "home-made" by the freelance dressmakers and tailors who sprang up like weeds without apprenticeships, throughout the Village. Every piece of clothing, from the skin to the outside, that was worn to church on Christmas morning, had to be new, brand new, for this occasion. And after church, we caught the bus and went into Town, and walked through the multitude of people, to Queen's Park, to listen to the Police Band under the direction of Captain Raison, an Englishman. Captain Raison was the best-liked man in the country, on Christmas morning. He had turned military musicians of the Police Band into a band playing calypsoes, and Christmas carols with a beat. We would walk through the Park, no snow in sight, and show off our new tailored suits of jackets and short pants, and shirts made by women, by the dressmakers, who sometimes, in the rush of things, mistook our measurements for our sisters' and made us blouses instead.

We would walk soft and in pain from our new shiny, cheap John White shoes which had *English Made* printed at the sweated, bladdered sides. If you were a high school boy, you made pains, and bore the pains of your shoes, to be visible and conspicuous, creaking up and down with fresh bladders on your feet, and eating "cocks" and "comforts" and "sweeties" and black sugar cakes, and white sugar cakes, and red sugar cakes, and rolly-pollies, made by the local confectioners, the selling women who looked like birds of paradise on this bright God-spelling morning. *"Comforts, toffees, pack o' nuts! Look muh here! Who calling? You want me, young fellow?"* Their voices on Christmas morning in the park, was like the breath of love. This was the practice in those days when the War was raging overseas.

I would meet my girl on this Christmas morning, and walk her off to a side, away from the throbbing bass drum in the Police Band, playing "Good King Wenceslas" as if it was a fox trot, near the pens where the Agricultural Society kept birds and rabbits that were brown, for taunts and gifts of peanuts from children and from women in love. And I would tell her, with my heart brimful with new love:

> "Roses are red
> Violets are blue . . ."

That was the limit of my tender-hearted, teenaged serious courtship. That was the license for that age of prowess. She would smile and blush, and touch the frills of her new white frock, and laugh and chew the fresh roasted peanuts I had bought for her, out of my life-time savings, one bright shilling with a King's head on it, my pocket money on Christmas Day.

Our parents did not allow us to go to horse racing. Horse racing on the Garrison Pasture was for "big people"; adults and crooks, and women who "picked fares," and for pimps. The Garrison Pasture was known also as a place where men and women did "things" at night, when the moon wasn't shining. The Races were horses running round a circle of wooden rails, on grass. And shouting and betting; and fights. Men and women sold fruits and "sweets," and bets, and each other; and there would be gambling under make-shift tents: cards and dice and cursing. And there was never a Race-Day that didn't end in bloodshed, and tottering men who had lost their way home, from the kick of the "steam" and the "darrou" they had drunk from too many bottles.

"Man, fire one!"

"Gimme the kiss-me-arse snapglass and let me show yuh I can fire one with yuh, man!"

And all these people congregated in the middle of the Pasture, while the horses ran around them; and while the people betted money on games of chance, trying and failing to find the Ace of Spades, or one polished seed from under a tot.

They raised their heads from their fortunes, sometimes, when a race was being run. Once a boy was trampled by a horse, and the entire congregation of people cried and said, "Oh Jesus Christ, the horse kill-he dead, dead, dead, be-Jesus Christ!" And when the next race started, they forgot the boy.

But our races, the races we boys organized in our Village, were better. The girls made the silks for the jockeys, and the boys made the whips. The whips were made from the spines of the palm leaf and woven together by cord. The cord was dyed in many colors. At the end of our whips, we always had a piece of rubber. We called it the tongue. The colors for our whips, like the colors of our kites which came out around Easter, like harmless birds of prey, angry only at the trees and the telephone wires, were made from the juice of the berry of the spinach vine; and from soaking colored paper in water. Nobody had ever seen real dye.

The fastest boys were the "horses." A piece of strong string was tied around the waist, as the reins. Our race course was the distance round the main building of the Girls' School. No girl was allowed by us to be a jockey, or a "horse." We did not play with girls, on our Village "Race Day." We held derbies of ten or more "horses" with their jockeys running behind them at break-neck speed, and *brek-toe* speed, at full gallop round the rock-infested school house. The jockeys wore their caps with peaks turned up, because they thought it made them look like the real jockeys on the Garrison. Their silks were ordinary shirts, too big, pulled out from the waist so that they would billow in the wind. They were splashed with stripes and crosses and bright colors, made of sashes.

The "horses" and the jockeys stood at the tape, stomping the ground, foaming at the mouth, ready to tear around the school. The jockeys shouted, "Now, sir! Now, sir!" And some "horses" who forgot they were "horses," disagreed and shouted "Not yet, sir! Not yet sir!" because their trousers were falling down. Or because they saw a large rock planted savagely in the ground over which they had to run. After each race, these rocks took toll and nails out of our big toes. There would be toes with broken nails, and with no nails at all, and some with big pieces of flesh ripped out of them. And some of us now, have large flattened big toes, the result of these races round the St. Matthias Girls' School. . . .

Combermere was far from my mind these days. I went to the beach, with the boys, and sat in the sun all day, pretending to be a fisherman. We caught crabs and "sea-beefs" off the reefs, and from the black slimy pipe that ran for miles, it seemed, from the shore out far, on its way to Canada and America. Canada existed only in apples. Far out of view. The black slimy pipe was filled with the sewage of the Town and the hotels and the white people's homes. We would stand on this pipe and fall off, and pretend we were drowning, and shout, "Help, help! Helpppp!" and watch the men and the bigger boys come, like fish through the rough life-saving waves, doing *the crawl*. And then, we would dive from their view, and come up again, like a silent submarine, to emerge on the spluttering beach, catching our cocky breaths, laughing and screeling and jeering and bragging, "Man, I can swim like a shark! Drown, wha'?"

Once, the cockiest among us bragged, "Man, I could swim like a shark-and-a-half." He drowned the first week of the next vacation. And we buried him in the graveyard of the church beside the school. None of us went to the beach that vacation.

"Once upon a time, and a very long time, there was a boy who uses to go up the Hill every evening. And when all the people in the Village was cooking and cutting their food, and just before the sun went down behind the sea, this boy would shout-out, 'Wolf! Wolf!' and the people would run and leave their food, and run up the Hill to rescue the boy. And the boy would laugh, and say, 'How could there be a wolf? You ever heard of wolves in Barbados?' And the men and women would go back down the Hill. And the next evening, the boy would go up the Hill, to get his sheep, and when the sun went down, he would shout-out, 'Wolf! Wolf,' and the people would leave their food, and run up the Hill, and he would laugh and tell them no wolves ever lived in Barbados, and the people would go back down the Hill. And this went on for days and days. And one day when the sun had just gone down behind the sea, and the sky look dark, the boy screel-out, 'Wolf! Wolf! A real wolf!' And the people went on eating their food, and saying, 'That boy does really make we laugh. He going grow up to be a good comedian, one o' these days! Wolves in Barbados? He tell we so himself, more than one time, there ain't no wolves here. But that boy have a future as a comedian.' And the next morning, when the men and women went up the Hill to tie-out their sheep and goats, they saw an Alsatian dog eating-out the boy's guts. 'But I won't call this a wolf! You would call this a wolf?' I step 'pon the wire, and the wire won't bend, and that's the way my story end!"

Old Year's Night was the highest moment in our lives. Our mothers and every woman in the Village, our big sisters, aunts, uncles, and fathers, worked at some time, at some job, at the Marine Hotel.

The Marine Hotel was a huge building, white-washed in pink, with tall casuarina trees for miles and miles up in the blue sky; and at night, almost touching the stars which we counted, and never could count in our arithmetic of wonder, beyond five hundred, although the sages of little boys among us said, "If you ever count past five hundred stars, yuh going *dropdown* dead, yuh!" The women came home from the Marine, at all hours of the night, although it was just past nine. After midnight, was the time only ghosts and fowl-cock thieves walked the streets from the Marine, past the church which had a graveyard of dead Englishmen, and English vicars, and an English sailor which a tombstone called an "ensing." This Marine Hotel was our bread and butter. And when we ventured too close to its wall on Old Year's Night, the watchman, dressed in an old black jacket to suit the night, and rolled-up khaki trousers above the ankles, and who knew the lay and geography of each *glass-bottle* in the roads and lanes surrounding the grounds, this night-watchman would challenge us, and curse and say, "Where the arse wunnuh think wunnuh going?" And if we stood our ground, which we never did, and stated our mission, which he never accepted, we would end up running from him, with the fear of his bull-pistle in our back. We soon learned that we could take liberties with his responsibilities to guard the grounds of the Marine, only when he had a woman in the flower bed of blooming begonias.

On Old Year's Night, there would be balloons bigger and prettier and with faces painted on them, than we had ever seen before. And music played by the best dance bands in the country. Coe Alleyne's Orchestra, Percy Greene's Orchestra, and others. The music would be slipping over the high wall which was too high and too treacherous for us to climb. And we would stand, hundreds of boys and unemployed men, and some girls who were old enough to be out at night, and have boyfriends, and stand in the dew dressed in men's jackets, always black, to keep the dew from falling on our heads, and giving us consumption. Outside the free wall, we would dance to the music, and watch the white people inside, because the Marine was "blasted segregated." The men all wore black formal suits that turned them into undertakers. And the women were white in long dresses skating over the huge dance floor, slippery and dangerous from the waxing which the watchman had given it, the day before. "Woe be-tide the man who don't know a waltz from a trot, when he step 'pon that floor!" he would boast to us.

And we watched them from below the wall. And we dreamed of becoming powerful and rich, to join them, to be like them. The waiters, our "relatives," our family, are mingling among them now: men who were our fathers, uncles, and older brothers. And if we were looking at the right moment, we would see a wink cast in our direction, and in the wink, the promise of a turkey leg, or a rum, for the older boys. Perhaps, a funny hat, or a balloon that was not trampled at the stroke of midnight.

Once, one of them, braver than the watchman, and smarter, sneaked a leg of a turkey out to us, before the ball was over. And we chomped on the cold strange-tasting meat, all the way through "The Blue Danube," all the while making mincemeat with prettier steps than any of those trudging ladies and stumbling drunken gentlemen in the grand ballroom floor, waxed by the silent watchman standing some distance away from us.

Five minutes before midnight, it would become very quiet. Quiet like my old school, down the gap, fifty yards away, silent and asleep at this time of gravedigging darkness. The watchman would stand at attention. And when he knew that we had all seen him, he would walk through the midst of us like a general, like a plantation overseer; come right up to each one of us, twirling his stick like the drum-major in the Volunteer Forces, right in our faces, and say, "Don't mek no noise in front of the white people, you hear me?" Four minutes before midnight. And we can see the *musicianers* with their instruments at the ready, and the ladies and the gentlemen in the grand ballroom, skipping here and there, looking for husbands or for partners. And the lights would go off one by one, and suddenly the place is like a fairy-garden with only colored bulbs, and the balloons like beads of seawater on the skin. And then the counting in a collection of voices, ours and theirs inside. "Twelve . . . eleven . . . ten . . . nine . . ." The watchman refuses to join. All of us outside, counting in a Year that will bring us more War, and nothing like what it will bring the ladies and gentlemen on the other side of the wall. The counting is louder now. "Five . . . four . . ." And we continue to ignore the watchman, whom we had long ago nicknamed "Hitler." And suddenly he too joins in the counting. And then, on the stroke of midnight, the eruption of motorcar horns blowing, balloons popping; and waiting taxicabs honking, with a hint of deliberate impatience; and the ringing of bells, dinner bells and church bells; and the bursting of balloons, and the scuffling and fighting for the balloons thrown over the wall and floating in our direction; and the good fortune of a funny hat which has landed in our midst, and is barely destroyed, which we patched and for days afterwards, wore as a statement: "Man, you went to the Marine Old Year's Ball? I went, man. I got this hat. Look!" Or a noise-maker sneaked out from behind the wall, by a maid or a mother; and the boiled unsalted rice carried in paperbags; "them tourisses is people who suffer from sugar in the blood!"

We would walk back, happy, to our district, memorizing the night of magic and revelry and choruses and words to the most popular tune played by the Percy Greene Orchestra. *Goodnight Irene* . . .

"Percy blow that tenor sax like po'try, boy! You hear how he take them riffs in the first chorus? Pure po'try, boy!"

Day in and day out, I working my fingers to the bone in that blasted Marine, and I can't see myself getting nowhere for it. It's slavery. Tomorrow is Monday however, and the tourisses leffing. They going back up to Englund and Amurca. So, the hotel laying-off maids and butlers, left and right. You need school books. This Cawmere costing me a fortune in new books. I wonder where next term school fees coming from. If my sister in Panama don't send the little thing, boy, you *loss*. You seen the postman pass here recently? He pass for the week, yet? This Christmas you shouldda hear the amount o' money the people say the postmens thief. There ain't no money coming in this place, so I don't see how they could accuse the poor postmens, though. But it ain't no wonder if they thief, 'cause the Guvment pays them peanuts. Where am I going to get your school fees from this term, boy? Look! Come and write a letter to your aunt and find out what happen to the money-order she promise to send . . .

My mother sat at my elbow. I would smell the honor and the sweat of her hard labor. To write or to read was beyond the expectations the Village held out to her. Certain passages of the Bible she had probably learned by heart, she had them so often, at St. Matthias Girls' School, years before I was born. But she was careful that what she dictated to me to write down, was just what she said, and nothing more. She followed each turn and twist of the common pen with her eyes. Some marvelous instinct told her when I had completed a word; or when I ought to have done so.

The kerosene lamp was placed in the middle of the table. And she would squint her large beautiful eyes, just as we squinted ours at Combermere when we faced a difficult Latin word. The Bible was nearby. The Bible was always nearby. It was the only book, apart from mine, that was in our library. It was the only book I ever saw her look into: she would open the pages, turn her eyes up, and soon afterwards, fall asleep. The hieroglyphics of the printed word induced an opiate of slumber and weakness of the eyes. "Learn, learn," she always told me. "You must learn, son. You hear me? Learn. Learning is next to godliness."

The writing paper was fine, *English Made*, and suitable for air mail correspondence (we never wrote a local letter: we would walk with that message, or give it verbally, to a friend, to give to a friend, to give to the person. I never could understand why). The bottle of Quink ink was *English Made*. The pen nib was ready to be dipped into the rich majestic blue liquid, and I was ready to begin. . . .

"Yuh didn't forget the day o' the mont', eh, son?" She pronounced it *day-de-munt*. "And write pretty like how Mr. Thorpe at St. Matthias teach you." She then dictated the salutation:

My dear Aunt Eloise, I hope that the reaches of these few lines will find you in a perfect state of good health, as they leave me feeling fairly well at present.

No request for money, no matter how small, or large, or serious, or frivolous, could be made before these "presents" were communicated with sincerity and respect to my Aunt Ella. She had gone from our midst years and years ago, even before I was born. But Aunt Ella had remembered me and my mother. From the first memory of time, sitting at the table always covered by a cloth of many colors, during the week; and by a white linen cloth on Sunday (which she said she had "borrowed" from the Marine!), I would write this monthly dictation of love and respect and request. From that time, and until the time I would leave the country, a letter came to us, with the strange postage stamps of the Unites States of America, in an envelope of red, white, and blue trim, with waves of lines to show where and when it had been posted across the seas in the Canal Zone, and when it arrived in the Post Office, in the Public Buildings in Town. And it always contained a money order for five American dollars.

At Easter and at Christmas, it was ten dollars. Sometimes, she sent twenty.

My mother always dictated phrases like, "As I take this pen in hand, to write you these tidings," and "I am, dear Aunt Eloise, your loving nephew," in the letters to Aunt Ella.

Aunt Ella sent us a picture of herself, once. My mother said, "Boy, this is the woman who sending you to Cawmere. Kiss the ground she walk on, boy. Respect her." The picture showed her in a long dress, with a smile on her face, and something in her hand. She looked like my mother. My mother said, "She more older than me, though." But my mother never told me how old she was. And I never asked. Not even to this day. My mother was always telling me, "Ask no questions, hear no lies!" Or she would say, "Dogs amongst doctors," which puzzled me. When that was said, *Dog amongst doctors,* by an older person, I knew instinctively that it was time for me to leave the adults to themselves, and seek my own level of company. I never did find out, nor appreciate the association the old people made between dogs and doctors. It would be years before I would come across signs which read, *Indians and dogs not allowed,* and *Blacks and dogs not allowed!*

Hitler must have been winning the War. For all of a sudden sugar which we produced, was rationed. It became almost impossible to get, and very difficult to buy, unless the shopkeeper liked you. Flour, rice, corn meal for making *coucou,* a delicious weekend delicacy; matches; butter from Australia, salt beef, and English potatoes, all of a sudden, these foodstuffs disappeared from Barbados. Delcina chose as her morning working hymn, one written for the burial of the dead. *Now the Laborer's task is o'er.*

People in the Village counted the number of dead at sea. They memorized the famous battles; and the names of the local dead, in the air, serving with the Royal Air Force; for some of our men were now flying in the air, like birds, Delcina said, all over Germany. But those who fought on land, took the heaviest toll.

When Delcina heard all these news, she raised her voice higher, and sweeter, singing the burial of the dead.

There the tears of earth are dried;
There its hidden things are clear;
There the work of life is tried
By a juster Judge than here.
Father, in Thy gracious keeping
Leave we now Thy servant sleeping.

"And in case none of wunnuh don't know, I singing Hymn number four hundred and one, in *Hymns Ancient and Modern!*" she told the Village. Food became as scarce as the news of victories. Every night, on the BBC World News, we listened to the voice of Winston Churchill.

We turned to the green bushes among us. "If you don't have a horse," my mother said, "ride a cow." So, we made teas from the bushes we normally left growing wild. Miraculous Bush, made into tea, was all of a sudden, discovered to be good for the bowels. We ground sweet potatoes into flour. We processed, with the help of some homemade graters, cassava root. Both the "poisonous" cassava, and the "sweet" cassava; and we turned these formerly despised roots, into the most delicious *staple foods*. We had to turn our kerosene lamps down, if not out, at a certain time at night. Blackouts reached us from up in the Mother Country, and from the various "theaters of war." The Germans, the British said, were now in Caribbean waters. We got scared. *Sireens* sounded throughout the night, throughout the country. Searchlights would point into the sky at nightfall, and we would follow the line, and imagine German planes in it, and shoot them down, with our mouths. The three or four hundred men who were enlisted in the Barbados Volunteer Force were called into barracks, at the Garrison, to live and to prepare themselves for the defense of the British Empire, and to eat bully-beef and biscuits. All of a sudden we had an Army. The Police were put on alert. Sea-scouts became self-important, as they were taken deeper out into the Harbor, and told a few things by the Harbor Police. And our leader, Grantley Adams, sent a cable up to the King, His Brittanical Majestical George the Sixth, King of England, Northern Ireland, and the

British Possessions Beyond the Seas, and told the King, *"Go on England, Little England is behind you."* And from that day, we were known, with pride or with embarrassment, as "Little England."

The ships which contained our new school books, and the corn beef and the butter from Australia, were sunk on the black oily seas between here and there. Students at high schools, began to borrow text books, and copy out the entire books in longhand. Hitler, the watchman at the Marine, was fired. He was caught by the head watchman with a paperbag of flour. He said he was taking it for his wife and seven children. The women in the Village clapped their hands and said, "Serve the bastard right! Hitler used to report us for bringing out a chicken wing from the Marine! The thiefing bitch!"

We continued to write the names of German generals, and paint swastikas along the church wall. Some of my friends who were still under the headmastership of Mr. Ward said the list of the dead and the list of the lost at sea, grew longer every morning. Assemblies at morning were spent reading out these lists of the dead, and singing "Ride on, in Majesty," and in floggings.

And all of a sudden, at Combermere, a stranger appeared among us. Our new Headmaster. He was a drill sergeant of a man. For discipline, and for "administering" public floggings. We likened him to Himmler. He was military in bearing, tall as a casuarina tree in the grounds at the Marine; severe and cruel, both in looks and action. He became overnight the Gestapo of the secondary schools in the country. According to those masters who feared him, and disliked him, he was a man (some called him, in our hearing, "That tall lanky Limey") recently demobilized from the British Army, Colonial, Dominion & Overseas. He looked as devastating in his moustache, as Barclays Bank in Town. He had the un-Barbadian name of Major Noot! We did not know whether he was a Christian-minded man like our dear former Headmaster, the Reverend Armstrong. But he conducted Prayers in the Hall, and made us sing hymns only, from the book, *Hymns Ancient and Modern*, as the Reverend used to do. He was a severe-looking man. For the five years I was at Combermere, I never saw him dressed in anything but the suit of British Officer's khaki, without pips. He would thunder down the corridors in brown boots made from dead alligators or dead elephants. I always thought of thunder when I saw him coming. I did not think he liked any of us. We did not hate him. We didn't see him as a human being. He was an Englishman, sent down to us by the King, or by our leader, or by Churchill. We saw him as an Englishman. He drank more rum in one day than anybody else on the teaching staff. He liked rum and water and ice in a short glass.

My life became more ordered and organized during those tough War days. At five minutes to nine, we assembled in the Hall. We sat murmuring the tragedies and achievements of our little world, under our breaths. We sat on long wooden benches without backs, built by the school carpenter, and we whispered our plans and aspirations for the day. One day was like the next. Lists of the dead at sea, in the air, and on land. We talked like ventriloquists so that the school prefects at the head of the rows of benches would not give us "demerits for talking at Prayers." The assistant masters stood against the south wall, and looked bored. Major Noot had pinned a command on the Notice Board: it ordered *all* assistant masters out of the Common Room, where they played draughts, or threw dice, or talked about the women and the men of the previous night; made them come to Prayers. The first morning after this command, we saw several assistant masters for the first time in years. We thought some of them had been in wheel chairs in all this time of absence from Prayers.

Five hundred of us sang hymns ancient and modern every morning, listened to the short prayers from the *Book of Common Prayer*, heard about the King and his ministers, and that they should be spared from the Germans to lead us better, and then we were "dismissed."

When the Major wanted to "administer" a public flogging, the Lower School was "dismissed." The War was still raging overseas. The only evidence we had of it at Combermere, was the Major's British khaki uniform without the pips of rank. This strange Englishman, this Major formerly of the British Army, read no notices of the War at Assembly; and he did not show us the deeds and the exploits of the Allies. He seemed to know that the War had taken a turn for the worse, for the Allies. School now became a regiment. At St. Matthias, the headmaster was still ringing his dinner bell. Two teachers would pull out the large Map of the World, in front of all the boys. Then the headmaster showed them the current "theaters of war."

"Now, boys, what is the capital of Englan'?"

At the top of their voices the boys are still yelling, "London!"

"And who is the Allies?"

"Englunt and Russia and the British Empire, sir!"

The headmaster would still be smiling; and he is still running his chalk-covered hand, with the tuning fork in it, his beloved tuning fork, over the wide expanse of the millions of square miles, painted in red.

"What my hand passing over, boys?"

"The British Empire, sir!"

They know, as I knew it, with their eyes shut.

The headmaster is still smiling in that school, and looking gratified. He is smiling as if he is the owner of this vast empire of land, known to them by name and by position of a map.

"That is why the sun can never set on the British Empire!"

All those strange countries and strange cities and strange people, whose languages we did not know, but whose positions on the Map of the World, I was taught to learn by heart!

Sometimes, in a good mood, when his roses had won the First Prize at the annual Agricultural Exhibition, or when he had flogged half of the school with his soaked black snake, and was perspiring and was washed of whatever torment he had brought from his home that morning, my old headmaster would gather a few of us, the "good boys," round the Globe, and spin it around on its axis like a top, according to the geography book we read, and would complete for us, one revolution, in a slow spin. And we would see only the red of the British Empire to our unbelieving eyes. So large an Empire, to which the headmaster told us, we belonged as free people! *Our Empire!*

But the Major did not tell us we belonged to the Empire, not in that way.

Prefects, take posts!

It was a hot Monday morning. It had rained all weekend. Our school uniforms were damp. The school became silent and stiff. Like a concentration camp. The Head Boy and the Assistant Head Boy took up their positions, on either side of the headmaster's table, on the platform. The Major stood like a general in the middle of the platform. Behind him, I saw the three large French windows, always open to let in a breeze from the playing field, and from the canal at the edge of the playing field. The canal flowed slowly, floating the silt and the guts and the bodies of dead frogs and chickens, and children killed before birth, so some boys who lived in that district, said. It curdled our blood to hear such stories.

The Major was now like Goebbels. People were talking in whispers about the Jews and the concentration camps. It was mentioned one night, at the end of the BBC World Service News. The House Captains (we called the Houses, "sets"; A, B, C, and D), and the prefects stood in front of the platform, on our level, facing the trembling "culprits," those boys who were to be flogged publicly. The Assembly was now quiet, as a court-martial.

Suddenly, the shouts and laughter and the screams of students from the private school across the street, came in on us. We envied their rejoicing and softer discipline. A passenger bus changed gears and when the motor was quieter, we heard shouts and cursing, and a hawker singing out, "Get your okras, yuh yams, yuh nice bananas . . . . You want me, mistress?"

The Major was furious.

"Armstrong R. D., mentioned three times, *four* strokes!" he bellowed.

And little Armstrong tried to pull his shirt as far out of his pants as he could in the short frightening time from the benches to the steps of the guillotine. As he climbed the scaffold of three steps, he loosened his belt. If he had more time, he would have wet his face at the tap, in crocodile tears, and put himself at the mercy of the court; and hope that the sound of the tamarind rod on his damp mildewed khaki uniform would make such a loud noise and fool the Major General. But the Major intended to brutalize the small boy.

We sat and anticipated the force and the venom of the falling tamarind rod. We counted the number of blows with our eyes closed. Armstrong's eyes were closed even more tightly after the first blow.

But we knew that Armstrong was tough, was a "man." He was brave. He was not going to be a little boy, and cry. Not in front of three hundred boys . . . .

> . . . one afternoon after school, when the headmaster had already marched across the field to his house, one of the small "bad" boys got a Gillette razor, and "broke-and-entered" the headmaster's office. He got hold of the collection of freshly cut, and trimmed tamarind rods. The headmaster kept them on the top of the cupboard which contained the texts of the French course he taught in the Fifth Form. This "bad" boy, now a school hero, screwed each rod in the middle, just deep enough below the brown skin, to make them weak and breakable in the Major's hand. At the next "administering" of a public flogging, we all laughed under our breaths. The older boys said that it was after that, that the headmaster commanded the porter to get bamboo to flog us with. He had served in the Malaya theater of war, the Head Boy told us . . . .

. . . the tamarind rod breaks in his hand, after it flashes back from Armstrong's back. We laugh, because some boy has put a tamarind rod in between the bamboo. But just as fast, we are sad again, as the headmaster chooses one long, willowy bamboo from the collection on his table, with the *Book of Common Prayer*.

The last boy who faced the Major that morning, was mentioned thirty-six times. He got thirty-seven lashes, for having been mentioned thirty-six dishonorable times. And when the Major's hand fell on the boy's black backside, it was no less vicious and stinging than the first blow which Armstrong's khaki pants had reported more than one hour earlier.

That morning I became very sad for the freedom of our country. I wondered if the War would ever end. I waited for the BBC World Service News to tell me when Hitler was going to blow the Allies from the North Atlantic. I wondered when this demobilized Major was going to take a boat and sail back to England?

At the soaked end of the morning, we were all crying real tears: those who were flogged and those who had escaped the Major's wrath. A young very popular master, pretty with a football at centerforward, as he was pretty with a cover drive on the cricket pitch, broke down and cried. He cried in front of us all. He had been made to stand and witness his brother receive thirteen of the most vicious blows anybody outside of a prison or a slave plantation, or a movie about penal institutions, had ever received. *That tall lanky Limey!*

I was now in the third form. Life was becoming even more serious. A civil servant, a sanitary inspector, an overseer, an elementary school teacher, were coming into the focus of my educational accomplishments. I was under a chloroform of learning things which made no immediate and applied sense. Trigonometry was too hard for my head. We were introduced to the prose of Julius Caesar; and the verse of Virgil. A master who taught us English Literature, ranted and raved before us, in his love for Keats and Byron and Shelley and Milton. I wondered about my aunt Ella, in the Canal Zone alone, and without the Empire to protect her. Did my letter get through the German blockade? And I wondered about Milton, a boy in my village, who did not know about paradise, lost and regained, and who was not blind, and who was an expert at killing lizards and ground-doves. "You'll remain the savages you are, if you don't read the English poets!" I wondered whether Milton knew there was another Milton.

We learned French.

Je suis, tu suis, il suit . . .

"How many years have you, man?"

"I have thirteen, old man!"

"How are you carrying yourself?"

"I see you remember the reflective verb!"

"I carrying myself well, old man!"

The cow that jumped over the moon, and Mr. Twirly and Mr. Twisty the two English screws, were now years behind me, in elementary school. We learned "big" things at Combermere. Now, we memorized things about a Grecian urn; learned about a man with "resolution and independence" who walked beside a sea and picked up seashells. We picked welts and "sea-beefs," ourselves. The fools in our Village and the doatish old women had been doing this all their lives, and nobody in Barbados wrote a poem about their antics. They were committed to the Jenkins Mental Hospital. Hannibal, whom we loved (and no one told us he was black like us!), climbed mountains, and was smart. Alas, he lost one eye: *in occulo altero.* But he had crossed the Alps, one of the highest mountain ranges in the *whole whirl!* We loved Hannibal. The name was pure romance and "poultry" in our mouths. We named our pets and our favorites at home, Hannibal; and we walked about the school yard spouting *impedimenta* and *transgresserat,* and when we couldn't remember more by heart, we settled on *depuis longtemps.* We continued asking ourselves, "How many years have you?" And in all this time, not a word about the Allies and their fights and battles, from the British Major. We didn't know at first, that Mussolini was an Italian, a Roman. All the Italians we knew, were in books, dead; speaking a dead language; and wearing togas, and eating while lying on their sides; grapes from a bunch and wine from an urn. So, why a Grecian urn, and not a Roman one? We in Barbados, drank rum. We loved the Italians (and hated Mussolini) because they were like us; like the men in our Village, who loved rum and women more than work. And the Romans like our own men, talked and sang hymns ancient and modern, all drunklong. In Geography classes, we learned the exact place where the rancid butter we ate came from; and the potatoes which we called "English" potatoes; and the rotten, "high" skinny-bodied salt fish: Australia, Idaho and Newfoundland. We didn't realize Newfoundland was a part of Canada. We had heard that some of our men had emigrated there, to love and to live and to work and to die in the snow building a fort and squatting in a place named Africville, on gifts of land that was rocks. Sailors from English ships in the Harbor, came among us, and kicked us, and bruised our shins, and called us *darkies;* and didn't say "Sorry, old boy!" as we had been taught to say, on the playing field, by the British Major. We played against them, and beat them. They sometimes refused to obey the Umpire's decision. It was not the same game we were taught. But they were English, the Mother Country's men who were giving up their lives, "on beaches, in trenches" to keep us safe and free; and the entire world civilized and democratic.

One afternoon, I stood beside one of these English sailors, on the touchline of the football field at Combermere. He had a hand of bananas in his hand. Ten fat and juicy things. As the game progressed, I saw him eat all of them, except one. Then with a flick of his hairy wrist he threw the banana thirty yards into the canal. It would take days to float among the other obstacles in the foul water, unmolested down into the Harbor to the sea, where his man-of-war lay sleeping in Carlisle Bay. His arms were hairy like the monkeys' in our books. His arms had many blue-painted pictures on them. They looked like arrows piercing a heart; and some were naked women; and there was one picture that looked like a coat of arms. His skin was pale. I could see beneath the skin.

"I say, old chap," he said to me, "are there any whores, nearby?"

Even at this young witnessing time, I knew from the schoolboy gossip of adult matters, that the whores in Town did not like the English sailors. "Them Limeys? They are too blasted cheap!" With the help of the whores' experiences, we knew that the English was a strange tribe of a different kind. The English were cheap, the whores said. Cheapness came to mean, English. But in the classes at Combermere, we were taught that the best things were made by the English. *English Made. Made in England.* The clothes we wore; the books we read; the pencils we wrote with; the Quink ink; the book bags; the combs made from tortoise shell, which were too fine-toothed for our thick brand of hair; the medicines, and the Ferrol; the Wincarnis Wine which every self-respecting mother gave to her son, as a tonic, one spoonful every morning; and the ties around the necks; the perfumes, Evening in Paris and Cush-Cush; the skin powders and the Brilliantine which made our heads shine like stars, slicked-back, concealing the African kink in our hair. *Rule Britannia, Britannia rules the waves . . .*

> *For advertisers, the turn-of-the century fad for all things imperial was a god-send. The Empire was a permanent source of second-hand excitement, a stage show of exploration and warfare with all suffering either romanticized or removed. In the clothes suggested by the "Queen, Empire, and British Character," manufacturers had ideal material: dramatic, colorful, and flattering to patriotic self-esteem.*

The mustard in the bright yellow tin of Coleman's Mustard, with its red lettering, was used in our kitchen. But more often, the tin was acquired, already empty. She would wash it clean with Sunlight Soap, from the memory of Queen Victoria, because it was the best soap sold in Barbados. At this time, there was another Britannic Majesty on the Throne of England, George the Sixth however, but the people who made Sunlight were "soap makers by special appointment to Her Majesty," and they forgot to change the boast, when a new Monarch came along.

My mother bathed me herself, every first Sunday of the month, in a large tub made of wallaba wood, made in England; and scrubbed me clean with Pears Soap, made in England. Once, I saw the soap before it was opened from its wrapping, and I read in amazement and wonder, the short history on its label. *Nelson the hero of Trafalgar and Pears Soap have become the most familiar names in the English language.* I knew Nelson. He was the man who had shouted "England expects every man to do his duty!" He was shot by a cannon ball, and dying on a ship when he said these brave words. At that time, I did not know he was a fornicator. Had Miss Smith, my Sunday School teacher, who liked Nelson also, known this, she would have closed the book on his sin. She would have prayed for him, too. This expectation of duty was written in the history book, and at the base of the statue of Nelson, which stands in the middle of our capital, Bridgetown, looking out to sea, "to see what he can see," as we used to say when we passed the statue in Town. Nelson was dead hundreds of years before, but every small boy in Barbados giggled and laughed in the suds of Nelson's memory and history; and we would stand in the middle of a fishing boat, or perhaps with luck in life, on the deck of a schooner, and shout, "England expects every man to do his duty!" We were English. The allegiance and the patriotism that Mr. Grantley Adams had imprisoned us with, had been cabled to the Colonial Office in London. We were the English of Little England. Little black Englishmen.

Our masters at Combermere spoke with the accents of the gentlemen of England. When one of the younger masters passed the examination, the Intermediate to the Bachelor of Arts Degree, *External,* an examination which was set and corrected in England, all of a sudden he became very intelligent and educated. He spoke with an Englishman's accent. Because he was educated, and because he was our master, and because we too wanted to be educated, we therefore talked like little black Englishmen.

We had in our midst, the Major, a real, "true-true" Englishman, on whom to pattern the strange inflections of spoken English. We could not know at the time, because of the vast Atlantic which separated us from England, that the educated English speech we were imitating, was really working-class London fishsellers' speech. We, the black aristocracy of an unfree society, exchanged our native speech, for English working-class patois!

"Journey Back to the Source"

ALEJO CARPENTIER
(CUBA)

I

*"W*hat d'you want, pop?"

Again and again came the question, from high up on the scaffolding. But the old man made no reply. He moved from one place to another, prying into corners and uttering a lengthy monologue of incomprehensible remarks. The tiles had already been taken down, and now covered the dead flower beds with their mosaic of baked clay. Overhead, blocks of masonry were being loosened with picks and sent rolling down wooden gutters in an avalanche of lime and plaster. And through the crenellations that were one by one indenting the walls, were appearing—denuded of their privacy—oval or square ceilings, cornices, garlands, dentils, astragals, and paper hanging from the walls like old skins being sloughed by a snake.

Witnessing the demolition, a Ceres with a broken nose and discolored peplum, her headdress of corn veined with black, stood in the back yard above her fountain of crumbling grotesques. Visited by shafts of sunlight piercing the shadows, the gray fish in the basin yawned in the warm weed-covered water, watching with round eyes the black silhouettes of the workmen against the brilliance of the sky as they diminished the centuries-old height of the house. The old man had sat down at the foot of the statue, resting his chin on his stick. He watched buckets filled with precious fragments ascending and descending. Muted sounds from the street could be heard, while overhead, against a basic rhythm of steel on stone, the pulleys screeched unpleasantly in chorus, like harsh-voiced birds.

The clock struck five. The cornices and entablatures were depopulated. Nothing was left behind but stepladders, ready for tomorrow's onslaught. The air grew cooler, now that it was disburdened of sweat, oaths, creaking ropes, axles crying out for the oil can, and the slapping of hands on greasy torsos. Dusk had settled earlier on the dismantled house. The shadows had enfolded it just at that moment when the now-fallen upper balustrade used to enrich the façade by capturing the sun's last beams. Ceres tightened her lips. For the first time the rooms would sleep unshuttered, gazing onto a landscape of rubble.

Contradicting their natural propensities, several capitals lay in the grass, their acanthus leaves asserting their vegetable status. A creeper stretched adventurous tendrils toward an Ionic scroll, attracted by its air of kinship. When night fell, the house was closer to the ground. Upstairs, the frame of a door still stood erect, slabs of darkness suspended from its dislocated hinges.

II

Then the old Negro, who had not stirred, began making strange movements with his stick, whirling it around above a graveyard of paving stones.

The white and black marble squares flew to the floors and covered them. Stones leaped up and unerringly filled the gaps in the walls. The nail-studded walnut doors fitted themselves into their frames, while the screws rapidly twisted back into the holes in the hinges. In the dead flower beds, the fragments of tile were lifted by the thirst of growing flowers and joined together, raising a sonorous whirlwind of clay, to fall like rain on the framework of the roof. The house grew, once more assuming its normal proportions, modestly clothed. Ceres became less gray. There were more fish in the fountain. And the gurgling water summoned forgotten begonias back to life.

The old man inserted a key into the lock of the front door and began to open the windows. His heels made a hollow sound. When he lighted the lamps, a yellow tremor ran over the oil paint of the family portraits, and people dressed in black talked softly in all the corridors, to the rhythm of spoons stirring cups of chocolate.

Don Marcial, Marqués de Capellanías, lay on his deathbed, his breast blazing with decorations, while four tapers with long beards of melted wax kept guard over him.

III

The candles lengthened slowly, gradually guttering less and less. When they had reached full size, the nun extinguished them and took away the light. The wicks whitened, throwing off red sparks. The house emptied itself of visitors and their carriages drove away in the darkness. Don Marcial fingered an invisible keyboard and opened his eyes.

The confused heap of rafters gradually went back into place. Medicine bottles, tassels from brocades, the scapulary beside the bed, daguerreotypes, and iron palm leaves from the grille emerged from the mists. When the doctor shook his head with an expression of professional gloom, the invalid felt better. He slept for several hours and awoke under the black beetle-browed gaze of Father Anastasio. What had begun as a candid, detailed confession of his many sins grew gradually more reticent, painful, and full of evasions. After all, what right had the Carmelite to interfere in his life?

Suddenly Don Marcial found himself thrown into the middle of the room. Relieved of the pressure on his temples, he stood up with surprising agility. The naked woman who had been stretching herself on the brocade coverlet began to look for her petticoats and bodices, and soon afterward disappeared in a rustle of silk and a waft of perfume. In the closed carriage downstairs an envelope full of gold coins was lying on the brass-studded seat.

Don Marcial was not feeling well. When he straightened his cravat before the pier glass he saw that his face was congested. He went downstairs to his study where lawyers—attorneys and their clerks— were waiting for him to arrange for the sale of the house by auction.

All his efforts had been in vain. His property would go to the highest bidder, to the rhythm of a hammer striking the table. He bowed, and they left him alone. He thought how mysterious were written words: those black threads weaving and unweaving, and covering large sheets of paper with a filigree of estimates; weaving and unweaving contracts, oaths, agreements, evidence, declarations, names, titles, dates, lands, trees, and stones; a tangled skein of threads, drawn from the inkpot to ensnare the legs of any man who took a path disapproved of by the Law; a noose around his neck to stifle free speech at its first dreaded sound. He had been betrayed by his signature; it had handed him over to the nets and labyrinths of documents. Thus constricted, the man of flesh and blood had become a man of paper.

It was dawn. The dining-room clock had just struck six in the evening.

IV

The months of mourning passed under the shadow of ever-increasing remorse. At first the idea of bringing a woman to his room had seemed quite reasonable. But little by little the desire excited by a new body gave way to increasing scruples, which ended as self-torment. One night, Don Marcial beat himself with a strap till the blood came, only to experience even intenser desire, though it was of short duration.

It was at this time that the Marquesa returned one afternoon from a drive along the banks of the Almendares. The manes of the horses harnessed to her carriage were damp with solely their own sweat. Yet they spent the rest of the day kicking the wooden walls of their stable as if maddened by the stillness of the low-hanging clouds.

At dusk, a jar full of water broke in the Marquesa's bathroom. Then the May rains came and overflowed the lake. And the old Negress who unhappily was a maroon and kept pigeons under her bed wandered through the patio, muttering to herself: "Never trust rivers, my girl; never trust anything green and flowing!" Not a day passed without water making its presence felt. But in the end that presence amounted to no more than a cup spilled over a Paris dress after the anniversary ball given by the Governor of the Colony.

Many relatives reappeared. Many friends came back again. The chandeliers in the great drawing room glittered with brilliant lights. The cracks in the façade were closing up, one by one. The piano became a clavichord. The palm trees lost some of their rings. The creepers let go of the upper cornice. The dark circles around Ceres' eyes disappeared, and the capitals of the columns looked as if they had been freshly carved. Marcial was more ardent now, and often passed whole afternoons embracing the Marquesa. Crow's-feet, frowns, and double chins vanished, and flesh grew firm again. One day the smell of fresh paint filled the house.

V

Their embarrassment was real. Each night the leaves of the screens opened a little farther, and skirts fell to the floor in obscurer corners of the room, revealing yet more barriers of lace. At last the Marquesa blew out the lamps. Only Marcial's voice was heard in the darkness.

They left for the sugar plantation in a long procession of carriages—sorrel hindquarters, silver bits, and varnished leather gleamed in the sunshine. But among the pasqueflowers empurpling the arcades leading up to the house, they realized that they scarcely knew each other. Marcial gave permission for a performance of native dancers and drummers, by way of entertainment during those days impregnated with the smells of eau de cologne, of baths spiced with benzoin, of unloosened hair and sheets taken from closets and unfolded to let a bunch of vetiver drop onto the tiled floor. The steam of cane juice and the sound of the angelus mingled on the breeze. The vultures flew low, heralding a sparse shower, whose first large echoing drops were absorbed by tiles so dry that they gave off a diapason like copper.

After a dawn prolonged by an inexpert embrace, they returned together to the city with their misunderstandings settled and the wound healed. The Marquesa changed her traveling dress for a wedding gown and the married pair went to church according to custom, to regain their freedom. Relations and friends received their presents back again, and they all set off for home with jingling brass and a display of splendid trappings. Marcial went on visiting María de las Mercedes for a while, until the day when the rings were taken to the goldsmiths to have their inscriptions removed. For Marcial, a new life was beginning. In the house with the high grilles, an Italian Venus was set up in place of Ceres, and the grotesques in the fountain were thrown into almost imperceptibly sharper relief because the lamps were still glowing when dawn colored the sky.

VI

One night, after drinking heavily and being sickened by the stale tobacco smoke left behind by his friends, Marcial had the strange sensation that all the clocks in the house were striking five, then half past four, then four, then half past three ... It was as if he had become dimly aware of other possibilities. Just as, when exhausted by sleep-lessness, one may believe that one could walk on the ceiling, with the floor for a ceiling and the furniture firmly fixed between the beams. It was only a fleeting impression, and did not leave the smallest trace on his mind, for he was not much given to meditation at the time.

And a splendid evening party was given in the music room on the day he achieved minority. He was delighted to know that his signature was no longer legally valid, and that worm-eaten registers and docu-ments would now vanish from his world. He had reached the point at which courts of justice were no longer to be feared, because his bodily existence was ignored by the Law. After getting tipsy on noble wines, the young people took down from the wall a guitar inlaid with mother-of-pearl, a psaltery, and a serpent. Someone wound up the clock that played the *ranz-des-vaches* and the "Ballad of the Scottish Lakes." Someone else blew on a hunting horn that had been lying curled in copper sleep on the crimson felt lining of the showcase, beside a transverse flute brought from Aranjuez. Marcial, who was boldly making love to Señora de Campoflorido, joined in the cacoph-ony, and tried to pick out the tune of "Trípili-Trápala" on the piano, to a discordant accompaniment in the bass.

Then they all trooped upstairs to the attic, remembering that the liveries and clothes of the Capellanías family had been stored away under its peeling beams. On shelves frosted with camphor lay court dresses, an ambassador's sword, several padded military jackets, the vestment of a dignitary of the Church, and some long cassocks with damask buttons and damp stains among their folds. The dark shadows of the attic were variegated with the colors of amaranthine ribbons, yellow crinolines, faded tunics, and velvet flowers. A picaresque *chispero's* costume and hair net trimmed with tassels, once made for a carnival masquerade, was greeted with applause. Señora de Campoflorido swathed her powdered shoulders in a shawl the color of a Creole's skin, once worn by a certain ancestress on an evening of important family decisions in hopes of reviving the sleeping ardor of some rich trustee of a convent of Clares.

As soon as they were dressed up, the young people went back to the music room. Marcial, who was wearing an alderman's hat, struck the floor three times with a stick and announced that they would begin with a waltz, a dance mothers thought terribly improper for young ladies because they had to allow themselves to be taken round the waist, with a man's hand resting on the busks of the stays they had all had made according to the latest model in *Jardin des Modes*. The doorways were blocked by maidservants, stableboys, and waiters, who had come from remote outbuildings and stifling basements to enjoy the boisterous fun. Afterward they played blindman's buff and hide-and-seek. Hidden behind a Chinese screen with Señora de Campoflorido, Marcial planted a kiss on her neck, and received in return a scented handkerchief whose Brussels lace still retained the sweet warmth of her low-necked bodice.

And when the girls left in the fading light of dusk, to return to castles and towers silhouetted in dark gray against the sea, the young men went to the dance hall where alluring *mulatas* in heavy bracelets were strutting about without ever losing their high-heeled shoes, even in the frenzy of the guaracha. And it was carnival time, the members of the Arara Chapter Three Eyes Band were raising thunder on their drums behind the wall in a patio planted with pomegranate trees. Climbing onto tables and stools, Marcial and his friends applauded the gracefulness of a Negress with graying hair, who had recovered her beauty and almost become desirable as she danced, looking over her shoulder with an expression of proud disdain.

VII

The visits of Don Abundio, the family notary and executor, were more frequent now. He used to sit gravely down beside Marcial's bed, and let his acana-wood cane drop to the floor so as to wake him up in good time. Opening his eyes, Marcial saw an alpaca frock coat covered with dandruff, its sleeves shiny from collecting securities and rents. All that was left in the end was an adequate pension, calculated to put a stop to all wild extravagance. It was at this time that Marcial wanted to enter the Royal Seminary of San Carlos.

After doing only moderately well in his examinations, he attended courses of lectures, but understood less and less of his master's explanations. The world of his ideas was gradually growing emptier. What had once been a general assembly of peplums, doublets, ruffs, and periwigs, of controversialists and debaters, now looked as lifeless as a museum of wax figures. Marcial contented himself with a scholastic analysis of the systems, and accepted everything he found in a book as the truth. The words "Lion," "Ostrich," "Whale," "Jaguar" were printed under the copper-plate engravings in his natural history book. Just as "Aristotle," "St. Thomas," "Bacon," and "Descartes" headed pages black with boring, close-printed accounts of different interpretations of the universe. Bit by bit, Marcial stopped trying to learn these things, and felt relieved of a heavy burden. His mind grew gay and lively, understanding things in a purely instinctive way. Why think about the prism, when the clear winter light brought out all the details in the fortresses guarding the port? An apple falling from a tree tempted one to bite it—that was all. A foot in a bathtub was merely a foot in a bathtub. The day he left the seminary he forgot all his books. A gnomon was back in the category of goblins; a spectrum a synonym for a phantom; and an octandrian an animal armed with spines.

More than once he had hurried off with a troubled heart to visit the women who whispered behind blue doors under the town walls. The memory of one of them, who wore embroidered slippers and a sprig of sweet basil behind her ear, pursued him on hot evenings like the toothache. But one day his confessor's anger and threats reduced him to terrified tears. He threw himself for the last time between those

infernal sheets, and then forever renounced his detours through unfre-
quented streets and that last-minute faintheartedness which sent him
home in a rage, turning his back on a certain crack in the pavement—the
signal, when he was walking with head bent, that he must turn and enter
the perfumed threshold.

Now he was undergoing a spiritual crisis, peopled by religious
images, paschal lambs, china doves, Virgins in heavenly blue cloaks,
gold paper stars, the three Magi, angels with wings like swans, the
Ass, the Ox, and a terrible St. Denis, who appeared to him in his
dreams with a great space between his shoulders, walking hesitantly
as if looking for something he had lost. When he blundered into the
bed, Marcial would start awake and reach for his rosary of silver
beads. The lampwicks, in their bowls of oil, cast a sad light on the
holy images as their colors returned to them.

VIII

The furniture was growing taller. It was becoming more difficult for
him to rest his arms on the dining table. The fronts of the cupboards
with their carved cornices were getting broader. The Moors on the
staircase stretched their torsos upward, bringing their torches closer
to the banisters on the landing. Armchairs were deeper, and rocking
chairs tended to fall over backward. It was no longer necessary to bend
ones's knees when lying at the bottom of the bath with its marble
rings.

One morning when he was reading a licentious book, Marcial suddenly felt a desire to play with the lead soldiers lying asleep in their
wooden boxes. He put the book back in its hiding place under the
washbasin, and opened a drawer sealed with cobwebs. His schoolroom
table was too small to hold such a large army. So Marcial sat on the floor
and set out his grenadiers in rows of eight. Next came the officers on
horseback, surrounding the color sergeant; and behind, the artillery with
their cannon, gun sponges and linstocks. Bringing up the rear were fifes
and tabors escorted by drummers. The mortars were fitted with a spring,
so that one could shoot glass marbles to a distance of more than a yard.

Bang! . . . Bang! . . . Bang!

Down fell horses, down fell standard-bearers, down fell drummers. Eligio the Negro had to call him three times before he could be persuaded to go to wash his hands and descend to the dining room.

After that day, Marcial made a habit of sitting on the tiled floor. When he realized the advantages of this position, he was surprised that he had not thought of it before. Grown-up people had a passion for velvet cushions, which made them sweat too much. Some of them smelled like a notary—like Don Abundio—because they had not discovered how cool it was to lie at full length on a marble floor at all seasons of the year. Only from the floor could all the angles and perspectives of a room be grasped properly. There were beautiful grains in the wood, mysterious insect paths and shadowy corners that could not be seen from a man's height. When it rained, Marcial hid himself under the clavichord. Every clap of thunder made the sound box vibrate, and set all the notes to singing. Shafts of lightning fell from the sky, creating a vault of cascading arpeggios—the organ, the wind in the pines, and the crickets' mandolin.

IX

That morning they locked him in his room. He heard whispering all over the house, and the luncheon they brought him was too delicious for a weekday. There were six pastries from the confectioner's in the Alameda—whereas even on Sundays after Mass he was only allowed two. He amused himself by looking at the engravings in a travel book, until an increasing buzz of sound coming under the door made him look out between the blinds. Some men dressed all in black were arriving, bearing a brass-handled coffin. He was on the verge of tears, but at this moment Melchor the groom appeared in his room, his boots echoing on the floor and his teeth flashing in a smile. They began to play chess. Melchor was a knight. He was the king. Using the tiles on the floor as a chessboard, he moved from one square to the next, while Melchor had to jump one forward and two sideways, or vice versa. The game went on until after dusk, when the fire brigade went by.

When he got up, he went to kiss his father's hand as he lay ill in bed. The Marqués was feeling better, and talked to his son in his usual serious and edifying manner. His "Yes, Fathers"'s and "No, Fathers"'s were fitted between the beads of a rosary of questions, like the responses of an acolyte during Mass. Marcial respected the Marqués, but for reasons that no one could possibly have guessed. He respected him because he was tall, because when he went out to a ball his breast glittered with decorations; because he envied him the saber and gold braid he wore as an officer in the militia; because at Christmas time, on a bet, he had eaten a whole turkey stuffed with almonds and raisins; because he had once seized one of the *mulatas* who were sweeping out the rotunda and had carried her in his arms to his room—no doubt intending to whip her. Hidden behind a curtain, Marcial watched her come out soon afterward, in tears and with her dress unfastened, and he was pleased that she had been punished, as she was the one who always emptied the jam pots before putting them back in the cupboard.

His father was a terrible and magnanimous being, and it was his duty to love him more than anyone except God. To Marcial he was more godlike even than God because his gifts were tangible, everyday ones. But he preferred the God in heaven because he was less of a nuisance.

X

When the furniture had grown a little taller still, and Marcial knew better than anyone what was under the beds, cupboards, and cabinets, he had a great secret, which he kept to himself: life had no charms except when Melchor the groom was with him. Not God, nor his father, nor the golden bishop in the Corpus Christi procession was as important as Melchor.

Melchor had come from a very long distance away. He was descended from conquered princes. In his kingdom there were elephants, hippopotamuses, tigers, and giraffes, and men did not sit working, like Don Abundio in dark rooms full of papers. They lived by outdoing the animals in cunning. One of them had pulled the great crocodile out of the blue lake after first skewering him on a pike concealed inside the closely packed bodies of twelve roast geese. Melchor knew songs that were easy to learn because the words had no meaning and were constantly repeated. He stole sweetmeats from the kitchens; at night he used to escape through the stable door, and once he threw stones at the police before disappearing into the darkness of the Calle de la Amargura.

On wet days he used to put his boots to dry beside the kitchen stove. Marcial wished he had feet big enough to fill boots like those. His right-hand boot was called Calambín, the left one Calambán. This man who could tame unbroken horses by simply seizing their lips between two fingers, this fine gentleman in velvet and spurs who wore such tall hats, also understood about the coolness of marble floors in summer, and used to hide fruits or a cake, snatched from trays destined for the drawing room, behind the furniture. Marcial and Melchor shared a secret store of sweets and almonds, which they saluted with "*Urí, urí, urá*" and shouts of conspiratorial laughter. They had both explored the house from top to bottom, and were the only ones who knew that beneath the stables there was a small cellar full of Dutch bottles, or that in an unused loft over the maids' rooms was a broken glass case containing twelve dusty butterflies that were losing their wings.

XI

When Marcial got into the habit of breaking things, he forgot Melchor and made friends with the dogs. There were several in the house. The large one with stripes like a tiger; the basset trailing its teats on the ground; the greyhound that had grown too old to play; the poodle that was chased by the others at certain times and had to be shut up by the maids.

Marcial liked Canelo best because he carried off shoes from the bedrooms and dug up the rose trees in the patio. Always black with coal dust or covered with red earth, he devoured the dinners of all the other dogs, whined without cause, and hid stolen bones under the fountain. And now and again he would suck dry a new-laid egg and send the hen flying with a sharp blow from his muzzle. Everyone kicked Canelo. But when they took him away, Marcial made himself ill with grief. And the dog returned in triumph, wagging his tail, from somewhere beyond the poorhouse where he had been abandoned, and regained his place in the house, which the other dogs, for all their skill in hunting, or vigilance when keeping guard, could never fill.

Canelo and Marcial used to urinate side by side. Sometimes they chose the Persian carpet in the drawing room, spreading dark, cloud-like shapes over its pile. This usually cost them a thrashing. But thrashings were less painful than grown-up people realized. On the other hand, they gave a splendid excuse for setting up a concerted howling and arousing the pity of the neighbors. When the cross-eyed woman from the top flat called his father a "brute," Marcial looked at Canelo with smiling eyes. They shed a few more tears so as to be given a biscuit, and afterward all was forgotten. They both used to eat earth, roll on the ground, drink out of the goldfish basin, and take refuge in the scented shade under the sweet-basil bushes. During the hottest hours of the day quite a crowd filled the moist flower beds. There would be the gray goose with her pouch hanging between her bandy legs; the old rooster with his naked rump; the little lizard who kept saying "*Urí, urá*" and shooting a pink ribbon out of his throat; the melancholy snake, born in a town where there were no females; and the mouse that blocked its hole with a turtle's egg. One day someone pointed out the dog to Marcial.

"Bow-wow," Marcial said.

He was talking his own language. He had attained the ultimate liberty. He was beginning to want to reach with his hands things that were out of reach.

XII

Hunger, thirst, heat, pain, cold. Hardly had Marcial reduced his field of perception to these essential realities when he renounced the light that accompanied them. He did not know his own name. The unpleasantness of the christening over, he had no desire for smells, sounds, or even sights. His hands caressed delectable forms. He was a purely sensory and tactile being. The universe penetrated him through his pores. Then he shut his eyes—they saw nothing but nebulous giants—and entered a warm, damp body full of shadows: a dying body. Clothed in this body's substance, he slipped toward life.

But now time passed more quickly, rarefying the final hours. The minutes sounded like cards slipping from beneath a dealer's thumb.

Birds returned to their eggs in a whirlwind of feathers. Fish congealed into roe, leaving a snowfall of scales at the bottom of their pond. The palm trees folded their fronds and disappeared into the earth like shut fans. Stems were reabsorbing their leaves, and the earth reclaimed everything that was its own. Thunder rumbled through the arcades. Hairs began growing from antelope-skin gloves. Woolen blankets were unraveling and turning into the fleece of sheep in distant pastures. Cupboards, cabinets, beds, crucifixes, tables, and blinds disappeared into the darkness in search of their ancient roots beneath the forest trees. Everything that had been fastened with nails was disintegrating. A brigantine, anchored no one knew where, sped back to Italy carrying the marble from the floors and fountain. Suits of armor, ironwork, keys, copper cooking pots, the horses' bits from the stables, were melting and forming a swelling river of metal running into the earth through roofless channels. Everything was undergoing metamorphosis and being restored to its original state. Clay returned to clay, leaving a desert where the house had once stood.

XIII

When the workmen came back at dawn to go on with the demolition of the house, they found their task completed. Someone had carried off the statue of Ceres and sold it to an antique dealer the previous evening. After complaining to the trade union, the men went and sat on the seats in the municipal park. Then one of them remembered some vague story about a Marquesa de Capellanías who had been drowned one evening in May among the arum lilies in the Almendares. But no one paid any attention to his story because the sun was traveling from east to west, and the hours growing on the righthand side of the clock must be spun out by idleness—for they are the ones that inevitably lead to death.

Isolation/Inter-Caribbean Relations

*A*ll of Ana Lydia Vega's stories focus on the complexity of gender, race, and class issues in the region, in the context of inter-Caribbean relations. She weaves phrases in French, English, and Créole into her narratives, making the multilingual Caribbean, and the obstacles to communication it creates, an inevitable sub-theme.

In "The Day It All Happened" Death herself narrates episodes in the tragic legacy of fratricidal relations between Dominicans and Haitians across generations and national boundaries, under the shadow of U.S. intervention in both nations. Desperate economic circumstances lead the protagonist across the Mona Passage to remake his life in a third country, Puerto Rico, where the past inevitably catches up with him.

"Port-au-Prince, Below," structured as a grouping of tourist snap-shots on slides, reveals the heroic legacy of Haitian resistance, of L'Ouverture and Dessalines, under the twin assault of desperate Dominican hustlers and Puerto Rican tourists who search the capital for authentic "folklore." The first person narrative of a dark-skinned Puerto Rican woman exposes her alienation from the values of her middle class compatriots on "holiday," along with the shock of self-recognition, and subsequent awareness of the need to build bridges from Puerto Rico to other Caribbean nations, as well as to explore, rather than deny, those that already exist.

"The Day It All Happened"

ANA LYDIA VEGA
(PUERTO RICO)

Yes sir, I was there that day at exactly three o'clock in the afternoon when the air outside was like a snowcone compared to the boiling inferno inside that laundry. Steam hung from the eaves, clinging like cellophane. There were more pants in there than in the army. Or, at least, it seemed that way: things were going pretty well for Filemón Sagredo, Jr., in Puerto Rico. Dirty laundry was in abundance this side of the Mona Passage, and on Arzuaga Street in Río Piedras, full of Dominican kiosks and rooming houses, the hot *sancocho** and frozen papaya shakes flowed just like back in El Cibao. From time to time a wave of nostalgia for a tear-up-the-floor merengue and the sound of a down-home accent hit real hard, but you could always make a quick trip back to the Republic to see the folks and put in an appearance at the public square and even bring back a few straw mats to sell, make a little extra on the side, and get ahead, yeah.

And so, in the Quisqueya[+] Laundry luck had winked at him, from the very day he arrived, numb with fear, on the shores of Eden, just above Bramadero Bay.

That son of a bitch Grullón had let him out far from shore so as not to risk his own hide. And Filemón, along with the other five illegals,

---

  * A stew of tubers, vegetables, and meat popular in the Dominican Republic, Puerto Rico, and Cuba *(ajiaco)*.

  [+] Aboriginal name for the Dominican Republic.

had had to swim the rest of the way in, scaring off the sharks with promises to the Virgin of Altagracia.

On the beach, another class of shark attacked him. He had to hand out wet dollars like so many blessings so he wouldn't end up in jail with all the others.

Bribes aside, the little trip had cost him well over five hundred dollars. It's a good thing that in Puerto Rico you're only poor if you want to be. There's no lack of jobs here, no. And you don't have to leave your back and your life in the damn canefields either. Anyone can get by, more or less, selling cones in a Chinese ice-cream shop, working as a short-order cook for some motherless Cuban, fixing flats in a compatriot's garage. Somehow or other, you can weather the storm. Until you can get hitched to some Puerto Rican broad and clear things up with Immigration. Or prosper in the day-to-day hustle and negotiate the official paperwork in exchange for a few hundred.

Yes sir, I was there in the flesh and saw it all when the big, tough-looking, Black guy squared off against Filemón Sagredo, Jr., with his sawed-off shotgun on his shoulder and said: "Félicien Apolon sends his regards."

The Dominican didn't even have time to open his mouth. He barely managed to take a step toward the clothes racks. The shotgun blast drowned out the scream of the woman who at that very moment was returning from the back room. But I'm sure of one thing: before he looked death in the eye, Filemón saw his father's face staring at him blankly from the past.

And don't you think this was all over money. The deceased was as punctual in paying his debts as Catholic school bells. Not money or women, no sir. Filemón was as light-fingered as the next guy, but he never picked up a woman that wasn't unclaimed and on the loose. This was a matter older and more serious than hunger itself. I could tell you myself, exactly, with all the details, what happened at Juana Mendez* so many years ago. I had gone over there—there's no cure for curiosity—on the very day it all happened.

It was during that bloody week everyone would rather forget. The Benefactor had called for the death of all Haitians up and down the

---

* A town in the Dominican Republic.

river that came to be known as "The Massacre."* The Dominicani-
zation of the border was under way. Any Dominican who considered
himself a patriot and a real man had to grab one of those filthy, no
good, miserable wretches who had taken the food off the plates of the
authentic sons and daughters of Duarte⁺ and bash his brains in.

By Friday night there was nothing left to carry the corpses in. There
were carts overflowing with dead bodies and drunken bands of pursuers
everywhere, incited by the scent of Haitian blood. Hiding under the
bed, in the dark, Félicien could hear the cries of his dying countrymen.
Some had been born on the wrong side of the border, the offspring of
Haitian immigrants and Dominican women. But when the final blows
were struck, no one bothered to ask anyone about their mothers.

In the next room, Filemón Sagredo, Sr., couldn't make up his mind
whether to denounce the Haitian or not. He had helped the man's son
to cross the river because Paula had asked him to. He had done it for
her, for her alone, because she was Dominican, besides being one hell
of a woman, even if she was living with a damn *cocolo*.⁺⁺ But when
Félicien asked for refuge, he had to think it over twice before murmuring a yes laden with indecision. The memory of his father who
had been killed in Haiti during the Yankee occupation stuck in this
throat, choking him.

He had been strung up by Péralte's henchman, and hung from the
mast where the Gringos' flag waved, denounced as a spy and a traitor.
Unjustly, of course. They had mistaken him for another Dominican,
a hotshot who had gone off to New York with a suitcase full of money.
I caught a glimpse of grandfather Filemón's feet, dancing their last
carabiné in the Haitian air. And I swear on the Constitution of the
Republic that with his last words he cursed the *madamo*** who killed

---

* A river separating the Dominican Republic and Haiti. In 1937, General Rafael
  Trujillo ordered the Dominican armed forces to massacre all Haitians found
  on the other side of the river, inside the Dominican Republic.
⁺ Juan Pablo Duarte, considered the father of the Dominican nation. He led
  the independence forces until he was exiled in 1844.
⁺⁺ In Dominican slang, a pejorative term for foreign cane cutters, from Haiti and
  the West Indies, and their descendants.
** A racist term for Haitians in general, used in the Dominican Republic.

his father during the third Haitian invasion. To avenge the death of his own father, of course, pierced through by a Dominican bayonet during Serapio Reinoso's time.

Filemón thought it over three times before he called in the hangmen who were circling the place like wolves. But blood is thicker than water. Dawn was just breaking when the door hinges creaked. A flash of sharpened blades filled the *batey.** And at six in the morning, Paula was scrubbing the floor with a brush, to make the thirsty floorboards cough up Haitian blood. And that is how Filemón Sagredo, Jr., descendant of so many Filemóns, victims and assassins, found himself face down on the floor of the Quisqueya Laundry of Río Piedras that fateful day.

The oldest of his two sons, standing in the doorway, stared out over the heads of the curious all the way down Arzuaga Street, where his father's past had just sped away in a black Chevrolet. At the wheel, Félicien Apolon, Jr., followed the trail of blood patiently traced by so many Féliciens, victims and assassins.

Everyone is wondering if it will rain again. If there's any news, you can always count on me. I know just about everything. I'm always there on the day it all happens.

---

* Barracks to house cane cutters on the grounds of a sugar mill.

"Port-au-Prince, Below"

ANA LYDIA VEGA

. . . sólo a veces Don Quijote
por chiflado y musaraña
de tu maritornería
construye una dulcineada

—Luis Palés Matos

Slide I
"It's not the heat, it's the humidity that gets you."

*A*n hour of sweat and dust. The Tonton Macoute sun beating down on the airport. Clothing struck to skin like a vampire's kiss. That dust that covers and strangles everything like a whitish nylon. The waiters rubbing water glasses with greasy rags like the face of the cockatoo *portorricensis* anticipating a meal of eggs and bacon. What a drag yesterday during the rain that began to fall out of the blue, pushing us under the arcades: cackling a capella. The pressure of craterous backsides against brightly colored polyester. The cockatoo bending over backwards in praise of the Haitians: so refined, so resigned, so cheerful, so attentive, so humble and—what for her is the height of cachet—so cultured that they even speak French. Then she breaks into a chorus of laments: what a shame, the poor things, it breaks your heart, Oh God, such misery. And the inevitable "Such is the bitter fruit of independence," at the end like an *Ite Missa Est*.

I deserved this. All forms of innocence bring on suffering. Like purifying oneself by teaching in the public school, like "Hey, Miss, you're looking so good," with his thing on the school desk. As if Angel Luis masturbating in the middle of a discussion of *La llamarada* weren't enough. It was my destiny to suffer this tourist's ordeal, this wonderful weekend in Hell. But *Johannes est nomen eius.* The asshole sacrificial lamb on San Juan's crest of arms bleats out its eternal soporific bolero.

I'm sorry, but it's hard not to feel like a movie star in the middle of this delegation of urban matrons: profusion of Chanel No. 5 and locks saturated with enough hair spray to withstand a hurricane. Dragging their husbands along behind, sporting corsages from Teacher's Day. Verbal diarrhea enlivened by the intermittent flash of a gold tooth. Today they'll want to know my zodiac sign. To scrutinize my Afro, searching for the fatal ancestor. Status is at issue: to challenge the amiability of the Puerto Rican people, the greatest of their national virtues, or twist your face up into a hypocritical, complicit, public-assistance smile. Let the Teachers' Association shoot me, pointblank. Anything would be better than the viscous drooling of this cockatoo on my arm. Stainless steel ovaries on wheels: I must survive this death blow in Haiti.

Slide II
"Oh my God, is it getting dark or is that a bunch of Blacks
over there . . ."

Port-au-Prince: a mangy dog stretched out on the pier. Rows of beggars harassing the passers-by who practically quiver with good intentions. Hands with dark backs and white palms, like a trumpetwood leaf. Open, twitching, conical, square, circular, fallen, maimed, raised, clinging to the window of a rental car as it speeds away in order to avoid contact.

Continually crossing oneself: from the throat to the belly to your weary tourist's eyes. Hands perpetually agitated. Older than the white warehouses left behind by the French colonists. Secular armies of bellies, without hope of redemption.

Slide III
"Even the Devil himself couldn't understand this patois."

Misery has a thousand tongues. All the voices ring out. The shrill cries of the market women, intent on the counting of the *gourdes*. The outcries in furious Créole of those fighting over the crumbs some Americans left on the table. Hoarse whispers like those of Wilfrid who is keeping guard in front of your hotel. Sticking out of his pocket, his own image immortalized on film by a Canadian's Polaroid.

"How much for the photograph?"

"Twenty, Madame."

"Twenty *dollars?* You're crazy."

"Ten goud', dix."

"Too expensive. I'll take your picture myself."

But before you could take aim with your homicidal lens, he disappeared with the speed of wounded pride. His shirt: a white dot at the end of the alley.

Slide IV
"You know Avenida de Diego is Fifth Avenue compared to this."

La Grand' Rue, a fat tapeworm in the belly of a hanged man. The mini-van taxis they call *tab-tabs* crossing it like bad omens, headed for John Brown Avenue. Polychrome commemorative tombstones on foreheads. Folkloric, according to Air France: ethnological Legba, Lord of the Crossroads, philosophical Bon Dieu Bon, pornographic "God in front, and me behind." The drivers push the pedestrians like sick cattle. They charge fifteen cents to pull you out of the sweat and the dust and transport you on blind, craggy roads up to the Cafolé

218

Olympus. There you have a petit punch, rice *jean-jean*, stuffed lobster à la Créole, and cherries in eau-de-vie. Satiety in Pétionville, surrounded by Hollywood-style mansions and colonial courtesy. Family guest houses wink painted eyes to the sound of native guitars. Inside Pétionville's enormous belly, maids in white uniforms place fresh fruit on the tables. The sky is scarlet with shame. And Port-au-Prince, below.

Slide V
"Does your husband let you travel by yourself, sweetheart?"

In front of the Hotel Acropolis there is a light-skinned mulatta, wearing her curly hair loose like Lola Flores. She approaches to sell me a wooden necklace. Ugly, poorly made. And she calls me *hermanita* with that syrupy accent the Dominicans have. Out of weakness, I hand her a peso and she tells me about the Puerto Rican who threw himself on her at noon. The one who's now stationed at the bar, drowning his guts in beer. We relive the ritual: my compatriot takes her up to his room, taking advantage of his wife's being out. On the stairs, he's got his hands all over her, from top to bottom. He feels the merchandise like an expert trafficker. He's as horny as a convict. Doors open. Mouths. Legs. The guy lunges boundlessly toward the bed. Pushing. Penetrating her. *Hermanita* loses her balance. She falls to the floor. The Puerto Rican is on top of her. Grunting. Snorting. Almost a death rattle.

"Take that thing off."

The he-goat roars an order, with a virile tug on her brassiere. His wish is instantly fulfilled. The brassiere falls in slow motion, with all the autumnal langor of gringo movies. And now the Puerto Rican is stuck like a leech to the Dominican fruit when, oh, Buñuel, a stream of warm milk stops him paradoxically in his tracks. He spits thickly, begins to slap the poor Altagracia, and lets out the following:

"You dirty whore, why didn't you tell me you were pregnant?"

Altagracia laughs now, and tells me that all Puerto Ricans are mystics, that Dominicans like mother's milk and the smell of salted cod. At this point the hero's wife arrives—hold on, mama—a moving display of lumps displaced by her girdle, a fanfare of jingling charm bracelets, showing him the five identical ashtrays she got for her five best friends, which she tirelessly bargained down to five American cents each. She complains of the sun, the humidity, the Créole, the noise, the beggars. And she gets teary-eyed at the air-conditioned memory of a day of shopping at the Plaza de las Américas mall back in San Juan.

Slide VI
"The best part was when they stuck their hands
in the fire."

Port-au-Prince rises before you like in a dream. All decorated with heroes. The Champs de Mars is deserted. Except for the soldiers shooting dice behind the doors of the Presidential Palace. The small crowd that gathered to hear the concert of military music had dispersed. The last chords disturb the night air:

> Grenadiers à l'assaut
> ça qui mouri z'affaire à yo . . .

The statues of L'Ouverture, Dessalines, and Christophe stand out like white perforations against the dark sky.

Everyone else has gone hunting for voodoo, like gringo tourists thirsty for chicken blood. Puerto Ricans living up to the standards of their U.S. passports. They took along a bottle of Don Q rum because Barbancourt tastes like perfume to them. And the spiritualist matrons tucked their envy away between their pubes and got to work messing with heads, taking on the difficult task of casting off menopause.

You insist on isolating yourself along with Haiti. The Haiti that went down in History. The Haiti that gives people goose bumps and makes their hearts beat like drums. Possessed by Ogún, with Dessaline's entire army riding cavalcade through your head, you want nothing less than to break the thread of time and see, in flashback, the so-called tree of liberty take root and grow. While another part of you, the wounded combat veteran, cries out that that's just minor-league intellectual romanticism.

At your side, the Runaway Black Slave menaces, with his short ankle chain and straight torch, reaching for the stars. It's only a statue facing the tanks that guard the white palace.

Up above, Pétionville yawns. The moon is impassively watching television. And you no longer commune with Boukman and Mackandal in the Cayman Woods. The howls of the living curdle your blood in Port-au-Prince.

Slide VII

"Low-life types and fools, that's all there was there."

The Choucoune Shack is jam-packed. Oh la la. But the orchestra's not bad, though the merengue leaves something to be desired. The matrons are all shaking their booty in vain. Gracefulness was forbidden to them by the Constitution of '52. And there go the Haitians, their belt buckles sparkling with the smooth but sure movement of the hips. The punch has gone to my head. The most crucial button holding my blouse together is threatening to pop, causing a dishonest exposure. You could say, in the most strictly physical sense of the term, that I feel good. The Puerto Rican husbands don't dare ask me out onto the dance floor under the watchful eye of the Mrs. I confess: this is a perverse coquetry on my part. But the truth is that there isn't a single one in the bunch that does anything for my libido. How can anyone get excited by the omnipresent image of those paterfamiliae watering the grama grass in the yards of their reinforced concrete cells in Bermuda shorts and tee-shirts. Finally one of the men rises and approaches me. He has the smile of a shoe salesman. He looks stoned. Ready to pierce my left flank with his barbs. His belly hits me seconds before his bad breath. Apocalyptic vision of the mammoth *portorricensis* before a giant plate of rice and beans. A vow of chastity would be preferable to the cackle of this executive type in my ear. In photo finish, I get up, run, and throw myself on the first body that blocks my escape. To find myself undulating to the beat of the Haitian merengue in the arms of a woman. Wagnerian crescendo. Avalanche of guffaws like when Shorty Castro recites a Mother's Day poem. Laughter that climbs like an efficient second-story man, and the volume increases and there are butterflies in my stomach and my legs are weak, and the rum and the music and my partner's confusion and the mammoth's frustration and the anger of the cockatoo and the ridiculous nature of colonial elections and the absurdity of this shopper's excursion to Hell.

I'm peeing buckets.

Slide VIII
"I'm sure I've seen you somewhere before."

Dies Irae. My Party membership stamped on my forehead. If you're a Communist, then you must be an atheist. If you're a feminist, you must be a dyke. If you're Black, you must be fast and loose. An absolute she-wolf. Oh God, the paranoia of the colonized mind. At any rate, they have the look of shock troops. They must be wondering what school I teach in so they can quarantine it. I should feel like an epic figure. Yet I'm more like a deflated happy birthday balloon. There's only one thing I want: to get the hell out of this place with its middle-class funeral atmosphere. So much crying and no one knows the dead man. The slightest noise irritates me. So does the slowness of the barman. The delayed flight. And the mournful prattle of my compatriots. The level of conversation has evolved a bit. It's not that it has grown more profound, but now that the suitcases are all bursting with souvenirs no one is giving the Haitians a thought. They're too busy singing "Preciosa" and "In My Old San Juan." With the glee of a reunion of the founders of the Popular Party. Picture the procession of Chevrolets bearing the single star of the Puerto Rican flag. Vocational counselors always carry a Stanford-Binet in their handbags. That's why they maintain that the per capita I.Q. of the Commonwealth is a lofty skyscraper, leagues higher than that of this leper's colony, doubly afflicted by its poverty and its Blackness. That's why they raise off-key Te Deums to the glory of the future Puerto Rican pope. And may the Guadeloupans' precious volcano erupt on them.

I think my travel companions have now graduated. They will receive their diplomas upon return. It will be a moving ceremony with caps and gowns. The cockatoo will show us her slides afterwards. Nothing like a trip through this mess of an archipelago to make you comprehend, at last, the vile gospel of the Cuban refugees: Miami is in sight.

Slide IX
"They've got to be kidding, fifty cents for a pack of gum!"

I make the rounds of the duty-free shop. With shackles on my tongue. I try on a pair of copper earrings. The nasal good-byes sound phonier than a debut in Casa de España.*

"Ou dominicaine?"

"Portoricaine."

"Aaaah. English, yes?"

Your head is once again filled with images of handkerchiefs, straw mats, nude statues, colored flutes, the smell of coffee, charcoal, oil; with embroidered white guayaberas, serpentine walks, earthenware jars, sewing machines, umbrellas, baskets, the sway of hips and buttocks. You would have liked to take another look at the murals of La Trinité, which one of the luminaries on the tour described as kindergarten scribbles. Port-au-Prince has wound you up again like a spinning top. And you find yourself in the market again, with that irrepressible desire to take a photograph possessing you like a mischievous, irreverent god. You piously remind yourself that misery is not folklore. You remember that you need a button and ask how much the first one you see costs. Five dollars, he says. He's a little man with a restless gaze. He's got you pegged: TURISTA. In spite of your color, in spite of your love. TURISTA: just like the others. You tell him no, with sadness in your gesture. You keep walking amid the crowd, hands, eyes that call. A little girl heads you off. She holds out her hand as if to take yours. A zombi's gaze. She slips something between your fingers. The five-dollar button: Papa sent it to you. You put your hand in your purse to give her something. She disappears. An idiotic euphoria comes over you. And you return to the hotel, relic in hand, refusing an autopsy. You're a walking puzzle of islands that have found one another again, falling into place, at last.

* A cultural center frequented by the elite of San Juan.—ED.

223

Slide X
"They'll never hook me in again."

Port-au-Prince is still down there, by the docks. Faithful to Mistress Death. You fix your gaze on the city from above until it faints away in the distance. Everything is blue and foam. Blue and clouds. The dilated uterine sky over San Juan awaits you. Relief. Even you feel it. Mea culpa. Haiti is a slap in the face, a challenge to your synthetic goodness. It is an unforgiving country. Every act is a guilty act, and pity is a luxury paid for at tourist prices.

San Juan will swallow you up again. Kindly, as only she knows how. In its quivering pudding of vague emotions. It will squeeze you without malice, with a broad, First Communion smile. Strong. Native. Hot. Strangling you with affection.

Down below, Port-au-Prince is setting like a shipwrecked sun.

"They say Spain is beauuutiiiful . . ."

Modern Life:
Alienation/Liberation

*J*n Caryl Phillips's *A State of Independence*, Bertram Francis returns to St. Kitts, considering a definitive repatriation, after twenty years in England. He arrives on the eve of the country's celebration of formal independence. In St. Kitts—a country whose capital appears, from the window of the airplane, "to be a neat and tropical Versailles," but "would seem little more than a sprawling mess when on the ground"—it was impossible to ignore "the existence of a conflict between the optimism of this imminent independence and the outward signs of a village still struggling to acquire the means to meet the most basic of needs." His observant eye and awareness of the contradictions that precipitated his "escape" to England twenty years earlier define his awkward and ultimately near-impossible return. Uneasy at home and uneasy in England, on this return he will be hurled toward an inevitable re-encounter with a childhood schoolmate turned corrupt politician. Yet Bertram Francis has come home with a sense of critical distance, a sharpened perspective, poised for a move toward liberation.

Chely Lima's characters move hesitantly through the modern landscape of urban Havana, not unlike the men and women of Silvio

Rodríguez's and Pablo Milanés's ballads. Young, urban, professional, and perhaps a bit "bohemian," they walk a tightrope between the desire for easy conformity to the traditional values of ingrained *machismo* and the ethos of independence and social equality of their own generation. In "Monologue with Rain," we encounter an appealing young woman—a motorcycle-riding, cigarette-smoking professional—and the tensions that caused a love affair to sour, recounted in flashback and interior monologue by the male protagonist, after his lover has gone.

"Common Stories" also centers on the failed love affair of two urban professionals, would-be writers, both married to others, who had met some time before at a literary workshop. Behind the initiation and demise of an affair, Chely Lima captures the texture of everyday life in the Vedado section of Havana, the nitty-gritty conflicts of interpersonal relations, family, work, and dreams among the literati of contemporary Cuba, for whom the tensions between the old and the new are palpable, and skillfully brought to life by the writer's craft.

"Passing," a prose poem by the Jamaican poet, novelist, and essayist Michelle Cliff, centers on an "ignorance of connections," held, seemingly lost, then found; the consciousness of a past, the knowledge of all that makes "assimilation impossible." In it, Cliff forcefully argues: "Passing demands quiet./ And from that quiet—silence." Her writing breaks the silence, redeeming the power of the word, the power of history acknowledged, of *spirit* against *isolation*, either "back home," in England, or in America.

From: A State of
Independence

CARYL PHILLIPS
(ST. KITTS)

It was twenty years since Bertram Francis had last seen the island of his birth. He leaned anxiously towards the window and tried to look through his neighbor. The woman was sleeping at an angle so awkward that Bertram felt as though he was peering through a climbing frame. She slept with her mouth open, which meant she snored, but the drone of the plane's engines ensured that nobody else could hear, even when she occasionally turned and her snore became a series of quick, low grunts. Bertram looked at her round, rather plump face. As she pulled in her chin, a second one formed and created a staircase that he felt sure many a tongue had slithered up. It was curious, thought Bertram, because from the neck down the rest of her body seemed both slender and firm. He imagined that some might mistake her for a woman ten years her junior, and that this would be her first time in the Caribbean, for in her lap she cradled a new, but already well-thumbed, guide to the area. Her flouting of regional ignorance somehow made him feel a little easier at the end of what had been a worrisome flight. He felt grateful that she was not a regular visitor who might have taken it upon herself to educate him about his own country and further disturb the feelings of guilt that lay inside him.

Almost imperceptibly the tone of the plane's engines changed. Then the aircraft began to bank to one side and despite the scaffolding of his neighbor's arms and legs Bertram saw sunlight bleeding through the clouds as they passed over the shoulders of the island. Below him lay a dense carpet of green forest, thin pools of mist entangled in the highest branches of the trees. And in a clearing he saw the crumbling stones and wild fern clusters of a disused sugar mill and broken-down Great House. They passed over a village whose corrugated iron roofs overlapped like the scales of a fish, and in the distance, beyond the village, Bertram saw the capital. He knew full well that from this height what appeared to be a neat and tropical Versailles would seem little more than a sprawling mess when on the ground. The plane began to bank to the other side, and Bertram now surveyed the shock-inducing blue of the Caribbean sea. The waves broke over the turquoise coral, and the people swam with only their severed heads visible. Then the plane lurched as it lost altitude, and Bertram's eyes closed as he imagined the long gray carpet unfolding beneath them.

The airport was small, though bigger than Bertram had expected. He had left by boat, for in those days the airport had been little more that a wooden shack in a canefield, the runway a curved gash someone had opened up with the blunt edge of a knife. Bertram remembered the first time he ever saw a plane land on the island, and how the entire classroom had stopped what they were doing and looked up in disbelief. Like a giant insect it whirred and circled overhead, then disappeared in the direction of a distant field. Everybody turned their attention back to the lesson, but each decided that after school they would try to be the first to see the plane close up. However, at the end of the day, Bertram's best friend, Jackson Clayton, announced that it was nothing but a piece of clumsy machinery. Bertram felt compelled to agree with him, and together they turned in the direction of home. It was not until some weeks later, when landings became more regular, and Jackson was at cricket practice, that Bertram was furtively able to view the plane (although he never admitted this small deception to his friend).

Now Bertram received priority disembarkation over those passengers merely in transit to one of the bigger islands to the south. He stepped down on to the apron and looked up at the mountains which posed as though in a family group. Above them the clouds drifted, crimson fortresses at peace. As the plane's engines died, the cicada-riddled hush of a late afternoon in the Caribbean overtook him.

The airport lounge was supported by clean white concrete pillars, each punctuated with round glassless holes. This helped the air to circulate freely, but the claustrophobia of the heat surprised Bertram. Not wishing to take off his jacket, Bertram concentrated on the signs that decorated the wall behind the desk of the immigration officer. Then he felt the first few drops of perspiration dribble from his armpits, catch the edge of his ribcage, and roll cold and wet toward his waist.

Welcome to Rum'n'Sun

And beneath this sign hung a second, and more assertive, placard.

INDEPENDENCE
Forward ever—Backward never

A blackboard and easel stood to the side of the desk. Someone had rubbed out a 4 and replace it with a 3, so the message now read:

PROUD, DIGNIFIED AND BLACK!
NONE CAN TAKE MY FREEDOM BACK!
Independence soon come—only 3 days more

The immigration officer seemed uninterested in anything. Like the other people who worked in the airport, his skin shone as though he had spent the day occupied with manual labour. Bertram looked at him, the young man's face seemingly vacant and uncluttered with thought, and wondered if he might be the victim of some form of lethargy-inducing sickness. He opened Bertram's passport, using the back of his palm to keep it flat, then glanced at the photograph, then up at Bertram, then back at the photograph.

"How long you planning on staying here?"

Bertram laughed, trying to remove some of the formality.

"I don't know, man. Maybe I come back to live."

"Alone?"

"Alone." Bertram said.

"You planning on working here to support yourself?"

"I look like a millionaire?"

The immigration officer stared blankly at Bertram, who now realized he would have to elaborate.

"Well, I don't know as yet. It depends on how things go."

The man stamped the passport, flicked it back shut, and silently handed it back to Bertram. As he turned to leave Bertram heard the man speak once more.

"Welcome home, Mr. Francis."

Bertram turned back to face him, but the young man was already attending to the next person in the queue. It was a severely-attired elderly woman. In the silence behind the mask of her face Bertram could tell she was a true national who had probably been to England only to see grandchildren. The speed with which she followed him down the steps towards the baggage reclaim section only served to confirm this in his mind for, unlike his, hers was a homecoming hastened by familiarity.

Bertram's two suitcases were waiting for him. He lifted them up on to the counter with other suitcases and boxes and parcels, whose battered states bore testament to much international scale-wrestling. The customs man looked at Bertram's luggage, but like his colleague at immigration he too seemed tired and indifferent. He enquired half-heartedly whether Bertram had anything to declare. Bertram shook his head. A huge cross was chalked on the side of both suitcases, and a brisk wave of the hand meant they were to be taken away.

"You need some help, man?"

A stocky, graying man in a sweat-stained shirt stood before Bertram. His trousers hung hopelessly at the crotch and were fat with turn-ups around the ankles.

"No, I can carry them alright."

"You sure you can manage?"

The man backed out of the customs hall, and Bertram stepped forward into the open air and stopped. He put down the suitcases and glanced at the hills in the distance, small white houses dotted up and around the backs of these gentle green giants. The stillness of the sea in the foreground looked, at this time of the day, like a mirror set ablaze. To his left the few people who waited by the arrivals gate stood and shielded their eyes from the now dying sun. They stared with interest at those who trickled through, wondering if they resembled half-forgotten relatives. Then they stared with dismissal, almost contempt, when it became clear they did not.

"Well, a taxi then? I can arrange one for you."

"I need to get to Sandy Bay."

"Well, that's no problem, man. You just wait here while I bring round the car."

The man limped, Bertram could now see that one leg was shorter than the other, across the grass verge and down to the tarmacked compound where he would collect his car. Bertram's eyes followed him, then he turned his attention to the poster that was pasted against the wall of the airport building. Peeling, and likely to flake apart at any moment, it advertised the forthcoming independence, and although the sun had sucked most of the ink from the paper much of it was still visible. If the man had not arrived with the taxi Bertram would have detached himself from the suitcases and gone across to take a closer look.

The taxi was a dark green Ford Corsair, a make of car Bertram had not seen for at least ten years. They were popular when he first arrived in England, but had rapidly become a joke car. Back on his home island the car seemed laughable to him, but the carefully polished exterior, and the reverence with which his self-appointed driver parked it, then waddled around to collect the luggage, made Bertram aware that in this society such a car was still a symbol of some status.

The man loaded the suitcases with a well-practiced ease. As he did so Bertram noticed the knuckles of his hands were little more than bruised knobs, as though he had been the victim of some medieval torture. Clearly, driving a taxi had not been his only vocation.

"So where it is you say you need to get to?"

"Sandy Bay," said Bertram. "You know where the Francis house is?"

The taxi driver pushed back his peaked cap and scratched his gray and wiry hair.

"The Francis house," he paused. "No, man, I don't seem to be able to place it."

"Well then, you just drive, and I going let you know as we get close to it."

"You want me to drive to Sandy Bay?" asked the man.

"You didn't hear me? Or maybe Sandy Bay done slide into the sea since I left."

"It's not going to cost you soft, you know. Gas don't be cheap. And the Government putting a tax on spare parts so I must charge you thirty dollars. If it isn't for the Government I let you take the trip for twenty, but they squeezing everyone these days."

Bertram quickly calculated that thirty dollars came to about eleven pounds. The alternative to taking the taxi was to wait for a bus, or to try and hitch a lift, but he had no idea whether a bus came to the airport, and there was nobody around whom he recognized.

"Thirty dollars seems alright to me," said Bertram.

He looked at the taxi driver, who replaced his hat and began to nod slowly as if to say, "Yes, Bertram, I agree with you, thirty dollars is alright."

Bertram opened the rear door and slid across into the seat. Before slamming the door he called impatiently to the driver:

"Well, you going stand there all day?"

The man looked at him, then checked the boot was properly shut. He came around to the driver's side, opened his door, then got in and started up the engine. The car jumped forward, the man obviously having some trouble with the clutch, then it began to ease its way smoothly down the hill towards the main road, Island Road. They turned left and joined the thin line of traffic streaming away from the capital and into the country.

"So tell me," said the driver, "how long it is since you been away?"

"Twenty years," replied Bertram.

Bertram noticed a roll of fat which bulged over the man's shirt collar.

"Well, one thing you going to have to remember," said the driver, "is that we don't rush things here. You rushing me too much, and I don't like to be rushed."

Bertram was slightly taken aback by the brashness of the voice. Then he noticed the man now looking back at him in the rearview mirror, so he sat forward in his seat.

"Listen, I'm only trying to rush you for I'm not sure if you're hearing what I'm saying to you."

"I know," said the man, not bothering to turn around. "I know why you're trying to rush me, but remember you're back home now and things do move differently here. I'm often picking up fellars who been living in England and America and all them places, and they coming back here like we must adjust to their pace rather than it's they who must remember just who it is they dealing with once they reach back."

"I know who it is I'm dealing with," said Bertram.

"Good," said the man, "for I don't be trying to make you feel bad. I'm just trying to help straighten you out."

Bertram sat back in his seat and looked out of the window. The man turned on the crackly radio and tuned it into the local station ZYZ, with its mixture of loud bass-oriented music and regional news. Bertram listened for a while, hoping that his exchange with the taxi driver had come to an end; then he turned all his attention to the island of his boyhood.

On the far side of the road there was little but sugar cane, which swam out flat like some vast economic blight. On the near side of the road the slack sea, the waves too sluggish to break. This one road hugged the perimeter of the island as though afraid to stray inland, and in the course of its thirty-mile circle it passed through a dozen irregularly spaced villages. Taking this particular route around the island meant that Sandy Bay, if Bertram remembered properly, would be the fifth village they would come to. Now, up ahead, he could see they were approaching the first. A few houses began to litter both sides of the road. Standing impassively outside them were small trouserless children with vests that just covered their distended bellies. Most went barefoot, but a few wore a solitary shoe which reminded Bertram that as children they used to joke that a child with only one shoe had a dead mother. Now, as he thought of his own mother, he found it disturbing to remember that he had once been amused by such humorless games.

The houses in this first village were wooden shacks painted all colors, as though a rainbow had bent down and licked some life into the place. They were framed by green vegetation which to Bertram's eyes seemed almost plastic in its perfection. He watched as a mother furiously beat a piece of rope across the back of a child's legs, the child silent, his face twisted in concentration. And then the taxi moved on past the snarling dogs. Bertram rolled down the window and listened to the music from both radio and throat, spiritually rich music for it came from the heart where people cried when they were happy and laughed when they were sad. They passed the stove-weary mothers putting braids in their small daughters' hair with metal comb and oil for tool and lubrication, their husbands squatting on wooden boxes before a tray of dominoes. Bertram looked at the cane cutters, who were now free for the day but still walked like condemned men with neither hope nor desire, their arms swinging loosely by their sides, as if they had just witnessed the world turn a full circle, knowing that fate no longer held any mystery for them. And he looked at the young girls waggling their hips crazily and throwing out their chests where breasts did not yet exist. Bertram found himself overwhelmed and disturbed by the bare brown legs, tired black limbs, rusty minds, the bright kinetic reds of the village signaling birth, the pale weary greens the approach of death. For a moment he could not admit to himself that he was home.

"People seem just as poor as they always been," said Bertram.

The man looked back at him but said nothing, as though unsure whether his passenger spoke from embarrassment or disappointment. Bertram caught the driver's look, but quickly turned away.

Although taken aback by the poverty of this village, it was the general optimism of the populace that now began to occupy Bertram's attention. In the midst of this tropical squalor, people were conscientiously repairing properties and dressing them with decorations. Others were whitewashing walls and cutting down overhanging branches. The tree trunks were painted white so they looked like long black legs sporting freshly laundered tennis socks. And the bunting was strung from branch to branch, from telegraph pole to telegraph pole, with the small flags of independence scattered everywhere. But it was impossible for Bertram to ignore the existence of a conflict between the optimism of this imminent independence, and the outward signs of a village still struggling to acquire the means to meet the most basic of needs, such as running water and proper lighting. He wondered if he was suffering from those same feelings of liberal guilt that he had always despised in some English people, or if in fact his thoughts did contain astute insights into the current state of the island.

As they moved into the heart of the next village, the taxi slowed down as the people grew thicker and claimed the outer fringes of the road as legitimate territory for their games and loitering. Then magically the people began to thin again, and the taxi was able to speed up and accelerate away into the country. The road was deserted, apart from the odd group of girls, their bodies slim as Coca-Cola bottles, making their way home from school in their regulation khaki uniforms. Following close behind them were the boys, their books balanced neatly on their heads to protect them from the sun. From the fields which skirted this section of the road curled great billowing clouds of smoke. The leaves were being burnt off the canestalks to make them easier to cut. The flames licked the air and the cindered canetrash spun in the wind. As they walked on the schoolchildren protected their eyes against the smoke. Then a bus crashed by, its engine aimlessly overrevved. Bertram watched as it bounced on its springs like an animated toy, stopping up the road ahead to set down a group of tired cutters. The old brakes hissed, cursed, then savored the relief of a moment's peace. Having taken its rest the bus shuddered and belched before disappearing behind a grayish mist of spent fuel.

Sandy Bay was the only village on the island, apart from the capital, Baytown, which possessed another road besides Island Road. The road was called Whitehall, but a thoroughfare less like London's Whitehall would be hard to imagine. It forked off left from Island Road, and the taxi immediately reduced speed as it entered the narrow highway. The road had been made because it led down to the pier, a rickety construction erected by a previous administration. The pier jutted out into the sea in the hope that it might facilitate trade with, and thus appease, the natives on one of the two sister islands, an island so far away that its low

outline could only be observed on the clearest of days. But this sister
island had refused to be mollified, and eventually she had insisted upon
her "freedom" from what she considered to be a double colonial yoke.
The British listened patiently to the islanders' pleadings, then decided
that the most practical thing to do would be to invade the sister island.
Six thousand paratroopers landed on an island barely six miles long, and
people woke up that morning and found it raining Red Berets. The
island's three policemen ran to the station and fought over two rifles.
And having restored order the British secured for this island its own
sovereignty, and Whitehall became an even narrower road, and the pier
at its end fell into disrepair.

"Stop by the ghaut," said Bertram.

"By the Sutton house there?"

The taxi driver pointed to a large concrete house that was painted
a blossomy orange. It was set so close to the road that the low wire
fence surrounding it looked like an embroidered hem. To squeeze
between it and the walls of the house would be difficult, it not
impossible, so all the fence served to do was make sure that the walls
of the house were not the edge of the road.

"I suppose so," said Bertram. "But I don't remember the house."

"You wouldn't," said the driver with satisfaction of one-upman-
ship. "It's only been there five of six years. But you remember the
Suttons?"

"Sure," said Bertram. Mr. Sutton had been a teacher at the Baytown Girls' High School, and his dominating wife had looked after the
Sunday School classes in Sandy Bay. He wondered if they were still
alive. If they were they would be old, but at least they had managed
to save enough money over the years to have a concrete house,
although something inside Bertram told him they were probably less
comfortable in this house than they had been in their wooden one. It
seemed that the desire for symbols of affluence touched even the
most pious of souls.

The taxi came to a halt, and the man screwed himself around in
his seat and scratched the gray bristles on his craggy face.

"I think we agreed upon thirty dollars, isn't it?"

Bertram lifted his backside from the seat and slipped a hand into his pocket. He peeled off a purple note and two green ones, and passed the money to the man, who received it with silence.

"You're not going to help me with the cases?" asked Bertram.

The driver got out of the car and Bertram followed. Having removed the suitcases he turned to Bertram, who was now looking overhead. An airplane streaked across the sky leaking a thin wisp of smoke, its noise rising and dying like that of a wave. Bertram knew now that he was alone, as he watched the jet that had brought him home continue its journey south.

"You needing a hand down the ghaut with these?"

"As far as the gate would be useful."

Bertram picked up the large suitcase and left the lighter one for the disabled man.

The ghaut was the ghaut of his childhood. A thin dusty path that led down into what could almost be considered a separate village. It was flanked on either side by tightly-crammed, ill-balanced, and blistered shacks that looked as though they might at any moment split open and reveal the bleakness inside. Underneath these houses played the children and fowls, while the sun-blackened adults tended to the sporadic yam or cassava plants that speckled the yard. Above them towered the stubborn breadfruit trees, pregnant with food, and together with the thick rubbery banana leaves, the wispier leaves of the palm, and the blazing red of the hibiscus, they created a spectacle of foliage through which only the sharpest spokes of light could penetrate. The air smelt of food being reheated in large blackened pots, and was stung with the faint echo of a vibrant drug. Running down the center of the ghaut were thin metal pipelines which Bertram realized were new to him, and he had to take extra care not to trip over them. Then, about halfway down on the right, he saw the house in which he had been born, the house in which he had grown up with his mother and his younger brother. It had recently received a lick of paint, or, more correctly, many licks. Bertram felt both glad that the place was being looked after, and appalled that the medley of colors was so distasteful.

"This is it," he said to the taxi driver as he put down his suitcase. The driver set down the other suitcase by the gate.

"You have everything?" he asked, clearly out of breath.

Bertram nodded. As he turned the man tugged at the waistline of his baggy pants, and Bertram watched him tack his way back up the ghaut towards his car.

Two small boys stood by the gate and looked up at Bertram. They both sported tee-shirts emblazoned with the new flag of independence. He looked at them and tried to imagine whose children they were, sure that their parents must once have been childhood friends, but he could not trace their origins. Then he looked down and noticed that they were standing with open palms. Although they asked for nothing, he realized they were begging and this annoyed him. Bertram picked up both suitcases.

The gate still hung drunkenly from its hinges. It creaked as he pushed it, and slammed loudly as the now-rusty spring flipped it back into place. The family house was little more than a two-roomed box built up on tiny pillars of bricks so that animals might find shade from the heat of the sun and shelter from the downpours during the rainy season. Four clearly unstable steps led to the front door, which in Bertram's memory had never been opened. Bertram could see the back of a chest of drawers which made the door impossible to open. The steps were for sitting on and talking to people who might lean over the fence.

Bertram left the two suitcases just inside the gate and made his way around to the back of the house. The kitchen stood in the middle of the dirt yard, the door open, the inside cluttered and untidy, reminding him of an English toolshed. A dog was licking out the contents of what Bertram imagined to be an empty pot of soup, so he bent and picked up a pebble. He tossed it and dashed the dog on the side of its head; then he watched as it scampered off, knocking over the pot as it did so. From inside the house no voice was raised to ask what was going on, no irate face appeared at the door, no item was thrown out to make doubly sure that the dog did not return. Bertram realized that either his mother was out, or she was sound asleep.

He climbed the steps that led to the back door, and brushed aside the curtain he remembered watching his mother hang when he was scarcely five years old. Then he stopped and looked around the cramped room. The same curling postcards and photographs, once colored, now yellow and white, were tucked under the same ceiling beams, were pinned to the same walls with the same drawing pins, were propped up against the same hymn books and unopened novels. The room disturbed him for it looked like a museum, but a special kind of museum where only he could be aware of the significance of the items on exhibition.

From the next room he could hear an uncomfortable breathing, as though the person were inhaling sand. Bertram eased back a second curtain (hung, if he remembered rightly, at the same time as the first) and stared at his mother. She lay on her back, arms by her sides, rigid as though Bertram ought to file past her rather than stand and look. It was a particularly warm evening and her face was puffed and wet with perspiration. As the breeze rose and swung the single light bulb, its glow caught his mother's skin and she held its reflection as though it were the most precious treasure on earth. But Bertram could see her face was thinner, the cheeks higher and more pronounced. Her hair was now a dignified silvery-gray, and the high veins on her arms criss-crossed as though a wire netting just below the skin were holding her together. She seemed at home in her bed, and Bertram wondered if the rest of her small house held any interest for her. It was impossible for him to judge the state of her mind as he had not heard from her in many years. Their letters to each other, though never frequent, seemed to have dried up like a river bed in summer. Whatever it was that had flowed between them had suddenly ceased, and Bertram's greatest fear was that he might return home and find that his mother had died and nobody, not even Dominic, had bothered to write and let him know. Then his mother stirred, and instinctively Bertram stood back and tried to find some shadow. But she did not open her eyes. She simply relaxed back into the same spasmodic pattern of breathing, and Bertram took this opportunity to retreat into the front room. Once there he hovered by the small settee, wanting to fold it out and lie down, but he thought he should first bring in the suitcases from outside.

The two boys still stood by the gate holding out their hands as though some form of paralysis had set in. Bertram looked at the suitcases, then at the two boys, then up and down the ghaut to make sure that nobody was watching. He pushed his hand into his pocket and, unsure as to why he was doing so, he gave the two boys ten pence each. They looked at the round silver coins that now lay in the middle of their palms, unable to decide to do with them. They did not recognize the coins but they looked valuable, big, and heavy. Then, presumably having assumed that they had been given something of great worth, they both quickly smiled and ran off as fast as they could before the man changed his mind. Bertram watched them, the tops of their short legs barely thickening out into dusty buttocks, their tee-shirts still white, knowing full well that by the time independence arrived these government gifts would be little more than soiled rags.

Bertram turned and picked up the suitcases. Then he saw that the dog had reappeared and was sitting and looking at him, as though guarding the door to the kitchen. He glared back and considered throwing yet another pebble, but it dawned on him that the animal might belong to his mother, so he strode past it and up the steps and into the house. The absurdity of his luggage became clear, for the two suitcases took up most of the floor area. He had no idea where he would eventually find space to unpack, and was uncertain about what would follow when he had done so. Bertram pushed both suitcases to one side and slumped on to the solitary chair, sleep stealing into his body. The tension of the flight and subsequent heat of a Caribbean day were beginning to oppress him. He tried to slouch in the high-backed wooden chair that his mother called "a preacherman chair," its plain structure giving off an unmistakable air of religious discomfort, but the small ball of fire at the base of his spine simply encouraged him to twist and turn until he finally resigned himself to this ordeal of pain. Bertram put his feet up on one of the suitcases, loosened the top button of his shirt, and slackened off his tie. Then he smiled inwardly as he realized that he had returned. There had been moments in the last twenty years when he felt sure he would never have the courage or the means to set foot once again on his island.

Bertram had left the island a wayward boy who had seized a final opportunity to fulfil his potential. Father Daniels, the English vicar, had seen to it that Bertram sat for the scholarship, even though nobody thought this restive boy could possibly succeed. A neighbor had told his mother that it was sinful to waste good ink and paper, but although she had never set any great store by academic achievement his mother was willing to defend either of her sons in anything they said they wanted to do.

On the morning of the scholarship examination his mother rose early to prepare for him a special breakfast, so he could at least start the day on equal footing with the other boys. She fried some plantain and saltfish, then cut up a ten-cents loaf and made a sauce for him to dip his bread into. Dominic, his younger brother, ate his meal in silence. Then he began to rush, as though anxious to eat more than Bertram, but when his mother shouted at him he threw down his fork, snatched up his bag, and sprinted off towards school.

"Dominic, come back here, you hear me! You don't even comb your hair as yet!"

In their mother's eyes this was by far the greater of the crimes he had committed. Bertram tried not to look up for he felt his brother's behavior was a deliberate ploy to upset him and make him lose concentration. So he continued to eat, and redoubled his efforts to think about the English, and the History, and the preliminary questions of Law that Father Daniels had been filling his head with for the last two years. Last year he had tried to convince Father Daniels that he was ready to take the examination, but Father Daniels had counter-argued that he liked to prepare a boy properly. Half-preparation was of no use to anyone. But in his heart Bertram had worried that by the time he was allowed to sit for the scholarship, he would be so old that people would laugh at him. And true enough when it was announced he would be doing so, some had laughed at him. At nineteen he was made to feel ancient, even though most of the others were nearly his age, two or three years out of school with some benevolent adult instructing them, either an old teacher or a friend of the family. And now, on this critical day, the twelve candidates were finely tuned and prepared, and expected to perform like racehorses.

Bertram found a desk at the back of the furthest column of six, across the aisle from his friend. Jackson Clayton was of stout medium build and the proud possessor of elegant good looks. Bertram had a gawkishly juvenile body, his neck like a slender stalk that held too weighty a flower. Jackson's features, in addition to his being the captain of the youth cricket team, meant he had little problem in attracting the girls. Why he was sitting the examination was a mystery to many, though of course most expected him to take the scholarship, he being somebody destined to succeed at anything he put his hand or mind to.

On one of those long evenings down by the abandoned pier, when Bertram would bowl to Jackson over after over of soft ball spin, so that his friend could practice dropping a dead bat on it and killing the kick on the ball, Jackson had admitted to Bertram that his father had threatened to beat him if he did not make an effort for the scholarship. Jackson claimed that he had protested forcibly, even though he knew full well he would finally lose out to the wishes of his father. And so, like Bertram, he had ended up taking tuition from Father Daniels, even though his greatest wish was to remain on the island and some day open the batting for the West Indies. It was a big ambition, in fact the biggest. Bertram had continued to bowl to him until the night began to mop up the blood from the sun, and in the distance the moon appeared, as yet unseen. He thought Jackson might some day make the team, but Bertram knew Jackson would never win the scholarship. It was pride alone that made him enter. The idea of being thought ignorant had been a greater spur than any threat of parental beatings, but Bertram said nothing for he never argued with his friend. He continued to bowl to him until the brooding trees waved their spreading heads in time with the rhythms of the sea breeze, and eventually it was too dark to continue.

Father Daniels was to be their invigilator. He stood at the front of the schoolroom and took a small paper knife to the brown package, which they all assumed contained their papers. Jackson rearranged his ruler and pencil, one behind the other, then turned to his friend.

"You feeling nervous, man?"

Bertram nodded. "I feel like all the knowledge is just draining out of my head."

"You lucky then, for I didn't never have none in my head to start with."

They both looked up at Father Daniels, his balding head catching the sun as he bent almost double and tried now to break manually into the envelope. He was a dignified man, unimposing in stature and modest of voice, a perfect combination for teaching boys in their late adolescence.

"You didn't listen to what Father Daniels been telling you?" asked Bertram.

"'Course I listened," said Jackson, "but I don't want to go to England. I have a job in the bank, and I have the bat, man. Anyhow, I hope you win for when you gone I going check for Patsy Archibald."

"How you know if I win I won't take she with me?"

"Don't chat shit, man. The scholarship fund don't provide for women."

"So what happen if the victor have a wife?"

Jackson picked up his pencil and pointed it at Bertram.

"You making joke with me, Bertram? You can't be serious about marriage to a girl like that."

"Like what?" snapped Bertram, indignation rising inside of him. "Like what?" he demanded.

Having finally opened the packet, Father Daniels now looked up at them both. His ruddy face was calm and he spoke quietly, a whisper that only just managed to reach the back of the room.

"Francis and Clayton, are you two boys interested in the scholarship paper or would you rather go outside and continue your discussion there?" He stared at them both, but neither said anything. "Well?"

"Sorry, Father Daniels," they chorused simultaneously.

Father Daniels looked hard at them; then having reasserted his authority he pulled the papers from the envelope and began to distribute them. Bertram sneaked a look at Jackson, who grinned. They had failed their first unscheduled test, and nobody would expect either of them now to pass the examination. The other ten boys sat in front, seemingly calm outside, but Bertram felt sure that inside they too were racked with nerves.

When Father Daniels reached Bertram he let his hand linger on the desk. He seemed loath to let go of the examination paper and, fed up with looking at his hand, it occurred to Bertram that perhaps Father Daniels wanted him to look up. When he did so Bertram read a private message. Father Daniels was clearly annoyed with him for what had just taken place, but he was also delivering a short final tutorial in which no words were necessary. His steely glare said everything. As Father Daniels made his way back towards the front of the class, Jackson turned to Bertram and inquisitively raised his eyebrows, but Bertram simply let a fraternal smile crease his face.

"You boys have three hours in which to complete the paper as best you can. I don't want to hear any talking or conferring. I don't want to see anybody looking at anybody else's paper, and I wish you all the best of luck. God's will shall prevail, and may the best young man succeed."

Bertram picked up his paper then froze, suddenly afraid to take a look and see what the three questions were that he would have to answer. He turned to his right and stared through the open door. Out at sea a pair of boats were making their way back to the island after a night of fishing. They were late, thought Bertram. Usually the boats had landed and the fish been sold by now, and without warning Bertram found his mind totally occupied with the various reasons that might explain their overdue arrival. A shark, an illness, a broken rudder, an extra large catch that had handicapped them? The options were almost endless, and for a few moments they proved more interesting than the paper in front of him. Above the boat he saw a giant bird carefully riding an air current. Then it dropped in a long and barely perceptible curve, and without a ripple it emerged with a large silver fish twice its size.

The papers were sent to England for marking, and it was two months before the boys were due to meet again in the schoolroom. In this time Jackson achieved the great honor of being selected to attend the West Indies youth team camp on a neighboring island. He was also invited to the Governor's house, and Jackson told Bertram that he had shaken hands not only with the Governor, but with the Governor's wife. He also claimed to have patted the white horse that the Governor kept around the back of the house, but Bertram knew there was no white horse. While Jackson's fame reached new heights, Bertram found himself grappling with the multiple problems of work, his brother, and most crucially, Patsy Archibald. Suddenly, as though he were being punished, Bertram's life became unbearably complicated.

He had found himself in a trough of depression after the scholarship examination, and so he left his job with the municipal department. This loss had troubled him little, as he had been not much more than a glorified litter collector in Stanley Park. And although his new job stacking shelves at Vijay's Supermarket was hardly much of an improvement, it did mean he had a few extra dollars in his pocket and some privacy in his work. At the end of the day he now began to hang around in Baytown, for he could afford to buy a beer, and stand up laughing in the street with the other young men, then go around the back of the treasury building and piss his spent water in a loud and lordly arch. But his leisurely behavior, although largely ignored by his mother, was something that began to drive a wedge between himself and Dominic.

Because of their father's perpetual absence, Dominic had come to depend upon Bertram more than a younger brother would normally do. They played together, ate together, slept and worked, they even lost their virginity together, having persuaded a local girl that if she did it twice it would be impossible for her to get pregnant. Bertram had gone first, then watched as Dominic conjured a stiffness into himself and entered. Bertram trusted his younger brother enough to tell him that this was his first time, although in the past he had lied to him, sure that Dominic needed to hear stories of fictional conquest in order to reinforce the notion of his older brother as a special being. But now that Bertram seemed to be spending more time in town after work, Dominic was becoming increasingly isolated. These days when he returned home from town, Bertram would often find his younger brother asleep, and in the morning loath to talk to him.

When Bertram started to see Patsy Archibald, Dominic became even more distant. They had both known Patsy for years, and although she was Bertram's age she was Dominic's friend too, for that was the way that it had always been. Like them, she was being brought up by just the one adult, although in her case it was not her mother but her aunt, for both parents had emigrated to Canada. One day, as they lay by the sea on the thin black scrap of sand that was a beach for the people of Sandy Bay, Bertram became aware of her in a manner which frightened him. He let her hand paddle in his palm, and the heat from her body aroused him. Then, having conquered his initial fear, he smiled at her and felt his body invaded with sexual longing. Suddenly the sole purpose of their afternoon involved divorcing themselves from Dominic. He was too adult for either of them to suggest he go to the shop or for a walk so, as the sun drew the strength from them like a giant sponge, they simply waited.

An hour later Dominic peeled himself off the sand and stood up. He was tall, and it was possible he might one day outgrow his brother. But Dominic was a nascent oak as opposed to a willowy sapling. He looked at the pair of them, lying flat on their backs and squinting up at the sky, then he brushed the sand from his legs and arms.

"It's too hot for me," he announced.

Bertram propped himself up on one elbow and tried to look as though he was in some way distressed by his brother's imminent departure.

"So where you going that don't be hot?"

"I don't know," said Dominic. "Probably back home to sit inside. I don't know how the two of you don't start to steam then cook."

Like Bertram, Patsy now propped herself up on her elbow. She continued to squint as she looked at Dominic.

"I know what you mean," she said. "But I going maybe lie here just a short while longer."

"Well, I can't take it no more," said Dominic.

He turned and left them. They both watched as he walked along the beach, then up the back of a small dune and out of sight. Patsy looked across at Bertram, and although he felt her eyes he could not meet them. Then he heard Patsy lower herself down onto the sand.

"You want to go now?" asked Bertram, his eyes firmly fixed upon the sea.

Patsy said nothing. Up above them a gull made a noise like an airborne cat. Then Bertram felt pressured by her silence into looking at her. When he did so he was sure that she had deliberately forced this quiet upon him so that he would have to make the first overtly suggestive move.

"So why you don't kiss me, Bertram?"

Bertram looked at her small and ideally-formed body, and his eyes caressed her high breasts. But he was still unsure of what was happening between them.

"Well?" said Patsy. "I know both you and Dominic had girls before, but it's you I want."

Bertram felt confused. "You ever take a man?" he asked.

Patsy laughed and sat up straight. She looked into Bertram's eyes as though shocked by his diffidence.

"Bertram, you honestly think that if I'd have had a next man I'd be waiting for you to touch me? Bertram, please do something or I going take fright and leave this place."

Bertram leaned forward and kissed her roughly, not because he felt a lack of sensitivity towards her, but because he was off-balance. Then he ran his hand clumsily along her leg, as though trying to wipe something off it, but Patsy trapped his hand with hers. She began to strip off his shirt, and as Bertram opened his mouth to speak she kissed silence into his body. Steering him towards her she encouraged him to stiffen, taut like a bow, then slowly she helped him to break into a thick milky predicament. She eased Bertram over to one side and lay back happy and at peace. But Bertram was restless, his mind turning over, his feet itching for he could feel the sand that had squeezed its way between shoe and sock.

When he returned home Dominic was sitting on the front steps that led nowhere, fanning himself with a coconut palm leaf. Bertram stopped at the gate. At first he simply looked as a neighbor's black pigs scampered to and fro, their snouts twitching, their eyes as ever wet. Then he could no longer tolerate the tension.

"You cool enough now?" asked Bertram.

Dominic glanced up at him. Then he looked back down at the space between his own feet.

"What's the matter, little man?" Bertram pushed open the gate. "Something the matter with Mummy?" Dominic neither spoke nor looked up. "You lost your tongue?"

"You fuck Patsy?" asked Dominic. "You wait till I gone to fuck her?"

Bertram sighed.

"I fucked her, but I didn't wait until you gone to do it. Or rather I did, but it's not something I planned."

Dominic was looking up at him now, his face contorted in hurt, and Bertram knew that whatever he said was bound to make it more painful for his brother. However, before he could say any more Dominic got to his feet and ran from him around the back of the house and slammed the door. He leaned against the gate and heard his mother angrily telling Dominic not to make so much noise. Bertram knew if he were to go in his presence it would only serve to trigger off his brother's fury once again, but as he looked around he knew he could not stand by the gate all night. So he chose instead to go for a walk, and soon he found himself outside the schoolroom.

Bertram walked around the front of the building and tried the door. It opened, and he resolved to go in and sit down until he felt secure enough that it would be all right to go back and confront both Dominic and his mother. But when he woke up it was morning, and the hand on his shoulder was that of Father Daniels, the same Father Daniels who stood before him on the morning that was to change his life.

Father Daniel looked at all twelve boys. He knew that to them two months must seem like a long time, but he found it difficult to believe that things had been decided so quickly, and that the critical letter had already arrived from England. He fingered the piece of paper and checked himself, realizing that he was playing with them for there was only the one name to read out, and he could hold that name quite comfortably in his head.

"The winner of this year's island scholarship is Bertram Francis of Sandy Bay."

All eyes turned on Bertram. Most were disbelieving, but some looked momentarily relieved, even pleased that it was not them. After all, Bertram knew that not every boy had wanted to sit the examination, parental ambition often being a cruel spur to childhood labor.

"He will be going to England," continued Father Daniels, "to pursue his chosen topic of study which, as I'm sure you're all aware, will be in the Law."

Father Daniels betrayed no emotion as he stared directly at Bertram.

"Well, I think you might all give your colleague a round of applause. His is an achievement worthy of your appreciation."

As they did so Bertram was filled with an inner conflict, unsure whether or not he should stand up to receive their congratulations. But mercifully their applause soon died away, and he was no longer required to make a decision.

Dominic was still at school when Bertram returned home with the good news. He picked his way down the ghaut and saw his angular mother carrying water from the standpipe to the kitchen. She wore a green headscarf which only seemed to accentuate the long rake of her face, and deepen the hollow blackness where her eyes should have been. There could be little doubt as to whose features Bertram had inherited. She looked up at him and spoke without breaking step.

"You not working today, then?"

Bertram felt certain that he had told her this was the day the results came through, but he could not be sure. Rather than imagine that his mother might have forgotten, he preferred to look upon himself as the one who had suffered an aberration of memory.

"I had to go up by the schoolroom to see Father Daniels."

"And what it is he have to say for himself?"

"He say I win the scholarship from the island to go to England."

His mother stopped and stared at him. For what seemed an age they said nothing to each other, then she spoke, although by now the focus of her eyes had slackened and Bertram could no longer be sure that she was looking at him.

"I'm proud of you, Bertram."

As though unable to think of anything else to say she turned and walked away, and Bertram felt sure that she did not understand the full implications of his achievement.

Bertram sat on the fence and looked up the ghaut. The line of his body fell from his narrow shoulders to his feet, with no discernible deviation either inward or outward. When he perched on the fence he did so as a bird, tucking one leg up under the other, flamingo-style.

He would not bother going to work today for there was too much to think about. Then he looked over into the next yard where a young boy tried to fly a kite which leapt feebly on the thin breeze before once more plummeting back to the ground. He watched for a while, then realized it would be hours before Dominic returned. He jumped down and decided to take a stroll. As Bertram passed up the ghaut he saw the marketwomen sitting in their well-groomed backyards, their breasts like blackening mushrooms, shrivelled, waterless, and undesirable. They were crouched, feet shrouded in outsize laceless shoes, flicking at the insects, aprons filthy, pockets bulging with useless change, and their broad straw hats only made complete by the occasional gaping hole. They had already been to Baytown and sold what bits of fruit and vegetable they had managed to gather or scrape up from the land, and now their day was done. Behind them, and stacked in discarded piles, lay rusting junk, and huddled beside the lumber their elevated shacks had their doors and windows thrown wide open trying to catch what little wind there was. The extremes of heat and rain, the habitual lashing from a hurricane or a movement of the earth, meant that these crooked dwellings seldom lasted long, but they did cast large pools of shadow in which animals were able to sleep.

Bertram looked at the marketwomen but kept walking until he reached Whitehall. Once there he glanced across the road and up and through the length of the village. But the shop doorways, the concrete steps, the grass verges, were strewn with sun-stunned villagers standing, sitting, drinking, ignoring the flies and the heat and dust, staring at nothing. It was the dull season around Sandy Bay so there was no longer cane to cut. Bertram decided to go back home and sit up on the fence. He was too familiar with the misery of the scenes that filled his eyes, and today of all days he wanted to think beyond them.

He sat again on the fence and tried hard to imagine what England would be like. He thought of how disciplined he would have to be in his study if he was to live up to what was now expected of him, not only by Father Daniels but by everyone on the island. These thoughts flashed backward and forward through the troubled cinema of his mind and before he knew it, time had slipped by and the sky began to darken.

When he finally saw Dominic the day was at an end. He was carrying a cricket bat so Bertram knew exactly what he had been doing. Dominic walked slowly, clearly exhausted at this late hour by what Bertram imagined to have been a keenly fought contest. He waited until his brother was right below him before speaking.

"You win the game?" began Bertram.

"We didn't play no match."

Dominic leaned the bat off against the fence, as though aware that they would probably be talking with each other for quite some while.

"We just play until the man is out and a next one to go in."

"I see," said Bertram, nodding aimlessly. "You bat?"

"Most of the night," said his brother, trying not to show any pride in his achievement. There was a chance, slim though it was, that Dominic might one day mature into a decent batsman. However, unlike Bertram's friend Jackson, it was not a goal he was actively pursuing to the exclusion of all others.

"Well, I have a piece of news I want to tell you before I tell anyone else."

Dominic looked over his brother's shoulder, enquiring as to whether or not Bertram had already told their mother his news. Bertram knew he would have to respond to this unasked question.

"I had to tell her first for you weren't here."

Dominic gave him an empty look which left Bertram unsure if his brother was interested in what he was trying to say to him. Then Dominic spoke.

"You capture the scholarship, right?"

Bertram nodded. "Who tell you?"

"Twelve of you sitting in the room when Father Daniels announce the winner. You think the other eleven going keep their mouth shut?"

Bertram was piqued that Dominic should speak to him in this way, but he was also secretly pleased that his brother should, for what he considered to be the first time, have outsmarted him.

"I see what you mean," said Bertram, in as generous a voice as he could muster.

Dominic picked up his bat and pushed open the crooked gate. He passed through into the yard and let the gate swing shut between him.

"You don't have nothing to say to me, then? No congratulations or anything of that order?"

Bertram realized he was letting Dominic know how upset he was, but he could not control himself. Dominic looked down and began to strike at the dust with the blade of his bat.

"This mean you're going to England?" asked Dominic.

"Of course it means I'm going to England," said Bertram. He leapt off the fence and circled around to face his brother.

"People don't take the scholarship examination to pass it and stay here. I'm going to England, but only for three years, four years at the most."

Dominic lifted his head, and his eyes met those of his older brother. Bertram knew that what had happened between himself and Patsy had soured their relationship, but this new blow was something that Dominic had clearly feared and half-anticipated for much longer. He looked hard at his younger brother, but it was as though Dominic could not find it within his heart to be angry at him. Bertram watched as Dominic let the bat slide through his hand, then with a quick flick of his wrist the wandering bat was back in his grip.

Dominic turned and walked off towards the house. Bertram's eyes followed him, still trying to understand his brother's distress, but he thought it best to leave him on his own for a few moments. Rather than leap back up on the fence, Bertram decided to take a walk up the ghaut and buy a beer at Mr. Carter's shop.

There was no street lighting in Sandy Bay, let alone ghaut lighting. Bertram edged his way up the ghaut, but he found it impossible to make this journey without treading on something uneven, although it was usually little more than a piece of broken cane lying chewed and rejected like a limb snapped in half. At the top of the ghaut some boys were sitting on the side of the road, soaking up whatever heat still lay unspent from the day. They waved to Bertram, more a gesture of new respect than a greeting or sign of imminent departure.

Leslie Carter's shop stood alone, its wooden walls thin with age, its roof inadequate. Outside, someone had nailed up a mosaic of bright enamel signs that advertised foreign beer, aspirins, and Pepsi-Cola. Inside, and carelessly displayed on the shelves, were the familiar packages of skin cream, soap powder, hair shampoo, all of them with healthy pink faces on the packets. On top of the counter Mr. Carter kept some cold meat, though it was regularly peppered with flies as he usually forgot to cover it once he had cut off a piece. And beside the meat was a large glass case in which there were cakes and stale patties.

The proprietor was folded over the shop counter. He wore his familiar orange vest and sported a tidemarked hat, the sort of hat a cowboy would wear, wide in the brim, tall in the crown. Bertram climbed the couple of steps and settled himself on one of the home-made stools. The ritual began. Mr. Carter knew exactly what Bertram wanted, but he would not be rushed into getting it until he was ready. He looked at Bertram and waited, as though listening to some night symphony heard solely by himself and his dog. Only when the last strains of this "music" had died away did he unfold himself and turn around. He lifted the lid of the freezer and took out a bottle of beer that was thinly frosted with ice. He slotted it into the wall-opener, as if ready to break off the neck of the bottle, and watched with infantile fascination as the metal cap fell obediently into the tin tray placed there for that purpose.

"Fifty cents."

Bertram pushed a dollar across the counter, and Mr. Carter picked it up as though this might be his last ever act. Tiredness flooded his every move, and to a stranger it might appear as though he were suffering from a debilitating disease that was eating away at either the muscles of his body or the fabric of his mind. But Bertram, like everyone else in the village, understood that this was just the way he was. There was no simpler or more complex explanation of his behavior than that. Mr. Carter had nothing to hurry for, he never had, and he never would. He slapped down Bertram's change, then he turned and once more folded himself over the counter. Bertram looked at him and realized that tonight there would be no conversation, for the second movement of Mr. Carter's night symphony had already commenced. He picked up the bottle and took a drink. The beer was so cold it tasted metallic and he gasped. Then he screwed himself around so he too could look out over the side street of Whitehall. The alternative was to continue staring at the cans of bully beef, and the soup, and the brown bags of sugar, and the countless packs of batteries that were piled up behind the food in anticipation of the cricket season. If there was one thing you could always rely upon Mr. Carter to have, it was batteries. To run out when a cricket match was coming up would lose him more custom than any amount of bad manners could possibly do.

When Bertram reached home the lights were off. He knew his mother would be asleep by now, but he was convinced that Dominic would still be awake. Bertram undressed in the yard. He stripped off down to his underpants, then carrying his clothes under one arm he curled himself around the door, through the curtain, and into the house. He could see Dominic lying bulky in their bed, his back turned towards him. And in the next room he could hear his mother breathing with the cracked discord that often kept him awake, especially on hot nights such as this one.

"You awake, Dominic?"

He tried to whisper, not wanting to further annoy his brother. But although Dominic did not reply, Bertram felt sure that he was awake and simply playing games with him. He waited a moment and listened as a rat thumped about under the house, then he slid into bed and asked him again.

"Dominic, you awake?"

This time Bertram spoke with more urgency. At first there was no reply, then Dominic stirred.

"Yes, I'm awake," he said.

"I didn't wake you, did I?" asked Bertram.

"I'm awake," said Dominic, in that same flat tone.

Bertram propped himself up and spoke once more.

"Look, you seem mad with me about winning the scholarship. You should be proud of me, man. I work hard for it, I thought you would be proud of me."

There was a long silence before Dominic replied. When he did so he spoke softly.

"I am proud of you," he said. "But I can't believe you really care what I'm thinking any more. It's like I'm just a something you knew once and you suddenly coming on like you're big now."

Although Bertram could not see his brother's face, he could feel the resentment in his voice.

"Dominic, you and me can't go on for the rest of our lives doing everything together."

"We used to."

"I know, but then things changed. I had to go to work, and I had to start to study for the scholarship and things." He paused. "Dominic, not everything can just carry on how it was, you know. Things always moving on but that don't mean we should fall out over them. We must learn to move in our own way too."

"I don't want to change."

"But that's just crazy, man!"

"You think you know everything now, don't you?!"

Dominic spun around to face him, his eyes rounded as though in fear.

"But you don't, you know. You're out with your new friends like I don't exist or nothing, but you're wrong. You're so wrong that you're going to regret treating me like this. Like I'm still a boy and I can't do nothing with you!"

Bertram watched as Dominic's mouth expelled the words his heart had kept locked up for so long. And as he watched he saw a cloud burst inside his brother's head and a tear begin to trickle from the grayness of his eyes. He reached out a hand to touch him, but Dominic recoiled as though Bertram's body was charged with an electricity that might damage him were he to come into contact with it.

"What's the matter?" asked Bertram.

Dominic stared back as though he hated his older brother. Then he snatched up the cover around his neck and twisted away from him. All Bertram could now see was Dominic's back, which he could not keep still enough to hide the fact that he was sobbing into the sheet he held so closely to himself.

And now Bertram sat in the same room, his feet on a suitcase, and he listened to his mother's voice which only just managed to rise high enough to be supported by the still and humid air.

"Who it is through there? Mrs. Sutton, it's you through there?"

Bertram reached up and loosened off his tie even further. His hands were itchy with dried sweat, and as he mopped his brow he realized he was caught in the fur-soft grip of a Caribbean night which had fallen quickly, as though in response to some unheard instruction. Outside he could see the clouds filtering the moon, and the shadows stood high like guards. Bertram listened to the chorus of insects, which he received as a constant roar. It disturbed him that he should have forgotten the pitch and echo of their massed voices, but it also reminded him of just how far he had traveled both in miles and time. He waited for a moment, unsure if his mother was going to call again; then he decided that his evasiveness might be frightening her.

His mother stared at him across the dimly lit room. Above her the swaying light bulb creamed everything in a pale yellow light. It hung from its beam, the wire twisted loosely around the wooden support as though a noose into which someone would soon slip their neck. His mother looked weary, her eyes glazed over with the age that had overtaken her during Bertram's absence.

"Hello, Mummy."

Bertram walked slowly towards her. He leaned over and kissed her on the forehead, but she did not respond. Then he perched, uninvited, on the side of her bed and took her thin hands in his, but still she stared back at him as though he were not really there.

"See, I told you I'd come back."

He laughed slightly, but his mother just looked at him. Then she dropped her eyes and began to roll her hands in the envelope of his, as though trying to make sure that her son was not simply a figment of her worn imagination.

"So you really done come back?"

"I've come back," said Bertram, this time trying to make it less of an announcement.

"And when you planning on taking off again?"

Bertram knew that his mother's apparently casual enquiry was framed so as to lure him into a false sense of security. He cleared his throat before answering.

"I don't know if I'm planning on taking off anywhere again. I was thinking that I might stay here and try and find a position in the society and make back my peace with the island."

He looked at his mother, but her gaze remained expressionless. Bertram felt obliged to continue, but he now found himself speaking to her as though trying to anticipate what she might be thinking.

"I know that twenty years is a long time to be away, but I feel that the time is right and I must seize the opportunity to help the new nation."

"Help them how? It's only the school certificate that you left here with that you bringing back, am I wrong?"

"No, you're not wrong, but I have some money. I've managed to save a little, which should enable me to start up a business of some kind."

"What kind of a business?"

It was only now that it became clear to Bertram his mother was speaking to him with an open contempt. And he discovered himself answering her with the polite manners of a schoolboy, as opposed to the self-assurance of a thirty-nine-year-old man.

"I don't know as yet what kind of a business, but something that don't make me dependent upon the white man."

His mother began to smile. And then she laughed, at first with confidence, then with more control as though unsure if the fragility of her body could support too much humor.

"So that's what England teach you? That you must come home with some pounds and set up a business separate from the white man?"

Bertram looked at her as sternly as he dared. He spoke now with an indignation fueled by his knowledge that she had seldom, in her sixty years on this earth, left Sandy Bay, let alone the island. To him her laughter was simply the cackle of ignorance, and he felt obliged to educate her.

"The only way the black man is going to progress in the world is to set up his own shops and his own businesses independent of the white man. There is no way forward for us if we keep relying on him, for we going continually be cleaning up his shit, and washing out his outhouse."

"I see," said his mother. "And what white man has Leslie Carter ever worked for? If you take a walk up the ghaut in your smart English suit and tie, you going see him bent double like a tree in a high wind over the same counter you left him behind. Is that what you mean by progress?"

Bertram scrutinized his mother, but he could see that she had already switched off from him. He waited in the hope that she might revive their conversation, but eventually he decided to stand up from the bed and leave her to sleep. However, Bertram had to ask his mother just one more thing.

"How is Dominic?" he asked. "He working still at the sugar factory?"

His mother's sigh was polluted with a high asthmatic whistle. Then she repeated Bertram's question.

"How is Dominic?"

After a few moments Bertram decided to speak out again.

"Well, Mummy. How is he?"

But Bertram could now see that his mother had fallen into a silence that made him wonder if she was sleeping. As he turned to take his leave her voice startled him.

"Your brother is well and waiting by the gate. We both going see him soon enough."

Bertram turned back. He watched as his mother folded in her lips so they all but disappeared. As she did so her wretchedness became evident.

In the morning Bertram found himself fully clothed and curled up fetus-style in the chair. Outside he could hear some children playing with a radio, spinning the dial from left to right, right to left, unable to decide upon any one station. He assumed that for them there would be no school today, and as the sun shot a dust-laden shaft through the window Bertram turned and thought of Dominic. He felt ashamed at having slept so soundly, but he knew that both nervous and physical exhaustion had finally taken their toll. Now he wanted to ask his mother more. He wanted to know how and when his brother had died, and why he had not been told. But as he first looked at, then smelt the circles of sweat under his armpits, he knew he would have to wash and change before he could do anything else.

Bertram tried to spring from the chair, but he felt his back protest. He would have to be less adventurous. He leaned forward, opened one of the suitcases and from it he pulled a shirt. As he stood up he caught a mercifully quick glimpse of himself in the badly-silvered mirror that was propped up on the small table. His face was shaped like an isosceles triangle, the most acute apex being his stubbled chin, his eyes set high in the remaining two angles. He scratched some sleep from the corner of one eye, decided not to shave, then admitted to himself that the idea of going around the side of the house and washing under the standpipe, as he had done as a youngster, no longer appealed to him. At the moment he was prepared to remain a little grubby, so he got dressed.

He plucked aside the curtain and peered into his mother's room, where she was still anchored to her dreams. Bertram wanted to wake her, but fear overcame him. In the end he retreated into the front room and searched around in the trouser pockets of his suit for a few Eastern Caribbean dollars. Then he quietly made his way down the back steps and out into the bright morning. The first thing he noticed was the dog lying by the door to the kitchen. He was sure now that it must belong to his mother, for the dog looked up at him as if he were a trespasser on its property. Then Bertram saw the two boys to whom he had given the ten-pence pieces. They stood by the fence and stared at him. As he left the yard and turned to walk up the ghaut, their eyes silently followed him. "They must know," thought Bertram, as a bolt of guilt passed through him. He felt uneasy, and wished that they had become angry or accused him of deception or something. But as it was, he could only worry about his future meetings with the boys.

At the top of the ghaut Bertram turned right into Whitehall. Mr. Carter was leaning over his counter, though characteristically he said nothing. Bertram smiled in his direction but it made little difference. He continued to walk up Whitehall, and although one or two people nodded at him the rest simply looked on, unsure as to whether this really was the Bertram Francis they thought it was. They squatted by the roadside, their eyes blurred and their feet swollen, watching their children drawing pictures in the dirt with pointed wooden sticks. And the children, they too looked at him. This puzzled Bertram until it occurred to him that in all probability they recognized a family likeness with Dominic. It was then that Bertram noticed some of the younger children seemed positively frightened, so he walked on at a quicker pace and listened as the villagers whispered to each other with dust-encrusted words.

The bus stop was where it had always been, outside the Browns' house and right across the road from the hospital. Though in reality there was no bus stop, just a place at the side of the road where horses and carriages had stopped long before the advent of the engine. Bertram looked across at the hospital and saw some workmen putting the final touches to an extension. A sign on the wall boasted that Princess Margaret, the Queen's representative, would be opening the "new" hospital as part of this week's independence celebrations. The workmen scurried back and forth, hurrying to finish their work, but both to the left and to the right Bertram could see that little else in Sandy Bay had changed. The same houses were there, and Bertram imagined that the same people were doing the same things inside them. Only the festive streamers and slogans, and the images of the new flag painted up on the stone walls, were unfamiliar. But when the bus arrived, Bertram noticed that at least one other aspect of life in Sandy Bay was new to his eyes, for this bus was clean and modern and trimmed with well-shined chrome. Bertram also noticed that it was not really a bus at all, but a refurbished Transit van with slick upholstery and a thumping hi-fi system. He climbed aboard and secured a seat by the offside window so he could look out to sea.

The bus was crowded with children taking advantage of their day off from school. Bertram looked at them and realized that they were probably from St. Patrick's. Due in part to its isolated position at the end of the island, this village had the reputation of harboring the most backward of all the island's people. As a child Bertram had taken part in the many jokes about St. Patrick's, but although he now recognized their triviality, he suspected that some people still made them. As he looked at the children and thought of St. Patrick's, the bus sped away and began its frenzied journey to town. Bertram immediately remembered the style of driving, a style which seemed to be denying the possibility that there might be a tomorrow, and at the same time asserting the fact that the driver was a "go-ahead" type of fellar. Each stop was sudden and threw passengers forward and careening into each other, each abrupt piece of acceleration designed to toss you from side to side and to impress upon you the fact that on this island speed was not measured by the speedometer, but by the number of bumps and bruises to the body.

As they raced towards Baytown, Bertram noticed that all the villages now seemed similar. There was generally a stop at the near end of the village, and one at the far end. Only at Middle Way was there also a stop in the center, for this village was slightly larger than the others en route, though nowhere near the size of Sandy Bay. A little way out of Middle Way they lurched over two small humpbacked bridges, which to the untutored eye might appear to have no meaning. But unlike most dwarfish countries, where the river is a sinewy muscle, the strength of the place, rivers on this island were almost permanently sunk beneath their sun-baked bellies. Yet in times of rain they suddenly flowed as a torrent of water from the mountains cascaded down the hillsides, and if it were not for these bridges the island's highway would be severed in two places.

Once they had passed through Butler's village, the bus was able to accelerate down the long straight piece of road and into the gentle bend that gave them a view of Baytown, which from this distance looked beautiful. Behind the capital, and on the horizon, the sole surviving sister island brooded, clouds hanging over her as though harnessed to the mountain peaks by thin invisible wires. When Bertram thought of Baytown he pictured a tropical ghost town, like those they used to study in the geography lesson of the movies. He would queue for hours with his school friends to watch the latest black and white westerns, the same movies they took their school nicknames from. Roy Rogers, Gary Cooper, Audie Murphy; Bertram had liked James Stewart best of all. His funny way of talking made Bertram feel sorry for him, but it also made him guess that to "play" James Stewart would ensure his always being the object of some attention from his friends. But Cripple-mouth was what they decided to call him, until Bertram swore blind that he hated James Stewart and would never see another of his films.

In reality Baytown bore little resemblance to a mid-Western watering hole. Father Daniels had taught Bertram that like most Caribbean towns, it was originally part slave-market and part harbor. It was primarily designed to facilitate the importation of Africans and the exportation of sugar, but over the years it had developed in three directions. Firstly, there were the well-patrolled middle-class estates of the possessors; neat, planned, perfumed, and often affording spectacular views of both the mountains and the sea. And then down by the harbor, and for a few streets in each direction, the low commercial buildings of trade and government. Finally, there existed a hellish and labyrinth-like entanglement of slums in which lived the dispossessed in their broken-down wooden buildings and under their rusty iron roofs. These dwellings were strung out like pebbles on a beach. They formed loosely-defined streets, some only wide enough to permit two cyclists to pass, and living self-consciously among them was always the odd concrete building whose slate roof sat a little easier on top. Streets that followed each other at random, streets in which awkward boys played cricket with no discipline, in which bad-tempered mongrels scoured every corner, crevice, crack for a morsel, in which hens played in drying and dried mud, and goats either wandered free or were tethered on chains so tight that one might as well have driven a bolt through the animals' heads into the thirsty earth. This area, which resembled the country in its poverty, had always impressed Bertram as the unassembled, peopled, animaled heart of Baytown.

"Monologue with Rain"

CHELY LIMA (CUBA)

J am walking in the dark. It's very late. It's raining and for some
reason the power is out in this part of the neighborhood. But I know
every inch of the street by heart, and every corner. And your smell is
everywhere. Not even the rain can wash it away; your scent sticks to
the wet earth and the open leaves. It must be that my own skin is
saturated with it. *Back then we hadn't begun to clash over everything yet,
and you were the marvellous woman I met at the party at work. Who could
have known that later everything would change so completely.*

(I knew it would be you. Come on in. You're soaking wet. Get out
of those clothes. The power just came back on. The towels are over
there.)

You made a good first impression. The sofa with you on it in the
corner. You dressed in a sweater and gray pants. I don't remember the
rest. You weren't wearing any makeup. And your hair was so simple,
so beautiful.

The walls seem to have sprouted a strange vegetation in the rain,
miniature jungles have grown up from the puddles and sidewalks. You
were the silhouette of a woman lost among sheets of rain in the
downpour.

*There you were, holding a glass, watching the others dance and laughing
to yourself, like a bandit, over things that you don't tell anyone so you can
keep them all to yourself and have a good laugh.*

263

(Hang your clothes to dry anywhere. Better yet, give them to me and I'll hang then outside so they'll dry faster. Would you like me to warm some milk or make you a cup of tea? I won't have any coffee until tomorrow.)

Your voice was warm, and a little hoarse. A small voice. You didn't even need to be a little drunk, like I was, to want to tie yourself up, hands and feet, and surrender to your mercy, your prisoner.

When the headlights of a passing car light up the neighborhood, the rain is like a concert of tinkling, breaking glass. I don't want to go home even though it's late. Even though you might be waiting for me on the stairs, sitting on one of the steps with your elbows on your knees and your chin cupped in one hand.

Then came the really good times, and even I have to admit, with all your defects, what a wonderful companion you are to go through life with because of the simple joy you put into all the things you do.

(I thought you said you were going to quit smoking. No, it doesn't bother me. The cigarettes are in the night table, on the left side. Bring me one too, Dania.)

For you, I can remember entire scenes as if I had filmed them while they were happening. You're on the edge of the bed, leaning over, with your legs folded over each other like a Buddha, and your hair covering your forehead. You are looking at yourself in the mirror.

The rain always sings when it falls on you, on your wet hair and your damp, slippery flesh. At this hour you could also be the silhouette of the one who's on duty for the Neighborhood Defense Committee, standing guard on the corner, opening and closing your eyes, daydreaming that you're a fish, alert in the ghostly world of the rainstorm.

You are fighting with somebody again—with one of those somebodies who sought you out and went after you despite all my silence, my bad temper, my curses—and you sit down on the edge of the chair and listen. All of a sudden you yell, wave your arms around, throw your cigarette down violently.

(My pajamas are enormous on you. Don't button the top. Come here. You are wonderful. I wanted you to come. I wanted you to do those things to me that you . . .)

264

If I keep this up I'll end up making a slide of every single moment and you'll tell me, like you did that time, that I'm a sentimental fool, that I'm spoiled, that I'm an asshole. That was the day I yelled at you on the street, and you looked at me unblinking, your eyes wide open, and disappeared for a week until I called you up because I couldn't stand it anymore.

The stairs are a tunnel of silence. My feet measure the distance between the steps by memory, they know every inch of this ground and even though my eyes are useless I keep trying to make things out in the dark with them. Outside the rain is like the body of a harp that doesn't sleep.

What can I do, woman, when you've gotten into my life and into my dreams without any consideration, and it's Dania who is not in my bed, and not at the table, and not here on a Sunday that has become inconceivably long.

(Don't stop, Dania. I don't know what it is you've got. You electrify me, as if you were sending shock waves through me. Dania, Dania, Dan.)

You did everything I didn't want you to do. You smoked enough for three, went out with your friends, you were independent, capable, told me you could handle things on your own whether I liked it or not, you bought that damn motorcycle . . . And you justified it all.

The hallway where I live is off limits to the rain. Right now the rain is so distant it only represents an exterior sound. I go on, immersed in a bubble of silence.

You justified everything. I couldn't ask you to quit smoking if I smoked myself. You could have friends. Why not? Why should I be jealous, if I was the only man you needed? You had no reason to be dependent on me, that would be absurd and even ignoble. You had your work and your own involvements with the Revolution. And the motorcycle. You were always so practical in your reasoning. If you were like that when I met you, like that when I fell in love with you, why should I want to make you change now? You had me there.

(I'm feeling hot now. Stay there, just like that. No, I'm not getting tired. You either?)

But Dania, what was I to do when my friends winked and laughed among themselves every time they saw me with you, me, who used to be such a tough guy around women? How do you think it made me look, with you smoking, wearing pants all the time, on a motorcycle? Me. You always responded that my friends were macho idiots, and that if it embarrassed me we just shouldn't go out.

I'm at my door. Behind it there could be a crocodile with open jaws or a big bunch of blue roses. You could be there naked looking at yourself in the mirror between two candles, and the light shining and flickering on your skin with red tones.

How much can a man take, Dania? How long can he put up with you until he explodes?

(Right now I would be telling you about what I did today. Like I used to do when we got into bed. But there's no one here. You're not here.)

But I need you in ways I wasn't even conscious of. No one to understand me, no one to listen to me and suggest things, no one to make love to, sleep with, laugh with, and be tender. No one like you. But I couldn't give in.

I have opened the door, and by coincidence, the lights came back on at the same time. There's nothing to do on this humid night. Behind the door your absence waits, like another rainstorm.

"Common Stories"

CHELY LIMA

1

a warm light bathed the furniture in the bedroom.

Roberto began to dress and Asela rested her elbow on the bed to watch him with eyes just opened and full of sleep.

"What?"

"Nothing. Go back to sleep. I didn't call you yet."

While he waited for the coffee to boil, he put his papers in order on the kitchen table.

The coffee bubbled over before it began to spill out over the edge of the pot.

That noise. Asela got out of bed.

Asela was pulling the robe over her shoulders and yawning.

"Why didn't you call me? Did the coffee boil over?"

They had breakfast in the kitchen under the streams of bright white light from the open window.

It is like an obligatory ritual every day to serve the milk, spread the butter on the bread.

"Are you coming home early today?"

"I think so. The seminar ends at five or six."

"I'll get home before you, either way."

"Why? Is there something that has to be picked up at the *bodega?*"

Roberto kissed her on the hair in a rapid gesture and left her sitting over an empty cup, reaching for the bread.

2

He looked up.

"Excuse me?"

"I was asking if this seat was taken."

She put her books down and hung her leather bag over the back of the chair.

"I think I know you from somewhere. I'm sure I've seen you before."

"I know you from somewhere too, but I'm not sure where."

"From the dormitory? No. The university?"

"I don't think so."

"Were we volunteers for the cane harvest together one summer?"

"No, that's not where we met either."

"You were at the contest for members of the writers' workshops they held two or three years ago, weren't you?"

"Yeah. And you were the guy I got into so many arguments with, weren't you?"

They both began to laugh.

"We almost ended up throwing books at each other."

"Are you doing any writing these days?"

"Yeah, but not much."

Roberto looked through his books, pulled out a few sheets of paper and handed them to her.

"Read this and tell me what you think later."

They had lunch together.

"What's your name?"

"Roberto."

"My name is Mayra. Listen, Roberto, the poems aren't bad but they lack grounding."

"Grounding?"

"Yes, a poem can't be made of air and things you learn in books; it has to be made of flesh, it has to pulsate, grab you, bite!"

"But poetry can be written in many different forms."

"No, it's not that. When you enter a poem, if it's a good one, you feel you can believe in it. That's the thing! You have to believe in what you are reading, and I don't believe in your poetry: you write yours from the accumulation of things you've learned, and that's all; you don't suffer through the process of the poetry or appease it."

"But I don't believe you have to suffer in order to write poetry."

They were staring at each other almost in rage.

"We speak different languages, you and I."

Roberto broke into a smile.

"We are going to end up biting each other. Why don't we go out for lunch?"

Mayra said yes and they continued walking.

3

What did I do with the key to the front door, it's never in the pocket where I put it in the morning. I must have lost it, here it is.

Asela was writing something in her notebook and Roberto leaned over to kiss her.

"I'll be done in a minute. I was preparing the chemistry classes and I wanted to get ahead. We'll eat right away."

"No, there's no hurry."

While he was undressing in the bathroom he remembered something and opened the door halfway.

"Did you go to the butcher's?"

"Yeah, I already picked up the meat."

Asela went into the bathroom and Roberto turned the shower head so she wouldn't get wet.

"If you're not too tired, do you want to go to the movies?"

"Sure, if you want."

On the way back from the theater, they walked through the parks near the sea wall, both of them lost in their own thoughts. Roberto was the first one to speak.

"Asela, do you think my poetry lacks life, substance? Do you think it's weak?"

She blinked.

"What? What are you talking about?"

He explained it all to her in detail as they dodged the cars, crossing the street to get to the sea wall.

"It all depends on each person's creative process, doesn't it? Anyway, is it worth getting all worked up about?"

Roberto stopped dead.

"No, I guess not."

4

The seminar dragged on and he and Mayra became inseparable so they could go on talking. They were caught in a great need to unburden themselves to one another and each phrase required new phrases of explanation, background, and those led to more phrases, until they found themselves writing notes to each other at night that became five- or six-page letters, proving a point they had fought over obstinately at lunch, over rolls they never got around to eating, pressed for time and unwilling to break up the dialogue in order to chew or raise a glass to their lips.

When Roberto put aside the poems he had crossed out, started again, and crossed out, in order to write to Mayra, the sensation would begin in his hands and rise to his head, caused by a chain of small memories, bursting one by one, like bubbles, and Roberto would see Mayra, hear her laugh and say no, her face so serious she would sometimes grow pale with indignation, when she suspected that he was laughing at her arguments. And if Asela, who worked with him at the dining room table at that hour, spoke to him or asked him a question, Roberto would look up at his wife, absent, as if he had been gone for centuries.

"Are you writing a novel?" Asela once asked.

Roberto knew it would be impossible to tell her what he was writing and for whom.

"Yes," he lied, "but it hasn't really taken shape yet."

When they were already in bed, and he had to face himself as he mulled over the day in his mind, Roberto was a bit surprised to have to admit that that was the first lie he had told his wife in a long time.

The next day he told Mayra about his wife.

"I love her very much. I love her . . . the way you love people, but sometimes we are very distant. Sometimes it seems like I'm all alone, because I can't talk with her about things . . . she doesn't understand."

"I know, I know."

"Asela is very smart. She's very good. She's the best thing that has ever come into my life."

"I'm very happy for you."

5

Tomorrow the seminar is over, Asela wants us to go to Aunt Rosa's house, it's been a month since we visited, tomorrow is Saturday and there's only a half day of classes, Mayra was asking me yesterday what she could do on Saturday night, wanted me to suggest a good movie or someplace to go, she's probably going out with someone, who knows who, someone to spend the evening with, I know they won't talk as much as we do, it must be a friend, or maybe she's going out by herself, it's none of my business anyway, it would be nice to take her to the play by . . . it would be nice to take her with us, but Asela would get bored with us, and besides Asela hasn't met her yet, I don't think they would get along, they are so different, but I am not going to leave Asela all by herself at home, and she wouldn't like us going out alone together, what does it matter, what a problem.

6

Mayra started gathering up the files that were in the desk.

The telephone to her left was ringing and she stuck her hand out, without looking up, reaching through the air for the cold body of the receiver.

"Hello."

"Mayra, it's Roberto."

"Roberto, hello, what's up?"

"How are you?"

"Fine, I'm fine. How are you doing?"

"Just fine. You know, we haven't seen each other for three days."

"Since the seminar ended."

"I have a million things to tell you."

"Me too."

"When can I see you?"

"When can *you?* You're the one with problems to deal with, at home, with your wife. I can see you anytime except during office hours."

"O.K., can I see you today?"

"All right. What time, and where?"

"Downtown, at Lonja del Comercio. My bus passes right by there. I'll be there at seven."

"Fine."

"See you, ciao."

"Ciao."

And he hung up.

7

A stream of people came through the doors of each bus that stopped. Mayra waited, looking at all the faces, but she didn't see him arrive until he was right next to her.

They greeted each other with an effusive handshake.

"How are you?"

"How are you doing?"

"Let's get out of here, it's too crowded."

They walked through the groups of people hurrying to catch the bus, through the frenetic blasts of car horns. Two streets later they emerged into the calm; it was silent in Cathedral Plaza.

"So, what's new?"

Roberto tried to speak, but didn't know what to say.

"You first."

She was tongue-tied too and they discovered that they had nothing to say to one another, but that it was magnificent just being together.

Mayra smiled.

"When I left work I was tired. Now I feel fine. You give me peace, Roberto."

"The perfect friendship," Roberto responded without noticing his tone of voice.

She looked at him as if she just realized something.

"Isn't it kind of . . . absurd?"

"Of course. That's the best thing about it."

8

There was the sound of aluminum clanking against the china on the shelf. Mayra pulled the sheet up over her head and tried to go back to sleep.

"Mayra." Ana María brought her some coffee in a glass.

"Thanks, sweetheart."

She drank it slowly, because it was so hot it burned. Víctor was screaming and crying in the dining room.

"What's the matter with him?"

"He doesn't want to sit with his grandmother and drink his milk."

Ana María took the glass away and Mayra got out of bed and left the room.

Her mother was rocking Víctor in her lap with the milk bottle in her hand.

"You spoil him, Mama."

"Poor thing, he's still sleepy."

In the bathroom, her brother César was shaving in front of the mirror.

"César, shave in the bedroom and let me use the bathroom."

"Shit, what a pain you can be."

When she came out of the bathroom it was her father who was rocking Víctor, who was calmer now.

Ana María was washing the dishes, in a hurry, in the kitchen.

"I'm going to be late, and by the time I finish dressing Víctor . . ."

"Leave the dishes. I'll rinse them. Go get Víctor ready."

The sound of buses and trucks was coming through the open window.

9

I'm always so sleepy at this hour, it would be nice to have someone next to me in bed right now, someone to keep me warm and speak softly to me until I fell asleep, Francis wasn't like that, he used to turn with his back to me, I would lie face-up, it made me so angry, what a stupid thing but it was one of the things that hastened our divorce, the little things, the little things are important, Ernesto doesn't pay much attention to details, well, sometimes, once he brought me a flower, and I can't stand flowers, only at a distance, so I had to find a way to leave it behind somewhere or throw it away without him noticing, Roberto's not much on details either, neither am I, to tell the truth, of course Roberto's nothing more than a friend, I don't know what he's like with his wife, but he's probably not very . . . her name is Asela, Roberto has never introduced me to her, we've never bumped into each other, at this hour I'm always so sleepy.

10

"Are you going out?"

"Ernesto is picking me up to go to the movies. And you guys, are you going out tonight too?"

"We don't know where yet. César wanted to see that movie, the one . . ."

"Come with us."

Ana María grabbed her lipstick and stood in front of the mirror.

"I'll let you know in a little while."

After the movies they went to Coppelia for an ice cream.

Mayra was raising the spoon to her mouth when she saw Roberto with Asela two tables away.

Roberto looked up and saw her, and Asela followed his glance, looking in the same direction.

That must be his wife.

Who could that be, why is he looking at her . . .
She's with a guy and a couple, I don't know any of them.

Mayra nodded at Roberto, and then again, but less pronounced, at Asela. Roberto waved good-bye lightly with his hand and Asela responded to Mayra's wave with her own.

"Who's that, Roberto?"

"Her name is Mayra. She's a girl I met at the seminar."

Roberto went back to his ice cream and Mayra went back to watching the foursome at the next table.

"Who are they, Mayra?"

"He's one of the people I met at the seminar, and she must be his wife."

11

Rain began falling on the city at dawn and it started to get cold.

Early that morning Roberto had a dream in which he and Asela were going round and round on a carousel. He woke up tired. He wanted to see Mayra.

"Mayra."

"Hello."

"Mayra, it's me, Roberto. I need to see you tonight."

"Oh, I had made plans to . . . oh well, it doesn't matter. Sure. What time?"

"Meet me at nine. Where's a good place, nearby? At La Lonja, like last time? No, I think we should meet at the square. Meet me at Cathedral Square."

12

"Ernesto?"

"No, it's not Ernesto. Who's calling, please?"

"Mayra, tell him it's Mayra."

"Hello."

"Ernesto?"

"Yes, Mayra. What's up?"

"I'm not going to be able to make it tonight."

"Why not?"

"I have to go and visit a friend of mine who is . . . sick."

"Want me to go with you?"

"No, that's all right, it's better if I go alone."

13

"Roberto."

He looked at her and finished buttoning up his pants.

"Are you going out?

"Yes."

"How come?"

"I'm just going over to see someone from work for a little while, to drop off some forms he has to hand in tomorrow."

"Do you want me to go with you?"

"No, I'm coming right back."

When he was at the door, about to leave, Asela called him again.

"What?"

"You're forgetting the forms."

Roberto looked down at his hands and remembered.

"Oh, yeah."

He pulled a few blank sheets out of the desk drawer, put them in an envelope, and left.

14

It was raining again.

Mayra was standing under one of the porticos in the square with her shoulder against a column.

"How are you?"

"Soaked."

They both laughed.

"I'm a little wet too."

"Where can we go that's nearby?"

"I don't know . . ."

"We could go to the Bodeguita. Let's go now, the rain's letting up a little."

In the Bodeguita there was a man with a solemn face drinking rum, and two foreign women talking in hushed voices without touching their glasses.

"What would you like to drink?"

"Whatever."

He asked the bartender for two *mojitos.**

"I had to see you."

"Why, did something come up?"

"No, everything's fine. And you?"

"Me too."

They fell silent until the bartender placed the two glasses down in front of them and then began a slow conversation, punctuated with names and dates.

It was about ten-thirty, after they had had seven *mojitos*, when Mayra noticed that it was pouring outside. The bar was spinning around her and Roberto was as tipsy as she was.

She leaned carefully against the barstool.

"Roberto, can you stand up?"

"I think so."

"Why don't you try?"

He placed his feet on the ground and grabbed hold of the bar firmly.

"I'm up, I'm up."

"But can you walk alright?"

"I don't know."

"It's just that I'm not sure I can walk under my own steam."

"I'll hold you up."

Roberto paid the bill and she leaned on him as they walked to the door.

A cold, light rain was falling.

"Let's walk. The rain will be refreshing."

* A drink made with rum, fresh spearmint, and lime juice.—ED.

But they were still a little dizzy so they stopped under the portico on the side of the cathedral and stayed there, close together, leaning on the stone wall.

Roberto sought out Mayra's forehead, her eyes, and then his mouth found hers.

They started to kiss.

15

We were dizzy, I don't know, it's so dark and I can barely make out Roberto's face, it's nice and warm, outside it was cold, but not Roberto, he was warm from head to toe, like he is now, he's dozed off, I can barely feel his head on my chest, his hair is so soft, it's getting long, who would have said that we'd end up in this explosion, my head is still spinning, I wonder what time it is, but if I move he'll wake up and it's so good to have him sleeping on my chest like this.

16

Asela sat up in bed and picked up the watch that was on the night table.

It was twelve minutes after two.

The rain had let up quite a while ago.

17

My head is clearer now, it must be very late, that scent must be perfume or a lotion she put on right between her breasts, did she fall asleep, poor thing, I don't want to wake her, I'll have to take her home, it's late and my sweet Mayra was so dizzy, she's breathing deeply, she must have fallen asleep, that perfume, I wonder if it's still raining?

18

The sound of footsteps in the hallway on this floor stopped just by the door and then the fumbling of keys in the lock.

Someone came in, closing the door very gently.

"Roberto. Roberto?"

He turned the bedroom light on.

"It's me."

Asela was staring at him.

"Did something happen?"

"No, it was pouring outside and I waited till the rain stopped. We were talking about problems on the job and I didn't realize how late it was."

She sniffed the air.

"Were you drinking?"

"We had a few drinks."

"There's milk in the kitchen, why don't you have some?"

"No, I'm not hungry."

"All right. Hurry up and turn off the lights. I'm sleepy."

"I'll be in in a minute."

19

"Let the night stretch on. I want to be with you."

"Why did all of this have to happen?"

"I was looking for you, Mayra, and you me, and we've been with lots of people and got mixed up, but . . ."

"Write to me, on the days we can't see each other, write to me."

20

Asela got up from the table covered with papers and went to the drawer for some fresh sheets, but there weren't enough there so she went to Roberto's desk.

The sound of running water was coming from the bathroom.

Roberto had left his pants on the bed and Asela found the key chain right away.

The desk drawer was crammed full of envelopes and folders and she went through their contents looking for blank sheets. One of the envelopes had letters in it.

Asela unfolded the first sheet. When Roberto came out of the bathroom he found her still standing there, with one of Mayra's letters in her hand. Her lips were trembling.

She looked up when she heard him come in, shaking her head gently.

"Ay, Roberto, Roberto."

And started to cry.

21

The telephone began to ring. The whole family was eating and watching television.

César was closest to it, so he answered.

"Hello, yes, hold on a second."

He handed the phone to Mayra.

"It's for you."

"For me? Who is it?"

"I don't know, some man."

The adventure series on television was making an indescribable racket and Víctor made noises along with it, in between bites, seated on his mother's lap.

"Hello."

She recognized Roberto's voice immediately, but he was very upset and she couldn't make out what he was saying.

She covered the end of the phone with her hand.

"Ana María, for God's sake, make the boy be quiet."

Roberto was breathing jaggedly into the telephone. Mayra tried to make out what he was saying.

"Asela . . . the letters . . . I couldn't deny anything . . . she's falling apart."

"Can you come over right now? Yes? I'll be waiting at the entrance to the building."

When she hung up everyone's eyes were fixed on her.

"So, what are you all staring at?"

She went into the bedroom to put on a pair of pants.

"Are you going out?" her mother mumbled.

"Yes."

"You're not going to finish eating?"

"No."

César shrugged his shoulders.

"She's nuts."

22

"Mayra."

They walked off together.

When they got to the corner they kissed.

Roberto rubbed his forehead.

"I had to tell her everything. What else could I do, she found your letters. I had never seen her like that. It was like she had collapsed. If she had at least yelled, made a scene. . . . But she won't even speak, doesn't reproach me for anything. She walks around like she's half dead."

"What shall we do now? Not see each other anymore?"

He stopped and leaned into her shoulders.

"I can't, I can't, I don't want to do that, Mayra. Why should I give you up?"

"What about her? Are you going to leave her?"

Roberto tapped at his chest with the tips of his fingers.

"I can't do that either. Asela has no family, she has no one but me. We've had a life together for seven years. In seven years you end up either loving or detesting the person who sleeps, eats, talks, and lives with you utterly, completely. I have no reason to detest her."

"All right. Enough. So what are you going to do?"

"I don't know."

They kept walking and turned on Acosta Street. When they got to the benches along the wall that borders Paseo Avenue, Roberto sat down and put his head on Mayra's belly.

"I want to go on seeing you."

"And does she know you're not going to stop seeing me?"

"No. But I'm not going to deny it either."

23

It's almost three o'clock, why do I feel like crying right now, on the street, it's embarrassing, Roberto and that woman, saying her name is like a slap in the mouth, we've been together seven years, could it be that time wears love down, but it didn't for me, I should tell him to go but what am I going to do without Roberto, and not even a child, that terrible disgrace of never having given birth, I'm starting again, it's so embarrassing to have people see me crying on the street, my handkerchief, it's three o'clock already, I'm late.

24

The sound of breaking glass came from the kitchen, and Roberto threw his book down and ran to the doorway, in a flash.

"Asela, what happened?"

She was looking, perplexed, at the pile of broken china and glass on the floor. She was very pale.

"It slipped out of my hands. I don't know how it happened."

For a while they just looked at each other, without saying anything, miserable.

Roberto held his arms out to her and Asela crossed the kitchen, stepping over the rubble of china, and fell onto his chest, desolate.

"Don't go, Roberto, don't go."

25

"Mayra."

"What, Mama."

"You're not going to eat anything?"

"I'm not hungry."

"Not even a glass of milk?"

"No."

The woman went over to the bed,
"Don't you feel well? Are you sick?"
"No, Mama."
"Is there some problem at work?"
"No."
There was a silence that lasted minutes.
Mayra turned her taciturn face away, avoiding her mother's eyes.
"What's the matter, baby?"
"Don't worry, Mama. It's nothing serious."

26

It was afternoon, and downtown was full of light.

There were less people than usual at the bus stop, waiting for the No. 19. Mayra was glancing distractedly from one passerby to the next when she spotted Asela, and Asela recognized her at almost the same time.

They faced each other with the same stupor and both made the same unconscious gesture, as if they were trying to grab hold of something. A bus opened its doors less than two steps from where Mayra was standing, and she let herself be carried on by the crowd.

Asela stood there at the bus stop, her throat tight, watching the bus drive away enveloped in exhaust fumes.

27

"This is the last time we'll see each other."

He merely nodded his head.

"That's how it's going to be. We're all cowards, the three of us, Roberto. Me, for staying with you, your wife, for the same reason, and you for having to go on with both of us. I want to break the triangle."

"You're so hard."

Yes—Mayra thought for a second—but none of us will escape my hardheadedness.

"Can you give me some time?"

"Some time? For what?"

"I don't know. To think about it. To tell you it's O.K."

"I still don't see why."

Because I don't want to let go of you Mayra, because I don't want to, because this might be the last piece of my youth, because I can't go back to the way things always were, because life is rough and I discovered it too late, to hell with my arrogant self-sufficiency, I'm helpless now with you there in front of me, beautiful.

"Mayra . . ."

"All right. If you want, tomorrow, but that will be the last time."

28

Asela was sitting on the couch, doing nothing, staring straight ahead.

"I'm back."

He closed the door, wearily.

"What are you doing there?"

"Nothing. I was waiting for you."

"Did you prepare tomorrow's classes?"

"Yes."

"Do you feel O.K.? You look strange."

She moved her hands nervously.

"There's nothing wrong with me. I sat down here to wait for you. Idiotic, isn't it?"

"No."

Roberto walked to the window and looked outside.

On the orange tile roofs and terraces of Old Havana, the lights began to go out.

"Passing"

MICHELLE CLIFF
(JAMAICA)

I

The mystery of the world is the visible,
not the invisible.
        —Oscar Wilde

Camouflage: ground lizards in the schoolyard rustle under a pile of leaves—some are deep-green, others shiny blue: all blend in. I fear they might be there—even when there is no sound.

To this day camouflage terrorizes me.

The pattern of skin which makes a being invisible against its habitat.

And—yes—this camouflage exists for its protection. I am not what I seem to be.

I must make myself visible against my habitat. But there exists a certain danger in peeling back. The diamondback without her mottled skin loses a level of defense.

The onlooker may be startled to recognize the visible being.
The onlooker may react with disbelief: sometimes, with recognition.

II

I am remembering: women in Jamaica asking to touch my hair.

On a map from 1740 which hangs above my desk I can see the place where my grandmother now lives. Old-womans Savannah. That is the place which holds colors for me. The other seems a shadow-life.

I am remembering: in the hard dirt in the bright sun between the house and the shed which is a kitchen my mother sat—after church—on a wooden crate. Under the box a headless chicken flapped its wings.

Quiet. Then she rose—removed the box. Plunged the carcass into boiling water to loosen the feathers.

She passed the carcass to her mother who cut and stewed Sunday dinner.

I watched this all in wonder. The two women were almost silent.

III

I thought it was only the loss of the mother—
but it was also the loss of others:
who grew up to work for us
and stood at the doorway while the tv played
and stood at the doorway while we told ghost-stories
and ironed the cloths for the tea-trays—
but this division existed even then—

Passing demands a desire to become invisible. A ghost-life. An ignorance of connections.

IV

In America: each year the day before school after summer vacations I sat on my bed touching my notebooks, pencils, ruler—holding the stern and sweet-smelling brown oxfords in my lap and spreading my skirt and blouse and underwear and socks before me. My mother would come in and always say the same thing: "Free paper burn now."

Such words conspire to make a past.
Such words conjure a knowledge.
Such words make assimilation impossible. They stay with you for years. They puzzle but you sense a significance. I need these words.

V

People call my grandmother the miracle of the loaves and the fishes. People used to fill the yard at dinnertime with their enamel bowls and utensils waiting to be fed. And she managed to feed them all. Whether rice or yam or green banana cooked in dried saltfish.

In America this food became a secret—and a link. Shopping under the bridge with my mother for cho-cho and cassava and breadfruit. And the New Home Bakery for hard-dough bread. Finding a woman who makes paradise plums.

My mother sees this. She says nothing.

Passing demands quiet. And from that quiet—silence.

VI

Something used by someone else carries a history with it. A piece of cloth, a platter, a cut-glass pitcher, a recipe.

A history and a spirit. You want to know when it was used. And how. And what it wants from you.

Passing demands you keep that knowledge to yourself.

VII

In Jamaica we are as common as ticks.
We graft the Bombay onto the common mango. The Valencia onto the Seville. We mix tangerines and oranges. We create mules.

Under British rule—Zora Neale Hurston writes about this—we could have ourselves declared legally white. The rationale was that it made us better servants.

This symbolic skin was carried to the United States where passing was easy.

Isolate yourself. If they find out about you it's all over. Forget about your great-grandfather with the darkest skin—until you're back "home" where they joke about how he climbed a coconut tree when he was eighty. Go to college. Go to England to study. Learn about the Italian Renaissance and forget that they kept slaves. Ignore the tears of the Indians. Black Americans don't understand us either. We are—after all—British. If anyone asks you talk about sugar plantations and the Maroons—not the landscape of downtown Kingston and children at the roadside. Be selective. Cultivate normalcy. Stress sameness. Blend in. For God's sake don't pile difference upon differ-ence. It's not safe.

Back on the island the deep-purple skin of the ripe fruit conceals a center which holds a star-shape. Sitting in the branches one afternoon with a friend we eat ourselves into an intimacy in which we talk about our families. He is fourteen and works for my grandmother. I am twelve. He tells me his grandmother was East Indian and therefore he is not completely black. I tell him I am white—showing my sunburnt nose—explaining only white skin burns. He laughs. Then we scuffle.

It is like trying to remember a dream in which the images slip and slide. The words connect and disconnect and you wake feeling senseless.

"No strange news," my grandmother often closes her letters.

We are not exotic—or aromatic—or poignant.
We are not aberrations. We are ordinary.
All this has happened before.

Part II

Theoretical Essays

Identity, Historiography, and the Caribbean Voice

$\mathcal{C}$. L. R. James's "From Toussaint L'Ouverture to Fidel Castro" is a masterful overview of the forces and tensions that have shaped Caribbean discourse from the Haitian to the Cuban revolutions, addressing the problems of historiography in terms of *focus*. James moves with ease and fluidity from the eighteenth century to the twentieth century, signaling as he goes along the ways in which the Caribbean has been misread, stressing that the "same myopic vision which failed to focus Africa is now peering at the West Indies." Yet within the Caribbean, James argues, this link is strong and the central role of Africa in the region's development "is documented as few historical visions are documented." The seminal figures James studies, from the Haitian Revolution to the present, have all been aware that "[t]he road to West Indian national identity lay through Africa." Having established and recognized this vital link, it then becomes clear that in the Caribbean, "the mass of people are not seeking an identity, they are expressing one."

Roberto Fernández Retamar takes up the same problematic in "Caliban: Notes Toward a Discussion of Culture in Our America." In it he examines history, identity, and the Caribbean voice through the prism of Shakespeare's drama *The Tempest*, and its symbolism for Latin America and the Caribbean, along with shifts in its interpretation across historical epochs. He revisits the myths and realities of conquest that have shaped Caribbean identity and reveals the world view implicit in identification with either Caliban, Ariel, or Prospero. Their drama has been replayed over and over in the evolving theories of Caribbean identity, which all too often, even when undertaken by Latin Americans and Caribbeans, "still took only the European world into account." The French Revolution and the Spanish-Cuban-American War of 1898, marking the decline of one empire and the ascendency of another, each contributed to a reading and reception of *The Tempest*, the drama of European conquest and colonization in the Caribbean. For Fernández Retamar, 1969 ushers in the era of a new reading, of a significant shift in the perception of culture and national identity in Latin America and the Caribbean; that is the year in which Caliban was taken up with pride as an American symbol, a Caribbean symbol, as "our symbol," by three Antillean writers, Aimé Césaire, Edward Kamau Brathwaite, and Roberto Fernández Retamar himself. Each author assumed the perspective of Caliban, rethinking history, culture, and identity from the viewpoint of "the *other* side, from the viewpoint of the *other* protagonist," from the perspective of the unconquerable. Fernández Retamar's essay on Caliban and culture can and should be read as an invitation to consider the Caribbean not in isolation but as part of the world, "a part of the world that should be looked at with the same attention and respect as the rest." That is precisely what each of the writers in this volume has done, and in so doing, the act of creation has also constituted a reinterpretation of history.

Michelle Cliff, in the essay that lends its title to this volume, makes explicit the very necessary links between the personal, the political, and the international context, in her own development as a Caribbean woman and a writer. She looks back across time and history in an attempt to "locate the vanishing point: where the lines of perspective converge and disappear. Lines of color and class. Lines of history and social context. Lines of denial and rejection." The need to explain *how* and *why* these lines were drawn led her to recover the real sources of meaning, those that inspired "Claiming an Identity They Taught Me to Despise," and "Caliban's Daughter or into the Interior," from among her *corpus* of essays that explore culture, resistance, and identity. Cliff concludes her essay, a powerful exploration of all that gives rise to the Caribbean voice, with a tribute to the complexity of the formation of identity—national, cultural, social, historical, personal—in the Caribbean. "There is no ending to this piece of writing. There is no way to end it. As I read back over it, I see that we/they/I may become confused in the mind of the reader: but these pronouns have always co-existed in my mind." And her eloquent appeal for a new configuration of we/they/I in the Caribbean articulates some of the elemental questions posed by all the writers represented in this volume.

From: The Black Jacobins

C. L. R. J A M E S
(TRINIDAD)

From Toussaint L'Ouverture to Fidel Castro

Toussaint L'Ouverture is not here linked to Fidel Castro because both led revolutions in the West Indies. Nor is the link a convenient or journalistic demarcation of historical time. What took place in French San Domingo in 1792–1804 reappeared in Cuba in 1958. The slave revolution of French San Domingo managed to emerge from

> . . . The pass and fell incensed points
> Of mighty opposites.

Five years later the people of Cuba are still struggling in the same toils.

Castro's revolution is of the twentieth as much as L'Ouverture's was of the eighteenth. But despite the distance of over a century and a half, both are West Indian. The people who made them, the problems and attempts to solve them, are peculiarly West Indian, the product of a peculiar origin and a peculiar history. West Indians first became aware of themselves as a people in the Haitian Revolution. Whatever its ultimate fate, the Cuban Revolution marks the ultimate stage of a Caribbean quest for national identity. In a scattered series of disparate islands the process consists of a series of uncoordinated periods of drift, punctuated by spurts, leaps, and catastrophes. But the inherent movement is clear and strong.

The history of the West Indies is governed by two factors, the sugar plantation and Negro slavery. That the majority of the population in Cuba was never slave does not affect the underlying social identity. Wherever the sugar plantation and slavery existed, they imposed a pattern. It is an original pattern, not European, not African, not a part of the American main, not native in any conceivable sense of that word, but West Indian, *sui generis*, with no parallel anywhere else.

The sugar plantation has been the most civilizing as well as the most demoralizing influence in West Indian development. When three centuries ago the slaves came to the West Indies, they entered directly into the large-scale agriculture of the sugar plantation, which was a modern system. It further required that slaves live together in a social relation far closer than any proletariat of the time. The cane when reaped had to be rapidly transported to what was factory production. The product was shipped abroad for sale. Even the cloth the slaves wore and the food they ate was imported. The Negroes, therefore, from the very start lived a life that was in its essence a modern life. That is their history—as far as I have been able to discover, a unique history.

In the first part of the seventeenth century, early settlers from Europe had made quite a success of individual production. The sugar plantation drove them out. The slaves saw around them a social life of a certain material culture and ease, the life of the sugar-plantation owners. The clever, the lucky, and the illegitimate became domestics or artisans attached to the plantation or the factory. Long before the bus or the taxi, the small size of the islands made communication between the rural areas and the urban quick and easy. The plantation owners and the merchants lived an intense political life in which the ups and downs of sugar and in time the treatment and destiny of the slaves played a crucial and continuous role. The sugar plantation dominated the lives of the islands to such a degree that the white skin alone saved those who were not plantation owners or bureaucrats from the humiliations and hopelessness of the life of the slave. That was and is the pattern of West Indian life.

The West Indies between Toussaint L'Ouverture and Fidel Castro falls naturally into three periods: I. The Nineteenth Century; II. Between The Wars; III. After World War II.

I. The Nineteenth Century

The nineteenth century in the Caribbean is the century of the abolition of slavery. But the passing of the years shows that the decisive patterns of Caribbean development took form in Haiti.

Toussaint could see no road for the Haitian economy but the sugar plantation. Dessalines was a barbarian. After Dessalines came Christophe, a man of conspicuous ability and within his circumstances an enlightened ruler. He also did his best (a cruel best) with the plantation. But with the abolition of slavery and the achievement of independence the plantation, indelibly associated with slavery, became unbearable. Pétion acquiesced in substituting subsistence production for the sugar plantation.

For the first century and a half of Haiti's existence there was no international opinion jealous of the independence of small nations; no body of similar states, ready to raise a hue and cry at any threat to one of their number; no theory of aid from the wealthy countries to the poorer ones. Subsistence production resulted in economic decay and every variety of political disorder. Yet it has preserved the national independence, and out of this has come something new which has captured a continent and holds its place in the institutions of the world.

This is what happened. For over a century after independence the Haitians attempted to form a replica of European, i.e., French civilization in the West Indies. Listen to the Haitian Ambassador, M. Constantin Mayard, in Paris in 1938:

French our institutions, French our public and civil legislation, French our literature, French our university, French the curriculum of our schools . . .

Today when one of us (a Haitian) appears in a circle of French-men, "welcome smiles at him in every eye." The reason is without doubt that your nation, ladies and gentlemen, knows that within the scope of its colonial expansion it has given to the Antilles and above all to San Domingo all that it could give of itself and its substance . . . It has founded there, in the mould of its own national type, with its blood, with its language, with its institutions, its spirit and its soil, a local type, an historic race, in which its sap still runs and where it is remade complete.

Generation after generation the best sons of the Haitian elite were educated in Paris. They won distinctions in the intellectual life of France. The burning race-hatred of pre-independence days had vanished. But a line of investigators and travelers had held up to international ridicule the hollow pretensions of Haitian civilization. In 1913 the ceaseless battering from foreign pens was reinforced by the bayonets of American Marines. Haiti had to find a rallying-point. They looked for it where it can only be found, at home, more precisely, in their own backyard. They discovered what is known today as Negritude. It is the prevailing social ideology among politicians and intellectuals in every part of Africa. It is the subject of heated elaboration and disputation wherever Africa and Africans are discussed. But in its origin and its development it is West Indian, and it could not have been anything else but West Indian, the peculiar product of their peculiar history.

The Haitians did not know it as Negritude. To them it seemed purely Haitian. Two-thirds of the population of French San Domingo in Toussaint's time had made the Middle Passage. The whites had emigrated or been exterminated. The Mulattoes who were masters had their eyes fixed on Paris. Left to themselves, the Haitian peasantry resuscitated to a remarkable degree the lives they had lived in Africa. Their method of cultivation, their family relations and social practices, their drums, songs, and music, such art as they practiced, and above all their religion which became famous, Vodun—all this was Africa in the West Indies. But it was Haitian, and the Haitian elite leapt at it. In 1926 Dr. Price Mars in his famous book *Ainsi Parla*

L'Oncle (This is What Uncle Said), described with loving care the way of life of the Haitian peasant. Rapidly, learned and scientific societies were formed. The African way of life of the Haitian peasant became the axis of Haitian literary creation. No plantation laborer, with free land to defend, rallied to the cause.

The Caribbean territories drifted along. At the end of the nineteenth century, Cuba produced a great revolution which bears the name "The Ten Years' War." It produced prodigies—no West Indian pantheon but will have among its most resplendent stars the names of José Martí the political leader and Maceo the soldier. They were men in the full tradition of Jefferson, Washington, and Bolivar. That was their strength and that was their weakness. They were leaders of a national revolutionary party and a national revolutionary army. Toussaint L'Ouverture and Fidel Castro led a revolutionary people. The war for independence began again and ended in the Platt Amendment of 1904.

It was just one year after the Platt Amendment that there first appeared what has turned out to be a particular feature of West Indian life—the non-political writer devoted to the analysis and expression of West Indian society. The first was the greatest of them all, Fernando Ortiz. For over half a century, at home or in exile, he has been the tireless exponent of Cuban life and *Cubanidad*, the spirit of Cuba. The history of Spanish imperialism, sociology, anthropology, ethnology, all the related sciences are his medium of investigation into Cuban life, folklore, literature, music, art, education, criminality, everything Cuban. A most distinctive feature of his work is the number of solid volumes he has devoted to Negro and Mulatto life in Cuba. A quarter of a century before the Writers' Project of the New Deal began the discovery of the United States, Ortiz set out to discover his native land, a West Indian island. In essence it is the first and only comprehensive study of the West Indian people. Ortiz ushered the Caribbean into the thought of the twentieth century and kept it there.

II. Between the Wars

Before World War I Haiti began to write another chapter in the record of the West Indian struggle for national independence. Claiming the need to recover debts and restore order, the Marines, as we have seen, invaded Haiti in 1913. The whole nation resisted. A general strike was organized and led by the literary intellectuals who had discovered the Africanism of their peasants as a means of national identity. The Marines left, and Negroes and Mulattoes resumed their fratricidal conflicts. But Haiti's image of itself had changed. "Goodbye to the Marseillaise," a famous phrase by one of the best-known of Haitian writers, signifies the substitution of Africa for France in the first independent West Indian state. Africa in the West Indies would seem to have been evoked by an empirical need and accidental circumstance. It was not so. Long before the Marines left Haiti, the role of Africa in the consciousness of the West Indies people had proved itself to be a stage in the development of the West Indian quest for a national identity.

The story is one of the strangest stories in any period of history. The individual facts are known. But no one has ever put them together and drawn to them the attention they deserve. Today the emancipation of Africa is one of the outstanding events of contemporary history. Between the wars when this emancipation was being prepared, the unquestioned leaders of the movement in every pubic sphere, in Africa itself, in Europe, and in the United States, were not Africans but West Indians. First the unquestioned facts.

Two black West Indians using the ink of Negritude wrote their names imperishably on the front pages of the history of our time. Standing at the head is Marcus Garvey. Garvey, an immigrant from Jamaica, is the only Negro who has succeeded in building a mass movement among American Negroes. Arguments about the number of his followers dispute the number of millions. Garvey advocated the return of Africa to the Africans and people of African descent. He organized, very rashly and incompetently, the Black Star Line, a steamship company for transporting people of African descent from the New World back to Africa. Garvey did not last long. His movement took really effective form in about 1921, and by 1926 he was in a United States prison (some charge about misusing the mails); from prison he was deported home to Jamaica. But all this is only the frame and scaffolding. Garvey never set foot in Africa. He spoke no African language. His conceptions of Africa seemed to be a West Indian island and West Indian people multiplied a thousand times over. But Garvey managed to convey to Negroes everywhere (and to the rest of the world) his passionate belief that Africa was the home of a civilization which had once been great and would be great again. When you bear in mind the slenderness of his resources, the vast material forces and the pervading social conceptions which automatically sought to destroy him, his achievement remains one of the propagandistic miracles of this century.

Garvey's voice reverberated inside Africa itself. The King of Swaziland told Mrs. Marcus Garvey that he knew the name of two black men in the Western world: Jack Johnson, the boxer who defeated the white man Jim Jeffries, and Marcus Garvey. Jomo Kenyatta has related to this writer how in 1921 Kenya nationalists, unable to read, would gather round a reader of Garvey's newspaper, the *Negro World,* and listen to an article two or three times. Then they would run various ways through the forest, carefully to repeat the whole, which they had memorized, to Africans hungry for some doctrine which lifted them from the servile consciousness in which Africans lived. Dr. Nkrumah, a graduate student of history and philosophy at two American universities, has placed it on record that of all the writers who educated and influenced him, Marcus Garvey stands first. Garvey found the cause of Africans and of people of African descent not so much neglected as unworthy of consideration. In little more than half of ten years he had made it a part of the political consciousness of the world. He did not know the word Negritude but he knew the thing. With enthusiasm he would have welcomed the nomenclature, with justice claimed paternity.

The other British West Indian was from Trinidad, George Padmore. Padmore shook the dust of the cramping West Indies from his feet in the early 1920s and went to the United States. When he died in 1959, eight countries sent representatives to his funeral, which was held in London. His ashes were interred in Ghana; and all assert that in that country of political demonstrations, there has never been a political demonstration such as was evoked by these obsequies of Padmore. Peasants from remote areas who, it could have been thought, had never heard his name, found their way to Accra to pay the last tribute to this West Indian who had spent his life in their service.

Once in America he became an active Communist. He was moved to Moscow to head their Negro department of propaganda and organization. In that post he became the best known and most trusted of agitators for African independence. In 1935, seeking alliances, the Kremlin separated Britain and France as "democratic imperialisms" from Germany and Japan, making the "Fascist imperialisms" the target of Russian and Communist propaganda. This reduced activity for African emancipation to a farce: Germany and Japan had no colonies in Africa. Padmore broke instantly with the Kremlin. He went to London where, in a single room, he earned a meagre living by journalism, to be able to continue the work he had done in the Kremlin. He wrote books and pamphlets, attended all anti-imperialist meetings and spoke and moved resolutions wherever possible. He made and maintained an ever-increasing range of nationalist contacts in all sections of African society and the colonial world. He preached and taught Pan-Africanism and organized an African Bureau. He published a journal devoted to African emancipation (the present writer was its editor).

This is no place to attempt a summary of the work and influence of the most striking West Indian creation between the wars, Padmore's African Bureau. Between the wars it was the only African organization of its kind in existence. Of the seven members of the committee, five were West Indians, and they ran the organization. Of them only Padmore had ever visited Africa. It could not have been accidental that this West Indian attracted two of the most remarkable Africans of this or any other time. A founder-member and a simmering volcano of African nationalism was Jomo Kenyatta. But even better fortune was in store for us.

The present writer met Nkrumah, then a student at the University of Pennsylvania, and wrote to Padmore about him. Nkrumah came to England to study law and there formed an association with Padmore; they worked at the doctrines and premises of Pan-Africanism and elaborated the plans which culminated in Nkrumah's leading the people of the Gold Coast to the independence of Ghana. This revolution by the Gold Coast was the blow which made so many cracks in the piece of African colonialism that it proved impossible ever to stick them together again. With Nkrumah's victory the association did not cease. After independence was signed and sealed, Nkrumah sent for Padmore, installed him once more in an office devoted to African emancipation and, under the auspices of an African government, this West Indian, as he had done in 1931 under the auspices of the Kremlin, organized in Accra the first conference of African states, followed, twenty-five years after the first, by the second world conference of fighters for African freedom. Dr. Banda, Patrice Lumumba, Nyerere, Tom Mboya, were some of those who attended the conference. Jomo Kenyatta was not there only because he was in jail. NBC made a national telecast of the interment of his ashes in Christiansborg Castle, at which Padmore was designated the Father of African Emancipation, a distinction challenged by no one. To the degree that they had to deal with us in the period between the wars, many learned and important persons and institutions looked upon us and our plans and hopes for Africa as the fantasies of some politically illiterate West Indians. It was they who completely misconceived a continent, not we. They should have learned from that experience. They have not. The same myopic vision which failed to focus Africa is now peering at the West Indies.

The place of Africa in the West Indian development is documented as few historical visions are documented.

In 1939 a black West Indian from the French colony of Martinique published in Paris the finest and most famous poem ever written about Africa, *Cahier d'un retour au pays natal* (Statement of a Return to the Country Where I Was Born.) Aimé Césaire first describes Martinique, the poverty, misery, and vices of the masses of the people, the lickspittle subservience of the colored middle classes. But the poet's education has been consummated in Paris. As a West Indian he has nothing national to be aware of. He is overwhelmed by the gulf that separates him from the people where he was born. He feels that he must go there. He does so and discovers a new version of what the Haitians, as had Garvey and Padmore, had discovered: that salvation for the West Indies lies in Africa, the original home and ancestry of the West Indian people.

The poet gives us a view of Africans as he sees them.

> ... my Negritude is not a stone, its
> deafness a sounding board for
> the noises of the day
> my Negritude is not a mere spot of
> dead water on the dead eye of
> the earth
> my Negritude is no tower, no cathedral
>
> it cleaves into the red flesh of the
> teeming earth
> it cleaves into the glowing flesh of
> the heavens
> it penetrates the seamless bondage of
> my unbending patience
>
> Hoorah for those who never invented
> anything
> for those who never explored anything
> for those who never mastered anything
>
> but who, possessed, give themselves up
> to the essence of each thing
> ignorant of the coverings but possessed
> by the pulse of things
> indifferent to mastering but taking the
> chances of the world ...

In contrast to this vision of the African unseparated from the world, from Nature, a living part of all that lives, Césaire immediately places the civilization that has scorned and persecuted Africa and Africans.

> Listen to the white world
> its horrible exhaustion from its
> immense labors

its rebellious joints cracking under
    the pitiless stars
its blue steel rigidities, cutting
    through the mysteries of the
    flesh
listen to their vainglorious conquests
    trumpeting their defeats
listen to the grandiose alibis of their
    pitiful floundering

The poet wants to be an architect of this unique civilization, a commissioner of its blood, a guardian of its refusal to accept.

But in doing so, my heart, preserve
    me from all hate
do not turn me into a man of hate of
    whom I think only with hate
for in order to project myself into
    this unique race
you know the extent of my boundless
    love
you know that it is not from hatred
    of other races
that I seek to be the cultivator of this
    unique race . . .

He returns once more to the pitiful specter of West Indian life, but now with hope.

for it is not true that the work of man
    is finished
that man has nothing more to do in the
    world but be a parasite in the world
that all we now need is to keep in step
    with the world
but the work of man is only just beginning
    and it remains to man to conquer all

the violence entrenched in the recesses
of his passion
and no race possesses the monopoly of beauty,
of intelligence, of force, and there
is a place for all at the rendezvous
of victory . . .

Here is the center of Césaire's poem. By neglecting it, Africans and the sympathetic of other races utter loud hurrahs that drown out common sense and reason. The work of man is not finished. Therefore the future of the African is not to continue not discovering anything. The monopoly of beauty, of intelligence, of force, is possessed by no race, certainly not by those who possess Negritude. Negritude is what one race brings to the common rendezvous where all will strive for the new world of the poet's vision. The vision of the poet is not economics or politics, it is poetic, *sui generis*, true unto itself and needing no other truth. But it would be the most vulgar racism not to see here an incarnation of Marx's famous sentence, "The real history of humanity will begin."

From Césaire's strictly poetic affinities* we have to turn our faces if even with distinct loss to our larger general purpose. But *Cahier* has united elements in modern thought which seemed destined to remain asunder. These had better be enumerated.

1. He has made a union of the African sphere of existence with existence in the Western world.

2. The past of mankind and the future of mankind are historically and logically linked.

3. No longer from external stimulus but from their own self-generated and independent being and motion will Africa and Africans move towards an integrated humanity.

It is the Anglo-Saxon poet who has seen for the world in general what the West Indian has seen concretely for Africa.

---

* Baudelaire and Rimbaud, Rilke and D. H. Lawrence. Jean-Paul Sartre has done the finest of critical appreciations of *Cahier* as poetry, but his explanation of what he conceives Negritude to mean is a disaster.

Here the impossible union
Of spheres of existence is actual,
Here the past and future
Are conquered, and reconciled,
Where action were otherwise movement
Of that which is only moved
And has in it no source of movement—

Mr. Eliot's conclusion is "Incarnation"; Césaire's, Negritude.

Cahier appeared in 1938 in Paris. A year before that *The Black Jacobins* had appeared in London. The writer had made the forward step of resurrecting not the decadence but the grandeur of the West Indian people. But as is obvious all through the book and particularly in the last pages, it is Africa and African emancipation that he has in mind.

Today (but only today) we can define what motivated this West Indian preoccupation with Africa between the wars. The West Indians were and had always been Western-educated. West Indian society confined black men to a very narrow strip of social territory. The first step to freedom was to go abroad. *Before they could begin to see themselves as a free and independent people they had to clear from minds the stigma that anything African was inherently inferior and degraded.* The road to West Indian national identity lay through Africa.

The West Indian national community constantly evades racial categorization. After Ortiz, it was another white West Indian who in the same period proved himself to be the greatest politician in the democratic tradition whom the West Indies has ever known.

Arthur Andrew Cipriani was a French Creole in the island of Trinidad who came into public life as an officer in a West Indian contingent in World War I. It was in the army that many of the soldiers, a medley from all the British West Indian islands, for the first time wore shoes consistently. But they were the product of their peculiar history. The speed with which they adjusted themselves to the spiritual and material requirements of a modern war amazed all observers, from General Allenby down. Cipriani made a reputation for himself by his militant defense of the regiment against all racism, official and unofficial. To the end of his days he spoke constantly of the recognition they had won. By profession a trainer of horses, it was only after much persuasion that, on his return home after the war, already a man over forty, he entered politics. He at once put himself forward as the champion of the common people, in his own phrase, "the barefooted man." Before very long this white was acknowledged as leader by hundreds of thousands of black people and East Indians. An utterly fearless man, he never left the colonial government in any doubt as to what it was up against. All who ever heard him speak remember his raising of his right hand and his slow enunciation of the phrase, "If I raise my little finger . . ." Against tremendous odds he forced the government to capitulate on workmen's compensation, the eight-hour day, trade union legislation, and other elementary constituents of democracy. Year after year he was elected mayor of the capital city. He made the mayoralty a center of opposition to the British Colonial Office and all its works.

Cipriani always treated West Indians as a modern contemporary people. He declared himself to be a socialist and day in day out, inside and outside of the legislature, he attacked capitalists and capitalism. He attached his party to the British Labour Party and scrupulously kept his followers aware of their privileges and responsibilities as members of the international labor movement. Cipriani was that rare type of politician to whom words expressed realities. Long before any of the other territories of the colonial empires, he not only raised the slogans of national independence and federation of the British West Indian territories, he went tirelessly from island to island mobilizing pubic opinion in general and the labor movement in particular in support of these slogans. He died in 1945. The islands had never seen before and have not seen since anything or anybody like him.

The West Indian masses jumped ahead even of Cipriani. In 1937, among the oil field workers in Trinidad, the largest proletarian grouping in the West Indies, a strike began. Like a fire along a tinder track, it spread to the entire island, then from island to island, ending in an upheaval at the other end of the curve, in Jamaica, thousands of miles away. The colonial government collapsed completely and two local popular leaders had to take over the responsibility of restoring some sort of social order. The heads of the government in Trinidad and

Tobago saved their administrations (but earned the wrath of the imperial government) by expressing sympathy with the revolt. The British Government sent a Royal Commission, which took much evidence, discovered long-standing evils, and made proposals by no means unintelligent or reactionary. As usual they were late, they were slow. Had Cipriani been the man he was ten years earlier, self-government, federation, and economic regeneration, which he had advocated so strenuously and so long, could have been initiated then. But the old warrior was nearly seventy. He flinched at the mass upheavals which he more than anyone had prepared, and the opportunity was lost. But he had destroyed a legend and established once and for all that the West Indian people were ready to follow the most advanced theories of an uncompromising leadership.

III. After World War II

Cipriani had built soundly and he left behind a Caribbean Labour Congress devoted to federation, independence and the creation of an enlightened peasantry. But what has happened to Castro's Cuba is inherent in these unfortunate islands. In 1945 the congress, genuinely West Indian, joined the World Federation of Trade Unions. But in 1948 that body split into the World Federation of Trade Unions of the East and the International Confederation of Free Trade Unions of the West. The split in the international split the Caribbean Labour Congress and it lost its place as the leader and inspirer of a genuinely West Indian movement. The British Colonial Office took the colored middle class under its wing. These gradually filled the Civil Service and related organizations; they took over the political parties, the old colonial system.

What is this old colonial system? It is the oldest Western relic of the seventeenth century still alive in the world today, surrounded on all sides by a modern population.

The West Indies has never been a traditional colonial territory with clearly distinguished economic and political relations between two different cultures. Native culture there was none. The aboriginal Amerindian civilization had been destroyed. Every succeeding year, therefore, saw the laboring population, slave or free, incorporating into itself more and more of the language, customs, aims, and outlook of its masters. It steadily grew in numbers until it became a terrifying majority of the whole population. The ruling minority therefore was in the position of the father who produced children and had to guard against being supplanted by them. There was only one way out, to seek strength abroad. This beginning has lasted unchanged to this very day.

The dominant industrial structure has been the sugar plantation. For over two hundred years the sugar industry has tottered on the brink of disaster, remaining alive by an unending succession of last-minute rescues by gifts, concessions, quotas from the metropolitan power or powers.

Sugar Manufacturers' "Grim Future"
From our Correspondent

Georgetown, Sept. 3

The British West Indies Sugar Association's chairman, Sir Robert Kirkwood, has stated here that cane manufacturers were facing a grim future and the position was reaching a stage where beet sugar production should be restricted to provide cane manufacturers with an enlarged market. Sir Robert pointed out that Britain's participation in the European Common Market should be no threat to sugar manufacturers provided preferences under the Commonwealth sugar agreement were preserved.

You would be able to read the same in any European newspaper at regular intervals during the last two hundred years. Recent official reports on the life and labor of the plantation laborer are moved to language remarkably similar to that of the non-conformist agitators against plantation slavery. There are economists and scientists today in the West Indies who believe that the most fortunate economic occurrence would be a blight that would destroy the sugar cane completely and thus compel some new type of economic development.*

* None will dare to say so publicly. He or she would be driven out of the territory.

As they have been from the first days of slavery, financial power and its mechanism are today entirely in the hands of metropolitan organizations and their agents.

Such a Westernized population needs quantities of pots, pans, plates, spoons, knives, forks, paper, pencils, cloth, bicycles, buses for public transport, automobiles, all the elementary appurtenances of civilization which the islands do not manufacture, not forgetting Mercedes-Benzes, Bentleys, Jaguars, and Lincolns. In this type of commerce the dominating elements are the foreign manufacturers and the foreign banks. The most revealing feature of this trade and the oldest is the still massive importation of food, including vegetables.

The few industries of importance, such as oil and bauxite, are completely in the hands of foreign firms, and the local politicians run a ferocious competition with each other in offering inducements to similar firms to establish new industries here and not there.

As with material, so with intellectual necessities. In island after island the daily newspaper is entirely in the hands of foreign firms. Radio and television cannot evade the fate of newspapers.

In 1963 the old colonial system is not what it was in 1863; in 1863 it was not what it had been in 1763 or 1663. The fundamentals outlined above, however, have not changed. But for the first time the system is now threatened, not from without but from within, not by communism, not by socialism, but by plain, simple parliamentary democracy. The old colonial system in the West Indies was not a democratic system, was not born as such. It cannot live with democracy. Within a West Indian island the old colonial system and democracy are incompatible. One has to go. That is the logic of development of every West Indian territory, Cuba, the Dominican Republic, Haiti, the former British colonies, the former French colonies, and even Puerto Rico, the poor relation of the wealthy United States.

The supreme wrong of West Indian politics is that the old colonial system has so isolated the ruling classes from the national community that plain, ordinary, parliamentary democracy, *suffused with a sense of national identity*, can remake the islands.

Statistics of production and the calculations of votes together form the surest road towards misunderstanding the West Indies. To which for good measure add the antagonism of races. The people of the West Indies were born in the seventeenth century, in a Westernized productive and social system. Members of different African tribes were split up to lessen conspiracy, and they were therefore compelled to master the European languages, highly complex products of centuries of civilization. From the start there had been the gap, constantly growing, between the rudimentary conditions of the life of the slave and the language he used. There was therefore in West Indian society an inherent antagonism between the consciousness of the black masses and the reality of their lives, inherent in that it was constantly produced and reproduced not by agitators but by the very conditions of the society itself. It is the modern media of mass communication which have made essence into existence. For an insignificant sum per month, the black masses can hear on the radio news of Dr. Nkrumah, Jomo Kenyatta, Dr. Julius Banda, Prime Minister Nehru, events and personalities of the United Nations and all the capitals of the world. They can wrestle with what the West thinks of the East and what the East thinks of the West. The cinema presents actualities and not infrequently stirs the imagination with the cinematic masterpieces of the world. Every hour on the hour all variations of food, clothing, household necessities, and luxuries are presented as absolutely essential to a civilized existence. All this to a population which over large areas still lives in conditions little removed from slavery.

The high material civilization of the white minority is now fortified by the concentration of the colored middle classes on making salaries and fees do the work of incomes. Sometimes a quarter of the population is crowded into the capital city, the masses irresistibly attracted by the contrast between what they see and hear and the lives they live. This was the tinder to which Castro placed a match. Historical tradition, education in the sense of grappling with the national past, there is none. History as taught is what it always has been, propaganda for those, whoever they may be, who administer the old colonial system. Power here is more naked than in any part of the world. Hence the brutality, savagery, even personal cruelties of the regimes of Trujillo and Duvalier, and the power of the Cuban Revolution.

This is the instrument on which perform all West Indian soloists, foreign or native. Take the French West Indian islands of Martinique and Guadeloupe. The colonial administration declared and acted for Vichy, the mass of the population for the Resistance. Vichy defeated, the islands whole-heartedly became departments of France, anxious to be assimilated into French civilization. But the hand of the Paris administration, notoriously heavy in the provincial administrations of France itself, is a crushing weight on any attempt to change the old colonial system. Today the mass of the population, disillusioned, is demanding independence. Their students in Paris are leading the struggle with blood, with boldness, and with brilliance available to all who use the French language.

The British system, unlike the French, does not crush the quest for a national identity. Instead, it stifles it. It formed a federation of its Caribbean colonies. But the old colonial system consisted of insular economies, each with its financial and economic capital in London. A federation meant that the economic line of direction should no longer be from island to London, but from island to island. But that involved the break-up of the old colonial system. The West Indian politicians preferred the break-up of the federation. Two of the islands have actually been granted independence. The Queen of England is their queen. They receive royal visits; their legislatures begin with prayers; their legislative bills are read three times; a mace has been presented to each of these distant infants by the Mother of Parliaments; their prominent citizens can receive an assortment of letters after their names, and in time the prefix "Sir." This no longer lessens but intensifies the battle between the old colonial system and democracy. Long before the actual independence was granted, large numbers of the middle classes, including their politicians, wanted it put off as far into the distance as possible. For the cruiser in the offing and the prospect of financial gifts and loans, they turn longing eyes and itching feet towards the United States.

The Caribbean is now an American sea. Puerto Rico is its show piece. Puerto Rico has the near-celestial privilege of free entry into the United States for their unemployed and their ambitious. The United States returns to the Puerto Rican government all duty collected on such staple imports as rum and cigars. American money for investment and American loans and gifts should create the Caribbean paradise. But if the United States had the Puerto Rican density of population, it would contain all the people in the world. Puerto Rico is just another West Indian island.

In the Dominican Republic there is no need to go beyond saying that Trujillo had gained power by the help of the United States Marines and all through the more than quarter-century of his infamous dictatorship he was understood to enjoy the friendship of Washington. Before the recent election of his successor, Sr. Juan Bosch, the French newspapers stated as an item of news that members of the left in the Dominican Republic (names were given) were deported to Paris by the local police, who were assisted in this operation by members of the FBI. Trujillo gone, Duvalier of Haiti is the uncrowned king of Latin American barbarism. It is widely believed that despite the corruption and impertinence of his regime, it is American support which keeps him in power: better Duvalier than another Castro.

Such a mass of ignorance and falsehood has surrounded these islands for so many centuries that obvious truths sound like revelations. Contrary to the general belief, the Caribbean territories taken as a whole are not sunk in irremediable poverty. When he was Principal of the University of the West Indies in Jamaica, Professor Arthur Lewis, former head of the faculty of economics at Manchester University and at the time of writing due to head the same faculty at Princeton, tried to remove some cobwebs from the eyes of his fellow West Indians:

> The opinion that the West Indies can raise all the capital it needs from its own resources is bound to shock many people, because West Indians like to feel that ours is a poor community. But the fact of the matter is that at least half the people in the world are poorer than we are. The standard of living in the West Indies is higher than the standard of living in India, or China, in most of the countries of Asia, and in most of the countries of Africa. The West Indies is not a poor community; it is in the upper bracket

of world income. It is capable of producing the extra 5 or 6 percent of resources which is required for this job, just as Ceylon and Ghana are finding the money they need for development by taxing themselves. It is not necessary for us to send our statesmen around the world begging for help. If help is given to us let us accept it, but let us not sit down and say nothing can be done until the rest of the world out of its goodness of heart is willing to grant us charity.*

The economic road they have to travel is a broad highway on which the signposts have long been erected. Sr. Juan Bosch began his campaign by promising to distribute the land confiscated from the baronial plunder of the Trujillo family. His supporters rapidly transformed this into: "A house and land for every Dominican." Not only the popular demand and modern economists, but British Royal Commissions during the last sixty years, have indicated (cautiously but clearly enough) that the way out of the West Indian morass is the abolition of the plantation laborer and the substitution, instead, of individual landowning peasants. Scientists and economists have indicated that an effective industry is possible, based on the scientific and planned use of raw material produced on the islands. I have written in vain if I have not made it clear that of all formerly colonial colored peoples, the West Indian masses are the most highly experienced in the ways of Western civilization and most receptive to its requirements in the twentieth century. To realize themselves they will have to break out of the shackles of the old colonial system.

I do not propose to plunge this appendix into the turbulent waters of controversy about Cuba. I have written about the West Indies in general and Cuba is the most West Indian island in the West Indies. That suffices.

One more question remains—the most realistic and most pregnant question of all. Toussaint L'Ouverture and the Haitian slaves brought into the world more than the abolition of slavery. When Latin Ameri-

* Study Conference of Economic Development in Underdeveloped Countries, August 5–15, 1957, University of the West Indies, Jamaica.

cans saw that small and insignificant Haiti would win and keep independence they began to think that they ought to be able to do the same. Pétion, the ruler of Haiti, nursed back to health the sick and defeated Bolivar, gave him money, arms, and a printing press to help in the campaign which ended in the freedom of the Five States. What will happen to what Fidel Castro has brought new to the world no one can say. But what is waiting in the West Indies to be born, what emerged from the womb in July 1958, is to be seen elsewhere in the West Indies, not so confused with the pass and fell incensed points of mighty opposites. I speak now of a section of the West Indies of which I have had during the past five years intimate and personal experience of the writers and the people. But this time the people first, for if the ideologists have moved closer towards the people, the people have caught up with the ideologists and the national identity is a national fact.

In Trinidad in 1957, before there was any hint of a revolution on Cuba, the ruling political party suddenly declared, contrary to the declaration of policy with which it had won the election, that during the war the British government of Sir Winston Churchill had given away Trinidad property and it should be returned. What happened is one of the greatest events in the history of the West Indies. The people rose to the call. Mass meetings and mass demonstrations, political passion such as the island had never known, swept through the population. Inside the chains of the old colonial system, the people of the West Indies are a national community. The middle classes looked on with some uncertainty but with a growing approval. The local whites are not like whites in a foreign civilization. They are West Indians and, under a strong impulse, think of themselves as such. Many of them quietly made known their sympathy with the cause. The political leader was uncompromising in his demand for the return. "I shall break Chaguaramas or it will break me," he declared, and the words sprouted wings. He publicly asserted to mass meetings of many thousands that if the State Department, backed by the Colonial Office, continued to refuse to discuss the return of the base, he would take Trinidad not only out of the West Indian Federation but out of the British association altogether: he would establish the independence of the island, all previous treaties entered into under the colonial regime would automatically become null and void, and thus he would deal with the Americans. He forbade them to use the Trinidad airport for their military planes. In a magnificent address, "From Slavery to Chaguaramas," he said that for centuries the West Indies had been bases, military footballs of warring imperialist powers, and the time had come to finish with it. It is the present writer's opinion (he was for the crucial period editor of the party journal) that it was the response of the population which sent the political leader so far upon a perilous road. They showed simply that they thought the Americans should quit the base and return it to the people. This was all the more remarkable in that the Trinidad people freely admitted that Trinidad had never enjoyed such financial opulence as when the Americans were there during the war. America was undoubtedly the potential source of economic and financial aid. But they were ready for any sacrifices needed for the return of the base. They were indeed ready for anything, and the political leadership had to take great care to do or say nothing which would precipitate any untoward mass intervention.

What was perhaps the most striking feature of this powerful national upheaval was its concentration on the national issue and its disregard for all others. There was not the slightest trace of anti-American feeling; though the British Colonial Office was portrayed as the ally of the State Department and the demand for political independence was well on the way, there was equally no trace of anti-British feeling. There was no inclination toward non-alignment, not even, despite the pressure for independence, anti-imperialism. The masses of the people of Trinidad and Tobago looked upon the return of the base as the first and primary stage in their quest for national identity. That they were prepared to suffer for, if need be (of this I am as certain as one can be of such things) to fight and die for. But in the usual accompaniments of a struggle against a foreign base, they were not in any way concerned. Not that they did not know. They most certainly knew. But they had had a long experience of international relations and they knew precisely what they wanted. Right up the islands, the population responded in the same way to what they felt was a West Indian matter. The press conference of the political leader was the most popular radio program in the West Indian islands. It was 1937–38 all over again. "Free is how you is from the start, an' when it look different you got to move, just move, an' when you movin' say that is a natural freedom make you move."* Though the British flag still blew above them, in their demands and demonstrations for Chaguaramas they were free, freer than they might be for a long time.

The West Indian national identity is more easily to be glimpsed in the published writings of West Indian authors.

Vic Reid of Jamaica is the only West Indian novelist who lives in the West Indies. That presumably is why he sets his scene in Africa. An African who knows the West Indies well assures me that there is nothing African abut Reid's story. It is the West Indies in African dress. Whatever it is, the novel is a *tour de force*. African or West Indian, it reduces the human problems of under-developed countries to a common denominator. The distinctive tone of the new West Indian orchestra is not loud but it is clear. Reid is not unconcerned about the fate of his characters. The political passions are sharp and locked in murderous conflict. But Reid is detached as no European or African writer is or can be detached, as Garvey, Padmore, Césaire were not and could not be detached. The origin of his detachment appears very clearly in the most powerful and far-ranging of the West Indian school, George Lamming of Barbados.

Confining ourselves strictly to our purpose, we shall limit ourselves to citing only one episode from the latest of his four powerful novels.

Powell, a character in *Season of Adventure*, is a murderer, rapist, and altogether criminal member of West Indian society. Suddenly, after nine-tenths of the book, the author injects three pages headed "Author's Note." Writing in the first person he accounts for Powell.

> Until the age of ten Powell and I had lived together, equal in the affection of two mothers. Powell had made my dreams; and I had lived his passions. Identical in years, and stage by stage, Powell and I were taught in the same primary school.

* *Season of Adventure*, by George Lamming.

And then the division came. I got a public scholarship which started my migration into another world, a world whose roots were the same, but whose style of living was entirely different from what my childhood knew. It had earned me a privilege which now shut Powell and the whole *tonelle* right out of my future. I had lived as near to Powell as my skin to the hand it darkens. And yet! Yet I forgot the *tonelle* as men forget a war, and attached myself to that new world which was so recent and so slight beside the weight of what had gone before. Instinctively I attached myself to the new privilege; and in spite of all my effort, I am not free of its embrace to this day.

I believe in my bones that the mad impulse which drove Powell to his criminal defeat was largely my doing. I will not have this explained away by talk about environment; nor can I allow my own moral infirmity to be transferred to a foreign conscience, labeled imperialist. I shall go beyond my grave in the knowledge that I am responsible for what happened to my brother.

Powell still resides somewhere in my heart, with a dubious love, some strange, nameless shadow of regret; and yet with the deepest, deepest nostalgia. For I have never felt myself to be an honest part of anything since the world of his childhood deserted me.

This is something new in the voluminous literature of anti-colonialism. The West Indian of this generation accepts complete responsibility for the West Indies.

Vidia Naipaul of Trinidad does the same. His Mr. Biswas writes his first article for a newspaper.

DADDY COMES HOME IN A COFFIN
U.S. Explorer's Last Journey
On Ice by M. Biswas

. . . Less than a year ago Daddy—George Elmer Edman, the celebrated traveler and explorer—left home to explore the Amazon.

Well, I have news for you, kiddies.

Daddy is on his way home now.

Yesterday he passed through Trinidad. In a coffin.

This earns Mr. Biswas, former agricultural laborer and keeper of a small shop, a job on the staff of this paper.

Mr. Biswas wrote a letter of protest. It took him two weeks. It was eight typewritten pages long. After many rewritings the letter developed into a broad philosophical essay on the nature of man; his son goes to a secondary school and together they hunt through Shakespeare for quotations and find a rich harvest in *Measure for Measure*. The foreigner may miss this bland reproduction of the *modus operandi* of the well-greased West Indian journalist, politician, prime minister.

Mr. Biswas is now a man of letters. He is invited to a session of local literati. Mr. Biswas, whose poetic peak is Ella Wheeler Wilcox, is bewildered by whiskey and talk about Lorca, Eliot, Auden. Every member of the group must submit a poem. One night after looking at the sky through the window Mr. Biswas finds his theme.

He addressed his mother. He did not think of rhythm; he used no cheating abstract words. He wrote of coming up to the brow of a hill, seeing the black, forked earth, the marks of the spade, the indentations of the fork prongs. He wrote of the journey he had made a long time before. He was tired; she made him rest. He was hungry; she gave him food. He had nowhere to go; she welcomed him . . .

"It is a poem," Mr. Biswas announced. "In prose."

. . . "There is no title," he said. And as he had expected, this was received with satisfaction.

Then he disgraced himself. Thinking himself free of what he had written, he ventured on his poem boldly, and even with a touch of self-mockery. But as he read, his hands began to shake, the paper rustled; and when he spoke of the journey his voice failed. It cracked and kept on cracking; his eyes tickled. But he went on, and his emotion was such that at the end no one said a word . . .

The West Indian had made a fool of himself imitating American journalism, Shakespeare, T. S. Eliot, Lorca. He had arrived at truth when he wrote about his own West Indian childhood, his West Indian mother, and the West Indian landscape. Naipaul is an East Indian. Mr. Biswas is an East Indian. But the East Indian problem in the West Indies is a creation of politicians of both races, seeking means to avoid attacking the old colonial system. The East Indian has become as West Indian as all the other expatriates.

The latest West Indian novelist is one of the strangest of living novelists. Beginning in 1958 he has just completed a quartet of novels.* He is from British Guiana, which is a part of the South American continent. There are nearly 40,000 square miles of mountains, plateaux, forest, jungle, savannah, the highest waterfalls in the world, native Amerindians, settled communities of escaped African slaves—all largely unexplored. For fifteen years, over this new territory, Wilson Harris worked as a land surveyor. He is a member of a typical West Indian society of 600,000 people which inhabits a thin strip of coastline. Harris sets the final seal on the West Indian conception of itself as a national identity. On the run from the police a young Guianese, half-Chinese, half-Negro, discovers that all previous generations, Dutch, English, French, capitalists, slaves, freed slaves, white and black, were expatriates.

> ". . . All the restless wayward spirits of all the aeons (who it was thought were embalmed for good) are returning to roost in our blood. And we have to start all over again where they began to explore. We've got to pick up the seeds again where they left off. It's no use worshipping the rottenest tacouba and tree-trunk in he historic topsoil. There's a whole world of branches and sensations we've missed, and we've got to start again from the roots up even if they look like nothing. Blood, sap, flesh, veins, arteries, lungs, heart, the heartland, Sharon. *We're the first potential parents who can contain the ancestral house.* Too young? I don't know. Too much responsibility? Time will tell. We've got to face it. Or else it will be too late to stop everything and everyone from running away

---

* *Palace of the Peacock, The Far Journey of Oudin, The Whole Armour, The Secret Ladder.* London: Faber & Faber.

and tumbling down. And then All the King's Horses and All the King's Men won't be able to put us together again. Like all the bananas and the plantains and the coffee trees near Charity. Not far from here, you know. A small wind comes and everything comes out of the ground. Because the soil is unstable. Just pegasse. Looks rich on top but that's about all. What do you think they say when it happens, when the crops run away? They shrug and say they're expendable crops. They can't begin to see that it's *us*, our blood, running away all the time, in the river and in the sea, everywhere, staining the bush. *Now* is the time to make a newborn stand, Sharon; you and me; it's up to us, even if we fall on our knees and *creep* to anchor ourselves before we get up."

There is no space here to deal with the poet in the literary tradition, or the ballad singer. In dance, in the innovation in musical instruments, in popular ballad singing unrivaled anywhere in the world, the mass of the people are not seeking a national identity, they are expressing one. The West Indian writers have discovered the West Indies and West Indians, a people of the middle of our disturbed century, concerned with the discovery of themselves, determined to discover themselves, but without hatred or malice against the foreigner, even the bitter imperialist past. To be welcomed into the comity of nations a new nation must bring something new. Otherwise it is a mere administrative convenience or necessity. The West Indians have brought something new.

> Albion too was once
> a colony like ours . . .

> . . . deranged
> By foaming channels, and the vain
>   expanse
> Of bitter faction.
> All in compassion ends.
> So differently from what the heart
>   arranged.

Passion not spent but turned inward. Toussaint tried and paid for it with his life. Torn, twisted, stretched to the limits of agony, injected with poisonous patent medicines, it lives in the state which Fidel started. It is of the West Indies West Indian. For it, Toussaint, the first and greatest of West Indians, paid with his life.

"Caliban: Notes Toward a Discussion of Culture in Our America"

ROBERTO FERNÁNDEZ RETAMAR
(CUBA)

A Question

a European journalist, and moreover a leftist, asked me a few days ago, "Does a Latin-American culture exist?"* We were discussing, naturally enough, the recent polemic regarding Cuba that ended by confronting, on the one hand, certain bourgeois European intellectuals (or aspirants to that state) with a visible colonialist nostalgia; and on the other, that body of Latin-American writers and artists who reject open or veiled forms of cultural and political colonialism. The question seemed to me to reveal one of the roots of the polemic and, hence, could also be expressed another way: "Do you exist?" For to question our culture is to question our very existence, our human reality itself, and thus to be willing to take a stand in favor of our irremediable colonial condition, since it suggests that we would be but a distorted echo of

* This article appeared for the first time in *Casa de Las Américas* (Havana), 68 (September–October 1971). It is that journal, and that issue specifically, to which the author refers in the text.

what occurs elsewhere. This elsewhere is of course the metropolis, the colonizing centers, whose "right wings" have exploited us and whose supposed "left wings" have pretended and continue to pretend to guide us with pious solicitude—in both cases with the assistance of local intermediaries of varying persuasions.

While this fate is to some extent suffered by all countries emerging from colonialism—those countries of ours that enterprising metropolitan intellectuals have ineptly and successively termed *barbarians*, *peoples of color*, *underdeveloped countries*, *Third World*—I think the phenomenon achieves a singular crudeness with respect to what Martí called "our *mestizo* America." Although the thesis that every man and even every culture is *mestizo* could easily be defended and although this seems especially valid in the case of colonies, it is nevertheless apparent that in both their ethnic and their cultural aspects capitalist countries long ago achieved a relative homogeneity. Almost before our eyes certain readjustments have been made. The white population of the United States (diverse, but of common European origin) exterminated the aboriginal population and thrust the black population aside, thereby affording itself homogeneity in spite of diversity and offering a coherent model that its Nazi disciples attempted to apply even to other European conglomerates—an unforgivable sin that led some members of the bourgeoisie to stigmatize in Hitler what they applauded as a healthy Sunday diversion in westerns and Tarzan films. Those movies proposed to the world—and even to those of us who are kin to the communities under attack and who rejoiced in the evocation of our own extermination—the monstrous racial criteria that have accompanied the United States from its beginnings to the genocide in Indochina. Less apparent (and in some cases perhaps less cruel) is the process by which other capitalist countries have also achieved relative racial and cultural homogeneity at the expense of *internal* diversity.

Nor can any necessary relationship be established between *mestizaje* ["racial intermingling, racial mixture"—ed. note] and the colonial world. The latter is highly complex[1] despite basic structural

1. See Yves Lacoste, *Les pays sous-développés* [The Underdeveloped Countries] (Paris, 1959), 82–84.

affinities of its parts. It has included countries with well-defined millennial cultures, some of which have suffered (or are presently suffering) direct occupation (India, Vietnam), and others of which have suffered indirect occupation (China). It also comprehends countries with rich cultures but less political homogeneity, which have been subjected to extremely diverse forms of colonialism (the Arab world). There are other peoples, finally, whose fundamental structures were savagely dislocated by the dire activity of the European despite which they continue to preserve a certain ethnic and cultural homogeneity (black Africa). (Indeed, the latter has occurred despite the colonialists' criminal and unsuccessful attempts to prohibit it.) In these countries *mestizaje* naturally exists to a greater or lesser degree, but it is always accidental and always on the fringe of the central line of development.

But within the colonial world there exists a case unique to *the entire planet:* a vast zone for which *mestizaje* is not an accident but rather the essence, the central line: ourselves, "our mestizo America." Martí, with his excellent knowledge of the language, employed this specific adjective as the distinctive sign of our culture—a culture of descendants, both ethnically and culturally speaking, of aborigines, Africans, and Europeans. In his "Letter from Jamaica" (1815), the Liberator, Simón Bolívar, had proclaimed, "We are a small human species: we possess a world encircled by vast seas, new in almost all its arts and sciences." In his message to the Congress of Angostura (1819), he added:

> Let us bear in mind that our people is neither European nor North American, but a composite of Africa and America rather than an emanation of Europe; for even Spain fails as a European people because of her African blood, her institutions, and her character. It is impossible to assign us with any exactitude to a specific human family. The greater part of the native peoples has been annihilated; the European has mingled with the American and with the African, and the African has mingled with the Indian and with the European. Born from the womb of a common mother, our fathers, different in origin and blood, are foreigners; all differ

327

visibly in the epidermis, and this dissimilarity leaves marks of the
greatest transcendence.

Even in this century, in a book as confused as the author himself
but full of intuitions (*La raza cósmica*, 1925), the Mexican José Vasconcelos pointed out that in Latin America a new race was being
forged, "made with the treasure of all previous ones, the final race,
the cosmic race."[2]

This singular fact lies at the root of countless misunderstandings.
Chinese, Vietnamese, Korean, Arab, or African cultures may leave the
Euro–North American enthusiastic, indifferent or even depressed.
But it would never occur to him to confuse a Chinese with a Norwe-
gian, or a Bantu with an Italian; nor would it occur to him to ask
whether they exist. Yet, on the other hand, some Latin Americans are
taken at times for apprentices, for rough drafts or dull copies of
Europeans, including among these latter whites who constitute what
Martí called "European America." In the same way, our entire culture
is taken as an apprenticeship, a rough draft or a copy of European
bourgeois culture ("an emanation of Europe," as Bolívar said). This
last error is more frequent than the the first, since confusion of a
Cuban with an Englishman, or a Guatemalan with a German, tends
to be impeded by a certain ethnic tenacity. Here the *rioplatenses*
appear to be less ethnically, although not culturally, differentiated.
The confusion lies in the root itself, because as descendants of
numerous Indian, African, and European communities, we have only
a few languages with which to understand one another: those of the

2. José Vasconcelos, *La raza cósmica* [The Cosmic Race] (1925). A Swedish
    summary of what is known on this subject can be found in Magnus Mörner's
    study, *La mezcla de razas en la historia de América Latina* [The Mixture of Races
    in the History of Latin America], Jorge Piatigorsky (Buenos Aires, 1969).
    Here it is recognized that "no part of the world has witnessed such a gigantic
    mixing of races as the one that has been taking place in Latin America and
    the Caribbean [Why this division?] since 1492" (15). Of course, what interests
    me in these is not the irrelevant biological fact of the "races" but the historical
    fact of the "cultures;" see Claude Lévi-Strauss, *Race et histoire* [Race and
    History] [1952] (Paris, 1968).

colonizers. While other colonials or ex-colonials in metropolitan centers speak among themselves in their own language, we Latin Americans continue to use the languages of our colonizers. These are the linguas francas capable of going beyond the frontiers that neither aboriginal nor Creole languages succeed in crossing. Right now as we are discussing, as I am discussing with those colonizers, how else can I do it except in one of their languages, which is now also *our* language, and with so many of their conceptual tools, which are now also *our* conceptual tools? This is precisely the extraordinary outcry that we read in a work by perhaps the most extraordinary writer of fiction who ever existed. In *The Tempest*, William Shakespeare's last play, the deformed Caliban—enslaved, robbed of his island, and trained to speak by Prospero—rebukes Prospero thus: "You taught me language, and my profit on't/ Is, I know how to curse. The red plague rid you/ For learning me your language!" (1.2.362–64).

Toward the History of Caliban

Caliban is Shakespeare's anagram for "cannibal," an expression that he had already used to mean "anthropophagus," in the third part of *Henry IV* and in *Othello* and that comes in turn from the word *carib*. Before the arrival of the Europeans, whom they resisted heroically, the Carib Indians were the most valiant and warlike inhabitants of the very lands that we occupy today. Their name lives on in the name Caribbean Sea (referred to genially by some as the American Mediterranean, just as if we were to call the Mediterranean the Caribbean of Europe). But the name *carib* in itself—as well as in its deformation, *cannibal*—has been perpetuated in the eyes of Europeans above all as a defamation. It is the term in this sense that Shakespeare takes up and elaborates into a complex symbol. Because of its exceptional importance to us, it will be useful to trace its history in some detail.

In the *Diario de Navegación* [Navigation logbooks] of Columbus there appear the first European accounts of the men who were to occasion the symbol in question. On Sunday, 4 November 1492, less than a month after Columbus arrived on the continent that was to be called America, the following entry was inscribed: "He learned also that far from the place there were men with one eye and others with dogs' muzzles, who ate human beings."[3] On 23 November, this entry: "[the island of Haiti], which they said was very large and that on it lived people who had only one eye and others called cannibals, of whom they seemed to be very afraid." On 11 December it is noted ". . . that *caniba* refers in fact to the people of El Gran Can," which explains the deformation undergone by the name *carib*—also used by Columbus. In the very letter of 15 February 1493, "dated on the caravelle off the island of Canaria" in which Columbus announces to the world his "discovery," he writes: "I have found, then, neither monsters nor news of any, save for one island [Quarives], the second upon entering the Indies, which is populated with people held by everyone on the islands to be very ferocious, and who eat human flesh."[4]

This *carib/cannibal* image contrasts with another one of the American man presented in the writings of Columbus: that of the *Arauaco* of the Greater Antilles—our *Taino* Indian primarily—whom he describes as peaceful, meek, and even timorous and cowardly. Both visions of the American aborigine will circulate vertiginously throughout Europe, each coming to know its own particular development: The Taino will be transformed into the paradisiacal inhabitant of a utopic world; by 1516 Thomas More will publish his *Utopia*, the similarities of which to the island of Cuba have been indicated,

3. Cited along with subsequent references to the *Diario* [Logbook], by Julio C. Salas, in *Etnografía americana: Los indios caribes—Estudio sobre el origen del mito de la antropofagia* [Latin American Ethnography: The Carib Indians—A Study of the Myth of Anthropophagy] (Madrid, 1920). The book exposes "The irrationality of [the] charge that some American tribes devoured human flesh, maintained in the past by those interested in enslaving [the] Indians and repeated by the chroniclers and historians, many of whom were supporters of slavery" (211).

4. *La carta de Colón anunciando el descubrimiento del nuevo mundo, 15 de febrero — 14 de marzo 1493* [Columbus's Letter Announcing the Discovery of the New World, 15 February–14 March 1493] (Madrid, 1956), 20.

almost to the point of rapture, by Ezequiel Martínez Estrada.[5] The Carib, on the other hand, will become a *cannibal*—an anthropophagus, a bestial man situated on the margins of civilization, who must be opposed to the very death. But there is less of a contradiction than might appear at first glance between the two visions; they constitute, simply, options in the ideological arsenal of a vigorous emerging bourgeoisie. Francisco de Quevedo translated "utopia" as "there is no such place." With respect to these two visions, one might add, "There is no such man." The notion of an Edenic creature comprehends, in more contemporary terms, a working hypothesis for the bourgeois left, and, as such, offers an ideal model of the perfect society free from the constrictions of that feudal world against which the bourgeoisie is in fact struggling. Generally speaking, the utopic vision throws upon these lands projects for political reforms unrealized in the countries of origin. In this sense its line of development is far from extinguished. Indeed, it meets with certain perpetuators—apart from its radical perpetuators, who are the consequential revolutionaries—in the numerous advisers who unflaggingly propose to countries emerging from colonialism magic formulas from the metropolis to solve the grave problems colonialism has left us and which, of course, they have not yet resolved in their own countries. It goes without saying that these proponents of "There is no such place" are irritated by the insolent fact that the place *does* exist and, quite naturally, has all the virtues and defects not of a project but of genuine reality.

As for the vision of the *cannibal,* it corresponds—also in more contemporary terms—to the right wing of that same bourgeoisie. It belongs to the ideological arsenal of politicians of action, those who perform the dirty work in whose fruits the charming dreamers of utopias will equally share. That the Caribs were as Columbus (and, after him, an unending throng of followers) depicted them is about as

5. Ezequiel Martínez Estrada, "El Nuevo Mundo, la Isla de Utopía y la Isla de Cuba" [The New World, the Island of Utopia, and the Island of Cuba], *Casa de las Américas* 33 (November–December 1965); this issue is entitled *Homenaje a Ezequiel Martínez Estrada.*

probable as the existence of one-eyed men, men with dog muzzles or tails, or even the Amazons mentioned by the explorer in pages where Greco-Roman mythology, the medieval bestiary, and the novel of chivalry all play their part. It is a question of the typically degraded version offered by the colonizer of the man he is colonizing. That we ourselves may have at one time believed in this version only proves to what extent we are infected with the ideology of the enemy. It is typical that we have applied the term *cannibal* not to the extinct aborigine of our isles, but above all, to the African black who appeared in those shameful Tarzan films. For it is the colonizer who brings us together, who reveals the profound similarities existing above and beyond our secondary differences. The colonizer's version explains to us that owing to the Carib's irremediable bestiality, there was no alternative to their extermination. What it does not explain is why even before the Caribs, the peaceful and kindly Arauacos were also exterminated. Simply speaking, the two groups suffered jointly one of the greatest ethnocides recorded in history. (Needless to say, this line of action is still more alive than the earlier one.) In relation to this fact, it will always be necessary to point out the case of those men who, being on the fringe both of utopianism (which has nothing to do with the actual America) and of the shameless ideology of plunder, stood in their midst opposed to the conduct of the colonialists and passionately, lucidly, and valiantly defended the flesh-and-blood aborigine. In the forefront of such men stands the magnificent figure of Father Bartolomé de las Casas, who Bolívar called "the apostle of America" and whom Martí extolled unreservedly. Unfortunately, such men were exceptions.

One of the most widely disseminated European utopian works is Montaigne's essay "De los caníbales" [On Cannibals], which appeared in 1580. There we find a presentation of those creatures who "retain alive and vigorous their genuine, their most useful and natural, virtues and properties."[6]

---

6. *The Complete Essays of Montaigne*, trans. Donald Frame (Stanford, Calif., 1965), 152.

Giovanni Floro's English translation of the *Essays* was published in 1603. Not only was Floro a personal friend of Shakespeare, but the copy of the translation that Shakespeare owned and annotated is still extant. This piece of information would be of no further importance but for the fact that it proves beyond a shadow of doubt that the *Essays* was one of the direct sources of Shakespeare's last great work, *The Tempest* (1612). Even one of the characters of the play, Gonzalo, who incarnates the Renaissance humanist, at one point closely glossed entire lines from Floro's Montaigne, originating precisely in the essay on cannibals. This fact makes the form in which Shakespeare presents his character *Caliban/cannibal* even stranger. Because if in Montaigne—in this case, as unquestionable literary source for Shakespeare—"there is nothing barbarous and savage in that nation . . . , except that each man calls barbarism whatever is not his own practice,"[7] in Shakespeare, on the other hand, *Caliban/cannibal* is a savage and deformed slave who cannot be degraded enough. What has happened is simply that in depicting Caliban, Shakespeare, an implacable realist, here takes *the other option* of the emerging bourgeois world. Regarding the utopian vision, it does indeed exist in the work but is unrelated to Caliban; as was said before, it is expressed by the harmonious humanist Gonzalo. Shakespeare thus confirms that both ways of considering the American, far from being in opposition, were perfectly reconcilable. As for the concrete man, present him in the guise of an animal, rob him of his land, enslave him so as to live from his toil, and at the right moment exterminate him; this latter, of course, only if there were someone who could be depended on to perform the arduous tasks in his stead. In one revealing passage, Prospero warns his daughter that they could not do without Caliban: "We cannot miss him: he does make our fire,/ Fetch in our wood, and serves in offices/ that profit us" (1.2.311–13). The utopian vision can and must do without men of flesh and blood. After all, *there is no such place.*

There is no doubt at this point that *The Tempest* alludes to America, that its island is the mythification of one of our islands. Astrana Marín, who mentions the "clearly Indian (American) ambience of the island,"

7. *Ibid.*

recalls some of the actual voyages along this continent that inspired Shakespeare and even furnished him, with slight variations, with the names of not a few of his characters; Miranda, Fernando, Sebastian, Alonso, Gonzalo, Setebos.[8] More important than this is the knowledge that Caliban is our Carib.

We are not interested in following all the possible readings that have been made of this notable work since its appearance,[9] and shall merely point out some interpretations. The first of these comes from Ernest Renan, who published his drama *Caliban: Suite de "La Tempête"* in 1878.[10] In this work, Caliban is the incarnation of the people presented in their worst light, except that this time his conspiracy against Prospero is successful and he achieves power—which ineptitude and corruption will surely prevent him from retaining. Prospero lurks in the darkness awaiting his revenge, and Ariel disappears. This reading owes less to Shakespeare than to the Paris Commune, which had taken place only seven years before. Naturally, Renan was among the writers of the French bourgeoisie who savagely took part against the prodigious "assault of heaven."[11] Beginning with this event, his antidemocratic feeling stiffened even further. "In his *Philosophical Dialogues,*" Lidsky tell us, "he believes that the solution would lie in the creation of an *élite* of intelligent beings who alone would govern and possess the secrets of science."[12] Characteristically, Renan's aristocratic and prefascist elitism and his hatred of the common people

8. In William Shakespeare, *Obras completas*, trans. Luis Astrana Marín (Madrid, 1961), 107–8.

9. For example, Jan Kott notes that "there have been learned Shakespearian scholars who tried to interpret *The Tempest* as a direct autobiography, or as an allegorical political drama" (*Shakespeare, Our Contemporary*, trans. Boleslaw Taborski, 2d ed. (London, 1967), 240.

10. Ernest Renan, *Caliban: Suite de "La Tempête." Drame Philosophique* [Caliban: "The Tempest" Suite. A philosophical Drama] (Paris, 1878).

11. See V. Arthur Adamov. *La Commune de Paris (8 mars–28 mars 1871): Anthologie* [The Paris Commune (8 March–28 March 1871): An Anthology] (Paris, 1959); and, especially, Paul Lidsky, *Les écrivains contre la Commune* [Writers Against the Commune] (Paris, 1970).

12. Lidsky, Paul, *Les écrivains contre la Commune*, 82.

of his country are united with an even greater hatred for the inhabitants of the colonies. It is instructive to hear him express himself along these lines.

> We aspire [he says] not only to equality but to domination. The country of a foreign race must again be a country of serfs, of agricultural laborers or industrial workers. It is not a question of eliminating the inequalities among men but of broadening them and making them law.[13]

And on another occasion:

> The regeneration of the inferior or bastard races by the superior races is within the providential human order. With us, the common man is nearly always a *declassé* nobleman, his heavy hand is better suited to handling the sword than the menial tool. Rather than work he chooses to fight, that is, he returns, to his first state. *Regere imperio populos*—that is our vocation. Pour forth this all-consuming activity onto countries which, like China, are crying aloud for foreign conquest. . . . Nature has made a race of workers, the Chinese race, with its marvelous manual dexterity and almost no sense of honor; govern them with justice, levying from them, in return for the blessing of such a government, an ample allowance for the conquering race, and they will be satisfied; a race of tillers of the soil, the black . . . a race of masters and soldiers, the European race. . . . *Let each do that which he is made for, and all will be well.*[14]

It is unnecessary to gloss these lines, which, as Césaire rightly says, came from the pen not of Hitler but of the French humanist Ernest Renan.

13. Cited by Aimé Césaire in *Discours sur le colonialisme* [An Address on Colonialism], 3d ed. (Paris, 1955), 13. This is a remarkable work, and I have made extensive use of its main ideas in this essay. (A part of it has been translated into Spanish in *Casa de las Américas* 36–37 [May–August 1966], an issue dedicated to *Africa en América* [Africa in Latin America]).
14. *Ibid.*, 14–15.

The initial destiny of the Caliban myth on our own American soil is a surprising one. Twenty years after Renan had published his *Caliban*—in other words, in 1898—the United States intervened in the Cuban war of independence against Spain and subjected Cuba to its tutelage, converting her in 1902 into her first *neocolony* (and holding her until 1959), while Puerto Rico and the Philippines became colonies of a traditional nature. The fact—which had been anticipated by Martí years before—moved the Latin American *intelligentsia*. Elsewhere I have recalled that "ninety-eight" is not only a Spanish date that gives its name to a complex group of writers and thinkers of that country, but it is also, and perhaps most importantly, a Latin American data that should serve to designate a no less complex group of writers and thinkers on this side of the Atlantic, generally known by the vague name of *modernistas*.[15] It is "ninety-eight"—the visible presence of North American imperialism in Latin America—already foretold by Martí, which informs the later work of someone like Darío or Rodó.

In a speech given by Paul Groussac in Buenos Aires on 2 May 1898, we have an early example of how Latin American writers of the time would react to this situation:

> Since the Civil War and the brutal invasion of the West [he says], the *Yankee* spirit had rid itself completely of its formless and "Calibanesque" body, and the Old World has contemplated with disquiet and terror the newest civilization that intends to supplant our own, declared to be in decay.[16]

The Franco-Argentine writer Groussac feels that "our" civilization (obviously understanding by that term the civilization of the "Old

15. See Roberto Fernández Retamar, "Modernismo, noventiocho, subdesarrollo" [Modernism, the Generation of 1898, Underdevelopment], paper read at the Third Congress of the International Association of Hispanists, Mexico City, August 1968; collected in *Ensayo de otro mundo* [Essay on a Different World], 2d ed. (Santiago, 1969).

16. Quoted in José Enrique Rodó, *Obras completas* [Complete Works], ed. Emir Rodríguez Monegal (Madrid, 1957), 193; this volume will hereafter be cited by page number in the text.

World," of which we Latin Americans would, curiously enough, be a part) is menaced by the Calibanesque Yankee. It seems highly improbable that the Algerian or Vietnamese writer of the time, trampled underfoot by French colonialism, would have been ready to subscribe to the first part of such a criterion. It is also frankly strange to see the Caliban symbol—in which Renan could with exactitude see, if only to abuse, the people—being applied to the United States. But nevertheless, despite this blurred focus—characteristic, on the other hand, of Latin America's unique situation—Groussac's reaction implies a clear rejection of the Yankee danger by Latin American writers. This is not, however, the first time that such a rejection was expressed on our continent. Apart from cases of Hispanic writers such as Bolívar and Martí, among others, Brazilian literature presents the example of Joaquín de Sousa Andrade, or Sousândrade, in whose strange poem, *O Guesa Errante*, stanza 10 is dedicated to "O inferno de Wall Street," "a *Walpurgisnacht* of corrupt stockbrokers, petty politicians, and businessmen."[17] There is besides José Verissimo, who in a 1890 treatise on national education impugned the United States with his "I admire them, but I don't esteem them."

We do not know whether the Uruguayan José Enrique Rodó—whose famous phrase on the United States, "I admire them, but I don't love them," coincides literally with Verissimo's observation—knew the work of that Brazilian thinker but it is certain that he was familiar with Groussac's speech, essential portions of which were reproduced in *La Razón* of Montevideo on 6 May 1898. Developing and embellishing the idea outlined in it, Rodó published in 1900, at the age of twenty-nine, one of the most famous works of Latin American literature: *Ariel*. North American civilization is implicitly presented there as Caliban (scarcely mentioned in the work), while Ariel would come to incarnate—or should incarnate—the best of what Rodó did not hesitate to call more than once "our civilization" (223, 226). In his words, just as in those of Groussac, this civilization was identified not only with "our Latin America" (239) but with ancient

---

17. See Jean Franco, *The Modern Culture of Latin America: Society and the Artist* (London, 1967), 49.

Romania, if not with the Old World as a whole. The identification of Caliban with the United States, proposed by Groussac and popularized by Rodó, was certainly a mistake. Attacking this error from one angle, José Vasconcelos commented that "if the Yankees were only Caliban, they would not represent any great danger."[18] But this is doubtless of little importance next to the relevant fact that the danger in question had clearly been pointed out. As Benedetti rightly observed, "Perhaps Rodó erred in naming the danger, but he did not err in his recognition of where it lay."[19]

Sometime afterward, the French writer Jean Guéhenno—who, although surely aware of the work by the colonial Rodó, knew of course Renan's work from memory—restated the latter's Caliban thesis in his own *Caliban parle* [Caliban speaks], published in Paris in 1929. This time, however, the Renan identification of Caliban *with* the people is accompanied by a positive evaluation of Caliban. One must be grateful to Guéhenno's book—and it is about the only thing for which gratitude is due—for having offered for the first time an appealing version of the character.[20] But the theme would have required the hand or the rage of a Paul Nizan to be effectively realized.[21]

18. José Vasconcelos, *Indología* [Indology], 2d ed. (Barcelona, n.d.), XXIII.
19. Mario Benedetti, *Genio y figura de José Enrique Rodó* [A Portrait of José Enriqué Rodó] (Buenos Aires, 1966), 95.
20. The penetrating but negative vision of Jan Kott causes him to be irritated by this fact. "Renan saw Demos in Caliban; in his continuation of *The Tempest* he took him to Milan and made him attempt another, victorious coup against Prospero. Guéhenno wrote an apology for Caliban-People. Both these interpretations are flat and do not do justice to Shakespeare's Caliban" (*Shakespeare, Our Contemporary*, 273).
21. Guéhenno's weakness in approaching this theme with any profundity is apparent from his increasingly contradictory prefaces to successive editions of the book (2d ed., 1945; 3d ed., 1962) down to his book of essays *Caliban et Prospero* [Caliban and Prospero] (Paris, 1969), where according to one critic, Guéhenno is converted into "a personage of bourgeois society and beneficiary of its culture," who judges Prospero "more equitably than in the days of *Caliban parle*" (Pierre Henri Simon, in *Le Monde*, 5 July, 1969).

Much sharper are the observations of the Argentine Aníbal Ponce, in his 1935 work *Humanismo burgués y humanismo proletario*. The book—which a student of Che's thinking conjectures must have exercised influence on the latter[22]—devotes the third chapter to "Ariel: or, The Agony of an Obstinate Illusion." In commenting on *The Tempest*, Ponce says that "those four beings embody an entire era: Prospero is the enlightened despot who loves the Renaissance; Miranda, his progeny; Caliban, the suffering masses [Ponce will then quote Renan, but not Guéhenno]; and Ariel, the genius of the air without any ties to life."[23] Ponce points up the equivocal nature of Caliban's presentation, one that reveals "an enormous injustice on the part of a master." In Ariel he sees the intellectual, tied to Prospero in "a less burdensome and crude way than Caliban, but also in his service." His analysis of the conception of the intellectual ("mixture of slave and mercenary") coined by Renaissance humanism, a concept that "taught as nothing else could an indifference to action and an acceptance of the established order" and that even today is for the intellectual in the bourgeois world "the educational ideal of the governing classes," constitutes one of the most penetrating essays written on the theme in our America.

But this examination, although made by a Latin American, still took only the European world into account. For a new reading of *The Tempest*—for a new consideration of the problem—it was necessary to await the emergence of the colonial countries, which begins around the time of the Second World War. That abrupt presence led the busy technicians of the United Nations to invent, between 1944 and 1945, the term *economically underdeveloped area* in order to dress in attractive (and profoundly confusing) verbal garb what had until then been called *colonial area*, or *backward areas*.[24]

22. See Michael Lowy, *La pensée de Che Guevara* [Che Guevara's Thought] (Paris, 1970), 19.

23. Aníbal Pónce, *Humanismo burgués y humanismo proletario* [Bourgeois Humanism and Proletarian Humanism] (Havana, 1962), 83.

24. J. L. Zimmerman, *Países pobres, países ricos: La brecha que se ensancha* [Poor Countries, Rich Countries: The Breech that is Widening], trans. G. González Aramburo (Mexico City, 1966), 7.

Concurrently with this emergence there appeared in Paris in 1950 O. Mannoni's book *Psychologie de la colonisation*. Significantly, the English edition of this book (New York, 1956) was to be called *Prospero and Caliban: The Psychology of Colonization*. To approach his subject, Mannoni has created, no less, what he calls the "Prospero complex," defined as "the sum of those unconscious neurotic tendencies that delineate at the same time the "picture" of the paternalist colonial and the portrait of 'the racist whose daughter has been the object of an [imaginary] attempted rape at the hands of an inferior being.' "[25] In this book, probably for the first time, Caliban is identified with the colonial. But the odd theory that the latter suffers from a "Prospero complex" that leads him neurotically to require, even to anticipate, and naturally to accept the presence of Prospero/colonizer is roundly rejected by Frantz Fanon in the fourth chapter ("The So-Called Dependency Complex of Colonized Peoples") of his 1952 book *Black Skin, White Masks*.

Although he is (apparently) the first writer in our world to assume our identification with Caliban, the Barbadian writer George Lamming is unable to break the circle traced by Mannoni:

Prospero [says Lamming] has given Caliban language; and with it an unstated history of consequences, an unknown history of future intentions. This gift of language meant not English, in particular, but speech and concept as a way, a method, a necessary avenue towards areas of the self which could not be reached in any other way. It is this way, entirely Prospero's enterprise, which makes Caliban aware of possibilities. Therefore, all of Caliban's future— for future is the very name of possibilities—must derive from Prospero's experiment, which is also his risk. Provided there is no extraordinary departure which explodes all of Prospero's premises, then Caliban and his future now belong to Prospero . . . Prospero lives in the absolute certainty that Language, which is his gift to

25. O. Mannoni, *Psychologie de la colonisation* [The Psychology of Colonialism] (Paris, 1950), 71; quoted by Frantz Fanon, in *Peau noire, masques blancs* [Black Skin, White Masks], 2d ed. (Paris [c. 1965]), 106.

Caliban, is the very prison in which Caliban's achievements will be realized and restricted.[26]

In the decade of the 1960s, the new reading of *The Tempest* ultimately established its hegemony. In *The Living World of Shakespeare* (1964), the Englishman John Wain will tell us that Caliban

has the pathos of the exploited peoples everywhere, poignantly expressed at the beginning of a three-hundred-year wave of European colonization; even the lowest savage wishes to be left alone rather than be "educated" and made to work for someone else, and there is an undeniable justice in his complaint: "For I am all the subjects that you have,/ Which once was mine own king." Prospero retorts with the inevitable answer of the colonist: Caliban has gained in knowledge and skill (though we recall that he already knew how to build dams to catch fish, and also to dig pig-nuts from the soil, as if this were the English countryside). Before being employed by Prospero, Caliban had no language: ". . . thou didst not, savage,/ Know thy own meaning, but wouldst gabble like/ A thing most brutish." However, this kindness has been rewarded with ingratitude. Caliban, allowed to live in Prospero's cell, has made an attempt to ravish Miranda. When sternly reminded of this, he impertinently says, with a kind of slavering guffaw. "Oh ho! Oh ho!—would it have been done!/ Thou didst prevent me: I had peopled else/ This isle with Calibans." Our own age [Wain concludes], which is much given to using the horrible word "miscegenation," ought to have no difficulty in understanding this passage.[27]

At the end of that same decade, in 1969, and in a highly significant manner, Caliban would be taken up with pride as our symbol by three

26. George Lamming, *The Pleasures of Exile* (London, 1960), 109. In commenting on these opinions of Lamming, the German Janheinz Jahn observes their limitations and proposes an identification of Caliban/negritude (see *Neo-African Literature,* trans. O. Coburn and U. Lehrburger [New York, 1968], 239–42).
27. John Wain, *The Living World of Shakespeare* (New York, 1964), 226–27.

Antillian writers—each of whom expresses himself in one of the three great colonial languages of the Caribbean. In that year, independently of one another, the Martinican writer Aimé Césaire published his dramatic work in French *Une tempête: Adaptation de "La Tempête" de Shakespeare pour un théâtre nègre;* the Barbadian Edward Brathwaite, his book of poems, *Islands,* in English, among which there is one dedicated to "Caliban"; and the author of these lines, an essay in Spanish, "Cuba hasta Fidel," which discusses our identification with Caliban.[28] In Césaire's work the characters are the same as those of Shakespeare. Ariel, however, is a mulatto slave, and Caliban is a black slave; in addition, Eshzú, a "black god-devil," appears. Prospero's remark when Ariel returns, full of scruples, after having unleashed—following Prospero's orders but against his own conscience—the tempest with which the work begins is curious indeed: "Come now!" Prospero says to him, "Your crisis! It's always the same with intellectuals!" Brathwaite's poem called "Caliban" is dedicated, significantly, to Cuba: "In Havana that morning..." writes Brathwaite, "It was December second, nineteen fifty-six./ It was the first of August eighteen thirty-eight./ It was the twelfth of October fourteen ninety-two./ How many bangs how many revolutions?"[29]

Our Symbol

Our symbol then is not Ariel, as Rodó thought, but rather Caliban. This is something that we, the *mestizo* inhabitants of these same islands where

28. See Aimé Césaire, *Une tempête: Adaptation de "La Tempête" de Shakespeare pour un théâtre nègre* [A Tempest: An Adaptation of Shakespeare's "The Tempest" for a Black Theater] (Paris, 1969); Edward Brathwaite, *Islands* (London, 1969); Roberto Fernández Retamar, "Cuba hasta Fidel" [Cuba until Fidel], *Bohemia,* 19 September 1969.
29. The new reading of *The Tempest* has become a common one throughout the colonial world of today. I want only, therefore, to mention a few examples. On concluding these notes, I find a new one in the essay by James Ngugi (of Kenya), "Africa y la descolonización cultural" [Africa and Cultural Decolonization], in *El correo* (January 1971).

Caliban lived, see with particular clarity: Prospero invaded the islands, killed our ancestors, enslaved Caliban, and taught him his language to make himself understood. What else can Caliban do but use that same language—today he has no other—to curse him, to wish that the "red plague" would fall on him? I know no other metaphor more expressive of our cultural situation, of our reality. From Túpac Amaru, *Tiradentes*, Toussaint-Louverture, Simón Bolívar, Father Hidalgo, José Artigas, Bernardo O'Higgins, Benito Juárez, Antonio Maceo, and José Martí, to Emiliano Zapata, Augusto César Sandino, Julio Antonio Mella, Pedro Albizu Campos, Lázaro Cárdenas, Fidel Castro and Ernesto Che Guevara, from the Inca Garcilaso de la Vega, the *Aleijadinho*, the popular music of the Antilles, José Hernández, Eugenio María de Hostos, Manuel González Prada, Rubén Darío (yes, when all is said and done), Baldomero Lillo, and Horacio Quiroga, to Mexican muralism, Heitor Villa-Lobos, César Vallejo, José Carlos Mariátegui, Ezequiel Martínez Estrada, Carlos Gardel, Pablo Neruda, Alejo Carpentier, Nicolás Guillén, Aimé Césaire, José María Arguedas, Violeta Parra, and Frantz Fanon—what is our history, what is our culture, if not the history and culture of Caliban?

As regards Rodó, if it is indeed true that he erred in his symbols, as has already been said, it is no less true that he was able to point with clarity to the greatest enemy of our culture in his time—and in ours—and that is enormously important. Rodó's limitations (and this is not the moment to elucidate them) are responsible for what he saw unclearly or failed to see at all.[30] But what is worthy of note in his case is what he did indeed see and what continued to retain a certain amount of validity and even virulence.

Despite his failings, omissions, and ingenuousness [Benedetti has also said], Rodó's vision of the Yankee phenomenon, rigorously situated in its historical context, was in its time the first launching pad for other less ingenuous, better informed and more fore-

30. "It is improper," Benedetti has said, "to confront Rodó with present-day structures, statement, and ideologies. His time was different from ours[;] . . . his true place, his true temporal homeland was the nineteenth century" (*Genio y figura de José Enrique Rodó*, 128).

sighted formulations to come. . . . the almost prophetic substance
of Rodó's Arielism still retains today a certain amount of validity.[31]

These observations are supported by indisputable realities. We
Cubans become well aware that Rodó's vision fostered later, less
ingenuous, and more radical formulations when we simply consider
the work of our own Julio Antonio Mella, on whose development the
influence of Rodó was decisive. In "Intelectuales y tartufos" [Intel-
lectuals and Tartuffes] (1924), a vehement work written at the age of
twenty-one, Mella violently attacks the false intellectual values of the
time—opposing them with such names as Unamuno, José Vasconcelos, Ingenieros, and Varona. He writes, "The intellectual is the
worker of the mind. The worker! That is, the only man who in Rodó's
judgment is worthy of life, . . . he who takes up his pen against iniquity
just as others take up the plow to fecundate the earth, or the sword to
liberate peoples, or a dagger to execute tyrants."[32]

Mella would again quote Rodó with devotion during that year[33]
and in the following year he was to help found the Ariel Polytechnic
Institute in Havana.[34] It is opportune to recall that in this same year,
1925, Mella was also among the founders of Cuba's first Communist
party. Without a doubt, Rodó's *Ariel* served as a "launching pad" for

31. *Ibid.*, 109. Even greater emphasis on the current validity of Rodó will be
    found in Arturo Ardao's book *Rodó: Su americanismo* [Rodó: His American-
    ism] (Montevideo, 1970), which includes an excellent anthology of the
    author of *Ariel*. On the other hand, as early as 1928, José Carlos Mariátegui,
    after rightly recalling that "only a socialist Latin or Ibero-America can
    effectively oppose a capitalist, plutocratic, and imperialist North America,"
    adds, "The myth of Rodó has not yet acted—nor has it ever acted—usefully
    and fruitfully upon our souls" ("Aniversario y balance" [An Anniversary and
    a Summing Up] [1928], in *Ideología y política* [Ideology and Politics] [Lima,
    1969], 248).
32. *Hombres de la revolución: Julio Antonio Mella* [Men of the Revolution: Julio
    Antonio Mella] (Havana, 1971), 12.
33. *Ibid.*, 15.
34. See Erasmo Dumpierre, *Mella* (Havana, c. 1965), 145; see also José Antonio
    Portuondo, "Mella y los intelectuales" [Mella and the Intellectuals] [1963],
    which is reproduced in *Casa de las Américas*, no. 68 (1971).

the meteoric revolutionary career of this first organic Marxist-Leninist in Cuba (who was also one of the first on the continent.)

As further examples of the relative validity that Rodó's anti-Yankee argument retains even in our own day, we can point to enemy attempts to disarm such an argument. A strange case is that of Emir Rodríguez Monegal, for whom *Ariel*, in addition to "material for philosophic or sociological meditation, *also* contains pages of a polemic nature on political problems *of the moment*. And it was precisely this *secondary* but undeniable condition that determined its immediate popularity and dissemination." Rodó's essential position against North American penetration would thus appear to be an afterthought, a *secondary* fact in the work. It is known, however, that Rodó conceived it immediately after American intervention in Cuba in 1898, *as a response to the deed*. Rodríguez Monegal says:

> The work thus projected was *Ariel*. In the final version *only two direct allusions* are found to the historical fact that was its primary motive force; ... both allusions enable us to appreciate how Rodó has *transcended* the initial historical circumstance to arrive fully at the essential problem: the proclaimed decadence of the Latin race.[35]

The fact that a servant of imperialism such as Rodríguez Monegal, afflicted with the same "Nordo-mania" that Rodó denounced in 1900, tries so coarsely to emasculate Rodó's work, only proves that it does indeed retain a certain virulence in its formulation—something that we would approach today from other perspectives and with other means. An analysis of *Ariel*—and this is absolutely not the occasion to make one—would lead us also to stress how, despite his background and his anti-Jacobianism, Rodó combats in it the antidemocratic spirit of Renan and Nietzsche (in whom he finds "an abominable, reactionary spirit" [224]) and exalts democracy, moral values, and emulation. But undoubtedly the rest of the work has lost the immediacy that its gallant confrontation of the United States and the defense of our values still retains.

35. Emir Rodríguez Monegal, ed., *Rodó* (Madrid, 1957), 193–93; my emphasis.

Put into perspective, it is almost certain that these lines would not bear the name they have were it not for Rodó's book, and I prefer to consider them also as a homage to the great Uruguayan, whose centenary is being celebrated this year. That the homage contradicts him on not a few points is not strange. Medardo Vitier has already observed that "if there should be a return to Rodó, I do not believe that it would be to adopt the solution he offered concerning the interests of the life of the spirit, but rather to reconsider the problem."[36]

In proposing Caliban as our symbol, I am aware that it is not entirely ours, that it is also an alien elaboration, although in this case based on our concrete realities. But how can this alien quality be entirely avoided? The most venerated word in Cuba—*mambí*—was disparagingly imposed on us by our enemies at the time of the war for independence, and we still have not totally deciphered its meaning. It seems to have an African root, and in the mouth of the Spanish colonists implied the idea that all *independentistas* were so many black slaves—emancipated by that very war for independence—who of course constituted the bulk of the liberation army. The *independentistas*, white and black, adopted with honor something that colonialism meant as an insult. This is the dialectic of Caliban. To offend us they call us *mambí*, they call us *black;* but we reclaim as a mark of glory the honor of considering ourselves descendants of the *mambí*, descendants of the rebel, runaway, *independentista* black— *never* descendants of the slave holder. Nevertheless, Prospero, as we well know, taught his language to Caliban and, consequently, gave him a name. But is this his true name? Let us listen to this speech made in 1971:

> To be completely precise, we still do not even have a name; we still have no name; we are practically unbaptized—whether as Latin Americans, Ibero-Americans, Indo-Americans. For the imperialists, we are nothing more than despised and despicable peoples. At least that was what we were. Since Girón they have begun to change their thinking. Racial contempt—to be a Creole,

36. Medardo Vitier, *Del ensayo americano* [On the Latin American Essay] (Mexico City, 1945), 117.

to be a mestizo, to be black, to be simply, a Latin American, is for them contemptible.[37]

This naturally, is Fidel Castro on the tenth anniversary of the victory at Playa Girón.

To assume our condition as Caliban implies rethinking our history from the *other* side, from the viewpoint of the *other* protagonist. The *other* protagonist of *The Tempest* (or, as we might have said ourselves, *The Hurricane*) is not of course Ariel but, rather, Prospero.[38] There is no real Ariel-Caliban polarity: both are slaves in the hands of Prospero, the foreign magician. But Caliban is the rude and unconquerable master of the island, while Ariel, a creature of the air, although also a child of the isle, is the intellectual—as both Ponce and Césaire have seen.

Again Martí

This conception of our culture had already been articulately expressed and defended in the last century by the first among us to understand clearly the concrete situation of what he called—using a term I have referred to several times—"our mestizo America:" José Martí[39] to whom Rodó planned to dedicate the first Cuban edition of *Ariel* and about whom he intended to write a study similar to those he

---

37. Fidel Castro, speech, 19 April, 1971.
38. See Kott, *Shakespeare, Our Contemporary*, 269.
39. See Ezequiel Martínez Estrada, "Por una alta cultura popular y socialista cubana" [Toward a Cuban Popular and Socialist High Culture] [1962], in *En Cuba y al servicio de la Revolución cubana* [In Cuba and at the Service of the Cuban Revolution] (Havana, 1963); "Martí en su (tercer) mundo" [Martí in his (Third) World] [1964], in *Ensayo de otro mundo, Cuba Socialista* 41 (January 1965); Noël Salomon, "José Martí et la prise de conscience latinoaméricaine" [José Martí and Latin America's Coming to Consciousness], *Cuba Sí* 35–36 (4th trimester 1970–1st trimester 1971); and Leonardo Acosta, "La concepción histórica de Martí," [Martí's Idea of History], *Casa de las Américas* 67 (July–August 1971).

devoted to Bolívar and Artigas, a study that in the end he unfortunately never realized.

Although he devoted numerous pages to the topic, the occasion on which Martí offered his ideas on this point in a most organic and concise manner was in his 1891 article "Our America." I will limit myself to certain essential quotations. But I should first like to offer some observations on the destiny of Martí's work.

During Martí's lifetime, the bulk of his work, scattered throughout a score of continental newspapers, enjoyed widespread fame. We know that Rubén Darío called Martí "Maestro" (as, for other reasons, his political followers would also call him during his lifetime) and considered him the Latin American whom he most admired. We shall soon see, on the other hand, how the harsh judgments on the United States that Martí commonly made in his articles, equally well known in his time, were the cause of acerbic criticism by the pro-Yankee Sarmiento. But the particular manner in which Martí's writings circulated—he made use of journalism, oratory, and letter but *never published a single book*—bears considerable responsibility for the relative oblivion into which the work of the Cuban hero fell after his death in 1895. This alone explains the fact that nine years after his death—and twelve from the time Martí stopped writing for the continental press, devoted as he was after 1892 to his political tasks—an author as absolutely ours and as far above suspicion as the twenty-year-old Pedro Henríquez Ureña could write in 1904, in an article on Rodó's *Ariel*, that the latter's opinions on the United States are "much more severe than those formulated by two of the greatest thinkers and most brilliant psycho-sociologists of the Antilles: Hostos and Martí."[40] Insofar as this refers to Martí, the observation is completely erroneous; and given the exemplary honesty of Henríquez Ureña, it led me, first, to suspect and later, to verify that it was due simply to the fact that during this period the great Dominican had not read, *had been unable to read*, Martí adequately. Martí was hardly *published* at the time. A text such as the fundamental "Our America" is a good example of this fate. Readers of the Mexican newspaper *El Partido Liberal* could have read it on 30 January 1891. It is possible that

40. Pedro Henríquez Ureña, *Obra crítica* [Critical Work] (Mexico City, 1960), 27.

some other local newspaper republished it,[41] although the most recent edition of Martí's *Complete Works* does not indicate anything in this regard. But it is most likely that those who did not have the good fortune to obtain that newspaper knew nothing about the article—the most important document published in America from the end of the past century until the appearance in 1962 of the Second Declaration of Havana—for almost twenty years, at the end of which time it appeared in book form (Havana, 1910) in the irregular collection in which publication of the complete works of Martí was begun. For this reason Manuel Pedro González is correct when he asserts that during the first quarter of this century the new generations did not know Martí. "A minimal portion of his work" was again put into circulation, starting with the eight volumes published by Alberto Ghiraldo in Madrid in 1925. Thanks to the most recent appearance of several editions of his complete works—actually still incomplete—"he has been rediscovered and reevaluated."[42] González is thinking above all of the dazzling literary qualities of this work ("the literary glory" as he says). Could we not add something, then, regarding the works' fundamental ideological aspects? Without forgetting very important prior contributions, there are still some essential points that explain why today, after the triumph of the Cuban Revolution and because of it, Martí is being "rediscovered and reevaluated." It was no mere coincidence that in 1953 Fidel named Martí as the intellectual author of the attack on the Moncada Barracks nor that Che should use a quotation from Martí—"it is the hour of the furnace, and only light should be seen"—to open his extremely important "Message to the Tricontinental Congress" in 1967. If Benedetti could say that Rodó's time "was different from our own . . . his true place, his true temporal homeland was the nineteenth century," we must say, on the other hand, that Martí's true place was the future and,

41. Ivan Schulman (*Martí, Casal y el modernismo* [Martí, Casal, and Modernism] [Havana, 1969] 92) has discovered that it had been *previously* published on 10 January 1891, in *La Revista Ilustrada de Nueva York*.

42. Manuel Pedro González, "Evolución de la estimativa martiana" [The Evolution of Martí's Critical Tools], in *Antología crítica de José Martí* [Critical Anthology of José Martí], comp. and ed. Manuel Pedro González (Mexico City, 1960), xxix.

for the moment, this era of ours, which simply cannot be understood without a thorough knowledge of this work.

Now, if that knowledge, because of the curious circumstances alluded to, was denied or available only in a limited way to the early generations of this century, who frequently had to base their defense of subsequent radical arguments on a "first launching pad" as well-intentioned but at the same time as weak as the nineteenth-century work *Ariel*, what can we say of more recent authors to whom editions of Martí are now available but who nevertheless persist in ignoring him? I am thinking, of course, not of scholars more or less ignorant of our problems but, on the contrary, of those who maintain a consistently anticolonialist attitude. The only explanation of this situation is a painful one: we have been so thoroughly steeped in colonialism that we read with real respect only those anticolonialist authors *disseminated from the metropolis*. In this way we cast aside the greatest lesson of Martí; thus, we are barely familiar with Artigas, Recabarren, Mella, and even Mariátegui and Ponce. And I have the sad suspicion that if the extraordinary texts of Che Guevara have enjoyed the greatest dissemination ever accorded a Latin American, the fact that he is read with such avidity by our people is to a certain extent due to the prestige his name has even in the metropolitan capitals—where, to be sure, he is frequently the object of the most shameless manipulation. For consistency in our anticolonialist attitude we must in effect turn to those of our people who have incarnated and illustrated that attitude in their behavior and thinking.[43] And for this, there is no case more useful than that of Martí.

I know of no other Latin-American author who has given so immediate and so coherent an answer to another question put to me by my interlocutor, the European journalist whom I mentioned at the beginning of these lines (and whom, if he did not exist, I would have

43. Nonetheless, this should not be understood to mean that I am suggesting that those authors who have not been born in the colonies should not be read. Such a stupidity is untenable. How could we propose to ignore Homer, Dante, Cervantes, Shakespeare, Whitman, to say nothing of Marx, Engels, or Lenin? How can we forget that even in our own day there are *Latin American* thinkers who have not been born here? Lastly, how can we defend intellectual Robinson Crusoism at all without falling into the greatest absurdity?

had to invent, although this would have deprived me of his friendship, which I trust will survive this monologue): "What relationship," this guileless wit asked me, "does Borges have to the Incas?" Borges is almost a reductio ad absurdum and, in any event, I shall discuss him later. But it is only right and fair to ask what relationship we, the present inhabitants of this America in whose zoological and cultural heritage Europe has played an unquestionable part, have to the primitive inhabitants of this same America—those peoples who constructed or were martyred by Europeans of various nations, about whom neither a white nor black legend can be built, only an infernal truth of blood, that, together with such deeds as the enslavement of Africans, constitutes their eternal dishonor. Martí, whose father was from Valencia and whose mother was from the Canaries, who wrote the most prodigious Spanish of his—and our—age, and who came to have the greatest knowledge of the Euro–North American culture ever possessed by a man of our America, also asked this question. He answered it as follows: "We are descended from Valencian fathers and Canary Island mothers and feel the inflamed blood of Tamanaco and Paramaconi coursing through our veins; we see the blood that fell amid the brambles of Mount Calvary as our own, along with that shed by the naked and heroic Caracas as they struggled breast to breast with the gonzalos in their iron-plated armor."[44]

I presume that the reader, if he or she is not a Venezuelan, will be unfamiliar with the names evoked by Martí. So was I. This lack of familiarity is but another proof of our subjection to the colonialist perspective of history that has been imposed on us, causing names, dates, circumstances, and truths to vanish from our consciousness. Under other circumstances—but closely related to these—did not the bourgeois version of history try to erase the heroes of the Commune of 1871, the martyrs of 1 May 1886 (significantly reclaimed by Martí)? At any rate, Tamanaco, Paramaconi, "the naked and heroic Caracas" were natives of what is today called Venezuela, of *Carib blood, the blood of Caliban*, coursing through their veins. This will not be the only time

---

44. José Martí, "Autores aborígenes americanos" [1884], in *Obras completas*, 8:336–37; hereafter cited as "AAA" in the text.

he expresses such an idea, which is central to his thinking.[45] Again making use of such heroes, he was to repeat sometime later: "We must stand with Guaicaipuro, Paramaconi [heroes of Venezuela, probably of Carib origin], and not with the flames that burned them, nor with the ropes that bound them, nor with the steel that beheaded them, nor with the dogs that devoured them."[46] Martí's rejection of the ethnocide that Europe practiced is *total*. No less total is his identification with the American peoples that offered heroic resistance to the invader, and in whom Martí saw the natural forerunners of the Latin American *independentistas*. This explains why in the notebook in which this last quotation appears, he continues writing, almost without transition, on Aztec mythology ("no less beautiful than the Greek"), on the ashes of Quetzacoatl, on "Ayachucho on the solitary plateau," on "Bolívar, like the rivers."[47]

Martí, however, dreams not of a restoration now impossible but of the future integration of our America—an America rising organically from a firm grasp of its true roots to the heights of authentic modernity. For this reason, the first quotation in which he speaks of feeling valiant Carib blood coursing through his veins continues as follows:

> It is good to open canals, to promote schools, to create steamship lines, to keep abreast of one's own time, to be on the side of the vanguard in the beautiful march of humanity. But in order not to falter because of a lack of spirit or the vanity of a false spirit, it is good also to nourish oneself through memory and admiration, through righteous study and loving compassion, on that fervent spirit of the natural surroundings in which one is born—a spirit matured and quickened by those of every race that issues from such surroundings and finds its final repose in them. Politics and literature flourish only when they are direct. The American intelligence is an indigenous plumage. Is it not evident that America itself was paralyzed by the same blow that paralyzed the Indian?

45. For instance, to Tamanaco he dedicated a beautiful poem, "Tamanaco of the Plumed Crown," in *Obras completas*, 22:237.
46. José Martí, "Fragmentos" [Fragments] [1885–95], in *Obras completas*, 22:27.
47. *Ibid.*, 28–29.

And until the Indian is caused to walk, America itself will not begin to walk well. ["AAA," 337]

Martí's identification with our aboriginal culture was thus accompanied by a complete sense of the concrete tasks imposed upon him by his circumstances. Far from hampering him, that identification nurtured in him the most radical and modern criteria of his time in the colonial countries.

Naturally, Martí's approach to the Indian was also applied to the black.[48] Unfortunately, while in his day serious inquiries into American aboriginal cultures (which Martí studied passionately) had already been undertaken, only in the twentieth century would there appear similar studies of African cultures and their considerable contribution to the makeup of our mestizo America (see Frobenius, Delafosse, Suret-Canale, Ortiz, Ramos, Herskovits, Roumain, Metraux, Bastide, Franco).[49]

---

48. See, for example, José Martí, "Mi raza [My Race] in *Obras completas*, 2:298–300, where we read:

> An individual has no special right because he belongs to one race or another: to speak of a human being is to speak of all rights. . . . If one says that in the black there is no aboriginal fault or virus that incapacitates him from leading his human life to the full, one is speaking the truth . . . , and if this defense of nature is called racism, the name does not matter; for it is nothing if not natural decency and the voice crying from the breast of the human being for the peace and life of the country. If it be alleged that the condition of slavery does not suggest any inferiority of the enslaved race, since white Gauls with blue eyes and golden hair were sold as slaves with iron rings around their necks in the markets of Rome, that is good racism because it is pure justice and helps to remove the prejudices of the ignorant white man. But there righteous racism ends.

And, further on, "A human being is more than white, more than mulatto, more than black. Cuban is more than white, more than mulatto, more than black." Some of these questions are treated in Juliette Oullion's paper, "La discriminación racial en los Estados Unidos vista por José Martí," [Racial Discrimination in the United States as seen by José Martí], *Anuario martiano* (Havana, 1971), which I was unable to use, since it appeared after these notes were completed.

49. See *Casa de las Américas* 36–37 (May–August 1966), a special issue entitled *África en América* [Africa in Latin America].

And Martí died five years before the dawning of our century. In any event, in his treatment of Indian culture and in his concrete behavior toward the black, he left a very clear outline of a "battle plan" in this area.

This is the way in which Martí forms his Calibanesque vision of the culture of what he called "our America." Martí is, as Fidel was later to be, aware of how difficult it is even to find a name that in designating us defines us conceptually. For this reason, after several attempts, he favored that modest descriptive formula that above and beyond race, language, and secondary circumstances embraces the communities that live, with their common problems, "from the [Rio] Bravo to Patagonia," and that are distinct from "European America." I have already said that, although it is found scattered throughout his very numerous writings, this conception of our culture is aptly summarized in the article-manifesto "Our America," and I direct the reader to it: to his insistence upon the idea that one cannot "rule new peoples with a singular and violent composition, with laws inherited from four centuries of free practice in the United States, or nineteen centuries of monarchy in France. One does not stop the blow in the chest of the plainsman's horse with one of Hamilton's decrees. One does not clear the congealed blood of the Indian race with a sentence of Sieyès"; to his deeply rooted concept that "the imported book has been conquered in America by the natural man. Natural men have conquered the artificial men of learning. *The authentic mestizo has conquered the exotic Creole*" (my emphasis); and finally to his fundamental advice:

> The European university must yield to the American university. The history of America, from the Incas to the present, must be taught letter perfect, even if that of the Argonauts of Greece is not taught. Our own Greece is preferable to that Greece that is not ours. We have greater need of it. National politicians must replace foreign and exotic politicians. Graft the world onto our republics, but the trunk must be that of our republics. And let the conquered pedant be silent: there is no homeland of which the individual can be more proud than our unhappy American republics.

"If I Could Write This in Fire, I Would Write This in Fire"

MICHELLE CLIFF
(JAMAICA)

I

We were standing under the waterfall at the top of Orange River. Our chests were just beginning to mound—slight hills on either side. In the center of each were our nipples, which were losing their sideways look and rounding into perceptible buttons of dark flesh. Too fast it seemed. We touched each other, then, quickly and almost simultaneously, raised our arms to examine the hairs growing underneath. Another sign. Mine was wispy and light brown. My friend Zoe had dark hair curled up tight. In each little patch the riverwater caught the sun so we glistened.

The waterfall had come about when my uncles dammed up the river to bring power to the sugar mill. Usually, when I say "sugar mill" to anyone not familiar with the Jamaican countryside or for that matter my family, I can tell their minds cast an image of tall smokestacks, enormous copper cauldrons, a man in a broad-brimmed hat with a whip, and several dozens of slaves—that is, if they have any idea of how large sugar mills once operated. It's a grandiose expression—like plantation, verandah, out-building. (Try substituting farm, porch, outside toilet.) To some people it even sounds romantic.

Our sugar mill was little more that a round-roofed shed, which contained a wheel and woodfire. We paid an old man to run it, tend the fire, and then either bartered or gave the sugar away, after my grandmother had taken what she needed. Our canefield was about two acres of flat land next to the river. My grandmother had six acres in all—one donkey, a mule, two cows, some chickens, a few pigs, and stray dogs and cats who had taken up residence in the yard.

Her house had four rooms, no electricity, no running water. The kitchen was a shed in the back with a small pot-bellied stove. Across from the stove was a mahogany counter, which had a white enamel basin set into it. The only light source was a window, a small space covered partly by a wooden shutter. We washed our faces and hands in enamel bowls with cold water carried in kerosene tins from the river and poured from enamel pitchers. Our chamber pots were enamel also, and in the morning we carefully placed them on the steps at the side of the house where my grandmother collected them and disposed of their contents. The outhouse was about thirty yards from the back door—a "closet" as we called it—infested with lizards capable of changing color. When the door was shut it was totally dark, and the lizards made their presence known by the noise of their scurrying through the torn newspaper, or the soft shudder when they dropped from the walls. I remember most clearly the stench of the toilet, which seemed to hang in the air in that climate.

But because every little piece of reality exists in relation to another little piece, our situation was not that simple. It was to our yard that people came with news first. It was in my grandmother's parlor that the Disciples of Christ held their meetings.

Zoe lived with her mother and sister on borrowed ground in a place called Breezy Hill. She and I saw each other almost every day on our school vacations over a period of three years. Each morning early—as I sat on the cement porch with my coffee cut with condensed milk—she appeared: in her straw hat, school tunic faded from blue to gray, white blouse, sneakers hanging around her neck. We had coffee together, and a piece of hard-dough bread with butter and cheese, waited a bit and headed for the river. At first we were shy with each other. We did not start from the same place.

There was land. My grandparents' farm. And there was color.

(My family was called *red*. A term which signified a degree of whiteness. "We's just a flock of red people," a cousin of mine said once.) In the hierarchy of shades I was considered among the lightest. The countrywomen who visited my grandmother commented on my "tall" hair—meaning long. Wavy, not curly.

I had spent the years from three to ten in New York and spoke—at first—like an American. I wore American clothes: shorts, slacks, bathing suit. Because of my American past I was looked upon as the creator of games. Cowboys and Indians. Cops and Robbers. Peter Pan.

(While the primary colonial identification for Jamaicans was English, American colonialism was a strong force in my childhood—and of course continues today. We were sent American movies and American music. American aluminum companies had already discovered bauxite on the island and were shipping the ore to their mainland. United Fruit bought our bananas. White Americans came to Montego Bay, Ocho Rios, and Kingston for their vacations and their cruise ships docked in Port Antonio and other places. In some ways America was seen as a better place than England by many Jamaicans. The farm laborers sent to work in American agribusiness came home with dollars and gifts and new clothes; there were few who mentioned American racism. Many of the middle class who emigrated to Brooklyn or Staten Island or Manhattan were able to pass into the white American world—saving their blackness for other Jamaicans or for trips home; in some cases, forgetting it altogether. Those middle-class Jamaicans who could not pass for white managed differently—not unlike the Bajans in Paule Marshall's *Brown Girl, Brownstones*—saving, working, investing, buying property. Completely separate in most cases from Black Americans.)

I was someone who had experience with the place that sent us triple features of B-grade westerns and gangster movies. And I had tall hair and light skin. And I was the granddaughter of my grandmother. So I had power. I was the cowboy, Zoe was my sidekick, the boys we knew were Indians. I was the detective, Zoe was my "girl," the boys were the robbers. I was Peter Pan, Zoe was Wendy Darling, the boys were the lost boys. And the terrain around the river—jungled and dark green—was Tombstone, or Chicago, or Never-Never Land.

This place and my friendship with Zoe never touched my life in Kingston. We did not correspond with each other when I left my grandmother's home.

I never visited Zoe's home the entire time I knew her. It was a given: never suggested, never raised.

Zoe went to a state school held in a country church in Red Hills. It had been my mother's school. I went to a private all-girls school where I was taught by white Englishwomen and pale Jamaicans. In her school the students were caned as punishment. In mine the harshest punishment I remember was being sent to sit under the *lignum vitae* to "commune with nature." Some of the girls were out-and-out white (English and American), the rest of us were colored—only a few were dark. Our uniforms were blood-red gabardine, heavy and hot. Classes were held in buildings meant to recreate England: damp with stone floors, facing onto a cloister, or quad as they called it. We began each day with the headmistress leading us in English hymns. The entire school stood for an hour in the zinc-roofed gymnasium.

Occasionally a girl fainted, or threw up. Once, a girl had a grand mal seizure. To any such disturbance the response was always "keep singing." While she flailed on the stone floor, I wondered what the mistresses would do. We sang "Faith of Our Fathers," and watched our classmate as her eyes rolled back in her head. I thought of people swallowing their tongues. This student was dark—here on a scholarship—and the only woman who came forward to help her was the gamesmistress, the only dark teacher. She kneeled beside the girl and slid the white web belt from her tennis shorts, clamping it between the girl's teeth. When the seizure was over, she carried the girl to a tumbling mat in a corner of the gym and covered her so she wouldn't get chilled.

Were the other women unable to touch this girl because of her darkness? I think that now. Her darkness and her scholarship. She lived on Windward Road with her grandmother; her mother was a maid. But darkness is usually enough for women like those to hold back. Then, we usually excused that kind of behavior by saying they were "ladies." (We were constantly being told we should be ladies also. One teacher went so far as to tell us many people thought Jamaicans lived in trees and we had to show these people they were mistaken.) In short, we felt insufficient to judge the behavior of these women. The English ones (who had the corner on power in the school) had come all this way to teach us. Shouldn't we treat them as the missionaries they were certain they were? The creole Jamaicans had a different role: they were passing on to those of us who were light-skinned the creole heritage of collaboration, assimilation, loyalty to our betters. We were expected to be willing subjects in this outpost of civilization.

The girl left school that day and never returned.

After prayers we filed into our classrooms. After classes we had games: tennis, field hockey, rounders (what the English call baseball), netball (what the English call basketball). For games we were divided into "houses"—groups named for Joan of Arc, Edith Cavell, Florence Nightingale, Jane Austen. Four white heroines. Two martyrs. One saint. Two nurses. (None of us knew then that there were Black women with Nightingale at Scutari.) One novelist. Three involved in whitemen's wars. Two dead in whitemen's wars. *Pride and Prejudice.*

Those of us in Cavell wore red badges and recited her last words before a firing squad in World War I: "Patriotism is not enough. I must have no hatred or bitterness toward anyone."

Sorry to say I grew up to have exactly that.

Looking back: To try and see when the background changed places with the foreground. To try and locate the vanishing point: where the lines of perspective converge and disappear. Lines of color and class. Line of history and social context. Lines of denial and rejection. When did *we* (the light-skinned middle-class Jamaicans) take over for *them* as oppressors? I need to see when and how this happened. When what should have been reality was overtaken by what was surely unreality. When the house nigger became master.

"What's the matter with you? You think you're white or something?"

"Child, what you want to know 'bout Garvey for? The man was nothing but a damn fool."

"They not our kind of people."

Why did we wear wide-brimmed hats and try to get into Oxford? Why did we not return?

Great Expectations: a novel about origins and denial. about the futility and tragedy of that denial. about attempting assimilation. We learned this novel from a light-skinned Jamaican woman—she concentrated on what she called the "love affair" between Pip and Estella.

Looking back: Through the last page of *Sula.* "And the loss pressed down on her chest and came up into her throat. 'We was girls together,' she said as though explaining something." It was Zoe, and Zoe alone, I thought of. She snapped into my mind and I remembered no one else. Through the greens and blues of the riverbank. The flame of red hibiscus in front of my grandmother's house. The cracked grave of a former landowner. The fruit of the ackee which poisons those who don't know how to prepare it.

"What is to become of us?"

We borrowed a baby from a woman and used her as our dolly. Dressed and undressed her. Dipped her in the riverwater. Fed her with the milk her mother had left with us: and giggled because we knew where the milk had come from.

A letter: "I am desperate. I need to get away. I beg you one fifty-dollar."

I send the money because this is what she asks for. I visit her on a trip back home. Her front teeth are gone. Her husband beats her and she suffers blackouts. I sit on her chair. She is given birth control pills which aggravate her "condition." We boil up sorrel and ginger. She is being taught by Peace Corps volunteers to embroider linen mats with little lambs on them and gives me one as a keepsake. We cool off the sorrel with a block of ice brought from the shop nearby. The shopkeeper immediately recognizes me as my grandmother's granddaughter and refuses to sell me cigarettes. (I am twenty-seven.) We sit in the doorway of her house, pushing back the colored plastic strands which form a curtain, and talk about Babylon and Dred. About Manley and what he's doing for Jamaica. About how hard it is. We walk along the railway tracks—no longer used—to Crooked River and the post office. Her little daughter walks beside us and we recite a poem for her: "Mornin' buddy/Me no buddy fe wunna/Who den, den I saw?" and on and on.

I can come and go. And I leave. To complete my education in London.

II

Their goddam kings and their goddam queens. Grandmotherly Victoria spreading herself thin across the globe. Elizabeth II on our tv screens. We stop what we are doing. We quiet down. We pay our respects.

1981: In Massachusetts I get up at 5 a.m. to watch the royal wedding. I tell myself maybe the IRA will intervene. It's got to be better than starving themselves to death. Better to be a kamikaze in St. Paul's Cathedral than a hostage in Ulster. And last week Black and white people smashed storefronts all over the United Kingdom. But I really don't believe we'll see royal blood on tv I watch because they once ruled us. In the back of the cathedral a Maori woman sings an aria from Handel, and I notice that she is surrounded by the colored subjects.

To those of us in the commonwealth the royal family was the perfect symbol of hegemony. To those of us who were dark in the dark nations, the prime minister, the parliament barely existed. We believed in royalty—we were convinced in this belief. Maybe it played on some ancestral memories of West Africa—where other kings and queens had been. Altars and castles and magic.

The faces of our new rulers were everywhere in my childhood. Calendars, newsreels, magazines. Their presences were often among us. Attending test matches between the West Indians and South Africans. They were our landlords. Not always absentee. And no matter what Black leader we might elect—were we to choose

361

independence—we would be losing something almost holy in our impudence.

> WE ARE HERE BECAUSE YOU WERE THERE
> BLACK PEOPLE AGAINST STATE BRUTALITY
> BLACK WOMEN WILL NOT BE INTIMIDATED
> WELCOME TO BRITAIN . . . WELCOME TO SECOND-
> CLASS CITIZENSHIP
> (slogans of the Black movement in Britain)

Indian women cleaning the toilets in Heathrow airport. This is the first thing I notice. Dark women in saris trudging buckets back and forth as other dark women in saris—some covered by loosefitting winter coats—form a line to have their passports stamped.

The triangle trade: molasses/rum/slaves. Robinson Crusoe was on a slave-trading journey. Robert Browning was a mulatto. Holding pens. Jamaica was a seasoning station. Split tongues. Sliced ears. Whipped bodies. The constant pretense of civility against rape. Still. Iron collars. Tinplate masks. The latter a precaution: to stop the slaves from eating the sugar cane.

A pregnant woman is to be whipped—they dig a hole to accommodate her belly and place her face down on the ground. Many of us became light-skinned very fast. Traced ourselves through bastard lines to reach the duke of Devonshire. The earl of Cornwall. The lord of this and the lord of that. Our mothers' rapes were the thing unspoken.

You say: But Britain freed her slaves in 1833. Yes.

Tea plantations in India and Ceylon. Mines in Africa. The Cape-to-Cairo Railroad. Rhodes scholars. Suez Crisis. The whiteman's bloody burden. Boer War. Bantustans. Sitting in a theater in London in the seventies. A play called *West of Suez*. A lousy play about British colonials. The finale comes when several well-known white actors are machine-gunned by several lesser-known Black actors. (As Nina Simone says: "This is a show tune but the show hasn't been written for it yet.")

The red empire of geography classes. "The sun never sets on the British empire and you can't trust it in the dark." Or with the dark peoples. "Because of the Industrial Revolution European countries went in search of markets and raw materials." Another geography (or was it a history) lesson.

Their bloody kings and their bloody queens. Their bloody peers. Their bloody generals. Admirals. Explorers. Livingstone. Hillary. Kitchener. All the bwanas. And all their beaters, porters, sherpas. Who found the source of the Nile. Victoria Falls. The tops of mountains. Their so-called discoveries reek of untruth. How many dark people died so they could misname the physical features in their blasted gazetteer. A statistic we shall never know. Dr. Livingstone, I presume you are here to rape our land and enslave our people.

There are statues of these dead white men all over London.

An interesting fact: The swearword "bloody" is a contraction of "by my lady"—a reference to the Virgin Mary. They do tend to use their ladies. Name ages for them. Places for them. Use them as screens, inspirations, symbols. And many of the ladies comply. While the national martyr Edith Cavell was being executed by the Germans in 1915 in Belgium (called "poor little Belgium" by the Allies in the war), the Belgians were engaged in the exploitation of the land and peoples of the Congo.

And will we ever know how many dark peoples were "imported" to fight in whitemen's wars? Probably not. Just as we will never know how many hearts were cut from African people so that the Christian doctor might be a success—i.e., extend a whiteman's life. Our Sister Killjoy observes this from her black-eyed squint.

Dr. Schweitzer—humanitarian, authority on Bach, winner of the Nobel Peace Prize—on the people of Africa: "The Negro is a child, and with children nothing can be done without the use of authority. We must, therefore, so arrange the circumstances of our daily life that my authority can find expression. With regard to Negroes, then, I have coined the formula: 'I am your brother, it is true, but your elder brother.'" (*On the Edge of the Primeval Forest*, 1961)

They like to pretend we didn't fight back. We did: with obeah, poison, revolution. It simply was not enough.

"Colonies . . . these places where 'niggers' are cheap and the earth is rich." (W.E.B. DuBois, "The Souls of White Folk")

A cousin is visiting me from Cal Tech where he is getting a degree in engineering. I am learning about the Italian Renaissance. My cousin is recognizably Black and speaks with an accent. I am not and I do not—unless I am back home, where the "twang" comes upon me. We sit for some time in a bar in his hotel and are not served. A light-skinned Jamaican comes over to our table. He is an older man—a professor at the University of London. "Don't bother with it, you hear. They don't serve us in this bar." A run-of-the-mill incident for all recognizably Black people in this city. But for me it is not.

Henry's eyes fill up, but he refuses to believe our informant. "No, man, the girl is just busy." (The girl is a fifty-year-old white woman, who may just be following orders. But I do not mention this. I have chosen sides.) All I can manage to say is, "Jesus Christ, I hate the fucking English." Henry looks at me. (In the family I am known as the "lady cousin." It has to do with how I look. And the fact that I am twenty-seven and unmarried—and for all they know, unattached. They do not know that I am really the lesbian cousin.) Our informant says—gently, but with a distinct tone of disappointment—"My dear, is that what you're studying at the university?"

You see—the whole business is very complicated.

Henry and I leave without drinks and go to meet some of his white colleagues at a restaurant I know near Covent Garden Opera House. The restaurant caters to theater types and so I hope there won't be a repeat of the bar scene—at least they know how to pretend. Besides, I tell myself, the owners are Italian *and* gay; they *must* be halfway decent. Henry and his colleagues work for an American company which is paying their way through Cal Tech. They mine bauxite from the hills in the middle of the island and send it to the United States. A turnaround occurs at dinner: Henry joins the whitemen in a sustained mockery of the waiters: their accents and the way they walk. He whispers to me: "Why you want to bring us to a battyman's den, lady?" (*Battyman* = *faggot* in Jamaican.) I keep quiet.

We put the whitemen in a taxi and Henry walks me to the underground station. He asks me to sleep with him. (It wouldn't be incest. His mother was a maid in the house of an uncle and Henry has not seen her since his birth. He was taken into the family. She was let go.) I say that I can't. I plead exams. I can't say that I don't want to. Because I remember what happened in the bar. But I can't say that I'm a lesbian either—even though I want to believe his alliance with the whitemen at dinner was forced: not really him. He doesn't buy my excuse. "Come on, lady, let's do it. What's the matter, you 'fraid?" I pretend I am back home and start patois to show him somehow I am not afraid, not English, not white. I tell him he's a married man and he tells me he's a ram goat. I take the train to where I am staying and try to forget the whole thing. But I don't. I remember our different skins and our different experiences within them. And I have a hard time realizing that I am angry with Henry. That to him—no use in pretending—a queer is a queer.

1981. I hear on the radio that Bob Marley is dead and I drive over the Mohawk Trail listening to a program of his music and I cry and cry and cry. Someone says: "It wasn't the ganja that killed him, it was poverty and working in a steel foundry when he was young."

I flash back to my childhood and a young man who worked for an aunt I lived with once. He taught me to smoke ganja behind the house. And to peel an orange with the tip of a machete without cutting through the skin—"Love" it was called: a necklace of orange rind the result. I think about him because I heard he had become a Rastaman. And then I think about Rastas.

We are sitting on the porch of an uncle's house in Kingston—the family and I—and a Rastaman comes to the gate. We have guns but they are locked behind a false closet. We have dogs but they are tied up. We are Jamaicans and know that Rastas mean no harm. We let him in and he sits on the side of the porch and shows us his brooms and brushes. We buy some to take back to New York. "Peace, missis."

There were many Rastas in my childhood. Walking the roadside with their goods. Sitting outside their shacks in the mountains. The outside painted bright—sometimes with words. Gathering at Palisadoes Airport to greet the Conquering Lion of Judah. They were considered figures of fun by most middle-class Jamaicans. Harmless— like Marcus Garvey.

Later: white American hippies trying to create the effect of dred in their straight white hair. The ganja joint held between their straight white teeth. "Man, the grass is good." Hanging out by the Sheraton pool. Light-skinned Jamaicans also dred-locked, also assuming the ganja. Both groups moving to the music but not the words. Harmless. "Peace, brother."

III

My grandmother: "Let us thank God for a fruitful place."
My grandmother: "Let us rescue the perishing world."

This evening on the road in western Massachusetts there are pockets of fog. Then clear spaces. Across from a pond a dog staggers in front of my headlights. I look closer and see that his mouth is foaming. He stumbles to the side of the road—I go to call the police.

I drive back to the house, radio playing "difficult" piano pieces. And I think about how I need to say all this. This is who I am. I am not what you allow me to be. Whatever you decide me to be. In a bookstore in London I show the woman at the counter my book and she stares at me for a minute, then says: "You're a Jamaican." "Yes." "You're not at all like our Jamaicans."

Encountering the void is nothing more or less than understanding invisibility. Of being fogbound.

Then: It was never a question of passing. It was a question of hiding. Behind Black and white perceptions of who we were—who they thought we were. Tropics. Plantations. Calypso. Cricket. We were the people with the musical voices and the coronation mugs on our parlor tables. I would be whatever figure these foreign imaginations cared for me to be. It would be so simple to let others fill in for me. So easy to startle them with a flash of anger when their visions got out of hand—but never to sustain the anger for myself.

It could become a life lived within myself. A life cut off. I know who I am but you will never know who I am. I may in fact lose touch with who I am.

366

I hid from my real sources. But my real sources were also hidden from me.

Now: It is not a question of relinquishing privilege. It is a question of grasping more of myself. I have found that in the real sources are concealed my survival. My speech. My voice. To be colonized is to be rendered insensitive. To have those parts necessary to sustain life numbed. And this is in some cases—in my case—perceived as privilege. The test of a colonized person is to walk through a shantytown in Kingston and not bat an eye. This I cannot do. Because part of me lives there—and as I grasp more of this part I realize what needs to be done with the rest of my life.

Sometimes I used to think we were like the Marranos—the Sephardic Jews forced to pretend they were Christians. The name was given to them by the Christians, and meant "pigs." But once out of Spain and Portugal, they became Jews openly again. Some settled in Jamaica. They know who the enemy was and acted for their own survival. But they remained Jews always.

We also knew who the enemy was—I remember jokes about the English. Saying they stank. saying they were stingy. that they drank too much and couldn't hold their liquor. that they had bad teeth. were dirty and dishonest. were limey bastards. and horse-faced bitches. We said the men only wanted to sleep with Jamaican women. And that the women made pigs of themselves with Jamaican men.

But of course this was seen by us—the light-skinned middle class—with a double vision. We learned to cherish that part of us that was them—and to deny the part that was not. Believing in some cases that the latter part had ceased to exist.

None of this is as simple as it may sound. We were colorists and we aspired to oppressor status. (Of course, almost any aspiration instilled by Western civilization is to oppressor status: success, for example.) Color was the symbol of our potential: color taking in hair "quality," skin tone, freckles, nose-width, eyes. We did not see that color symbolism was a method of keeping us apart: in the society, in the family, between friends. Those of us who were light-skinned, straight-haired, etc., were given to believe that we could actually attain whiteness—or at least those qualities of the colonizer which made him superior. We were convinced of white supremacy. If we failed, we were not really responsible for our failures: we had all the advantages—but it was that one persistent drop of blood, that single rogue gene that made us unable to conceptualize abstract ideas, made us love darkness rather than despise it, which was to be blamed for our failure. Our dark part had taken over: an inherited imbalance in which the doom of the creole was sealed.

I am trying to write this as clearly as possible, but as I write I realize that what I say may sound fabulous, or even mythic. It is. It is insane.

Under this system of colorism—the system which prevailed in my childhood in Jamaica, and which has carried over to the present—rarely will dark and light people co-mingle. Rarely will they achieve between themselves an intimacy informed with identity. (I should say here that I am using the categories light and dark both literally and symbolically. There are dark Jamaicans who have achieved lightness and the "advantages" which go with it by their successful pursuit of oppressor status.)

Under this system light and dark people will meet in those ways in which the light-skinned person imitates the oppressor. But imitation goes only so far: the light-skinned person becomes an oppressor in fact. He/she will have a dark chauffeur, a dark nanny, a dark maid, and a dark gardener. These employees will be paid badly. Because of the slave past, because of their dark skin, the servants of the middle class have been used according to the traditions of the slavocracy. They are not seen as workers for their own sake, but for the sake of the family who has employed them. It was not until Michael Manley became prime minister that a minimum wage for houseworkers was enacted—and the indignation of the middle class was profound.

During Manley's leadership the middle class began to abandon the island in droves. Toronto. Miami. New York. Leaving their houses and business behind and sewing cash into the tops of suitcases. Today—with a new regime—they are returning: "Come back to the way things used to be" the tourist advertisement on American t.v. says. "Make it Jamaica again. Make it your own."

But let me return to the situation of houseservants as I remember it: They will be paid badly, but they will be "given" room and board. However, the key to the larder will be kept by the mistress in her dresser drawer. They will spend Christmas with the family of their employers and be given a length of English wool for trousers or a few yards of cotton for dresses. They will see their children on their days off: their extended family will care for the children the rest of the time. When the employers visit their relations in the country, the servants may be asked along— oftentimes the servants of the middle class come from the same part of the countryside their employers have come from. But they will be expected to work while they are there. Back in town, there are parts of the house they are allowed to move freely around; other parts they are not allowed to enter. When the family watches the t.v. the servant is allowed to watch also, but only while standing in a doorway. The servant may have a radio in his/her room, also a dresser and a cot. Perhaps a mirror. There will usually be one ceiling light. And one small square louvered window.

A true story: One middle-class Jamaican woman ordered a Persian rug from Harrod's in London. The day it arrived so did her new maid. She was going downtown to have her hair touched up, and told the maid to vacuum the rug. She told the maid she would find the vacuum cleaner in the same shed as the power mower. And when she returned she found that the fine nap of her new rug had been removed.

The reaction of the mistress was to tell her friends that the "girl" was backward. She did not fire her until she found that the maid had scrubbed the teflon from her new set of pots, saying she thought they were coated with "nastiness."

The houseworker/mistress relationship in which one Black woman is the oppressor of another Black woman is a cornerstone of the experience of many Jamaican women.

I remember another true story: In a middle-class family's home one Christmas, a relation was visiting from New York. This woman had brought gifts for everybody, including the housemaid. The maid had been released from a mental institution recently, where they had "treated" her for depression. This visiting light-skinned woman had brought the dark woman a bright red rayon blouse and presented it to her in the garden one afternoon, while the family was having tea. The maid thanked her softly, and the other woman moved toward her as if to embrace her. Then she stopped, her face suddenly covered with tears, and ran into the house, saying, "My God, I can't, I can't."

We are women who come from a place almost incredible in its beauty. It is a beauty which can mask a great deal and which has been used in that way. But that the beauty is there is a fact. I remember what I thought of the freedom of my childhood, in which the fruitful place was something I took for granted. Just as I took for granted Zoe's appearance every morning on my school vacations—in the sense that I knew she would be there. That she would always be the one to visit me. The perishing world of my grandfather's graces at the table, if I ever seriously thought about it, was somewhere else.

Our souls were affected by the beauty of Jamaica, as much as they were affected by our fears of darkness.

There is no ending to this piece of writing. There is no way to end it. As I read back over it, I see that we/they/I may become confused in the mind of the reader: but these pronouns have always co-existed in my mind. The Rastas talk of the "I and I"—a pronoun in which they combine themselves with Jah. Jah is a contraction of Jahweh and Jehova, but to me always sounds like the beginning of *Jamaica*. I and Jamaica is who I am. No matter how far I travel—how deep the ambivalence I feel about ever returning. And Jamaica is a place in which we/they/I connect and disconnect—change place.

Selected Bibliography

OF PROSE WORKS BY THE AUTHORS INCLUDED
IN THIS VOLUME

Barnet, Miguel
    With Esteban Monteso. *Autobiography of a Runaway Slave.* Translated
        by Jocasta Innes. New York: Pantheon Books, 1968.
    Gallego. Madrid: Ediciones Alfaguara, 1986.
    La vida real. Madrid: Ediciones Alfaguara, 1986.
    Rachel's Song. Translated by Nick Hill. Willimantic, Conn.: Curbstone
        Press, 1991.
Carnegie, James
    Wages Paid. Havana: Casa de las Américas, 1976.
Carpentier, Alejo
    Tientos y diferencias. Montevideo: ARCA Editorial, 1967.
    The War of Time. Translated by Frances Partridge. London: Gollancz,
        1970.
    Concierto barroco. Madrid: Siglo XXI de España, 1974.
    Reasons of State. Translated by Frances Partridge. New York: Knopf,
        1976.
    Consagración de la primavera. Mexico: Siglo XXI Editores, 1979.
    La novela latinoamericana en vísperas de un nuevo siglo y otros ensayos.
        Mexico: Siglo XXI, 1981.
    The Chase. Translated by Alfred Mac Adam. New York: Noonday
        Press, 1989.
    Explosion in a Cathedral. Translated by John Sturrock. New York:
        Noonday Press, 1989.
    The Kingdom of This World. Translated by Harriet de Onis. New York:
        Noonday Press, 1989.
    The Lost Steps. Translated by Harriet de Onis. New York: Noonday
        Press, 1989.
    The Harp and the Shadow. Translated by Thomas Christensen and
        Carol Christensen. San Francisco: Mercury House, 1990.
Clarke, Austin Chesterfield
    Amongst Thistles and Thorns. Toronto: McClelland & Stewart, 1965.
    When He Was Free and Young and Used to Wear Silks. Toronto: Anansi,
        1971.
    The Meeting Point. Boston: Little, Brown, 1972.
    Storm of Fortune. Boston: Little, Brown, 1973.
    The Bigger Light. Boston: Little, Brown, 1975.

The Prime Minister. London: Routledge & Kegan Paul, 1978.

Growing Up Stupid Under the Union Jack. Toronto: McClelland & Stewart, 1980.

Proud Empires. London: Gollancz, 1986.

Cliff, Michelle

The Winner Names the Age, ed. New York: Norton, 1978.

Claiming an Identity They Taught Me to Despise. Ithaca, N.Y.: Firebrand, 19XX.

No Telephone to Heaven. New York: Dutton, 1987.

The Land of Look Behind: Prose and Poetry. Watertown, Mass: Persiphone, 1980.

Abeng. New York: Penguin Books, 1991.

Fernández Retamar, Roberto

Algunos problemas teóricos de la literatura hispanoamericana. Cuenca: Casa de la Cultura Ecuatoriana. Núcleo del Azuay, 1981.

"Our America and the West." In *Social Text,* No. 15, Fall 1986, pp. 1–25.

Caliban and Other Essays. Translated by Edward Baker. Minneapolis: University of Minnesota Press, 1989.

James, Cyril Lionel Robert

Minty Alley. London: M. Secker & Warburg, 1936.

"The Artist in the Caribbean." Mona, Jamaica: University College of the West Indies.

The Black Jacobins: Toussaint L'Ouverture and the San Domingo Revolution. New York: Vintage Books, 1963.

Appendix to *Tradition, the Writer and Society,* by Wilson Harris. London: New Beacon Publications, 1967.

Kas-Kas: Interviews with Three Caribbean Writers in Texas. Edited by Ian Munro and Reinhard Sander. Austin: University of Texas at Austin, 1972.

Beyond the Boundary. New York: Pantheon Books, 1983.

At the Rendezvous of Victory (Selected Writings). London: Allison & Busby, 1984.

Cricket. Edited by Anna Grimshaw. London: Allison & Busby, 1989.

Essay and Lectures by C. L. R. James: A Tribute. Mona: Dept. of Extra-Mural Studies, University of the West Indies, 1989.

Lima, Chely

Monólogo con lluvia. Havana: Unión de Escritores y Artistas de Cuba, 1981.

With Alberto Serret. *La desnudez y el alba.* Havana: Editorial Letras Cubanas, 1989.

Mir, Pedro

> *Tres leyendas de colores: ensayo de interpretación de las tres primeras revoluciones del Nuevo Mondo*. Santo Domingo: Editora Nacional, 1969.
>
> *El gran incendio*. Santo Domingo: Ediciones de TALLER, 1974.
>
> *La gran hazaña de Limber*. Santo Domingo: Ediciones Sargazo, 1977.
>
> *Cuando amaban las tierras comuneras*. Mexico: Siglo XXI Editores, 1978.
>
> *¡Buen Viaje, Pancho Valentín!* Santo Domingo: Ediciones de TALLER, 1981.

Phillips, Caryl

> *Crossing the River*. London: Bloomsbury, 1983.
>
> *The Shelter*. Oxford: Amber Lane Press, 1984.
>
> *A State of Independence*. New York: Farrar, Straus & Giroux, 1986.
>
> *Higher Ground: A Novel in Three Parts*. New York: Viking, 1989.
>
> *The Final Passage*. New York: Penguin Books, 1990.
>
> *Cambridge*. New York: Knopf, 1992.

Schwarz-Bart, Simone

> With André Schwarz-Bart. *Un plat de porc aux bananes vertes*. Paris: Editions de Seuil, 1967.
>
> *The Bridge of Beyond*. Translated by Barbara Bray. New York: Atheneum, 1974.
>
> With André Schwarz-Bart. *Hommage à la femme noire*. Belgium: Editions Consulaires, 1988.
>
> *Between Two Worlds*. Translated by Barbara Bray. Portsmouth, N.H.: Heinemann Educational Books, 1992.

Vega, Ana Lydia

> With Carmen Lugo Filippi. *Vírgenes y mártires*. Río Piedras: Editorial Antillana, 1981.
>
> *Encancaranublado y otros cuentos de naufragio*. Río Piedras: Editorial Antillana, 1983.
>
> *Pasión de historia y otras historias de pasión*. Buenos Aires: Ediciones de la Flor, 1987.
>
> *Falsas crónicas del sur*. Río Piedras: Editorial de la Universidad de Puerto Rico, 1989.
>
> *El tramo ancla: ensayos puertorriqueños de hoy*, ed. Río Piedras: Editorial de la Universidad de Puerto Rico, 1989.

Permissions

Acknowledgments

Excerpt from *Autobiography of a Runaway Slave* by Esteban Montejo; ed., Miguel Barnet; trans., Jocasta Innes. Copyright © by The Bodley Head Ltd. Reprinted by permission of Pantheon books, a division of Random House, Inc.

Excerpt from *Between Two Worlds* by Simone Schwartz-Bart; trans., Barbara Bray. Copyright © 1992 by Heinemann International Literature and Textbooks. Reprinted by permission of Heinemann Publishers (Oxford).

Excerpt from *Cuando amaban las tierras comuneras / (When They Loved the Communal Lands)* by Pedro Mir; trans., Pamela Maria Smorkaloff. Copyright © 1978 by Siglo XXI Editores, S.A. Reprinted by permission of Siglo Veintiuno Editores, S.A. Mexico.

Excerpt from *Growing Up Stupid Under the Union Jack* by Austin Clarke. Copyright © 1980 by Austin Clarke. Reprinted by permission of Harold Ober Associates Incorporated.

"Journey Back to the Source," from *War of Time* by Alejo Carpentier; trans., Frances Partridge. Copyright © 1970 by Victor Gollancz, Ltd. Reprinted by permission of Harold Matson Company, Inc.

"The Day It All Happened" ("El día de los hechos") by Ana Lydia Vega; trans., Ana Lydia Vega with Pamela Maria Smorkaloff; and "Port-au-Prince, Below" ("Puerto Príncipe abajo") by Ana Lydia Vega: trans., Pamela Maria Smorkaloff. From *Vírgenes y mártires* by Carmen Lugo Filippi and Ana Lydia Vega. Copyright © 1981 by Carmen Lugo Filippi and Ana Lydia Vega. Reprinted by permission of Ana Lydia Vega.

Excerpt from *A State of Independence* by Caryl Phillips. Copyright © 1986 by Caryl Phillips. Reprinted by permission of Farrar, Straus & Giroux, Inc.

"Passing" and "If I Could Write This in Fire, I Would Write This in Fire," from *The Land of Look Behind* by Michele Cliff. Published by Firebrand Books, Ithaca, New York 14580. Copyright © 1985 by Michelle Cliff. Reprinted by permission of Firebrand Books.

Excerpt from "Caliban: Notes Toward a Discussion of Culture in Our America" in *Caliban and Other Essays* by Robert Fernandez Retamar; trans., Edward Baker. Copyright © 1989 by the University of Minnesota. Reprinted by permission of the University of Minnesota Press.